Orwellian Ireland

Corstown – MMVIII

Dedicated to Bernadette Reston, Heather Rieken and Katrina Rabinovich

This is the 7th edition 10 January 2008 and the 1st print edition.
ISBN 978-0-9556812-0-2
Corrected a few spelling mistakes et alia for this edition, November 2018.

CONTENTS

INTRODUCTION

If the modern Irish state could point to any one moment to define its birth that would be the day that the new Irish police force marched into Dublin Castle and took control of the organs of the state that had ruled over Ireland, sometimes with more fear than justice, for some 700 years. Many of the new recruits to the fledgling Irish police force were present that day, all of them full of the awesome weight of history and giddy with the hope and expectation of a risen nation. One of their number was William Geary who a few years later was to rise to the rank of Superintendent in the gardai and it is maybe his life story that encapsulates for some the deep problems that were to develop in the justice system of the emerging Irish state. The story goes that he was posted to Clare only to be summarily dismissed from his job without any explanation or any trial. He then spent all the years from 1934 till his death in 2004 trying to find justice. He was to end up writing to pretty much every single Minister for Justice that the Irish state ever had, always been ignored, or sent on his way with the myriad of insulting excuses and coverups that so many Irish people have had occasion to experience. He ended up at his death with a few heavily censored and incomplete files and a hollow apology for an incident that occurred some 75 years before. Never getting any real answers or evidence all he could do was explain to all that would listen how he had been setup by Davey Neligan, the first head of the Irish Secret Service, a person that drew a pension from the British Secret Service on his retirement for services that are by no means clear.[i]

Nobody ever gets any real answers as to what those intelligence agencies really do in Ireland, or who they genuinely answer to, but we can always guess and in that spirit I hope the references and links in this book might throw up a few clues. I would like to thank indymedia.ie for hosting the articles that this work is based on and also many many thanks for all the comments that they attracted from people like Barry, Seán Ryan, Eamonn Crudden, Jeff, Mary Kelly and Fergal Gallagher. Many thanks to my parents also and all who know me.

Brian Nugent B.A.
Co. Meath
16 November 2005

CHAPTER 1

Some thoughts on reading the book Stasiland and applying it to Ireland

The international bestselling book 'Stasiland', by Anne Funder, has once again brought to the fore the concept of a whole modern state being secretly subservient to its domestic intelligence agency. While doubtless many Irish people see no reason to draw a comparison between East Germany and Ireland I nonetheless think that there are disturbing similarities between these two states, and echoes of Stasi practices all too visible in the Irish political scene. Don't forget that to its citizens East Germany was supposed to be the great economic success story of the Communist Bloc, combining an industrial powerhouse with a workers paradise, or so their controlled media claimed at the time. (They were assisted in this brainwashing by constantly quoting government statistics which only much later, after the state fell, were found to be entirely falsified.) Obviously East Germany had elections national and local, political parties large and small, coalition governments, a supposedly free media in a 'workers paradise' but those institutions were clearly subordinate to the secret police, and surely even the most legalistic and naive German could have see through that? Of course there were dissidents in Germany who tried to warn the populace, but all too often they were dismissed as lunatics for outlining just how corrupt an apparatus the state really was, because that story contrasted too much with what the public were used to hearing from their mass media.[1] (What are now known in the west as conspiracy theorists?)

The true extent of this betrayal of the people only became apparent when the state fell at the end of 1989. In Leipzig for example on the 4th of December the people rushed into the secret police (the Stasi) offices climbing the staircases and overpowering the few guards they expected to find the files that had held their secrets for so long.[2] The first sight that greeted them though was not paper but row upon row of small filled glass bottles like some anatomy lab rather than a police headquarters. They were looking at the dirty underwear taken in burglaries and other means from the houses of all the 'dissidents' (meaning uncorrupt politically aware people) in Leipzig. That was a headscratcher even for the most extreme of the conspiracy theorists. It turns out that the Stasi wanted them as samples for their sniffer dogs who would use them to track the people corresponding to the samples.[3] And then they learned, as the book 'Stasiland' has shown, that the extent and power of these intelligence agencies was far in advance of even the most extreme suspicions that the people had prior to being able to see the files.

But could a modern western country really become subservient to its secret intelligence agencies? Consider Peru:

> "Which of the democratic checks and balances – opposition parties, the judiciary, a free press – is the most critical? Peru has the full set of democratic institutions. In the 1990s, the secret-police chief Vladimiro Montesinos systematically undermined them all with bribes. We quantify the checks using the bribe prices. Montesinos paid television-channel owners about 100 times what he paid judges and politicians. One single television channel's bribe was four times larger than the total of the opposition politicians' bribes. By revealed preference, the strongest check on the government's power was the news media."[6]

And it proved no protection from the secret police chief who is widely considered to be a CIA asset. In short it might be too safe an assumption to assume that stasi like activities couldn't happen here.

The first thing to note about Irish intelligence agencies is that it might be a naive assumption to think that they are controlled by Irish people in Ireland. It turns out that the control of the main domestic intelligence agency 'Security and Intelligence', then known as C3, was formally handed over to the British government in the form of MI5 at a secret meeting at Baldonnel airport in early 1974.[7] The reason given was naturally the suppression of terrorism. Turns out that at that time the main terrorism in the state was being carried out by the British intelligence agencies themselves, including the attacks that led to the passing of the 'Offenses Against the State' act.[8] It seems that this agreement is still in force. C3 in turn controlled Garda Special Branch and some army officers from Irish army intelligence, known as G2, found themselves unpromoted because they were 'cautious of the apparently unquestioning alliance between some senior Garda officers and British intelligence.' An interesting phoenix article that discusses this subject notes this information from a legal source who has seen the evidence given to the Barron enquiry on the Dublin and Monaghan bombings:

> "For years, a cabal of senior Garda officers, controlled by a foreign intelligence agency (MI5) directed state policy in many crucial areas, often against the better interests of citizens who were quite unaware of what was happening."

Maybe people wouldn't stand for the kind of practices that occurred in East Germany, but they aren't likely to be objecting to something they know nothing whatsoever about. The article goes on to state that army intelligence officers from G2 believe that one senior garda, in cooperation with MI5, had tried to oust the then Taoiseach Jack Lynch. MI5 in the UK meanwhile are known, as the article points out, to have bugged 10 Downing Street and broken into the private home of Harold Wilson, one of the few recent British Prime Ministers to question the atlantic consensus. Not long ago I read a report of an Irish business man who wanted to speak to somebody in charge of security at Dublin Airport as he wanted to question some point about the ID he had shown. The person he was introduced to turned out to be English and admitted that he worked for a British intelligence agency. A statement from the Gardai, I think, was issued later claiming he had been on some 'training exercise' in Ireland.[9] Meanwhile with respect to the American government here again is my much thumbed Phoenix Annual 2004 (p.68):

> "How much the hear no evil, see no evil policy towards the US by the Garda Siochana and Irish military intelligence (G2) is due to political influence, indolence or something more sinister, is hard to determine. Certainly, in the last 10 years, links have developed between American intelligence agencies and the Gardai and defence forces which need to be examined. Most of the senior officers in Garda HQ have been trained by the FBI at Quantico near Washington, where they come into contact with CIA operatives."

In the absence of a look at those files it is obviously difficult to determine the extent or nature of the domestic intelligence agencies in Ireland but I think it might be instructive to look at two practices that the Stasi revealed and try to guess are they happening in Ireland.

One of the most startling revelations the files revealed was that the Stasi were using chemicals and radioactive substances on their version of "terrorist suspects" (i.e. the dissidents.) as a kind of secret tag that could be monitored by hidden Geiger counters. As reported in the New Scientist magazine:

> "The Stasi files revealed that dissidents were labeled with radioactive substances in a number of ways. If people could not be sprayed with a radioactive solution the spies would label their cars, documents or paper money, according to Becker.
> If the floors of rooms used for meetings by dissidents could be treated, the Stasi could follow anyone who attended." [10]

Of course this had the effect of badly damaging the health of the dissidents, an effect which was no doubt excused as necessary for the security of the state but very bad news for those people unfortunate enough to be treated that way. For example the Stasi irradiated banknotes this way and calculated that if a person had more than two notes in his pocket: "the effect on his fertility `came close to castration.'"

The question is, is this practice, or some combination of it, being used right now by the western powers? One of the radioactive substances used was apparently scandium-64 and according to an article by the well known author Gordon Thomas it is now being used by the Israelis against the Palestinians,[11] where it is described as "highly lethal over a lengthy period as it permeates clothing with gamma radiation".

In America this general substance comes under the misleading heading of nonlethal weapons. The New York Times, for example, reported on this subject on October 29, 2002 the time of the Russian theatre siege, saying:

> "In interviews yesterday, senior American authorities and private experts said the agent used by the Russians was probably similar to one of a small arsenal of nonlethal weapons that the United States is quietly studying for use by soldiers and police officers against terrorists. Scientists said the United States had conducted research on Fentanyl, a well-known drug with many medical applications, as a human incapacitant for nearly a decade...
>
> A main contractor in the work is the Institute for Emerging Defense Technologies at Pennsylvania State University. Andrew Mazzara, the institute's director, said that nonlethal weapons 'are used for peacekeeping, humanitarian assistance, noncombatant evacuation, hostage rescue, and domestic law enforcement and corrections facilities.'" [12]

It certainly seems possible that the use of radiation on suspects is part of the 'small arsenal' mentioned. In the UK and Ireland meanwhile I have seen two straws in the wind that seem to point this way. Firstly here is a quote from a book by Martin McGartland the RUC Special Branch's famous agent in Belfast in the 80s:

> "The Special Branch had discovered a 'magic' spray which they would daub on the roof of a suspect car. The spray, invisible to the naked eye, could be picked up by a device fitted into a helicopter, and the mark would remain visible for a couple of weeks even if the car was washed and polished. It was one of the SB's most successful weapons in tracking IRA suspects and was the reason why so many IRA members were caught traveling around the country in what they thought were safe vehicles." [13]

What could that be except a radioactive spray? Invisible to the naked eye and yet can be tracked by a helicopter? And if they are using it on cars how else are they using it? This second reference is from a memo sent to Turkish security forces from Aims Ltd a private British security company "which has close links to British intelligence and the SAS",

8

and leaked to the Sunday Times in 1999:

"'Radiation detection. This is a method in which a radioactive source is placed in the target and the source is then monitored.

This can be done by aircraft or satellite. The downside is that the target succumbs to radiation poisoning in approximately 21 days. This has been used by certain nations when they have released PoWs.'

A security official involved in the deal said Aims proposed to irradiate the prisoners from a source hidden in a metal box on a table in an interrogation cell."[14]

Of course there are no prizes for guessing who the SAS got to practice this on first. As the above indicates they are remarkably cavalier with the health of those they classify as a threat to the state many of whom doubtless were never charged with any offence, because maybe they never committed any. In truth it is impossible to properly figure out if these substances, or devices, are used in Ireland but the above, I think, clearly shows that there is a use of chemical (and biological?) weapons by the security forces against people they don't like in western countries.

Unfortunately, with the advance of science and the amount of time and money that say the American government pours into this type of technology, the chances are that what the Stasi were using might be old hat although the idea of chemically tagging someone might be still popular. For example maybe if those new 'see through' type of surveillance devices that are now rolled out in ports and airports were commonly used for human surveillance then it might be desirable for the security forces to use some type of chemical to mark people in a way that would be particularly visible to such a device, in the same way that X-rays of blood vessels can be seen only after the patient has swallowed some drink that contains heavy metals like barium. Heavy metals being I suppose the best candidates for such a substance. It needn't be complicated to administer, for example a broken thermometer can throw up a very effective cloud of dangerous mercury vapour, mercury being a metal that vapourises into air at room temperature. Anyhow we can only guess in the absence of real facts from those secretive agencies.

Either way it's clearly worthy of remark that so many people caught up in the troubles in Northern Ireland claim now to be suffering from ill health as a result of coming into contact with the security forces. You can see this in the recent reports of republican prisoners dying of cancer who blame the experimental gas that was used during a prison riot in the 70s and also the ongoing complaints from people living near the watch towers in South Armagh.[15] You could also follow the logic of this and wonder whether or not this ill health in those perceived as 'enemies of the state' is something the authorities really dislike?

So much for the secretive poisoning of 'terrorist suspects' in the name of surveillance by the Stasi, the second tactic that the Stasi employed that I hope to look at is the question of isolating the 'dissidents'.

Basically the Stasi as the domestic intelligence agency were involved in watching and reporting to the state on the activities of that I suppose independent minded and therefore troublesome group of people that we now know as dissidents. No doubt they always justified this surveillance of such a large group of (basically harmless) people by hyping them up as a great threat to the security of the state. That of course is true of all domestic intelligence agencies everywhere in any era. But, contrary to what some might think, these agencies are not just glorified peeping toms, they also aim to actively prevent their 'suspects' from having any political impact. Among other ways, what they try to do is to isolate groups and individuals.[16]

To explain this I will try to give a hypothetical example. Lets take Anthony Coughlin [17] the well known opponent of further EU integration who we now know was monitored by Irish army intelligence prior to the first European Community referendum despite the fact that everybody knows he never had any involvement at any time with any paramilitary groups etc and you can be sure that the Irish state knew that but was spying on him anyway. (I wish to point out all this is genuinely hypothetical, I don't know much about Anthony Coughlin personally.) So they go about their merry way in the usual manner, following people on the street, intercepting mail and telephone calls, viewing banking records and any relevant files in any government departments etc building up quite a picture on their suspect as all these agencies do. But they have a problem. He simply isn't doing anything wrong and not breaking the law as is probably the case 99 per cent of the time these agencies are monitoring people. But the state would doubtless like very much to get the EEC referendum passed and would not be looking favorably on poor old Anthony doing his best to highlight the pitfalls in signing away so much of our sovereignty. So they still want to stop him and yet the whole idea of monitoring people in order to bring charges in court, which is what law enforcement people are supposed to be doing, is a non starter here. So to address this kind of problem some bright spark in some agency at some unrecorded moment in history thought up this idea of isolating people. They simply take the picture they have built up about the person, and the powers they are using in watching him, and attempt to restrict his ability to have a political impact.

Top of the list in a western country of course is financial isolation and pressure. So that letter that was intercepted in the mail, which they are constantly monitoring, with the lucrative or indeed any job offer gets lost in the post. The same possibly goes for checks in the mail, deadly for any small business. Whereas when they are just monitoring someone they can check out a person's place of employment by numerous discreet ways as part of this isolation process they might take a different approach. Some more high profile visits to his/her employer with questions that indicate what a troublemaker the target is might be in order, and obviously could give an employer cold feet about continuing to employ the person. Any small business person is very vulnerable to the vagaries of the complicated and strictly applied tax code in this country. Troubles on that front could easily devastate a self-employed person.[18] Nearly everybody has to interact as well with one or other government department, which in some shape or form regulate all professions and businesses in the state, and harm might come their way from there.[19] The net effect of course is that a person with little money is maybe not able to get around to meetings and publish things like Anthony Coughlin has done in successive European campaigns. It is very effective at times of high costs of living such as modern Ireland of course. It might also leave a person very vulnerable to some new 'financial assistance', with strings attached, from their erstwhile enemies.[20] Also there are eras when not having employment is considered the ultimate social sin and can damage a person's credibility by itself.[21]

This financial isolation and pressure can be aggravated by social isolation which is also of course useful for its own sake in this context. Clearly not having a car, place to stay, computer or whatever is not much of a problem when you are among a wide circle of friends and family who could lend a hand but very difficult to deal with for a person on his own. To achieve this social isolation they basically resort to slander, whispering campaigns, inaccurate information spread by the agencies themselves.[22] To take up a phrase that was used to describe slander against the 'Daily Ireland' newspaper they simply accuse people of being either mad, bad or dangerous to know or some horrible mixture of all three.[23] Of course the agencies can use the information that they already would have gleaned on a persons family and acquaintances to tailor their slander at just the right concerns or prejudices of their listeners.[24] They also probably do this early and often, *early* because first impressions of a person or his activities count better than later ones and *often* to reinforce the slander so that it is taken eventually as a kind of widely acknowledged truth. They might also be able to use some technological wizardry to make their case. For example conceivably an older person being maligned as 'past it' could be slipped something that could cause temporary confusion in him/her, in order to reinforce the slander.[25] Obviously doctored documents sound or video could be easily deployed here to discredit the victim, as it will likely never be seen by him/her never mind shown in court and therefore easily forged.[26] The two basic categories of slander:

Mad of course is the old standby of the eastern bloc agencies but it clearly has also been used in the west/[27] It combines a neat way to discredit what a person is saying with a smoother passage to a locked cell

11

than the judicial system can sometimes give. As a nice Orwellian twist a person that alleges some kind of grand state conspiracy against himself/herself is likely to get there all the sooner.

Bad in Ireland probably means claiming that a person is a member of a paramilitary organisation when they are not, like classically in the case of Pat Finucane, or maybe whispering that a person is connected to the drug trade. This kind of thing could be useful in the event of a person being killed as well since some statement along the lines that the victim was 'known to the police' can scare away too much public interest and disquiet, which thankfully has not succeeded in the case of the above mentioned solicitor. In the case of a high profile person this could be done through the organs of the media rather than at a personal level. This might also manifest itself in false charges being laid against the victim.[28] Here is the Phoenix magazine's recent impression of the influence the Gardai in Ireland can have in the media:

> "Many of the Garda problems stem from a culture of secrecy and media manipulation which has evolved as a result of 30 years of largely political policing in the North. The regular Garda practice of demonizing suspects and bringing them, in the absence of courtroom proof, to nudge-and-wink trial in the media, still goes on. An example of this unofficial, symbiotic relationship between certain gardai and the media – and not just various tabloids – came in the classic 'Sunday World' report that the then emerging Donegal scandal was an IRA plot to discredit Special Branch."[29]

Also as part of the ongoing surveillance it might be possible to change the nature of the surveillance in a way that assists this process. While before, on entering a hotel say, he/she might be watched discreetly by some nondescript person glancing up from his paper the other side of the ornamental flowers now an operative could noisily approach staff or the management inquiring about the whereabouts of their 'suspect' and just between themselves outlining a terrible saga of infamy culminating in the odd bout of kleptomania in hotel rooms! So getting in the early slander.[30]

Finally a little bit of more formal and official state interference might be in order as part of this policy of isolation. In the Soviet Union for example they had a system of internal passports so clearly a person not in good standing might be refused permission to travel about which is doubtless helpful in restricting their political influence. The same was especially true of exit visas to travel abroad. Meanwhile in many western countries it is increasingly the case that without proper ID you cannot book a room, open a bank account, and even enter pubs and clubs.

12

Of course in theory there is no problem getting such ID, but 'bureaucratic' difficulties could arise.[31] Obviously this might become even more of an issue with the talk of biometric IDs being compulsory for doing nearly anything in years to come.

As well as the footnotes to the above I have seen the following which seems to indicate that this is practiced in the west. This is a quote from a former 'US intelligence agent trained at a national level' in describing the results of research by her into a number of reported cases of harassment presumably by an intelligence agency in the US:

> "Isolation of the individual from members of his/her immediate family-virtually assured when highly focused forms of ... harassment commence.
>
> Progressive financial impoverishment, brought on by termination of the individual's employment, and compounded by expenses associated with the harassment."[32]

Whistleblowers would seem a common term in the west for those which we refer to in the east as dissidents. Here is a description of what happens to whistleblowers usually in the UK according to Liam Clarke the well known Sunday Times journalist:

> "In Britain whistleblowers such as White are generally subjected to a campaign of character assassination. It is suggested they are crooks or Walter Mitty-type characters, and they then face years of expensive litigation to clear their names."[33]

Of course the Stasi and the KGB had a lot of other weapons in their armoury like assassination, I have just concentrated on these two tactics. I just hope that people would agree with me that these practices should be prevented from taking root in Ireland as immoral and in any civilised country illegal and might join with me in condemning them.

Footnotes

i. Mentioning David Neligan: http://www.limerick-leader.ie/issues/20040110/interview.html also see http://www.tuppenceworth.ie/Politics/geary.htm. Describing the censored state of the documents he received prior to the apology see http://www.ireland.com/newspaper/newsfeatures/1999/0227/archive.99022700 074.html.
The list of pensions that David Neligan received is from Tim Pat Coogan, *Michael Collins: A Biography* (London, 1990), p76:
"..he was drawing five pensions when I [Coogan] first met him in the 60s – an old IRA pension, one from the RIC, the Irish police force, the Irish Civil Service, and the British Secret Service."
(I don't mean to suggest though that Neligan was particularly dishonest, personally I think that Broy – who pretty much succeeded him in the post – was a more suspect character.) Also Justin Keating has stated that: "I... take for granted that when the British left Ireland in 1922, they left sleepers behind them in a whole lot of serious locations and that those sleepers, as I call them, have successors."(http://www.irlgov.ie/oireachtas/Committees-29th-D%E1il/jcjed-wr-debates/scbr020304.htm).

1. If you feel the need to speculate on these issues, and apply them to Ireland, you might like to note that at the time of the Emmett Stagg affair it was reported that the Gardai have a practice of passing onto headquarters any details that might be considered compromising for at least some politicians. This was said to be in order to protect the politician from possible blackmail. (The Irish Council on Civil Liberties called this a "very sinister development"-Irish Times 10/3/94). Also with respect to the banks and Charles Haughey it was noted that his financial affairs were handled "at the highest level in the bank" apparently because of the sensitive position that Haughey held, and it was dealt with   remarkably   generously.   (http://archives.tcm.ie/irishexaminer/1999/02/18/ihead.htm)

2. www.bbc.co.uk/education/languages/germany_insideout/east1.html

In Ireland the files held in great secrecy by Special Branch date from the Fenian troubles of the 1860's.
(http://www.atholbooks.org/archives/publicarchives/pastlabcom/labcomjan04.h tml quoting The Phoenix 19/12/2003.)

Meanwhile one historian, Christy Campbell, had only intermittent and heavily censored access to secret service files relating to Ireland of the 1880s held in the PRO London.(Christy Campbell, *Fenian Fire* (London, 2002), p.xxi, also see chapter 4 footnote 106 of this work). Nonetheless he was able to figure out that the 'outrages' and terrorism that had Britain and Ireland in thrall at that time were actually part of elaborate plots by British Intelligence figures. Their activities were attributed to the nefarious activities of Irish dynamitards who were in fact nearly all in the employ of various branches of the British government, and used by them for political purposes. And that's only the files in the PRO, secret service papers that show some of the bribery that passed the Act of Union were kept so secret that their "very existence was not revealed to the modern PRO until nearly 200 years later." ('History, Journal of the Historical Association 'Jan 1997 Vol.82 no.265 p.225) Closed for the same 200 years were the court martial records of the 1798 rebellion (Brian Barton, *From Behind a Closed Door* (Belfast, 2002), p.31.). From which you might deduct that the secrecy these files are kept in are not paranoia but important in keeping Irish people clueless about what really went on during their supposedly violent history.

In Puerto Rico, a country dominated by the United States, the authorities had files on over 100,000 people:
"Over half a century the police unit built up a vast network of informers--everyday people like the victims themselves. Other governmental and private institutions also provided information for the files. ...
Information in the carpetas [secret police files] allegedly was used to deny employment or take other punitive actions such as unlawful arrests against Puerto Ricans from every walk of life, from students and teachers to farmers and cab drivers, lawyers and artists.
...
When the dossiers were released in 1992, many islanders--including school teachers, union leaders and writers--were shocked to learn that friends, neighbours and family members had secretly spied on them for years.
One client of Hey Maestre, a 16-year-old high school student, had books and other materials confiscated in Puerto Rico after attending an international socialist youth activity in Finland. He claims authorities then expelled him from school and blocked his admission to college.

The carpetas also were used in child custody hearings and employment interviews. And in some cases, entire families were drawn into the web of state spying because one member was considered 'subversive.' " (http://www.latinamericanstudies.org/puertorico/carpetas.htm quoting the Washington Post dec 28 1999.)

3. Of course if these tactics are employed now in advanced western countries they are highly likely to be using the various types of electronic 'noses' that have been developed rather than dogs. The reference is from the book 'Stasiland'.

4. This whistleblower has shown that political prisoners in Belmarsh prison in London have in practice no privacy from the security forces for legal matters:
Richard Tomlinson, *The Big Breach; From Top Secret to Maximum Security* (Moscow, 2001), p.185.

In Donegal supposedly private communications between solicitor and client were in fact deliberately bugged by the gardai:
http://www.unison.ie/irish_independent/stories.php3?
ca=9&si=646979&issue_id=6472 .

5. This is a sample of some of the serious issues the Morris Tribunal is examining, which might be of interest in this context:
Anonymous Allegations SITECONTENT_113.pdf .page 1..[allegations made by one or multiple gardai – the source to Howlin is said to be a serving Dublin garda, the source to Higgins a retired Donegal garda – of garda corruption being investigated by the Morris Tribunal, inter alia:]
"(ii) When working with these two high ranking members of An Garda Síochána he was alleged to have been given the job of producing evidence by unlawful means to prove a case beyond reasonable doubt whenever such evidence "had to be got";
(iii) In this regard a large number of convictions were achieved by planting evidence and it is alleged that both of the high ranking Gardaí were aware that the member under investigation was the source of trumped up evidence used in this manner;
(iv) The member under investigation gained from his actions of producing trumped up evidence which secured convictions in that he had paid to him extra expenses in the form of unworked overtime/travelling and subsistence allowances which continued up to 1998 and that he was given blanket permission to claim such expenses;"

Also a report by Barry O'Kelly in the Sunday Business Post Jan 29 2002 on the trial of a person accused of one of the most serious crimes in modern Irish history makes interesting reading. It's not stated there but reported at the time that one of the witnesses in the case during the trial stated that he gave false testimony because of intimidation by the Gardai.
(archives.tcm.ie/businesspost/2002/01/20/story57787728.asp)
(The witness discussed at: http://www.indymedia.ie/newswire.php?
story_id=68131&comment_order=asc&save_prefs=true)

6. "How to subvert democracy, Montesinos in Peru"
http://www.cesifo.de/pls/guestci/download/CESifo+Working+Papers+2004/CE
Sifo+Working+Papers+April+2004/cesifo1_wp1173.pdf

7. "The Phoenix" July 2003 Vol 21 no 14 p 8-10. This agreement was first revealed to the public in Ireland, as far as I know, by Fred Holroyd at a meeting of 'Justice for the Forgotten' in Dublin on the 27th June 2003. It was not reported in the media. Major Holroyd was told this by a Doctor Hugh Thomas who served as medical officer for the large British contingent at the discussions at Baldonnel.

8. See both above listed sources. That is also the Phoenix article mentioned

next in the text.

9. I regret I have forgotten which newspaper I read that in.

10. http://216.87.7.9/Intel%20Bulletin/Intel%20Bulletin%20020010105.htm

11. http://64.233.161.104/search?
q=cache:oqWY3afKkKUJ:lists.village.virginia.edu/cgi-
bin/spoons/archive_msg.pl%3Ffile%3Ddeleuze-guattari.archive/deleuze-
guattari.0104%26msgnum%3D75%26start%3D6930%26end
%3D7035+scandium-64&hl=en

12. http://www.cognitiveliberty.org/dll/knockoutgas2.htm

13. Martin McGartland, *Fifty Dead Men Walking* (London, 1998), p.269.

14. Sunday Times 31st October 1999.

15. On the gas used:
http://www.geocities.com/collusion2000_1999/news7.html
Where the local people have been driven to putting up road signs trying to
highlight the cancer and health problems they say are being caused by devices
used in those towers. (see
http://homepage.eircom.net/~eirenua/jun97/saoirse3.htm). Gerry Conlon (in his
book *Proved Innocent* (London, 1990)) also said that he was sometimes
poisoned while a prisoner in England.
A recent example of mercury poisoning (the victim was a Russian
businessman) is reported on by Wayne Madsen:
http://discussions.ghanaweb.com/viewtopic.php?start=15&t=36884, and
another curious modern example of long term gas poisoning comes from Los
Angeles involving a weed killer gas used to poison members of the Ritual
Abuse Task Force: http://www.reflectionsinthenight.com/alex_2.htm .

16. I have not seen this practice explained explicitly anywhere, just in passing
in 'Stasiland'. I have written it partly from that book and partly from the
sources noted in the footnotes. One writer who feels that KGB tactics like this
are used in the west is Julianne McKinney, who served with the DIA in Berlin
during the Cold War:
"KGB strategies were addressed in some detail during these discussions [dis-
cussions entitled "Understanding the Solzhenitzyn Affair: Dissent and its Control in the USSR" at Georgetown University]. It was noted that the KGB's success depended on the extensive use of informant networks and agent provocateurs; and, following Brezhnev's rise to power, on the use of drugs and psychi-
atrists for further purpose of manipulation and control. Shadowing, bugging,
slandering, blacklisting and other related tactics were also cited as serving
KGB purpose. Participants in the conference agreed that the KGB's obvious

intent was to divide and isolate the populace, to spread fear, and to silent dis-
senters.

Agencies of our own government are on record as having employed precisely
these same tactics on a recurrent basis. The Church and Rockefeller Committee
Hearings in the mid-70's purportedly put an end to these practices. Based on
recent developments, it would appear that the CIA's and FBI's Operations
MKULTRA, MHCHAOS and COINTELPRO (the focus of these Senate Committee and Vice-President-level Hearings) were instead merely driven underground. We are now in contact with a total of 25 individuals, scattered throughout the United states, who firmly believe they are being harassed by agencies
of the U.S. Government. Others have been brought to our attention whom we
will be contacting in the future. The majority of these individuals claim that
their harassment and surveillance began in 1989.
...
Four months ago, when this Project commenced, we approached these complaints of government harassment and experimentation with an admitted "high
degree of caution." We are no longer skeptical.
The growing numbers of independent complaints and the similarities between
those complaints cannot be ignored."
(http://www.naicr.org/aps/McKinney.htm).
(Other interesting links on the same type of subject are available at
http://www.naicr.org/aps/index.shtml .)

17. Article by Ryle Dwyer at IrishExaminer.com 8/1/2005.

18. This testimony of Thomas Gilmartin at the Mahon tribunal is possibly of
interest here, bearing in mind that he had some very dramatic things to say
about politicians in Ireland, none of it complimentary to the powers that be:
"A No, I didn't get profit. I was actually made bankrupt through skullduggery.

Q 433 We'll come to that in a moment. As far as this is concerned, that you
made profit and what is more important about this is that these documents
show that the driving force behind your involvement in these two investments
was to make a massive profit on a small investment.

A Wrong. That was not the driving force at all. I could have been – I had a 20
million pound deal in Milton Keynes going on, which I lost due to the skullduggery in this country. I didn't need the bank.

Q 434 But as far as the question of you ending up without any money is concerned, that was not to do with Quarryvale –

A It was to do with Quarryvale, and Frank Dunlop and false information supplied to the British Inland Revenue by your client and his merry men.

Q 435 That, I would suggest to you, is a ridiculous suggestion.

A No, it's not ridiculous. It's an absolute fact, and I will prove it.

Q 436 Did the inland –

A It's an absolute fact and I'll prove it.

Q 437 Did the Inland Revenue make you bankrupt?

A The Inland Revenue in England did on a false claim, supplied by one Mr. Frank Dunlop, the government press secretary, and Mr. O'Callaghan's sidekick.

Q 438 So Mr. O'Callaghan – you seem to portray yourself as the victim at every stage in relation to this. The Inland Revenue took proceedings against you and bankrupted you; is that correct?

A That's correct, on false information, and I can prove it. I lost a 20 million pound deal in Milton Keynes, as well as an office block that I had already built and paid for, due to a false claim. And the law in England is – when it comes to an Irishman, you're guilty until proven innocent. I didn't get justice there and I didn't get justice here."

(TUESDAY, 16TH MARCH 2004, CONTINUATION OF QUESTIONING OF MR. THOMAS GILMARTIN BY MR. MAGUIRE., SITECONTENT_255.pdf p.75-76 www.flood-tribunal.ie)

Gerald Reaveley James is a businessman and was chairman of a leading weapons manufacturer called Astra Holdings plc from 1980 to 1990. He was both investigated by the Inland Revenue and had great troubles with the DTI as a result of getting mixed up with the UK intelligence agencies. In his opinion a climate of fear exists in the UK with respect to them and other departments of state, a climate where:
"Politicians and civil servants and other leading figures who get out of line can be surveyed or bugged and then threatened, blackmailed, framed up or worse."
(http://www.elc.org.uk/papers/2000James.doc)

19. Major Holroyd at the above mentioned Dublin meeting also stated that Dr Hugh Thomas was set up on false charges by the state who claimed he had defrauded the NHS as part of his practice as a doctor. He luckily managed to show that some of the documents the state were using were forged. Apparently he detected it by seeing a wrong sized welsh dragon on the forms.

Also Pat Rabitte in the Dail has highlighted the case of farmer John Fleury. It is a truism in the farming community that their economic troubles are in large measure caused by a politically powerful oligopoly in the meat processing industry and to counteract that the only recourse they have are live cattle exports. Unfortunately some time ago the shipping companies refused to export any cattle and some people including Mr. Fleury brought them to court to compel them to allow the exports and were successful, so making many enemies it seems. He highlighted his subsequent strange problems with the Department of Agriculture, which has a very powerful impact on the life of a farmer, on the Vincent Browne radio show. Pat Rabbitte was contacted while Mr. Fleury was trying to protect his house from the banks. (www.gov.ie/debates-03/13May/Sect2.htm). This is from the Farmers Journal 17 May 2003:
"The issue of a witch hunt on Fleury by the Department of Agriculture was raised in the Dail by Pat Rabbitte Leader of the Labour Party. "Over 160 sum-

monses against Mr Fleury are still outstanding in circumstances that are reminiscent of the summary spree against Donegal publican, Mr Frank Shortt," said Mr Rabbitte.
...
Among the allegations that have been made by the Defence at a previous hearing is that the "Prosecution presented a false test result" and that of "Alleging alterations being made to cattle passports which they knew were not altered"."(http://www.farmersjournal.ie/2003/0517/news/currentedition/othernews.htm) .

20. Again at that meeting Major Holroyd said he had been approached to take up a very lucrative job offer as security consultant for Rank Xerox with 150,000 pounds offered up front tax free. It is clear that this would be on the understanding that he stopped making his allegations of abuses in the intelligence system in Northern Ireland. This was after he had been through the difficulties described below.

He also related the story of an unnamed Dublin journalist who initially gave a lot of publicity to some of the issues he raises but as a result lost his job, couldn't pay the mortgage, gave up and is now working for a very right wing paper.

These are some of the experiences of activists in the 32 County Sovereignty Movement:
"In recent weeks the RUC/PSNI have increased their campaign of harassment against anti-agreement republicans in Belfast. A number of republicans have lost their jobs as a result of the RUC special branch having a "word in the ear" of the men's employer. One can only speculate what lies and insinuations the branch have been telling these employers or indeed if threats have been made against them to make them comply. This tactic has long been used against republicans in the Free State and signifies a new level of desperation on behalf of the British security services. The aim of this tactic is quite clear, give up the defence of the republican position or we will starve you and your families. Enormous pressure is already being brought to bear on those who still defend the republic through an on-going campaign of demonisation, ostracisation, imprisonment and of course the recent spate of abductions by counter revolutionaries. Not content with this the Brits are determined to get their extra pound of flesh by victimizing the partners and children of republicans. The Brits must know that few republicans are likely to be put off by the prospect of financial hardship now when they have endured everything that the Brits have thrown at them in the past, but there may be a more sinister motive at work. In the past a number of members of the 32 County Sovereignty Movement have been approached with offers of financial inducement when in times of difficulty, indeed one member whose work regularly takes him to England is constantly approached with offers to help pay his travel expenses!" (The Sovereign Nation 2004 http://www.32csm.org/SovNation1.pdf).

21. At the same Dublin meeting listed above Major Holroyd mentioned how

they at times make it difficult for him to get employment and then sneer that he cannot hold down a job. Major Holroyd did describe this generally as a process of 'isolating' people (his word) but he didn't go into any detail and in fact used the word in a slightly different context.

From his book 'War without honour' p128: "I then lost my job at Group Four [Security]. I was in the office when a call came through from an officer in the Metropolitan Anti-Terrorist Squad, with a message that was to be passed to my superiors. It was quite simple: I was a dangerous disaffected ex-officer and could not be trusted. I went to see my boss shortly afterwards. He asked me to leave, saying they could not afford to upset people in the Security Services since they relied on the goodwill of the police, especially in London." He lost his job doing security for Marks and Spencers much the same way. Even in Rhodesia MI5 tried to banjax his employment by telling the security services out there that he was an MI6 agent spying on them (ibid p123). He states that MI5 "thrive on peoples insecurity – what their victims are afraid to lose. In my case I have lost everything anyway. I remain extremely poor, and live frugally."(ibid p147).

Malcolm Kennedy, a man with a long dispute with the London police centering around trials during which "every category of police document in the case had, since 1990, been suppressed, gone missing, or been forged" according to Michael Mansfield QC, believes his phone, which he depends on to run a small business, is routinely cut off "to damage his business, keep him impoverished and to put him under psychological pressure." (http://www.red-star-research.org.uk/malcolm.html).
He is mentioned here by the BBC where he says he knows of this happening to many miscarriage of justice campaigners.
(http://news.bbc.co.uk/1/hi/uk/3051792.stm).

John Burnes "a post-grad student at the time, he had his grant withdrawn; and, after training as a teacher, he was blocked by MI5 from teaching." He accidentally found out about MI6 money laundering (http://www.lobster-agazine.co.uk/articles/security.htm).

Richard Tomlinson the MI6 dissident talks about this kind of harassment in Switzerland which was done at the behest of his former employers:
"I later discovered the full extent of their double standards: every time I went for a job interview, Jourdain [a Commandant in the Swiss Federal Police] rang the company afterwards and told them not to employ me." Richard Tomlinson, *The Big Breech, From Top Secret To Maximum Security* (Moscow, 2001), p.224.

22. It seems the Stasi particularly enjoyed spreading false rumors that a person was a Stasi informant. (.http://64.233.161.104/search?
q=cache:JPIoNL09Ec4J:www.utopie1.de/stasi/heinrich/englisch1.htm+&hl=en

stasi tactics)

23. Daily Ireland Thursday February 10 2005 article by Jude Collins p.15. He says that some of the abuse heaped on the paper was so 'early' it was before the paper was actually launched.

24. Richard Tomlinson for example, the MI6 whistleblower, claims that private detectives hired by MI6 told his landlady and friends in Italy that he was a convicted paedophile. He also states that MI6 threatened him with lifelong harassment.
(www.chiark.greenend.org.uk/pipermail/ukcrypto/2001-Febrary/014745.html)

According to evidence at a recent libel trial in Cork, Brendan O'Brien, the RTE journalist, received an unsolicited telephone call from Noel O'Flynn TD while he was interviewing two gardai in the course of a programme unflattering to the Gardai. In it the FF TD referred to one of the retired gardai as having mental problems and the other as having been thrown out of the force for alcoholism and stealing. Jerry McCarthy, one of the gardai, slandered managed to win the libel case showing this to be completely untrue. The TD told O'Brien that he had "heard he was meeting with a garda" but no further details are reported as to how he knew to ring the journalist at that time. (home.eircom.net/content/unison/national/4225483?view=Printer) One of the gardai, Jack Doyle, was particularly concerned about aspects of a drug shipment that came via Cork to Urlingford in Kilkenny. Some of the drugs apparently went missing despite considerable garda knowledge of the circumstances of the importation. (http://www.missingpersons-ireland.freepress-freespeech.-com/primetimeonurlingforddrugs.htm)

25. The use of drugs that effect the mind in various ways is testified to by Major General Jan Sejna who described over 50 intelligence operations where drugs were used like that. He defected from Czechoslovakia in 1968 and had formerly being the head of the Defense Council Secretariat and Chief of Staff to the Minister for Defence in that country. This link also notes that the CIA conducted research in the 1950s into inter alia drugs that could "cause mental disturbance" and "diminish ambition and working efficiency". (www.apfn.net/messageboard/12-06-03/discussion.cgi.20.html).

Gene 'Chip' Tatum, a US covert operator and pilot, said that his group from the US used a type of drug to disorientate a Nicaraguan politician called Adolfo Calero. Then when he was in this dazed state he participated in homosexual acts that these operatives filmed in order to blackmail or slander him later. (http://www.theconspiracy.us/cati3/0014.html) Notice how this story matches closely the account that Russian presidential candidate Ivan Rybkin has recently given about his experiences in Kiev. (http://www.chinadaily.com.cn/english/doc/2004-02/14/content_306087.htm)

26. This is exactly what occurred to Sir Roger Casement with the black diaries which many people still consider to be forged and which were shown around to influential people to counteract sympathy for him before he was hung. They were never shown in court or to him or to the general public at the time. Considering then views on homosexuality he was clearly painted thus as mad and bad and consequently dangerous to know.

Consider also the case of Peter Foster the partner of Carole Caplin, an adviser with ready access to the Prime Minister, who got the full tabloid treatment recently. A number of telephone conversations said to have been intercepted between him in Australia and his mother in Dublin were reported verbatim in the Sun newspaper. Fosters' supporters stated that a number of different phone calls were mixed up together and "strategically edited" in a way that presented a completely misleading picture. Peter Foster describes his experiences thus:

"Over the last few weeks papers have reported: I am an agent for Mossad, I am facing extradition to Australia to face criminal charges, I sold emails to the Daily Mail, I am the father of twins I've never seen, my business in Australia was founded on drugs money, I sent an email to Paul Walsh attempting to tie the Blairs into my product, I have a brother called Paul, I was touting to sell my story to the British media for 100,000 pounds ...

And tomorrow I now hear it will be suggested I am gay. I could go on but none of these things are true. But I had no chance to challenge these lies. Where did they come from? Could it be I had to be discredited by the establishment?"(politics.guardian.co.uk/cherie/story/0,12713,861220,00.html)

Note the smooth relationship between the intelligence agencies, the only people who realistically could have recorded the conversations, and the tabloids. Incidentally it is said they were bugged in Dublin where Louise Pelloti Peter's mother lives. The Sun decided not to run the transcripts in its Irish edition.

Philip Agee the famous CIA dissident was very busy in the agency forging documents (Philip Agee, *Inside the Company, CIA Diary* (London, 1975)).

Captain Tom Clonan was told by a senior Irish army officer that "character asassination is a legitimate tactic [when an institution's back is to the wall]" when he complained of his treatment at the hands of the army. He was "confronted by the apparatus of the state" when he tried to highlight research he had done into sexual harassment in the army. The government even tried to leak a document to the media as part of this campaign to defame his character. (Programme 8 in Whistleblowers series, broadcast on RTE1 2nd September 2007 http://www.rte.ie/radio1/whistleblowers/1156941.html .)

27. The poet Ezra Pound was said to have been placed in a psychiatric hospital in Washington for many years as a result of making some powerful enemies. Quoting Eustace Mullins:

"Well I met a political prisoner, a man who had been imprisoned because he stood up for the Constitution of the United States: a poet named Ezra Pound.

And he had been incarcerated, without trial, in St. Elizabeth's Hospital in Washington, D.C."(www.soren.org/gov/eustace.html)

Meanwhile it has been alleged in a new Irish magazine that some of the former patients in the Magdalen Laundries have been housed in dubious circumstances in Grangegormon mental institution in Dublin ('Irish Crime' vol.1 issue.7 Dec-Jan 2004/05 p11) There have been lots of rumours that some of the abuse suffered by children in religious institutions was connived at by powerful politicians and civil servants. See also the article entitled "Abusers to be named on the net" by Carmel Hayes in the 'Kilkenny People' June 1997.

Sheenagh McMahon, describing some of her experiences in Donegal: "people were saying she is mad like..." It was written about her that she was a 'scorned woman' etc etc. Later, after she was vindicated in the Tribunals, she was accepted in Buncrana which made "a change from the isolation." (Whistleblowers Programme 4, RTE Radio 1 27th Nov. 2006 http://www.rte.ie/radio1/whistleblowers/rams/2006/27november.smil .)

Fr Gerard McGinnity, a whistleblower in the Catholic church, described how he had to go to the trouble of leaking to the media a favourable psychiatrist's report, to try and counteract the slander he was getting. Before that he described how he was removed on a sabbatical away from Maynooth, to separate him from his colleagues no doubt, and then forced, by Cardinal O'Fiaich, to resign his employment as Dean of Maynooth. (Whistleblowers Programme 2, broadcast on RTE 1 on 14 August 2006 http://www.rte.ie/radio1/whistleblowers/1102941.html .)

Also note the campaign of disinformation via private briefings by CIA agent Brian Latell on Capitol Hill accusing President Aristide of Haiti of seeking treatment for mental problems and subsequently leaked to the media. "It turned out that the time during which the CIA report alleges Aristide was treated at a Canadian hospital falls within the same period that Aristide was studying and teaching in Israel." (http://www.globalresearch.ca/articles/RIE402A.html)

These are some of the experiences of Robert Dougal Watt an auditor in the EU:
 "The Court has certainly done its best to discredit me; publicly denying all my allegations, publicly promising disciplinary procedures, and off-the-record insisting that I am as mad as a hatter.
...If I return to work without public acknowledgment by the Court that my allegations of 22 April are soundly based, then I assume I will be disciplined, and possibly bankrupted by Mr [B]'s claim of defamation."

Of course another point is that under the kind of stress people in this situation are likely to encounter problems can arise which can be easily and deliberately misinterpreted. Mr Watt begins one of his letters thus:

24

"However, I feel I should point out straight away – given the nature of the contents of this letter, and given that in my understanding you have been deliberately misled to date regarding my mental state – that neither my doctor in Luxembourg, nor my doctor in Scotland, has diagnosed me as paranoid or in any way, "mad". I have been prescribed beta-blockers and sleeping pills for stress, and an anti-depressant for anxiety; but both doctors have assured me that stress and anxiety are the rational responses of an individual who finds him/herself in circumstances such as mine. This stress and anxiety arise from much more than worry about holding on to my job and pension entitlements – which I knowingly placed at risk on 22 April; but from concern over the physical well-being of my family and myself – which I did not knowingly place at risk."

and is driven to finishing his letter:

"I conclude, I am not paranoid; only terrified.

Yours faithfully,

R Dougal WATT
Auditor
17 June 2002"
(http://www.justresponse.net/DougalWatt3Sep02.html)

Major Fred Holroyd actually has a whole chapter called 'Political Psychiatry' in his book based on his treatment by the various British intelligence agencies. He was forcibly detained at Musgrave Hospital Belfast and then imprisoned effectively at the British army's psychiatric hospital at Netley. As you can imagine Major Holroyd, who is a very traditional army man, spent a lot of time protesting that 'this wasn't Soviet Russia' and that 'you cannot do this to a serving British officer'. Unfortunately he was wrong about that. Apparently he is not the only case:
"Subsequently I was contacted by a former gunner officer who had been tasked to calibrate 25 pounder guns just prior to the Suez operation. On the completion of his task he was forcibly incarcerated at Netley in order to isolate him and preserve the secret of the forthcoming invasion of Egypt...his army career was ruined by those two weeks he spent in a mental hospital which were forever recorded on his military record. I can only wonder how many other innocent officers and soldiers have been held at Netley for political reasons, and how many lives have unnecessarily been blighted by the abuse of psychiatry in the forces."(p107).
To clarify Holroyd's career and position in Ireland since it might seem a little confusing to some: He was a Captain (he became a Major in the Rhodesian and later Zimbabwean army) in a regular British army regiment stationed in Asia where he wasn't particularly happy among other reasons because he felt "quite alienated within the mess" for refusing to join the Freemasons. So he applied for a a post as a Military Liaison Officer with the army in Northern Ireland.

25

This would involve intelligence coordination between the army and RUC Special Branch. For this he was trained as an intelligence officer at the Joint Services training school at Ashford in Kent where he was lectured by among others the famous Kitson. After graduating there he was approached to join the CIA along with two other graduating captains, but he declined the offer. He was then posted to Armagh during 1973-5 as part of a unit that handled the liaison between the army and each RUC division known as a Special Military Intelligence Unit headed by a Colonel in RUC headquarters at Knock. So he passes between the RUC Special Branch in Portadown (who assured him that his role was only to pass information on to the army on a need to know type basis) and the army in the form of the 3rd Infantry Brigade HQ at Lurgan (who made it clear that he was really an army man and wasn't to trust Special Branch!). His written rules emphasized the primacy of Special Branch but as time went on and his knowledge of RUC corruption grew he probably felt a bit like his predecessor who resorted to breaking into the RUC filing cabinets. He was then approached to work for MI6, his controller being Craig Smellie operating out of army HQ at Lisburn all the while continuing his work as a military intelligence officer as a useful cover. Later after a power struggle he was passed from MI6 to MI5. For the latter two agencies -at least – he operated agents both north and south of the border. Finally he had frequent contact with the SAS who were remarkably prominent and powerful both as a military force and separately in the intelligence sphere, their exact role being not always very clear. So obviously he has explicit inside knowledge of all the big beasts of British Intelligence that operate in Ireland and elsewhere. To give you an idea about the kind of information they obviously did not want him to talk about here is an anecdote he later picked up about an SAS NCO called 'ginge' that he sometimes worked with:

"The NCO had been tasked to keep surveillance on an old man who was thought to be giving assistance to the IRA. After a week or so of following the man he became bored and one night, as the man was returning home from the pub on his push-bike the NCO ran him over in a land-rover. Removing the lights from the victims bike, the NCO reported a fatal 'traffic accident'. A coroner's court attended by the NCO wearing an ordinary regimental, non SAS uniform, returned a verdict of accidental death, on the grounds that the man had no light on his bike in poor visibility. The NCO gained some notoriety in his unit and was thereafter referred to as 'Genie and his magic lamp'."

He is also on the record as saying this about the power of the UK intelligence agencies:

"The politicians can't bring the intelligence community under control because in many cases they are being blackmailed or owe their positions to these very same people. There are also many media people on the security services books." In general he talks about "frightened good people" being crushed by the intelligence agencies.

(Fred Holroyd and Nick Burbridge, *War Without Honour* (Hull, 1989), p.13,29-40,85,98,107, http://lindahome.freeuk.com/donovansview/ireland.html and the last quote from the above mentioned Dublin meeting.)

In the case of Major Wallace it was revealed by Clive Ponting that the MOD set up a special committee inside the ministry to coordinate the slander of him. They mainly portrayed him as a 'Walter Mitty' and delusional type figure. One of Wallace's claims was for example that he was a sky diving enthusiast and regularly parachuted as a PR exercise for the army. So the MOD briefed that that was typical of the way he just made things up and it was discovered that there were no files in his name in the British Parachuting Association as their should be in that regulated sport, so justifying the MOD's claims. It took Paul Foot the late journalist to check with the international association who hold duplicate copies of the records to find out that they knew all about him and this showed that the British association had been burgled deliberately as part of the discrediting campaign. Such is the way the system works unfortunately.
(http://planetquo.com/The-Wilson-Plots)

The late Zviad Gamsakhurdia, the first democratically elected leader of Georgia, was hit by widespread western media reports saying he suffered from "apparent madness" and even talk of setting up an international symposium to determine his mental health. The webpage set up by his supporters calls it 'Slandercraft'.(http://www.geocities.com/shavlego/slander.html) He had fallen out with the American government just before he was ousted in a coup. One of the few incoming leaders of the former Soviet states who had no connections with the old communist party he expresses interesting opinions on events at that time here:
http://www.geocities.com/shavlego/zg_1d.html and his letters http://www.-geocities.com/shavlego/lett_1.html .
He lists 'Bush, Baker, Genscher, Kohl' as siding with the USSR at the time which presumably means they also cooperated with the strategy of slander etc. He also stated once that he believed Gorbachev himself was behind the Soviet Union coup and furthermore that most of the leaders of the newly independent states in the eastern block were in fact communist stooges, the exceptions being himself and Landsbergis in Lithuania. He is also known in much of the western media as a dictator which is difficult to understand considering he was in office for only about a year during which he won parliamentary elections with c. 60 percent of the vote and presidential elections with 86 per cent.

A New Labour Councillor at Hetton-le-Hole, Tyne-Wear called Maurice Kellett had many run ins with well connected local business people including demanding at the council that some freemasons should declare their interest in lands that were being discussed. He has been repeatedly threatened with sectioning under the Mental Health Act for his pains. He has been informed by hospital staff that "You buck the establishment and it will buck you back".
(http://www.usenetbot.com/viewtopic/421492/Maurice-Kellett-The-Facts and http://www4.all-usenet-archive.com/pages/34101.html)

It has been alleged that the late police whistle blower Andy McCardle was forcibly detained and drugged at the State Hospital, Carstairs, apparently because he held some "delusional belief" that involved the state and drug smuggling (http://hardware.mcse.ms/archive125-2005-1-139401.html). He died in their custody in December 2004.

James Heny Graf an ex-employee of the New York State Department of Mental Hygiene describes how his former employers would trawl though federal and local intelligence databases seeking discrediting information on people. Forging information accusing people of being "mentally incompetent" was particularly common it seems. Here is a few quotes from his account:
"They made up whatever lies they needed to, told people whatever they needed to tell them in order to make them refuse to listen to me or cooperate with me. ...Though never charged with a crime in any state or nation, though never the subject of any mental competency hearing, I became nevertheless the butt of prejudicial presumption, mindless ridicule, criminal obstruction, and senseless discrimination."
...
"Over the years, my former employers enjoyed frequent contact with law enforcement and intelligence agencies, including the military. My workplace in the 1980s became a hotbed of covert intelligence activity. In alignment with Reagan Administration policies, these forces concerned themselves primarily with "fighting terrorism" and the "war on drugs." Their definition of "terrorism" was loose, to say the least".
"...my employers, wishing to rid themselves of this troublesome "left-leaning" speech therapist, used their contacts in federal agencies to focus attention on me."
"Throughout the 1980s, my agency's egregiously unscrupulous administrators used all the power and influence at their disposal to eliminate employees they didn't like. Obscenely intrusive, unbelievably extensive "lifestyle" investigations became a powerful administrative tool for staff reduction through intimidation – blackmailing, blackballing, and blacklisting. When they could not unearth real evidence, the "evaluators" simply invented it. Claims of "national security" and "police business" assured universal cooperation and secrecy. The process is practically identical to the system of psychiatric discreditation that prevailed in the last days of the Soviet Union..."
(http://pub17.ezboard.com/fhumanrightsfrm2.showMessage?topicID=8.topic)
(http://www.angelfire.com/j/jhgraf/hereshow.html)

Eric Shine a Federal Officer in the U.S. Merchant Marine has alleged that "The Department of Homeland Security has prosecuted me for over the last year at great expense to many parties and programs, for being "medically/ mentally incompetent" and without so much as a hearing." He is alleging widespread corruption in that area. (http://www.the-catbird-seat.net/EricShine.htm).
"Plus, the DHS/ USCG have seized medical records, falsified medical records, put out 'Be On Look Out' warning posters on me saying that I "may be dangerous" and more."

Army Reserve Lt. Jullian Goodrum was further confined in a locked psychiatric ward on the advise of military officials after he had "asked for an investigation into the death in Iraq of a 22-year-old soldier in his 212th Transportation Company."(http://www.upi.com/view.cfm?StoryID=20040525-111343-1697r)

A US army sergeant requested his commander to investigate abuses against some Iraqis that he had witnessed:
"instead, the company commander accused him of lying and threatened to have him examined by a psychiatrist if he did not withdraw the request in 30 seconds. When he refused to withdraw the request, the company commander confiscated his weapon, withdrew his security clearance, placed him under 24 hour surveillance, and had him examined by the psychiatrist."
http://www.abc.net.au/news/newsitems/200503/s1318789.htm

28. This seems a very common practice. See for example the experiences of Rodney Stich, a veteran of WW2 and a noted writer on abuses in the aviation industry and other areas in American society. Summing up an episode in his book 'Defrauding America' a reviewer notes:
"As a result of Stich's continuous whistle blowing, retaliation ensued when his assets were seized (to take away the funding of Stich's activist activities) through misuse of chapter 11 bankruptcy proceedings, and his refusal to "surrender" eventually led to him being sentenced to prison on trumped up charges."(the amazon.com page on "Defrauding America..." by Rodney Stich)

While Colin Wallace, another panelist at the above mentioned Dublin meeting and formerly a senior figure in the liaison between the security forces and the media in northern Ireland, is such a famous case they wrote a book about it (Paul Foot, *Who framed Colin Wallace* (London, 1989)). Major Colin Wallace was particularly trying to tell people that the government permitted Kincora and he also asks as Tim Dalyell MP related in the House of Commons: "why do we allow Army-related intelligence services to harass politicians? This was long before the world had heard of Peter Wright; it is the reason why Wallace was thrown out of Northern Ireland, and then harassed." (www.parliament.the-stationary-office.co.uk/pa/cm198889/cmhansrd/1989-10-18/Debate-6.html and www.parliament.the-stationary-office.co.uk/pa/cm198889/cmhansrd/1989-06-08/Debate-5.html)

Mark Barnsley was also stitched up on false charges as a political activist in the UK (http://flag.blackened.net/revolt/mark.html) .

29. The Phoenix Annual 2004, p 62.

30. Ralph McGehee the ex-CIA agent who revealed a lot of that agencies nefarious goings on in Thailand describes such a process as happening to him. He points out that: "I suppose the internal justification for their actions is to inves-

tigate me in a 'counterintelligence' investigation," he wrote in one message, "but their actions are so blatant, its real purpose can only be to intimidate me." (http://www.parascope.com/articles/1197/mcgehee3.htm)
His experiences in the CIA are described here:
http://home1.gte.net/res0k62m/mcgehee.htm

31. A political activist from the UK, who was arrested just before the Mayday protests in Dublin, had her passport confiscated as one of her bail conditions although she was only charged with trespassing. The case took forever to get to court and without such ID she couldn't even claim social welfare. (https://www3.indymedia.org.uk/en/2004/05/291959.html)

Eamonn Delaney, who used to work in the Department of Foreign Affairs, revealed that there is a blacklist there to prevent certain people from ever claiming Irish passports despite being eligible for them. He at any rate seemed to regard it as quite arbitrary the criteria that caused some people to go on the list and that it seemed to grow every year. Some people involved in custody disputes or owing money to the Department of Foreign Affairs were also on it. Also "sometimes if you looked up a famous gangland or IRA name you'd find not only that name but an entire family."(Eamonn Delaney, *Accidental Diplomat, My years in the Irish Foreign Service* (Dublin, 2001), p.41.)

Also the post 9-11 steps taken on air travel in America that are supposed to restrict travel by 'terrorist suspects' have actually impeded travel by people like Cat Stevens and Edward Kennedy, a 71-year-old Milwaukee nun and peace activist, and Barbara Olshansky, an attorney with the left-leaning Center for Constitutional Rights, who has been: "subjected to strip- and full-body searches every time she's flown since 9/11, even though she has no criminal record." (http://www.cbsnews.com/stories/2004/04/06/terror/main610466.shtml   and http://www.jdlasica.com/blog/archives/2003_08_03.html)

32. http://home.att.net/~mcra/microwav.htm
Association of National Security Alumni December 1992 Julianne McKinney.

This person is an expert in the use of those strange devices like those used in the famous microwave attack by the Soviet Union on the US embassy in Moscow mentioned by Henry Kissinger:

"In April 1976, Secretary of State Henry Kissinger sent the following telegram to the US Embassy in Moscow: "Beginning in 1960, the Soviet Union directed high frequency beams of radiation at the US Embassy in Moscow which were calculated not to pick up intelligence, but cause physiological effects on personnel. It has been verified that the effects are not temporary. Definitely tied to such radiation and the UHF/VHF electromagnetic waves are: (A) Cataracts, (B) Heart attacks, (C) Malignancies, (D) Circulatory problems, and (E) Permanent deterioration of the nervous system. In most cases, the after-effects do not

become evident until long after exposure – a decade or more.""""
(http://www.wanttoknow.info/mindcontrollers10pg)

In the McKinney quote I am guilty of leaving out the adjective electronic as I am trying to extrapolate the idea that these agencies aim for isolation in their targets, from the speculation that they use these devices to achieve it. I'm not saying there is no justification in what she says. It seems those gadgets were used extensively during the Cold War, after all Ms McKinney is rumored to have run agents out of Berlin for the Pentagon, during those years. To get a list of the sort of technology I am talking about I recommend this manual www.us-afa.af.mil/inss/OCP/ocp15.pdf. Note the url, the af.mil is the official web space of the American air force, hence the list it supplies is clearly taken seriously by at least one branch of the US government. This is the title:

"NONLETHAL WEAPONS:
TERMS AND REFERENCE
USAF Institute for National Security Studies
USAF Academy, Colorado

Robert J. Bunker
December 1996

We believe you will find this reference book to be a useful addition to the current literature on nonlethal weapons. Its target audience is individuals who deal with military operations other than war, special operations, or weapons procurement and sales."

As you see from that last quote the only areas really left are some type of law enforcement /intelligence capacity. I cannot describe all the technologies because there are so many different types of horrible devices pointed at people to make them ill or catch them like microwaves, infrared, ultrasound etc all described here in a clinical sobriety. Here is a few to give you some idea of how wide-ranging this is. From the spooky:
"Hologram, Death. Hologram used to scare a target individual to death. Example, a drug lord with a weak heart sees the ghost of his dead rival appearing at his bedside and dies of fright."

to the mind boggling:
"Biotechnical, Neuro-Implant. Computer implants into the brain which allow for behavioral modification and control. Current research is experimental in nature and focuses on lab animals such as mice"

or just disagreeable:
"Biotechnical, Malodorous Agents. Foul-smelling gases and sprays such as hydrogen sulphide (H2S) or a compound known as NaS8 which is used in making plastics. Could be delivered by a grenade. Past work on "cultural specific"

agents has also been undertaken [356,529]. See also Biotechnical, Project Agile"

or ambitious:
"Theoretical, New Gunpowder Revolution. The perception that the wide scale application of nonlethal technology on the battlefield will be as significant as the fielding of gunpowder based firearms during the European Renaissance"

As you can see under the heading nonlethal can lay a multitude of evils:
"Biotechnical, Genetic Alteration. The act of changing genetic code to create a desired less-than-lethal but longterm disablement effect, perhaps for generations, thereby creating a societal burden."

As far as I know the simple truth is that the use or otherwise of these devices in Ireland is simply unknown, but hopefully unlikely.

33. http://www.allaboutaccount.com/finding-a-secret-bank-account-in-a-divorce.html quoting from www.timesonline.co.uk/article/0,,2091-1452653,00.html .
Detective Sergeant John White and his informant Paddy Dixon have alleged that Garda authorities permitted the Omagh bomb 'to go through' .They "also allege that a clandestine deal between the Irish government and the Real IRA just weeks after the bombing led to charges being dropped against eight men arrested following the explosion." (http://observer.guardian.co.uk/nireland/story/0,11008,1066420,00.html)

I have concentrated in this account on the known activities of some intelligence agencies but possibly the real pattern of these networks comes from the experiences of P2 in Italy. As everybody knows this is a masonic lodge which controlled much of Italian politics in the post war period, possibly set up and certainly backed by the CIA, exercising effective control for its own ends the domestic Italian intelligence agencies and affiliated with the senior English Grand Lodge in London. So maybe this policy of isolation that I describe can be carried out by a wider group than simply a state controlled domestic intelligence agency. Robert Dougal Watt an auditor with EU Court of Auditors describes an atmosphere in the EU where the freemasons/mafia/ and western intelligence agencies seek to dominate and influence the political life of the EU. Here is some of his analysis of P2 and its leader Gelli:

"As part of this general US policy, from 1947 onwards the US Office of Strategic Services, forerunner of the CIA, undertook a number of initiatives designed to secure the defence of Western Europe from these twin threats of internal communist subversion and Soviet invasion.

Freemasonry – persecuted by Hitler, Mussolini and Vichy – was revived in post-1945 continental Europe with the support of US covert agencies. These encouraged freemasonry as "secret networks" of society's powerful: useful for combatting internal communist subversion, by covert as well as overt means; and foreseen as useful for anti-communist civil resistance, in the event of Soviet invasion and occupation.

US covert agencies were also instrumental in resurrecting the mafia – crushed by Mussolini – as a bulwark against communism in Italy's impoverished south. Until c.1970, the mafia fulfilled this role, to which it owed its origins in the nineteenth century: of combating those enemies of the established order against whom the authorities could or would not act; in return for implicit toleration of their extortion and other rackets.
...
The P2 conspiracy was initially attributed to KGB subversion – every Italian political party was compromised by the scandal, with the exception of the Communist Party. However, this attribution – traceable directly to the Italian secret services, themselves compromised by P2; indirectly to the CIA; and also promulgated by British secret services – was discredited by the following Italian parliamentary enquiry. Upon the basis of a detailed study of Gelli's personal history and secret service dossier, the enquiry concluded "that Gelli himself must belong to the secret services, since this is the only logical explanation for the cover they gave Gelli, both in a passive way (not gathering information on him) and an active one (not providing information about him to political authorities who requested it)" (quoted in Short, p550). However, given that Venerable Master Gelli himself was "puppet-master" of all three of Italy's secret service chiefs, his status seems to have been greater than merely "national". In this light, it can be deduced that P2 owed its origins to US "cold war" policy, in a period when the Italian Communist Party was receiving one third of the electoral vote, and rising in popularity. This conclusion is consistent with US action following revelation of the conspiracy; pressure was applied on the Italian government by NATO, to keep in post the senior military, naval, air force and secret service chiefs compromised by the scandal, ostensibly due to a need to maintain stability during a period marked by uncertainty in the Middle East." (http://www.justresponse.net/DougalWatt3Sep02.html and the links therein, note that Mr Watt has written three documents on this subject, and his own experiences, all of which are extremely interesting and all three should be read by anyone interested in the EU.
http://www.freemasonrywatch.org/P2.html for more on P-2 .
http://www.skepticfiles.org/socialis/cosiga3a.htm for evidence of CIA involvement.)

P-2 being a Masonic lodge, and in good standing with the Grand Lodge in London as told to Mr Watt, is maybe relevant to this practice of isolation. Here for example is an account of some Masonic practices, related by a senior Civil Servant in Whitehall to Stephen Knight:

"'It is not difficult to ruin a man,' he said. 'And I will tell you how it is done time and again. There are more than half a million brethren under the jurisdiction of Grand Lodge.

Christopher explained that Masonry's nationwide organization of men from most walks of life provided one of the most efficient private intelligence networks imaginable. Private information on anybody in the country could normally be accessed very rapidly through endless permutations of masonic contacts – police, magistrates, solicitors, bank managers, Post Office staff ('very useful in supplying copies of a man's mail'), doctors, government employee bosses of firms and nationalized industries etc., etc. dossier of personal data could be built up on anybody very quickly. When the major facts of an individual's life were known, areas of vulnerability would become apparent. Perhaps he is in financial difficulties; perhaps he has some social vice – if married he might 'retain a mistress' or have proclivity for visiting prostitutes; perhaps there is something in his past he wishes keep buried, some guilty secret, a criminal offence (easily obtainable through Freemason police of doubtful virtue), or other blemish on his character: all these and more could be discovered via the wide-ranging masons network of 600,000 contacts, a great many of whom were disposed to do favours for one another because that had been their prime motive for joining.

Sometimes this information gathering process – often involving a long chain of masonic contacts all over the country and possibly abroad – would be unnecessary. Enough would be known in advance about the adversary to initiate any desired action against him.

I asked how this 'action' might be taken.

'Solicitors are very good at it,' said Christopher. 'Get your man involved in something legal – it need not be serious – and you have him.' Solicitors, I was told, are 'past masters' at causing endless delays, generating useless paperwork, ignoring instructions, running up immense bills, misleading clients into taking decisions damaging to themselves.

Masonic police can harass, arrest on false charges, and plant evidence. 'A businessman in a small community or person in public office arrested for dealing in child pornography, for indecent exposure, or for trafficking in drugs is at the end of the line,' said Christopher. 'He will never work again. Some people have committed suicide after experiences of that kind.'

Masons can bring about the situation where credit companies and banks withdraw credit facilities from individual clients and tradesmen, said my informant. Bank can foreclose. People who rely on the telephone for their work can be cut off for long periods. Masonic employees of local authorities can arrange for a person's drains to be inspected and extensive damage to be reported, thus burdening the person with huge repair bills; workmen carrying out the job can 'find' – In reality cause – further damage. Again with regard to legal matters, a fair hearing is hard to get when a man in ordinary circumstances is in financial difficulties. If he is trying to fight a group of unprincipled Freemasons skilled in using the 'network' it will be impossible because masonic Department of Health and Social Security and Law Society officials can delay applications for

Legal Aid endlessly.

'Employers, if they are Freemasons or not, can be given private information about a man who has made himself an enemy of Masonry. At worst he will be dismissed (if the information is true) or consistently passed over for promotion.'

Christopher added, 'Masonic doctors can also be used. But for some reason doctors seem to be the least corruptible men. There are only two occurrences of false medical certificates issued by company doctors to ruin the chances of an individual getting a particular job which I know about. It's not a problem that need greatly worry us like the rest.'

...you finish up not knowing who you can trust. You can get no help because your story sounds so paranoid that you are thought a crank, one of those nuts who think the whole world is a conspiracy against them. It is a strange phenomenon. By setting up a situation that most people will think of as fantasy, these people can poison every part of a person's life.

...

When that happens [complete isolation] and they are without friends wherever they look, they become easy meat. The newspapers will not touch them'.

'There is no defence against an evil which only the victims and the perpetrators know exists.'"

(http://www.tlio.demon.co.uk/masons.htm)

Its by no means just the Stasi in East Germany that has shown the possible role of intelligence agencies in a modern state as you can see from the experiences of many western countries like Switzerland:

"Suddenly, as if from nowhere, the squeaky-clean image that postwar generations had of themselves and their country was shown to have been an illusion. In 1989 ...[among other scandals] it emerged that the Swiss secret police had been keeping hundreds of thousands of files on individuals under the guise of monitoring anti-patriotic activity. In 1999, an accountant in the defence department under investigation in a multimillion-franc fraud case – the largest in Swiss history – turned out to be an intelligence agent, and claimed he had withdrawn the money on the orders of his boss to fund the secret training of a shady battalion of highly armed agents for purposes unknown."

(http://switzerland.isyours.com/e/guide/contexts/sonderfall.html)

This is the 'secret files affair', some 700,00 of them. (http://virtor.bar.admin.ch/en/rec/the/sta.aspx)

In New Zealand 31 historians and political scientists are complaining that access to secret police files are less open and unrestricted than "those of the former Soviet Bloc."

(http://www.aranz.org.nz/SITE_Default/SITE_publications/papers_online/rachels_intelligence_article.asp)

In Germany:

"Releasing statements from two of the key people who managed their financial affairs since the 70's, the party opened a Pandora's Box of secret accounts, safe deposit boxes in Switzerland and million mark payments made via intelligence services to political parties in Spain and Portugal.
...
THE German secret service employed two figures in the Kohl scandal, it has emerged, something that raises questions about the possible involvement of intelligence agents in the channelling of foreign funds into party coffers. The two businessmen pivotal to the financing scandals in the Christian Democratic Union are the arms dealer Karlheinz Schreiber, who admits handing over quantities of cash to party leaders, and Dieter Holzer, who admits having received the equivalent of £16 million for his part in securing an East German refinery contract for Elf Aquitaine. Western intelligence sources say that both were on the books of the Munich-based Bundesnachrichtendienst (BND), the equivalent of MI6." (http://www.kc3.co.uk/~dt/kohl.htm)

In France they have only recently found out about what you might call a secret secret intelligence unit that reported directly to Mitterand. French journalist: "Plenel's phone was tapped by a secret anti-terrorist unit which reported directly to Mitterand after the reporter wrote a series of articles pinpointing the role of French agents in the blowing up of the Greenpeace vessel Rainbow Warrior off New Zealand in 1985. Plenel was one of several people including journalists, lawyers, politicians and a noted model and film actress whose telephone conversations were monitored from 1982 to 1986 by the anti-terror unit." http://www.freemedia.at/wpfr/Europe/france.htm)

Meanwhile some regular practices in France are quite astonishing:
"One of the most illustrative [of French 'raison d'etat'] is the use of the "special fund" representing 0.1% of the state budget, which is granted to each new government. This serves, as is known by everybody, to finance political campaigns and secret operations (as disclosed recently, sometimes with political scope) by the DGE (French State Secret Information Services). This is with total impunity and without any accountability (money is distributed in bank notes)."
{ http://www.transparency.org/working_papers/country/france_paper.html)

In Britain they most certainly aren't releasing secret police files but nonetheless we might be able to speculate on what they contain. Here is a revealing account of MI5 and the miners strike by Fern Lane in the Guardian May 5 2004: http://www.cpa.org.au/garchve04/1181miners.html .

CHAPTER 2

The O'Hara family, Adrienne McGlinchey and Kathy O'Beirne.

The O'Hara family from Meath were astonished to be greeted at their door recently by the gardaí, who, accompanied by a court order, proceeded to take their children into care, very much against their wishes. They feel, it is clear from the media reports, that this step was taken because they had begun to speak out in condemnation of the bad public services available for their autistic children. Mr and Mrs O'Hara will now have to undergo a psychological examination if they hope to keep custody of their children. It is not known what criteria was given by the state that could explain what causes it to insist on this step apart from the fact that the couple had gone public with their frustrations about the health and education service. This has caused some disquiet as Dolores O'Riordan, a grandmother of an autistic child, has written in a letter to the Irish Independent: "To add insult to injury, I read that in order to regain custody of their children, the parents have had to agree to a psychological assessment. Are we now living in a totalitarian state?"[1] There is also many references to other families in the same situation that seem to have been silenced by these means. While it is pure speculation, one wonders if that will prove to be an intrusive and far reaching examination and whether or not any negative results of it might get leaked to other departments or to the media. Of course a totally in depth analysis like this would be something few people could survive without some sticking points. I guess most people are also aware of the serious allegations that autism is caused by the MMR vaccine, including genetic tests conducted in TCD that link the strain of measles used in the vaccine to the strain of measles found in autism sufferers. The latest information on the O'Hara family is that the children were released home "on the grounds that the parents would have no further contact with the media."[2]

The other case I thought I'd mention was the interview of Adreinne McGlinchey on the Late Late Show.[3] Her story is that she was arrested one night on false terrorist charges and held by the Gardai in Donegal. When she got out and spoke to her family she found out that they had already been given a lurid story by the gardai claiming that she was in the IRA and unfortunately they believed the gardai. So in a huff she left the house and sustained herself for a time elsewhere cashing some cheques from a family chequebook to tide her over. Then she was arrested on a charge of stealing the money from her family. Her family had agreed to sign a document alleging this theft on the basis that the gardai had told them that the money was going to the IRA. She didn't know that that was the only reason her family were making the claim about the cheques, and the gardai were constantly telling her how her family were out to get her and prosecute her over the money. So now she was isolated from them and also from the law because the law, in the form of the powerful garda special branch, were pressing false charges on her related to her non existent membership of the IRA. Hence she was unable to resist pressure put on her to become a kind of fake IRA informer. Her garda handlers meanwhile were acquiring a great reputation as being experts on terrorism in Donegal. This isn't so surprising when you consider that they were basically creating it. They were manufacturing the explosives, purchasing all the materials, supplying all the weapons and ammunition, faking arms finds, it has been alleged even explosive attacks across the border etc. Incidentally she of course was not a terrorist nor were her family or anything like that but it is a political family, Adrienne's father was a Senator for a while. When the story began to emerge and get some publicity she describes how she was then accused of being a 'Walter Mitty' kind of person who just made the whole thing up.[4] One reason as well why she felt she couldn't get out of this trap was simply that whenever she complained about anything she got a punch in the face from her Garda handler.[5]

When I was writing up this 'strategy of isolation' tactic that seems to be used by intelligence agencies east and west I left out references to that kind of physical intimidation not knowing how common it was. But in fact threatening phone calls particularly is something you come across quite often when reading up on the experiences of dissidents. What makes me wonder now that it must be a common thing is the reference recently to Dana's experience in politics in Ireland. Her last Presidential run clearly showed that she was very disliked by the powers that be in Ireland and was blatantly frozen out by the system with only a tiny number of voices like Michael Ring prepared to stand up for the idea of a presidential election with her in the race. Apparently she is now stating that behind the scenes of her life in Irish politics she was receiving death threats against her and her family.[6]

One Irish person who has to cope with this kind of thing all the time apparently is Kathy O'Beirne who is trying to highlight the case of the former Magdalen victims being incarcerated in Irish mental institutions. She "has received constant threats after she decided to go public with her allegations." The threats are to "not rock the boat" and "not to talk to anybody about what happened to Elizabeth". This last is a reference to the recent death of Elizabeth Keegan as described in a recent magazine article:

> "Rita Nolan, Elizabeth Keegan and several other Magdalen victims have died in circumstances, which to this layman [the journalist] at least, seem disturbing."
> [Kathy is quite certain that Rita Nolan was not insane although she suffered panic attacks, as Kathy says:]

"Wouldn't you if you were locked up all your life simply because you were raped or abused by someone in authority?... there are many beautiful young laundry girls in that unit [in Grangegorman] who don't even know their own names because they are so heavily drugged. They are not even allowed to speak to each other."

Its the state that imprisons these people, not the church, and you cannot help thinking that its hardly the religious orders who are really threatening Kathy. Anyhow she "says she was obstructed all the way by the church authorities and Health Board officials. Their attitude was, she says, to leave the past alone."
"Despite changing her phone numbers four times and complaining to the police, the threats continued in a more serious and frightening way."[7]

I know I shouldn't generalise but I know of only one case where the perpetrators of this kind of ongoing threatening phone call harassment were unmasked. One of the Donegal families who were getting this treatment employed a private investigator and he managed to trace the source of the calls from phone records. It turned out that they came from the home phone number of a garda who has admitted that an informer of his made the calls while he was there.[8]

There must a pattern in all this somewhere!

Footnotes

1. Irish Independent 18 March 2005, p35.

2. On the autism vaccine link: http://www.autismconnect.org/news.asp?
itemtype=news&section=000100010001&page=30&id=4849 and the latest on
the family: http://www.indymedia.ie/newswire.php?story_id=72934 .

3. RTE1, March 18 2005.

4. It is now I think totally accepted by everyone that there is nothing wrong
with Adrienne's mental health but this didn't stop the state from erring badly
on this score at the time, as her sister Karen has pointed out in a comment at
http://www.indymedia.ie/newswire.php?story_id=69044. She got the 'mad'
slander while the McBreartys got the 'bad' one. Here is an example of the kind
of media publicity she got in the Sunday Independent (Nov 10 2002) based on
an opening statement given to the Morris tribunal:
"ADRIENNE McGlinchey, the source of allegations at the Morris tribunal that
two gardai killed cattle dealer Richie Barron, has emerged as a pathetic "Walter Mitty" character.
...[quoting Counsel for the tribunal:] 'As this narrative progresses it might be
reasonable, we feel, to have doubts in relation to her self-acclaimed role as terrorist and as informer, and to wonder how she might appropriately have been
handled.' [Of course her story started by being arrested by the gardai, there was
therefore nothing 'self-acclaimed' about her case.]
 He then unfolded a picture of the bizarre and pathetic lifestyle of the 37-year-
old daughter of former Fianna Fail senator Bernard McGlinchey.

He recounted the evidence of Det Sgt Michael Keane: "Adrienne McGlinchey
could be described as a Walter Mitty type person. She always liked to draw attention to herself. At times she would go on a spree of drinking and. .. would
drink herself stupid.

"It was a regular occurrence to observe Adrienne McGlinchey on her own or in
the company of Yvonne Devine, dashing across the roadway, hiding in cars, in
hedges, laneways etc. .. At night time I encountered her carrying small objects
similar to the component parts contained within a commercial radio or TV,
torches and batteries; in some cases the batteries were taped together."

As a result of this bizarre behaviour, Miss McGlinchey was arrested on many
occasions, including six times under the Offences Against the State Act, when
found in possession of suspicious-looking objects. On most of these occasions,
senior officers intervened to have her released.
...
The tribunal was able to contact the taxi driver, who said he was well aware
that the two were involved in eccentric behaviour. They were, he said, "two

loony bins"."
(http://www.unison.ie/irish_independent/stories.php3?
ca=36&si=866977&issue_id=8316).

5. see also http://www.emigrant.ie/article.asp?
iCategoryID=177&iArticleID=9831 and
http://archives.tcm.ie/businesspost/2003/06/01/story344592683.asp.

6. Irish Independent,18 March 2005, p3.

7. Aodhan Madden, *What happened to Rita Nolan? / Another victim locked away in Grangegorman dies in strange circumstance.* Irish Crime Vol.1 issue 7, Dec-Jan 2004/5 p.8-11.
It should be stated though that Hermann Kelly, in his book *Kathy's Real Story* (Dunleer, 2007), has persuasively cast serious doubt over the integrity of Kathy O'Beirne's allegations.

8. http://archives.tcm.ie/businesspost/2003/10/19/story629480993.asp .

CHAPTER 3

Orwellian Ireland

"I believe that spies, the security services, in the world generally, are becoming increasingly powerful and that our civil liberties are being eroded." – former Irish government minister Justin Keating.

This chapter is an attempt to put flesh on those bones. I attempt to list some of those agencies active in Ireland, to list some of the powers they can and do use to make life difficult for those that cross them and to look at some of the technology they have access to. I also point out their role in influencing the western media. In the following chapter and appendix I try to show the controlling role of those agencies in Irish paramilitary groups with some international comparisons to this type of intelligence agency support for 'terrorist' groups that they are ostensibly opposing. An Orwellian island in an Orwellian world.

Intelligence Agencies in Ireland

MI6

I guess I could start with MI6. It has been the subject of a recent book by Stephen Dorril from which we find that they "keep on file indiscretions, however politically sensitive, of crown servants, MP's etc." There is also a department of MI6 dedicated to planting false stories in the media as former agent Richard Tomlinson states:

"I/OPS looks after MI6's media contacts, not only to provide cover facilities but also to spin MI6 propaganda. For example they mounted a smear operation against the Egyptian candidate, Boutros Boutros-Ghali, who was regarded as dangerously francophile by the CIA. The CIA are constitutionally prevented from manipulating the press so they asked MI6 to help. Using their contacts in the British and American media, I/OPS planted a series of stories to portray Boutros-Ghali as unbalanced, claiming that he was a believer in the existence of UFOs and extra-terrestrial life."

It is said to have had a leading role in politics in both parts of Ireland during the early years of the troubles and it appears to have continued this role behind the scenes. For example there is this reference from the former foreign correspondent of the Daily Mirror which if true would certainly rewrite a controversial chapter in the recent history of Ireland:

"Until then [1972] responsibility for the British government's intelligence organisation rested with MI6, Britain's Secret Intelligence Service, which had mainly been confined to political operations in the Republic. It was MI6 that was responsible for setting up the arms deal that led to the trial of Irish government ministers Charles Haughey and Neil Blaney."[1]

I have got most of these references from Phoenix magazine in Dublin, Ireland's answer to Private Eye and we would be very much in the dark as to these agencies if that magazine wasn't around. This is an account from the magazine of Jan 14 1994 referring to some 'close liaison' between Martin McGuinness and Michael Oatley of MI6:

[Michael Oatley is] "the manager in fact of private investigators with offices in Saville Row [Kroll Associates]. He first met McGuinness in 1972 in Cheyne Walk, Chelsea, when he was a high-flyer at MI6 headquarters in Century House. A year later he became second in command at British Secret Service (MI6) headquarters in Northern Ireland at Laneside, Craigavad.

Since then, McGuinness and Oatley have got together regularly over the years in secret, and at one time (during the 1981 hunger strike) met on an almost daily basis. More recently, Oatley and McGuinness met in Donegal in 1990. It was that meeting which sparked the ongoing peace process of the Hume-Adams talks, a Downing Street declaration, and speculation about a peace deal.

Officially, Oatley retired as a Controller (one of the highest ranks in the Secret Service) in 1991 on reaching the age of 56. However, never a man to let friendships die, he kept in regular contact with Martin – with consequences which we are now reading about.

When historians peruse British archives relating to Irish events, they may find that the codename MOUNTAIN CLIMBER keeps cropping up in connection with the Hume-Adams talks and subsequent events. MOUNTAIN CLIMBER is the house name in the Secret Service for Michael Oatley."[2]

MI6 in particular are said to be quite fond of privatising out some of their more sensitive operations to private security firms [3] and presumably Kroll Associates is one such private security firm in light of the above described links. Kroll has an incredible international reach[4] and is called in by many governments and large corporations to get them out of whatever security problem they are faced with. For example in 2004 Abbey National, the big UK financial house, had a problem in that a whistle blower was distributing a letter which detailed some 'conspiracy theory' involving their treasury department. So they called in Kroll and now they no longer have that problem. Not since the suggested source of the leak took a dive from the 5th floor balcony of their London HQ while being interviewed by Kroll.[5]

MI5

Then there is obviously MI5 which is the main agency seeking to micro-manage the political life of the UK. It recruited 25 agents for example to infiltrate the very small Socialist Workers Party.[6] Tony Benn once said that if a British citizen wrote two letters to his local paper complaining about parking spaces that MI5 would open a file on him/her. [7] It is also said that they have a file on any person who goes up for local or national election.[8] Also "it is common knowledge amongst journalists that MI5 has a very close relationship with London's Fleet Street hacks. The Security Service has at least two agents working in every major newspaper office."

There is also a lot of talk of cliques operating and using the resources of the various agencies to run campaigns of their own and famously this is what happened to MI5 in the 70s and 80s as revealed by people like Colin Wallace and Peter Wright. At that time a right wing clique secretly operating within MI5 ran a campaign known as 'Clockwork Orange' to influence the political life of the UK by using the vast information available to MI5 to slander those they disliked, as described in one of their planning documents:

> "Given the following, it is clear that the campaign for the next general election will be heavily dominated by the personality factor, and every effort should be made to exploit character weaknesses in 'target' subjects, and in particular:
> (a) Financial misbehaviour
> (b) Sexual misbehaviour
> (c) Political misbehaviour"[9]

Here is an account from the Phoenix on MI5 in the Republic:

> "[Gardai] discovered an extensive MI5 operation which had been set up from London. MI5 activities in the Republic are normally run from either Belfast, covering the Border counties, or from the British Embassy – or 'station' as it is called by its agents – in Ballsbridge. Such is the scale and significance of the current operation

however, that it is being run from London, with the Merrion Road station being unaware even of its existence. Areas in which the Branch have detected MI5 activity include Dublin, Limerick, Offaly, Wicklow, Meath and Galway.

Other MI5 teams that the Branch have uncovered include a couple masquerading as husband and wife who bought an expensive house in Dublin 4. Another team has operated from Stillorgan, both with employment in the Dublin area. Other operatives have been monitored working for a private security firm in the Dublin 2 area. All are described as extremely intelligent, with 'good' accents, and are usually, but not exclusively, drawn from Britain and Northern Ireland. They tend to present themselves as business people with highly qualified technical credentials, often in the computer industry.

MI5 targets in this campaign are widespread; some are obvious – ie, Sinn Fein and the IRA – while others are more alarming, according to the Branch, who believe they have targeted the business and political community. They have even forged links with some of Dublin's top criminals, a development which has caused equal consternation among the IRA and Branch alike.

In the past MI5 have successfully placed agents in the Provos, and, according to garda sources, have recruited one well-known former Sinn Fein leader in a Border county. The current operation has netted several more, including at least four direct agents now working for them inside the Provos in the South. One of their tasks is to promote divisive political issues inside Sinn Fein. The method of contact and recruitment is often unsubtle, with direct approaches being made to Provo members from people describing themselves variously as journalists offering "expenses" for assistance in researching articles about Sinn Fein. Goldhawk has possession of letters from bogus British-based media agencies offering such inducements to Dublin Republicans.

One intriguing aspect of the operation is that MI5 is not confining itself to the Provos. Anybody with political, military or commercial influence is regarded as a desirable target for their agents, and the area they have had most success in penetrating is the business community.

Most intriguing of all, however, is that MI5 have even descended to fraternising with top Dublin criminals. The

45

Branch monitored one meeting between MI5 agents and a known drugs dealer from north County Dublin at a hotel near the airport, and believe that the drugs dealer was relaying information about IRA members. The suspicion is that the arrests of various Dublin criminals and their couriers in England has led to such contacts and the vulnerability of the criminals to such approaches. MI5 is known to engage extensively with criminals in Britain as part of their intelligence gathering activities there. Both the IRA and the Branch are especially nervous at this strange coalition between Dub crims and Brit spooks."[10]

Of course one reason to target the business community is that it could operate as a cut out mechanism in their attempts to influence Irish politics. What I mean is that they can use a business person to bribe a politician say and the hand of MI5 behind the bribe will not be readily visible. MI5 have clearly a big Irish presence and even on the appointment of Manningham Buller as the Director they recruited another 200 agents to work on Irish affairs.[11]

CIA
Then there are a number of references to the big American agencies in Ireland. The CIA is possibly the most famous of those groups and the one with the most power internationally. In the New York Times in 1977 it was reported by John Crewdson that they controlled:

"at least one newspaper in every foreign capital at any given time," one C.I.A. man said, and those that the agency did not own outright or subsidize heavily it infiltrated with paid agents or staff officers who could have stories printed that were useful to the agency and not print those it found detrimental.

In fact, the CIA's influence in the international media was probably much greater than its influence in the U.S. This was because the CIA was prohibited by law from certain actions in the U.S., whereas it was relatively unrestrained outside the country."

At least before the above mentioned legal bar was introduced the CIA played a leading role in controlling the media as this quote from William Colby, the late director of the CIA, indicates:
"The Central Intelligence Agency owns everyone of any significance in the major media." [12] In the UK it was reported by the Guardian:

".. in 1991 journalist Richard Norton-Taylor revealed the existence of a list of something like 500 prominent Britons, including around 90 in the media, who were in the employ of the CIA, and paid through the old friend of the intelligence services, the BCCI."

Some other CIA practices can be seen in this reference from the CIA dissident Victor Marchetti showing their influence on the Italian Secret Services:

"They are trained, for example, to confront disorders and student demonstrations, to prepare dossiers, to make the best possible use of bank data and tax returns of individual citizens, etc. In other words, to watch over the population of their country with the means offered by technology. This is what I call techno-fascism."
13

As regards Ireland it is rumoured that concern to cover up CIA-Garda links is behind the delay in investigating the issue of garda collusion in the death of the RUC officers Breen and Buchanan, from Phoenix again:

"It is from here [the Dundalk garda question] that the story of CIA-Garda cooperation is likely to emerge if the man against whom allegations in relation to Breen and Buchanan is asked under oath, and in public, to recall his life and times in the Special Branch."[14]

It is presumably this CIA-Garda Special Branch connection that the magazine is referring to when it hints at garda involvement in the Equatorial Guinea coup affair.[15] Its also rumoured that many intelligence forms have gone missing that detail this corrupt relationship between the CIA and Garda Special Branch. The affair includes over 100 Irish passports given to the CIA.[16]

FBI
As regards the FBI most senior officers in the gardai have been trained by them, for example the current Garda Commissioner Conroy is a graduate of the FBI Academy and the FBI National Executive Institute. It maybe noteworthy that at the time of his press conference on the Northern Bank Raid he was described on RTE's Prime Time by reporter Jim Cusack as being a strong believer in "intelligence driven policing". Of course this is considered a good thing but it might also be an insight into the kind of FBI tactics that the gardai are using and on that front it might be worthwhile to look at some extracts from a book on FBI tactics

that was endorsed by Phillip Agee, the most important whistleblower in CIA history, as a "must handbook" for all activists. It was written by Brian Glick a lawyer to many activists and now an associate professor of law at Fordham University in New York. It states that these practices continue today but most of the official information relates to the 60s because it was released in the general anti-intelligence agency atmosphere in the US in the mid 70s:

> "While much FBI and police harassment was blatant during the 1960s, and surveillance and infiltration was suspected, talk of CIA-style covert action against domestic dissidents was generally dismissed as "paranoia." It was not until the 1970s, after the damage had been done, that the sordid history of COINTELPRO began to emerge."

> [Supposedly a counter intelligence programme it was found in later Senate Hearings that it was] "adopted for use against perceived domestic threats to the established political and social order."

> "When congressional investigations, political trials, and other traditional legal modes of repression failed to counter the growing movements, and even helped to fuel them, the FBI and police moved outside the law. They resorted to the secret and systematic use of fraud and force to sabotage constitutionally protected political activity. Their methods ranged far beyond surveillance, amounting to a home front version of the covert action for which the CIA has become infamous throughout the world.

> FBI Headquarters secretly instructed its field offices to propose schemes to "expose, disrupt, misdirect, discredit, or otherwise neutralize" specific individuals and groups. Close coordination with local police and prosecutors was strongly encouraged. Other recommended collaborators included friendly news media, business and foundation executives, and university, church, and trade union officials, as well as such "patriotic" organizations as the American Legion.

> 1. Infiltration: Agents and informers did not merely spy on political activists. Their main purpose was to discredit and disrupt. Their very presence served to undermine trust and scare off potential supporters. The FBI

and police exploited this fear to smear genuine activists as agents.

2. Psychological Warfare From the Outside: The FBI and police used myriad other "dirty tricks" to undermine progressive movements. They planted false media stories and published bogus leaflets and other publications in the name of targeted groups. They forged correspondence, sent anonymous letters, and made anonymous telephone calls. They spread misinformation about meetings and events, set up pseudo movement groups run by government agents, and manipulated or strong-armed parents, employers, landlords, school officials and others to cause trouble for activists.

3. Harassment through the Legal System: The FBI and police abused the legal system to harass dissidents and make them appear to be criminals. Officers of the law gave perjured testimony and presented fabricated evidence as a pretext for false arrests and wrongful imprisonment. They discriminatorily enforced tax laws and other government regulations and used conspicuous surveillance, "investigative" interviews, and grand jury subpoenas in an effort to intimidate activists and silence their supporters."

4. Extralegal Force and Violence: The FBI and police threatened, instigated, and themselves conducted break-ins, vandalism, assaults, and beatings. The object was to frighten dissidents and disrupt their movements..."

No doubt the educational link has led to a close relationship between the two groups, there is one reference for example to a garda security audit of Shannon airport "arranged by their friends in the FBI on a nod and wink basis." [17]

The Pentagon

The US military control a number of important intelligence agencies like the Defence Intelligence Agency, Centra Spike and, in the case of the US Navy, the Office of Naval Intelligence. Obviously the US army has had a major impact all around the world since WWII and it would clearly be impossible to summarise all their policies or assets but I thought that this particular secret directive issued by the Pentagon in 1970 deserves a wider audience. It seems to me anyway to carry a potentially sinister meaning as related here by Daniele Ganser, a Senior Researcher at the Center for Security Studies at the Swiss Federal Institute of Technology Zurich, who starts with a quote from the directive which he gets ultimately from an Italian parliamentary inquiry into Italy's powerful P-2 masonic lodge:

' "There may be times when Host Country Governments show passivity or indecision in the face of communist subversion and according to the interpretation of
the US secret services do not react with sufficient effec-
tiveness. Most often such situations come about when
the revolutionaries temporarily renounce the use of
force and thus hope to gain an advantage, as the leaders of the host country wrongly consider the situation to
be secure. US army intelligence must have the means
of launching special operations which will convince
Host Country Governments and public opinion of the
reality of the insurgent danger."

Ongoing research now investigates whether the United
States have according to this directive promoted terrorism in Western Europe carried out through the network
of the secret NATO armies in order to convince European governments of the communist threat. "These
special operations must remain strictly secret", the US
Field Manual FM 30-31B concludes. "Only those persons who are acting against the revolutionary uprising
shall know of the involvement of the US Army in the internal affairs of an allied country. The fact, that the involvement of forces of the US military goes deeper
shall not become known under any circumstances." '

The Pentagon has also been found to have its fingers in the cookie jar
of the mass media when one of its units, the 4th Psychological Operations Unit, was discovered to have employees in CNN and National
Public Radio in the US. This isn't the first time that that psyops unit was
found to be involved in the domestic US media:

"In a case that demonstrated how PSYOP can be used
to manipulate political debates within the United States,
five soldiers from the 4th Group were dispatched to
Washington, D.C., in 1985-86, to work with an "Office
of Public Diplomacy" created by the Reagan National
Security Council. The office promoted the administration's controversial Central America policies, in particular the contra war against Nicaragua's Sandinista government.

According to declassified documents, the soldiers assisted the office's efforts to assess and influence media
coverage of contra funding debates in key congressional districts, using their skills for spotting "exploitable

themes and trends" and offering "intelligence analysis and production of persuasive communications" to Reagan's public-diplomacy team."

As regards Ireland here is a reference from Phoenix (Annual 2004 p.68):

> "The US military attaché in Dublin is a respected guest at monthly meals with G2 officers in McKee Barracks, while his informal visits to Defence Forces GHQ at Parkgate are more frequent. ...[Shannon etc] may not be unconnected with the cosy relationship between the Pentagon's representative in Dublin and the top brass in the Defence Forces."[18]

14th Intelligence Company

This is one of two British intelligence agencies which operate exclusively in Ireland North and South and is controlled directly by 10 Downing Street. This direct link is obviously surprising because usually it is said that the PM's office controls the intelligence agencies via the Joint Intelligence Committee. As it happens that is not the only function of that committee because recently it has been revealed in the Sunday Times that the chairman of this JIC, at present Michael Packenham third son of Lord Longford, has his own large committee to exert preassure on the UK media. How it exerts this pressure exactly is I guess unknown but we do have a reference to the influence the JIC has over the BBC from Dorril's book on MI6:

> "During national security alerts the D[irector] G[eneral]'s office will receive a direct 'subtle' briefing on behalf of the JIC from the resident Security Service [MI5] liaison officer on "the line to take" in terms of what would, and would not be in the national and operational interest to broadcast."

The agency is called the 14th Intelligence Company and is closely associated with the SAS with about 150 members:

> "The 14th Intelligence and Security company, known to it's secretive members as 'The Det' (short for Detachment, another cover name) is still part of the group of ad hoc units involved in various dirty tricks on both sides of the border. The Det's speciality is covert methods of entry, bugging and unattributable killings. Like the now better known FRU it is an "all arms" group which is British military terminology for a unit which draws members from naval, air force or army personnel."

[It is considered to be] "The oldest Dirty Tricks British army unit in the North"..."The Det was the most political formation in the British forces because of its unique chain of command and control...rested ...with the Director of Special Forces who reported direct to Downing Street." [19]

Force Research Unit

The other group that is based exclusively in Ireland is the Force Research Unit which is under the aegis of the Ministry of Defence in London (incidentally MI6 is under the Foreign Office and MI5 is run by the Home Office.) Like all these other groups the MOD is said to have quite an influence in shaping media stories and we know the name of one unit under that ministry that was involved in this during the run up to the Iraq war. It is called the Rockingham Cell and has been mentioned by the late David Kelly, Scott Ritter and Brigadier Richard Holmes its job being to amass as much skewed intelligence as possible about the mythical Iraqi WMD which was then leaked to the media to mislead the public into supporting an invasion of Iraq. It apparently operated in conjunction with another group in MI6 whose purpose Scott Ritter explained to Nicholas Rufford in The Times:

"'The aim was to convince the public that Iraq was a far greater threat than it actually was...Stories ran in the media about secret underground facilities in Iraq and ongoing programmes (to produce weapons of mass destruction).They were sourced to western intelligence and all of them were garbage."

...Ritter had previously met the MI6 officer at Vauxhall Cross, the service's London headquarters. He asked Ritter for information on Iraq that could be planted in newspapers in India, Poland and South Africa from where it would "feed back" to Britain and America.' [20]

The now famous Force Research Unit is also an outcrop of the British army's Intelligence Corps and was said to have been founded about 1979. It is now thought to have been involved in the one IRA killing that created the most public outrage in the Republic during the troubles: the death of Tom Oliver in Omeath in 1991. But what the local people didn't at the time realise was the extent and power of these intelligence agencies behind the scenes, and the close cooperative relationship they have with all the Irish paramilitary groups.[21] What we now know is that it was one FRU agent that caught Oliver, by putting a bug in a public phone box, and another FRU agent that tortured and killed him to death.[22] Here are a few references to the FRU and its leader Colonel Kerr:

"Brigadier Kerr was head of the hush-hush Force Re-

search Unit (FRU), an ad hoc military intelligence formation set up shortly after Mrs Thatcher's election as
British premier in 1979. One of the aims of the FRU
was to defeat the IRA by implementing a counter-terror
strategy, ie intimidating the Catholic population into
withholding support for republicanism.
Having armed them with clandestine weapons smuggled from South Africa, details of which are contained
in the Stevens report, the FRU used loyalist agents to
murder many non-involved nationalists, including high-
profile Belfast solicitor, Pat Finucane.
...

[General Sir Frank] Kitson has given for posterity a
body of written work explaining how local agents (called
indigenous forces in his magnum opus, Low Intensity
Operations) had been used in Kenya, Cyprus and
South Yemen to terrify rebel sympathisers.
Kerr became involved in counter-terror operations in
1972 when he joined the ad hoc covert operations
group, the Military Reaction Force (MRF) as a captain,
serving under the 39th Brigade commander, the then
brigadier, Frank Kitson.
...

Later, when Mrs Thatcher personally organised British
military as well as political strategy in Ireland after the
IRA hunger strikes, Kerr, promoted to lieutenant
colonel, took command of the counter terror group,
subsequently renamed and reorganised as the Force
Research Unit. Like another controversial colonel, Oliver North of Iran-Contra fame, Kerr was moving in high
political circles, outside the normal military chain of
command. Mrs Thatcher visited his secret unit headquarters at Lisburn (time and date noted in the unpub-
lished bit of the Stevens report) to speak to him about
his work and shake the hands of his operatives at an
informal party from which other military officers, including those senior to Kerr, were excluded, according to
the pseudonymous FRU non-commissioned officer,
Martin Ingram. Among Tory honchos who had personal
knowledge of Kerr and his secret unit were Tom King,
then Northern Secretary, and Douglas Hogg, reportedly
interviewed recently by Sir John Stevens about the Finucane assassination and related MRF activities.
All of this has huge implications for modern Irish history
and for contemporary politics in London. In the first
place, the British-inspired spin (embraced by the Dublin

chattering classes and peddled by the media for 30 years) that the noble British were standing as peace-keepers between two tribal factions engaged in an in-comprehensible religious war has been revealed for the myth that it is. British spies, with the approval, or possi-bly on the direction of at least some political leaders, were running a campaign of sectarian assassination since the days of Edward Heath, the Downing Street in-cumbent when the first dirty tricks unit, Kitson's MRF, was set up." [23]

Special Branch

As regards domestic agencies it has been stated that Special Branch, 'controls' Garda HQ [24] and that the practices of the secret police domi-nate the actions of the gardai. This is seen in the use of slander for ex-ample. From the Phoenix at the time of the succession to Commission-er Byrne:

"In the conspiratorial world of political policing, anony-mous tip-offs, mysterious alliances and byzantine plots are the stock-in-trade. The choice of recipients of leaks is interesting. In the normal course of events, a smear campaign against a politician or a subversive would be given verbally to a selected journalist who would run the story but this cannot be done when the smear sto-ries are about litigatious senior garda officers. Instead, the anonymous scribes have targeted politicians and lawyers in the hope that their gossip might eventually reach ministerial ears."[25]

Most of the Garda Commissioners since the 70s have come from this world of 'political policing', this is a description of former Commissioner Byrne as one example:

"Byrne's line of business has been hush-hush opera-tors in an elite cadre of detectives who have, because of their unique security responsibilities, a particular in-sight into the inner workings of the state and the modus operandi of politicians." [and in reference to the US plane immobilised at Shannon:] "The deflection of criti-cism onto politicians, who had assumed security could be safely left to the commissioner and garda intelli-gence experts, has shown yet again Byrne's talent for media manipulation."[26]

It is perfectly obvious to this observer anyway that the gardai have a controlling interest in large sections of the Irish media. This is much more so than any Irish politician or party as far as I can see. For example while allowing for the genuine grief of the McCabe family you cannot help wondering if no other person had been killed as a result of the troubles in the last 10 years except Garda McCabe. Certainly the countless Catholics killed North and South at the hands of what we now know to be the British government's proxy armies don't seem to interest the Irish media very much.

It is also said RUC Special Branch was very powerful "through its control of certain sections of the media". The Phoenix specifically alleges this in regard to the local offices of the BBC and the Sunday Times.[27]

No doubt Irish politicians are very conscious of this power in the hands of the secret police North and South and are careful not to cut across it. With reference to the Dublin and Monaghan bombings it is said that "Fianna Fail is scared of certain senior gardai who are most averse to public scrutiny of the force's negligence in 1974 as well as the subsequent disappearance of files on the inquiry from garda stations."[28]

Torture figures largely as well in the revelations that have emerged from Donegal and elsewhere. The three women mentioned in the McGlinchey case were all assaulted by the gardai: Adrienne repeatedly by her 'handler'; Yvonne Devine her friend had to be hospitalised after being held in a garda station and during which time Adrienne could hear her screams from the neighbouring room; and Karen McGlinchey was assaulted by a number of men wearing balaclavas who raided her house and seized documents which were later found to be in the possession of the gardai.[29] In the McBrearty case garda White remembers hearing the screams of Frank McBrearty junior when he was detained in the garda station.[30] Roisin McConnell arrested as part of that case "claimed to have been beaten, told she would lose her infant child, forced to pray for forgiveness and subjected to psychological torture that led to her being hospitalised in a psychiatric institution. She remains deeply traumatised."[31] Even in the Abbeylara scandal it was revealed that John Carthy was also afraid of the gardai because he had been beaten up in Granard garda station.[32] The death of John O'Shea in Kerry, shortly after being released from garda custody, has also caused disquiet.[33] Meanwhile the European Committee for the Prevention of Torture is on the Irish authorities case because of "compelling evidence of brutality to prisoners."[34] In the North of course the practice of torture has been so widespread that in international military training manuals they teach the 'Ulster techniques'.[35]

Legal Powers

Before the Mayday protests in Dublin in 2004 a number of anti war activists were followed around by Garda Special Branch as they attempted to hand out leaflets in a Dublin estate. As recorded on indymedia:

> "The scene attracted some local kids who hung around the guards as we headed off. Afterwards they caught up with us and said they had heard one of the cops saying he'd check with the council to see if they could find some by-lay against leafleting!"[36]

Of course this is no big deal but the fact is that it is symptomatic of the thinking of western intelligence and police agencies. Their instinct is to look for any state rule or regulation that they can then use to harass groups or people that they want to oppress. Clearly the point is that nobody can raise the cry of a police state or political oppression because of course the intelligence agencies stay in the background. So in any future court proceedings that those protesters would face the judges and the media are not going to entertain 'conspiracy theories' about state harassment all they will say is that the law is the law and everybody has to abide by it blah blah blah. So in order to see what powers those agencies have in a western country it is more instructive to look at the kind of arbitrary laws and state powers that are out there, that they can manipulate, rather than looking at specific anti-dissident or anti-protester legislation.

A simple example is that the local authorities in Ireland have introduced some 'anti-litter' regulations about postering and leafleting that of course seem necessary and don't attract much disquiet in the media. But in fact they have then been used in a very heavy handed fashion against protesters and small parties to such a degree that its pretty clear that that was who they were aiming the legislation at. After all with such an at times controlled and manipulated media the simple ruse of using posters is arguably the only way of getting one's point across.[37]

Driving completely legally in Ireland is well nigh impossible if all the rules and regulations are applied strictly. Regulations like car insurance are also almost impossibly expensive for some categories of driver. So for example Owen Rice, who is being harassed as a protester, has been jailed repeatedly but always for alleged offences that the media and judges would not describe as interfering with free speech, which is how Owen sees it. This includes being arrested for dangerous driving while actually asleep in his car. He was arrested 10 times in 9 months in 2003 for these kind of spurious charges which frequently accompany serious beatings and the gardai are quite open with him about the real reason for these arrests and assaults:

> "But seriously, officers up to the rank of Superintendant have told me quite candidly in 2003 that I will be arrested until such times as I learn to be "careful about what you say"."[38]

The laws relating to public houses and night clubs seem incredibly onerous nowadays and it would strike you as virtually impossible for an owner of such an establishment to stay in business very long unless he formed a close 'relationship' with the gardai. These include serious laws on opening hours, the age of patrons, even children accompanied by adults etc. They have been described by a former justice minister as the 'most draconian laws in Europe'.[39] In fact gardai now enter public houses and will prosecute the owners for 1,500 euro if they find anybody drunk there.[40] The McBrearty and Shortt families in Donegal claim that the gardai used these kinds of laws to harass them. It was revealed a short while ago on the Late Late Show that Frank McBrearty senior believes this was caused to the two families because he and the Shortt family refused to pay protection money to the gardai.[41] Here is an account of the case by Senator Jim Higgins of FG:

> "The tribunal may be called the Morris tribunal but to the ordinary citizen and in the public's perception it is the McBrearty tribunal. It is about the manner in which the State deliberately set out to accuse Frank McBrearty junior and his cousin, Mark McConnell, of a murder they never committed. It is about the State's vendetta against them and their licensed premises by bringing more than 160 liquor licensing charges against them, hauling them before court after court only to have each charge subsequently withdrawn by the Director of Public Prosecutions but, as a consequence, wrecking their business. It is about the emotional trauma and torture visited by the State on an innocent family which has been left with psychological scars that will never be erased. It is about the truth and whether the State, having wrongfully slandered, victimised and destroyed the McBrearty family, is now prepared to grant them the level of legal representation to which they are clearly and constitutionally entitled in order to establish who was responsible for what happened and the reason such a despicable and evil plot was contrived and persisted with."[42]

Of course one of the points to be made in general about charges made against ordinary people is that unless they are very wealthy they aren't likely to be able to afford to keep up legal proceedings against a state body and in these circumstances probably will never find justice.[43] This is exemplified by the story of those that have taken court cases against the gardai. Phoenix magazine revealed in March this year that there are some 750 cases pending against the gardai in the High Courts and Circuit Courts alleging things like "wrongful arrest, harassment, and personal injuries resulting from garda assaults against civilians"[44]. Of the cases settled so far this year no admission of liability was conceded and the compensation awards ranged from 250 euro to 6,000 euro. On the other hand there are also c.1,500 civil actions being taken by members of the gardai against the state alleging things like 'personal trauma' incurred while on duty. The average payout there is running this year at 65,000 euro per garda.

The McBrearty case also highlights the heavy use of slander by the intelligence agencies. In that case Garda Special Branch even went to the trouble of getting leaflets printed to be distributed in the local area slandering that family.[45]

The tax system is clearly another arm of the state that can be used against dissidents. It doesn't help either if the general public are conditioned to react with horror when even a minor lapse of the hugely complex tax laws are committed by someone. For example Michael Lowry was drummed out of Fine Gael very fast on the grounds that he had not declared in tax improvements that had been made to his house by builders working for Ben Dunne who owed him money as part of Lowry's refrigeration business. He disputed the value that Ben Dunne placed on those improvements and in the meantime he obviously felt he shouldn't declare it in tax until such time as a proper figure for the work done was agreed. Bear in mind that some people spend many years trying to understand Irish tax law, which gets more complex every year, and not every small business man should be assumed to know all the ins and outs of it. It seems to me not that amazing a decision on Lowry's part. Just before his downfall over this tax thing Michael Lowry felt he was under surveillance by some parties who were concerned to stop his attempts at rooting out corruption in the semi-state sector.[46]

Now we have very draconian laws on tax collection implemented by the Criminal Assets Bureau who basically have the power to take every penny off you and then compel you to go to court to try to prove your innocence in accounting for how you earned the money. In theory this was only supposed to be used on big drug dealers but in fact the CAB have been involved in most of the major political controversies of the last few years. They scrutinised the affairs of people like the farmer blamed for bringing in the Foot and Mouth[47] disease to Louth and Ray Burke and neither seem to meet the definition of the wealthy drug smugglers that everybody thought would be the only targets of the CAB. In the case of George Redmond the CAB intervened and held him for a while refusing the Flood Tribunal access to his documents which were only handed over eventually "after a rather bitter struggle" by the Tribunal against the CAB.[48] The Kelly family in Limerick clearly feel that the CAB work in concert with garda harassment.[49]

The drug trade has generated more examples of draconian legislation that can be used to harass people. Here is an account on that from Barry on indymedia:

"Lets put it this way, I don't use drugs, never have. Even when I was at college I was a stick in the mud and said no and just stuck to the drink instead...
But I've been searched by Guards in the street for drugs over 30 times in the last 8 years. I wasn't intoxicated, rude or threatening. I wasn't in possession of drugs. I have no crininal convictions and have never been before a court for anything, ever. But I was in possession of a political opinion the British and Irish state disliked. So the 26 county police stop me in the street claiming they believe I have drugs on my person and search me. Thats an abuse of power and an abuse of process. Thankfully I dont live in the 26 counties so it only happens every now and again.

At least when the Brits and RUC stopped and searched you they tell you its because you're a no good fenian bastard and don't spout bollocks about drugs.

All these quick fix laws which are slavishly copied from the British will ultimately end up being used against the wider population, those who for whatever reason have views the state would like to see crushed. Such as people with old fashioned ideas like ... its not nice to be dropping bombs on arab kiddies and notions about Irish neutrality and such like. And dont forget Irish special branch abused their power to intimidate the families of the Dublin Monaghan massacre at one time as well. An unaccountable police force with even more powers that no one can question."[51]

Anybody facing possible serious drug charges could also be vulnerable to blackmail. That blackmail is used by the gardai has been established by Karen McGlinchey who has pointed out that a garda under oath at the Morris tribunal admitted that they used the threat of a conviction to pressurise Adrienne McGlinchey [52] while Martin Ingram in his book has stated that blackmail of this sort is the stock in trade of the RUC Special Branch.[53] Michael Tanner, who was recently convicted for 15 years for trading cannabis, has claimed "he was set up by the gardai".[54] Somebody has been leaking some really interesting information on this subject to the Phoenix:

"Indeed, there have been many signs that a cosy relationship exists between particular detectives and clever criminals.

The upper crust of the drugs world claim that certain gardai operate what is known as the TOS (Three--in-One System). This allows a drug- or cigarette-smuggling informant to run two loads in without interference, while the third is seized by agreement. This is a simple explanation of what is a complex and variable arrangement where "controlled shipments" are allowed into the State in return for intelligence. The dangers for corruption in this secret-deal system are obvious, but it remains in place despite [Assistant Commissioner Gerry] Hickey's new rules. The only threat to it so far has been vigilant Customs officers who are not in on the scheme – and who occasionally stumble on "controlled" importations, with embarrassing results for gardai –...
Some TOS gougers went on to greater rewards in 2004...[goes on to describe two big drug importers in Spain with close and continuing garda links.]"[55]

There are further details on this in Phoenix Sept 13 2002 where it is described how a former senior IRA man now in Amsterdam imports large amounts of drugs into Ireland, through Wexford, drawing on a close relationship with the gardai and who makes arrangements for the latter to seize a small proportion of the shipments and prosecute "only one or two small time operators" to make them look good. It works the same as the Spanish operation according to the Phoenix.[56] Declan Griffin who was shot dead in a contract style killing in 2003 had won a court case showing that drugs he was found with at Dublin airport were imported with the full assistance of the garda authorities. Journalists who tried to figure out this drug-garda connection have been threatened with jail if they don't hand over notes they made about the case and customs officers found their files on the subject went missing.[57] Sean Dunne who has gone missing in Spain in 2004 is described by Phoenix as being a similar case. Information that the CAB had on him "regularly got into the wrong hands" presumably the magazine means the information was used by the potential assassins that shot him 7 times in Ratoath Co.Meath.[58]

In any case returning to my theme of arbitrary state powers there is also the planning laws and building regulations which again are severely enforced especially in the rural ring around Dublin. In fact many small businesses or local people trying to build housing feel it is impossible to get planning permission unless they cosy up to some 'golden circle' that seem to have no such problems. If they aren't on this inside track they are treated to endless 'bureaucratic' delays and harassment. For example a common reason for refusing permission is to claim that the local road is in too bad a repair to support the extra traffic of a house. The local road of course would also be under the management of the council who then refuse to repair it![59] In the media the powers that be like to characterise these problems as been caused by environmentalists like An Taisce but in fact only a minuscule number of planning applications are objected to by that body or by any other party on environmental grounds. Here is Dr. Ciaran Pairceir talking about this in Cavan:

"As for the majority of people around here, they are far from bad; they are often just afraid. They are horrified at what happens. This fear has been deliberately engendered by the 'powerful' people, the ones who make decisions, through whose greasy, grubby little hands money passes. These people are miserable cowards, but the 'good people' around here know that if they object they run the risk of being victimised. If they apply for planning permission it will be turned down, or delayed while a litany of technicalities are satisfied. They may well be visited by the Fire Officer, and officials will examine the obligatory notices in person and in microscopic detail."[60]

Incredible as it seems it appears that even the Minister for Justice Michael McDowell is himself being faced with what looks like politically inspired harassment of this type with respect to his holiday home in Roscommon. It is supposed to have been built two metres lower than proposed and for that aberration a poorer person, building the house on a high mortgage for example, could easily be bankrupted.[61] We get a running commentary in Phoenix about the gardai harassing McDowell because of some pretty minor changes he is thinking of introducing. Meaning the gardai it is stated that:
"McDowell is no-one's fool when it comes to knowing how and by whom the media has been manipulated."[62]
"His [McDowell's] unpopularity with some sections of the media has been exploited ruthlessly by the hidden hands in the Phoenix Park who have been quick to leak information which shows him an autocrat and a man driven by personal ambition. His bruising row with a tabloid-Garda Siochana alliance..."[63]

There are plenty of other arbitrary state laws and regulations that can be rolled out to hit people if necessary. Health and Safety legislation seems to be used against some businesses in a very arbitrary fashion for example. Even fire regulations could be used. A leaked document prepared by a police intelligence unit in England dedicated to 'monitoring' New Age travelers and rave party goers made the claim that "fire services were useful in producing prohibition notices".[64] Which means doubtless that the police were secretly working behind the scenes in getting the 'fire services' to issue those notices. One activist arrested before the Mayday protests in Dublin 2004 was arrested on a charge of trespassing. That charge is so arbitrary the gardai in court never even presented evidence from the property owner. In fact they didn't even know who was the property owner.[65] More protesters arrested at that time were falsely charged with loitering and being drunk and disorderly.[66]

The new ASBO laws now in force in the North, and soon to be so down here, are also incredibly arbitrary and of course are used against political 'undesirables'.[67] The ASBO is granted under civil law so normal criminal standards of proof are not necessary but if you break the Order, and 40 per cent of people affected do, then you go to jail as a criminal. It is this legal mousetrap effect that has led to so many people being jailed under this legislation:

"Asbos also deny people the right to have a jury hear the evidence and decide on guilt or innocence. They also allow hearsay or gossip to be given in evidence. In these circumstances the police know that the local magistrate is likely to grant an order. Only 3% of applications for Asbos have been refused. The result is imprisonment for votes. It is a national scandal that as a result of Asbos 10 young people a week are being jailed, and that beggars and prostitutes are being imprisoned even though begging and prostitution are non-imprisonable offences."

Another legal mousetrap that can be used against groups is the use of court injunctions which are rolled out to hit almost any organisation that tries any form of peaceful protest in Ireland right now. This is where a High Court judge can issue a temporary court order demanding a group cease a certain activity prior to the hearing of a case. It is primarily a matter of judicial discretion as to what order is made and the punishments that can be inflicted on anybody breaching the injunction are pretty limitless including, as at Rossport, imprisonment and, as in the case of the farmers at the meat plants, huge daily fines. Its no good arguing the merits of a case or one's constitutional rights because that might be only relevant to the full court hearing. Of course the point is that once the form of protest has been crushed by the injunction then the full court hearing becomes a kind of irrelevancy with the pressure being off the other side.[68]

Family law is another area where there is an array of incredibly arbitrary state powers which are exercised in Ireland in conditions of great secrecy. There is plenty of evidence that this has fostered an atmosphere of false allegations and legal abuses that the parties cannot remedy because they are prevented from suing their legal representatives due to the in camera rule. Unfortunately this secrecy is now very popular in the Irish court system as this quote from a frustrated Paddy Doyle indicates:

> "We have an illegal bond of silence placed upon every victim who seeks redress for what they endured. It is a fact this ban on the imparting of what occurs within the Redress Board would not be tolerated anywhere else in the world and the Redress Board Committee and the Irish Judicial System know this only too well. I have in my possession a letter indicating that what I have just said is true. Special advantages which the Redress Board have in Ireland would be considered illegal outside the boundaries of that God forsaken Country. Try to get any Solicitor representing Survivors to test its legality in court." [Meaning it appears that they simply cannot find any solicitor who will take on the state over this.][69]

In the US the family courts have been used against dissidents. The CIA whistle blower Michael Riconosciuto was threatened with this when he revealed details of CIA corruption, from his affidavit:

> "Videnieks [of the US Justice Department] forecasted an immediate and favorable resolution of a protracted child custody dispute being prosecuted against my wife by her former husband, if I were to decide not to cooperate with the House Judiciary Committee investigation."[70]

It is also reported that some bizarre twists of family law were used against Rodney Stich to curtail his dissident activities.[71] It has been alleged as well that Mark Harris has been jailed for family law offences (seeing his children etc) because he campaigned against injustices in the English courts. In Ireland Sheenagh McMahon has stated that she was threatened with being deprived of her children because of what she was saying about the gardai in Donegal.[72]

There is one fascinating example from the farming community of the power of some state bodies. Farmers frustrated at the fact that so much of the EU money goes to line the pockets of an oligopoly in the food processing industry demanded that the powers and resources of the Competition Authority be improved to tackle the situation.[73] So the government obliged giving extra powers and manpower to that body. Then in a classic Orwellian manoeuvre the Authority turned around and used those powers against the farmers. Now every time the farmers protest at the low income they get in dairy [74] or beef [75] or cereals [76] the Competition Authority turns up to harass them, demanding photographs of people on the protests and threatening to or taking prosecutions against them. The theory is that the farmers in protesting are gathering together in an anti-competitive manner to influence prices. This is despite the fact that those arrested would represent a tiny percentage of the overall market in that produce and are only protesting in the same way that trade unions seek higher wages.[77] Meanwhile the investigation into the processing industry seems to have been forgotten. Except by the farmers who are reading in their papers about leading members of the Irish meat processing industry describing how in their opinion one person has taken secret measures to attain a monopoly in that trade.[78]

Use of Modern Technology

It is clear that the way people use modern technology has greatly expanded the power of these agencies. Where a few years ago people used cash now a lot of transactions are by credit card and this obviously provides a whole raft of data that the agencies can use. The information required of tax and social welfare authorities also expands all the time and that can also be combined to provide quite a picture of a person.

Similarly as people do research on the internet, as opposed to in libraries, the capacity to monitor a person's research greatly increases. It is reported by Alain Lallemand in the Belgian newspaper Le Soir that as part of the Echelon network the western agencies monitor all internet traffic at the main internet exchanges.[79] Note that some people would say that monitoring all internet traffic in this way is impractical because of the huge computer power needed but I beg to differ when the way this is probably accomplished is considered. There is no requirement to store the actual data that would travel across the exchanges, as web page requests for example, all you need to do is store the IP numbers and details of who is requesting a given webpage on a given date. The data actually on the webpage can always be looked up again later by those agencies using a comprehensive web archive like www.archive.org which in all probability they use. So in other words they are only storing web addresses and corresponding IP numbers of people who read the pages, not the raw data, and this can be stored as something like a simple flat text file which of course requires very little computer space. In so far as the contents of emails are unique (meaning they are probably capable of screening out spam and forwarded emails very successfully) they would have to be stored but again (until the recent advent of broadband) they were usually not very large and I think it is within the scope of Echelon to cache them in their entirety.

One problem would have been internet voice calls which would clearly be unique to each conversation and could potentially be large files possibly even scattered over a number of exchanges. It is interesting that the capability of using the internet this way has been around for ages but only in the last few years has it been given any publicity, which maybe a valuable time delay for the agencies to get in place monitoring facilities for this traffic.

One final serious problem would be the matching of IP addresses (which are kinda the phone numbers used for all internet transactions) to actual people which presents many problems bearing in mind that normal dial up users are often given a separate randomly chosen IP address for every online session. There are two points I would make here.

First of all clearly Echelon has access to phone data as well as internet data so this combined with information in the IP address could tell them a lot. What I mean by this is take for example a hypothetical bucksheen called Peader O'Clancy going on the internet in some smallish town like Dungarvan and posting some risqué political stuff on the net using one of the ISPs that allocate random IP addresses. So if the intelligence agencies using Echelon wish to trace the internet packets they are watching on the internet back to a specific person the first clue they have is the detail thrown up by a reverse DNS lookup of the IP numbers which would show something like 22-ju-987.dungarvan.core.eircom.net. As you can see in practise the address itself will narrow things down to quite a small area. Of course the agencies also know the time the specific internet traffic flowed and the ISP used which is given also in the IP address. So using the phone log data from the phone companies it will show so many people who called into the ISP dial up number and were still connected to that number in the Dungarvan area at that particular time.[80] This clearly narrows their search quite a lot and in practise I'm sure if Peadar is one of those activist types they hate so much then probably they know all about him and will recognise his name from any small list that would be thrown up by such a search. But there is another point and that is the question of to what degree they cache the actual content of all phone calls which I will discuss in a minute. If the agencies can call up in some form the actual phone call then they can probably use an automated way of pulling out of the tapes of the phone call the details of an internet login session and specifically the numbers for the downloaded dynamically allocated IP address. They could do this for each of the phone calls in the Dungarvan list mentioned until they narrow down poor old Peadar who had thought he was safe using an anonymous ID in his web posts.

The second point is the question of the relationship between the ISPs and the intelligence agencies. I have assumed above that the ISPs are independent and value the privacy of their customers but in fact there is a lot of legislation or arm twisting out there which makes it probable that the various agencies and the ISPs have a close relationship. In the UK it was revealed in the Sunday Times that all UK ISP's have had to install a special hardwire link to MI5 headquarters.[81] They hardly go to that trouble without also putting in place some measures which allow MI5 to match the IP numbers to given users.

As mentioned above the main programme which coordinates the

monitoring of telecommunications traffic for the big western powers is known as Echelon. It is well known that all international phone calls are routinely intercepted by that network using facilities like the NSA plant at Menwith Hill in England and also GCHQ in Cheltenham near London. The main route by which a lot of this traffic is intercepted is via satellites that are run for NSA by the huge Maryland agency known as the National Reconnaissance Office. All this is very well known but I don't think the full implications of the kind of technology they are using are properly appreciated by most people. Take for example the question of satellite monitoring of phone calls. I suspect a lot of people think then that that refers to satellite calls either made from satellite phones or international calls routed over satellites. They monitor those calls as well but the fact is that they monitor via satellite the ordinary landline calls of many countries. This is done because a lot of those calls in all countries travel across microwave relay links which are line of sight towers that the phone companies use to bounce calls around the country because of their convenience not requiring as they do any landline cables. What happens is that the signal that is directed by microwave at a receiving tower continues on after that into space and there the NSA can position a satellite and pick up the telephone conversations.[82] Eircom do use microwave relays to route internal landline voice calls in Ireland.[83] Furthermore all the Irish and international mobile phone companies use microwaves to bounce mobile calls between their masts. So depending on the architecture of the eircom network it is at least possible that Echelon monitors all Irish internal and international landline and most definitely mobile phone calls. The western agencies have also developed since the 70s the capacity to tap into underwater telephone cables.[84]

Another issue when you look at the technology available is the question of whether they store copies of the calls they intercept. In fact if you agree that these agencies can do anything they want behind all their secrecy and that they would use whatever technology is available to the fullest extent possible then you can come to some startling conclusions. It strikes me that probably they store copies of all conversations that they intercept, which could easily be all voice calls on the island of Ireland, and keep the copies for as long as they like. The NSA for example has no legal restrictions on doing this: "information on US persons ...cannot be kept longer than a year, information on foreign citizens can be held eternally."[85] The real question is can they do it technologically bearing in mind that they have of course access to data storage technology at least somewhat more advanced that currently available to ordinary computer users.[86] So possibly they are using now the type of technology that IBM announced as theoretical in 2002[87] and exhibited in 2005.[88] This is the technology to store a terrabyte of data on a chip the size of a postage stamp. A terrabyte could store about 130,000 hours of telephone conversations.[89] Bear in mind that the NSA computer capacity is not calculated by numbers of computers but rather by the acreage of the computer space and in the 60s it was 5 and a half acres and was reported to be doubling every decade form there.[90]

So incredible as it seems it is technologically, and for them morally, feasible that they keep copies of every single telephone conversation held over the last few years on the island of Ireland. Anybody who would hold data on that scale would clearly have enormous power to use that information to blackmail people (including the capacity to retrospectively trawl through a persons past life before he or she came to the attention of those agencies) and to anticipate the actions of political opposition groups etc. And be under no illusions people that is certainly what those organisations use that information for.[91] As the New Statesman reported in 1988 with respect to a US Congressional investigation into Echelon:

> "Since then, investigators have subpoenaed other witnesses and asked them to provide the complete plans and manuals of the ECHELON system and related projects. The plans and blueprints are said to show that targeting of US political figures would not occur by accident, but was designed into the system from the start."

While more recently GCHQ, which runs the UK arm of Echelon, was found to be intercepting any data they could on the delegations of Angola, Cameroon, Chile, Bulgaria, Guinea and Pakistan to the Security Council to help the "US's "QRC" – quick response capability" in some 'dirty tricks' against those diplomats.[92] In Ireland this is the atmosphere described in Phoenix July 1 2005 p.8:

> "That many politicians are afraid of An Garda Siochana was evident by their silence or abscence during voting on the [new Garda] Bill. For some it may be trepidation of powerful vested interests like publicans and pharmacists who might effect their electoral prospects. For others there may be a feeling that their personal secrets are locked away in CSB [Crime and Security Branch] archives, ready to be leaked should they act against "national security" by undermining the Garda supremacy.

> Just as MI5 spies on the British Royals for "security reasons" (as revealed during the Charles and Diana affairs) the CSB as a matter of routine files vast amounts of information not only on politicians, but on many others who could not by any stretch of the imagination be regarded as subversives or criminals. Not too long ago both the Law Society and the Bar Council complained about the tapping of solicitors and barristers phones

while some journalists phones continue to be tapped.

> It is doubtful if Michael McDowell's fear of tackling the Garda head on is similar to that of some backbenchers and other ministers, although he has been on the receiving end of Garda leaks about his family and he angrily dispensed with the Garda static protection at his home for a time."

It is well known also that the telephone conversations are put through automated speech to text recognition systems and this has been done at least since the early 80s.[93] Similarly voice recognition is used and it appears they had that technology since about 1979. This means they can track a particular person by flagging his unique voice pattern as he tries to speak on any phone on any platform that they are monitoring. This is from Margaret Newsham an NSA dissident living in Texas: "As early as 1979 we could track a specific person and zoom in on his phone conversation while he was communicating."[94]
So all those movies that have the principals using call boxes to avoid detection are a bit mute when it comes to the technology available to the NSA and GCHQ.

Phoenix magazine when it described Echelon not long ago referred to a system called Enternet meaning the deployment of new technology that allows the agencies to interfere with the computers of people using the internet.[95] Presumably in cooperation with some large software companies they provide a kind of global hacking capability to the NSA and GCHQ et al:
"But ECHELON now has an "active" component which allows NSA or GCHQ analysts to covertly "hack" into information on the hard disks of computers linked into any telecommunications system, including the Internet."
Microsoft for example were discovered some time ago to have a close working relationship with NSA.[96] This came about because Microsoft felt it was illegal for them to export out of the US technology that could potentially be used as encryption that the US couldn't break. The question is how far does this legal pressure, and the secret relationship it fostered, go in terms of their products. Note as well the way in which Microsoft go to considerable lengths to hide from the user the extent to which their software caches key personal data.[97] This presumably is done under pressure from law enforcement bodies that are then supplied with all the information necessary to get access to the data later. Some of the main suppliers of anti-virus and internet security software also have remarkable holes in their security scans ostensibly because the software that they deliberately fail to detect is made by the same company as the anti-virus software. An employee of one of those companies claimed once that it was done under pressure from the US gov-

ernment but he quickly felt the need to retract that claim.[98]

It is even possible that the story of modern snail mail mimics that of email with a huge state apparatus of secret police using automated systems to hoover up any compromising information that they can glean from the post. Both the UK and the US have a tremendous legacy of secretly spying on any dissident activity of their citizens by reading their mail. In the UK this was revealed in the Spycatcher book where for the first time a shocked UK public found out that MI5 had offices in all the regional sorting centres where they monitored all the mail in a very widescale fashion.[99] The CIA have had the capacity for some time to read mail without opening it and have deployed this technology in the past on a large scale in the US.:[100]

> "In the 1960's and early 1970's, large numbers of American dissidents, including those who challenged the condition of racial minorities and those who opposed the war in Vietnam, were specifically targeted for mail opening by both agencies [FBI and CIA]. In one program, selection of mail on the basis of "personal taste" by agents untrained in foreign intelligence objectives resulted in the interception and opening of the mail of Senators, Congressmen, journalists, businessmen, and even a Presidential candidate."

The above is from the final report of the Church committee of the US Senate April 23 1976. It refers specifically to widespread 'warrantless' mail opening:

> "Despite the stated purpose of the programs, numerous domestic dissidents, including peace and civil rights activists, were specifically targeted for mail opening."[101]

In any case the point is that now the Royal Mail in the UK is using handwriting recognition software supplied by Lockheed Martin[102] a company described as the leading supplier of "monitoring equipment to the espionage agencies" in the US.[103] An Post in Ireland is also using handwriting recognition to some degree and the extent to which these developments have anything to do with monitoring by intelligence agencies is something that we can only speculate on.[104]

But there is one flaw in all this that I think I should address. Western intelligence agencies clearly have access to a vast array of data on any person they want to target but the downside is that they may have access to more information than they could possibly absorb. So its all well and fine having 160,000 hours of phone conversations on a stamp sized chip but listening to all that, or even reading it as an automated transcript, is clearly going to be beyond the manpower that most agencies could deploy. Some would say that this then drastically limits the practical impact of this technology in the actions of western intelligence agencies. Fair enough but here are a couple of thoughts that should be borne in mind.

The first is that the amount of manpower that you can see governments in the west deploying against their dissident citizens can be surprisingly high. During the protests in the summer of 2004 for example some would say that the amount of gardai deployed on expensive overtime to over police a few harmless protesters worked out at about 3 to 1. That's 3 gardai for every protester in case you were wondering was it the other way around. Clearly if that is mimicked in the shadowy world of the intelligence agencies monitoring these protesters then they could successfully plough through most of this mountain of surveillance data.

The second point is that faced with this mountain of information the intelligence agencies have no doubt invested a lot of time in developing computer systems to analyse the data automatically and show up the interesting information only. For example describing the situation north of the border:

> "In Northern Ireland, over the past 30 years, British intelligence was overwhelmed with information. It developed "knowledge management" software to handle the raw material from Operation Vengeful – the Big Brother network which produced a vast daily flow of facts on vehicle and personal movements from overt and covert observation posts, CCTV cameras, vehicle checkpoints and house raids."[105]

The question is what does that particular software look like and what does it do exactly? At a simple level we have the Echelon system of flagging particular keywords used in any telephone conversation fax or email and which seems problematic and ineffectual.[106] Its not surprising to discover for example that one Canadian housewife went onto a terrorist watch list when she described on the telephone once how her son had 'bombed' in a performance in the school play.[107]

But I'm sure as these type of systems have been refined they could now work very powerfully. So imagine for example a computerised system that was set to detect the interests and level of knowledge of a particular target using, without human intervention, intercepted telephone conversations of that person. For example it could flag the use of unusual words to accurately build up a picture of their subject. So anybody can talk about insomnia on the phone but if words like ciracadian rhythms are present then the software could identify the subject as having medical knowledge or interest. This could extend into every area like football where if in conversations a person is using the names of particular little known players all the time then he/she could be flagged as a football nut etc etc. So these robotic systems can no doubt be very accurate and useful. This might also be combined with psychologically modeling and profiling that the UK and US agencies are so fond of.

Furthermore the range of information could be deployed in a few simple effective displays that could help a lot. Take credit card information for example. Recorded there is the time and location of the person using the credit card as is the data from cash machines which also are reported to store video of the person taking out money. Imagine if they had permanent geographic information of the location of the cash machines combined with the location of at least some of the businesses that took the money on the credit card then they could throw up on a screen a map of where a person was at a given time going back as far as they had the bank data for. Unusual patterns of interest would be easy to discover from that. I don't personally know to what extent closed circuit video data, from the many cameras run by the gardai around Ireland, are stored or linked together but obviously there is great scope here as well for some combined mapping and visualisation on a large scale.

Maybe we should take another hypothetical case to see how this kind of information can be used e.g. the mayday protests of 2004. It seems likely that as the protesters gathered on the Navan Road the signals from their mobile phones were noted. Then as they dispersed the gardai possibly tracked the same phones as they moved away from the protest, and took the opportunity of a time when the signal was isolated enough to identify it from other signals to get the specific identity of the person using the phone, by stopping their car on a routine traffic issue or whatever. Then they can use the historic information from the phone signal to see where they came from to the protests, listen to the historic cache of phone calls from that phone as I speculate and definitely they could monitor a cache of text messages to build up a profile of that person. Furthermore by looking at the pattern of how the phone signals group together before and after the protest you can clearly see who normally hangs out with who etc. So with only one specific piece of surveillance data you can tell quite a lot quite quickly. The degree that this data is routinely used by even the smaller western intelligence agencies can be seen from *The Times* of 1997 which quotes this from *Sonntags Zeitung* of Zurich in the context of stating that Swiss police have been secretly tracking mobile phone users through the telephone companies:

> "Swisscom [the state-owned telephone company] has stored data on the movements of more than a million mobile phone users and can call up the location of all its mobile subscribers down to a few hundred metres and going back at least half a year," the paper reports, adding: "When it has to, it can exactly reconstruct, down to the minute, who met whom, where and for how

long for a confidential tte--tte." [108]

But this is in fact only the beginning of understanding the degree of surveillance that can be done using a mobile phone which is about the only product that has been heavily subsidised for sale in Ireland and the UK. Mobile phones can be silently turned on when the user has turned it off and then used to locate the user or to pick up sound in the vicinity of the phone. Yes folks believe it or not mobile phones can be silently activated as bugging devices, that is they can be turned on any time anywhere to record and transmit conversations picked up around the phone. The only way to stop it is to disable the phone by e.g. taking out the battery. As described turning it off makes no difference. To clarify this is not just conversations made with the phone, we are talking about bugging people who have the phone on them but aren't using it in a telephone conversation. This is all digital mobile phones using the GSM protocols not phones tampered with beforehand. It is reported that they are turned on by any party that can transmit to the phone special activation codes that are secretly built into the GSM network protocols. One small US intelligence agency in Colombia did this for example by transmitting to mobile phones from small aircraft silently circling in the sky thousands of feet above the phone. Centra Spike is the name of a US agency that works directly for the Pentagon and is here described working in Colombia:

> "There was another nifty secret feature to Centra Spike's capability. So long as their target left the battery in his cell phone, Centra Spike could remotely turn it on whenever they wished. Without triggering the phone's light or beeper, the phone could be activated so that it emitted a low-intensity signal, enough for the unit to get a fix on its general location. They would activate the phone briefly when their target was most likely sleeping, then move the plane into position to monitor any calls he might make when he awoke." [109]

From the BBC:

> "But today's spies are also able to convert conventional phones into bugs without the owners' knowledge.
> ...
> Mobiles communicate with their base station on a frequency separate from the one used for talking. If you have details of the frequencies and encryption codes being used you can listen in to what is being said in the immediate vicinity of any phone in the network.
> According to some reports, intelligence services do not

72

even need to obtain permission from the networks to get their hands on the codes.
So provided it is switched on, a mobile sitting on the desk of a politician or businessman can act as a powerful, undetectable bug."[110]

In fact this idea of using phones as secret bugging devices of the areas the phone is located in has a long and interesting history dating back to the good old landline or POTS era. The story starts with this guy in New York who invented a bug in the mid60s that could be placed in a phone. At the time one of the great aims of people developing bugging devices was to get ones that didn't need batteries so the beauty of this bug was that it drew power from the telephone line and so it could be used indefinitely. Hence some called it the infinity bug. But it had other features that made it unique. To understand how it worked think about an average phone sitting in a kitchen say. Obviously if anybody receives a call and leaves the phone off the hook by putting the receiver down on a table e.g. then the person at the other end of the phoneline can hear everything going on in the room. But it transpires that the difference between a phone being on and off hook like this relies on some small and easily tampered with components. So the inventor rigged the phone in order that when a call would come through his little device would activate first and if it noted a particular signal at the beginning of the call then it would stop the ringer activating and instead silently put the phone off hook and so allow the caller to listen to sounds in the room. Since the activating signal had to come in the normal way as a sound over the phone network the inventor used a distinctive sound not usually heard in a conversation. He rigged it that his bug would respond to a blast from an harmonica that the caller would give just after he dialed the number. Hence another name the 'harmonica' bug. This was all described in elaborate detail in articles like in Esquire magazine from 1966.[111] What was not revealed however until a long time later was that the western intelligence agencies were using the device with some important modifications. At least since the early 70s they had used it to bug rooms without having to tamper with the target phone at all. They achieved the same effect as the New York inventor by placing a device along the phoneline before it reached the target phone usually either the dropline from the telegraph poll, or junction box in a housing estate, or phone switchboard. It activated similarly by reading signals sent by a call to the target number and it could turn on or off the receiver on the victims phone by complicated duplexing of various frequencies along the phoneline from their gadget to the targets handset. The upshot is that from at least the very early 70s the US intelligence agencies could bug any room they liked using the phone line, without having to place any device whatsoever in the room, or tampering in anyway with the phone in the room, which as far as the user was concerned would also continue to work normally. That they had this technology for so long unknown to pretty much everybody gives you some insight into the kind of advanced technology that the western agencies have access to.[112] This was realised in paramilitary circles in Belfast as late as 1991 [113] and in political circles in Dublin sometime later.[114] It is now stated that ISDN lines have built in the capacity for the intelligence agencies to automatically bug rooms via those lines. This at the touch of a button in the phone company or agency offices.[115]

So we can only speculate what sort of surveillance technology they have access to now. For example it has even been discovered that modern consumer colour printers secretly print a code on each page with information designed to be read by intelligence agencies or law enforcement.[116] Satellite surveillance is obviously a very important area as Margaret Newsham says: "Since our satellites could in 1984 film a postage stamp lying on the ground, it is almost impossible to imagine how all-encompassing the system must be today."[117] Here is an MI5 officer being quoted in reference to some highly symbolic surveillance technology used in Ireland:

"There are homes in this Blessed Isle where the occupant sits to watch his television, which we have rigged so that the television is watching him".[118]

It is also stated there that MI5 in Ireland can install a miniaturised video camera inside a light switch. In fact Tony Geraghty, the author and ex SAS man that quotes those references, says that about 1 million people in the North are monitored using sophisticated surveillance.

That sort of figure shows you that Ireland is very much a country under the spotlight of this new Orwellian world. So reader beware! You are being watched...:-)

Footnotes

I refer to two earlier articles in these footnotes i.e. 'Stasiland' article (Chapter 1) at: http://www.indymedia.ie/newswire.php?story_id=68750 and 'O'Hara' (Chapter 2) at http://www.indymedia.ie/newswire.php?story_id=69044 .There is extensive comments added in later to both articles.

1. The Keating reference is from his submission to the Joint Committee on Justice, Equality, Defence and Women's Rights of the Oireachtas of the 2 March 2004 (http://www.oireachtas.ie/viewpda.asp? fn=/documents/Committees29thDail/jcjedwr/020304.htm). The quotes from Dorril are in fact from censored passages from his book available here: http://web.archive.org/web/20040127115740/http://www.politrix.org/foia/mi6/ mi6-restored.htm. See comments at the Stasiland article site for a discussion of MI6 and the early part of the troubles. The Tomlinson quote is from Richard Tomlinson, *The Big Breech, From Top Secret To Maximum Security* (Moscow, 2001), p.72. I/OPS played a major role in smearing him as well as he details throughout his book. The arms trial reference is from Nicholas Davies, *Dead Men Talking* (Edinburgh, 2005), p.47. Davies was a good friend of Princess Diana whom he had known even before she dated Prince Charles and he is now working on a book which claims that she was murdered by MI5. (http://www.royalarchive.com/index.php? option=com_content&task=view&id=1467&Itemid=2)

2. p.12 See also http://irelandsown.net/News11.htm quoting Ed Moloney in the Sunday Tribune 24 bSept 2000.

3 Richard Tomlinson, *The Big Breach / From Top Secret to Maximum Security* (Moscow, 2001), p.231.

4 http://www.krollworldwide.com/about/history/notable/

5 http://www.finextra.com/fullfeature.asp?id=552

6. http://www.bilderberg.org/sis.htm referring to David Shayler's book. See also the kind of surveillance of political actions mentioned on this site:http://tash.gn.apc.org/watched1.htm This site lists the various intelligence groups: http://www.informationclearinghouse.info/article4464.htm

7. He stated that on camera in a documentary I saw, but I cannot remember its name I'm afraid.

8. http://politicalbetting.com/index.php/archives/2004/12/email_form.php? p=541

From Michael Bettaney of MI5: "In pursuing its domestic policy, the govern-

ment relies on the aid of a security service which cynically manipulates the definition of subversion and thus abuses its charter so as to investigate and interfere in the activities of legitimate political parties, the trade union movement and other progressive organisations."
(http://web.archive.org/web/20021207061306/www.wakeupmag.co.uk/articles/ sstate4.htm Wakeup magazine in general makes very good reading on this subject)

9. The quote on MI5 in newspaper offices is from:
http://64.233.183.104/search?
q=cache:lZ3Wl_f12bEJ:www.infowars.com/pdfs/order_ch.PDF and see also this long discussion by Tony Gosling an ex BBC journalist and secretary of Bristol NUJ on MI5 and the media:http://www.bilderberg.org/infotrib.txt and for clockwork orange:
http://web.archive.org/web/20021207061114/www.wakeupmag.co.uk/articles/s state3.htm. On the subject of cliques in the intelligence agencies in general here is Richard Tomlinson ex MI6:
"There's an arrogant faction inside MI6, part of the Eton/Oxford/Guards clique, who see themselves literally as defenders of the realm – and for them, that means the royals." (http://www.thetruthseeker.co.uk/article.asp?ID=83) and from the same source:
"Although contact between MI6 and the Royal Household was officially only via the Foreign Office, I learnt while in MI6 that there was unofficial direct contact between certain senior and influential MI6 officers and senior members of the Royal Household. I did not see any official papers on this subject, but I am confident that the information is correct. I firmly believe that MI6 documents would yield substantial leads on the nature of their links with the Royal Household,"(http://www.thetruthseeker.co.uk/article.asp?ID=2)
 from the Gosling article op. cit. there is this from an MI5 officer describing the situation to an ex MI5 man Gary Murray:
"To make matters worse, we have our own subversive clique within the service, who are a law unto themselves." For the CIA see under Peru in the Appendix. Tomlinson's references to the Royal family have a remarkable echo in the Netherlands where it was revealed by a member of that royal family that the Queen has some little known influence over their intelligence agencies:
"What had emerged, in a feud between Queen Beatrix and estranged family members, are accusations that the queen had ruined their livelihoods with a sustained campaign of slander that involved the use of the courts. So-called Princess Margarita, niece to the queen, alleged that Beatrix was a tyrant who had ignored and insulted her and her husband because she disapproved of their marriage. Margarita's husband said that he had been the victim of "psychological terror." He described the queen as drinking excessively and falling asleep at her birthday party. The couple also say that their home was bugged and their mail intercepted by the Dutch intelligence service." (http://www.centreforciti-zenship.org/monarchy/mon7.html)

10. Phoenix March 11 1994 p3. From the same magazine Sept 23 2005: "Could it be that a full and frank investigation of the Ludlow affair by a public inquiry will discover how easily the unaccountable and unsupervised Garda State security system (C3-CSB) can be suborned at present by a financially powerful organisation like MI5."

11 Phoenix Feb 11 200520p.15.

12. The Crewdson quote is from http://dynalinks.3v8.net/link/13177 .The Colby quote is cited from David McGowan, *Derailing Democracy* (Common Courage Press, Monroe, Maine, 1999), mentioned at this website: http://www.newdawnmagazine.com/articles/why_the_media_lie.html .You see the depth of research that David McGowan has done for that book by reading the introduction here: http://www.thirdworldtraveler.com/Democracy/Derailing_Demo.html .

13. The Guardian quote: (http://www.cpa.org.au/garchve04/1181miners.html) and Marcetti: http://web.archive.org/web/20031005233651/www.wakeupmag.co.uk/articles/cia6.htm. This is Marcetti on some media practises of the CIA:
"A few months ago, in March, there was a meeting at CIA headquarters in Langley, Va., the plush home of America's super spooks overlooking the Potomac River. It was attended by several high-level clandestine officers and some former top officials of the agency. The topic of discussion was: What to do about recent revelations associating President Kennedy's accused assassin, Lee Harvey Oswald, with the spy game played between the U.S. and the USSR? (Spotlight, May 8, 1978.) A decision was made, and a course of action determined. They were calculated to both fascinate and confuse the public by staging a clever "limited hangout" when the House Special Committee on Assassinations (HSCA) holds its open hearings, beginning later this month. A "limited hangout" is spy jargon for a favorite and frequently used gimmick of the clandestine professionals. When their veil of secrecy is shredded and they can no longer rely on a phony cover story to misinform the public, they resort to admitting – sometimes even volunteering some of the truth while still managing to withhold the key and damaging facts in the case. The public, however, is usually so intrigued by the new information that it never thinks to pursue the matter further...But once again the good folks of middle America will be hoodwinked by the government and its allies in the establishment news media." (http://www.spartacus.schoolnet.co.uk/JFKsturgis.htm).
For more info. on the CIA see:
http://www.counterpunch.org/gibbs04072003.html,
http://home.att.net/~Resurgence/CIAtimeline.html, http://www.cia-on-campus.org/nsa/nsa2.html and
http://www.geocities.com/CapitolHill/Congress/7727/cia.htm. This site contains most of the text of the Rolling Sone article of Oct 20 1977 by Carl Bernstein entitled "The CIA and the media":

http://www.unknownnews.net/hh030102.html .

14. Phoenix 2004 Annual p.68

15. Phoenix Aug 13 2004 p.8

16. Phoenix Mar 11 2005 p.8

17.
http://www.thirdworldtraveler.com/Third_World_US/COINTELPRO60s_WA
H.html, http://www.justice.ie/80256E01003A02CF/vWeb/pcJUSQ5Y2F6U-en
and http://www.amazon.com/gp/reader/0896083497/ref=sib_dp_pop_ex/104-
0477615-2294306?%5Fencoding=UTF8&p=S00D#reader-link. The reference
to Shannon airport is from Phoenix April 25 2003 p.7 .

18. The Pentagon directive is called FM 30-31B and was issued by General
Westmoreland in 1970, the quotes are from
http://www.buergerwelle.de/pdf/secret_warfare_and_natos_stay_behind_armie
s.htm. Also from that page:
"The history of FM 30-31B itself is remarkable. The Pentagon document first
surfaced in Turkey in 1973 where the newspaper Baris in the midst of a whole
range of mysterious acts of violence and brutality which shocked the Turkish
society announced the publication of a secretive US document. Thereafter the
Baris journalist who had come into the possession of FM 30-31B disappeared
and was never heard of again. Despite the apparent danger Turkish Colonel Ta-
lat Turhan two years later published a Turkish translation of the top-secret FM
30-31 and revealed that in Turkey NATO's secret stay-behind army was code-
named "Counter-Guerrilla" directed by the Special Warfare Department. From
Turkey the document found its way to Spain where in 1976 the newspaper Tri-
unfo, despite heavy pressures to prevent the publication, published excerpts of
FM 30-31B upon the fall of the Franco dictatorship. In Italy on 27 October
1978 excerpts of FM 30-31B were published by the political magazine L'Eu-
ropeo, whereupon the printed issues of the magazine were confiscated. The
breakthrough for the document came arguably not in the 1970s, but in the
1980s, when in Italy the secret anticommunist P2 Freemason lodge of Licio
Gelli was discovered. Among the documents seized by the Italian police
ranged also FM 30-31B. The Italian parliamentary investigation into P2 decided to publish FM 30-31B in the appendix of the final public parliamentary report on P2 in 1987."
...
[From the Footnote references to the document:] Regine Igel, Andreotti. Politik
zwischen Geheimdienst und Mafia (1997), p. 346. Igel offers in her German
translation the full text of the top secret US FM 30-31B in her book on Giulio
Andreotti and the US subversion of Italy (Appendix, pp. 345-358). The English
quotes offered above are the author's translation of Igel's text. Igel's source is
the original English version of the FM 30-31B as contained in the collected

documents of the Italian Parliamentary Commission of Inquiry into the US-linked P2 secret lodge which was discovered in 1981 (Commissione parlamentare d'inchiesta sulla loggia massonica P2. Allegati alla Relazione Doc. XXIII, n. 2-quater/7/1 Serie II, Vol. VII, Tomo I, Roma 1987, pp. 287-298). The document FM 30-31B is dated 18 March 1970, Headquarters of the US Army, Washington DC, and signed by General of the US Army William C Westmoreland.

The psyop references are from http://www.indyweek.com/durham/2000-07-05/cover.html .

19. The quote from Dorril is at http://web.archive.org/web/20040127115740/http://www.politrix.org/foia/mi6/mi6-restored.htm. The reference to the JIC and Michael Packenham is from http://www.unclenicks.net/bilderberg/www.bilderberg.org/sis.htm quoting the Sunday Times of 21 May 2000. The Det quotations are from Phoenix June 6 2003 p.16 and Aug 13 2004 p.16. It was said to have been disbanded at this time but if the pattern of those agencies is anything to go by then it probably just changed its name.

20. The Ritter quote is from http://www.tvset.org/wmd-uk_00.html quoting The Times 28/12/2003. The Rockingham Cell is described at http://www.sundayherald.com/print34491.

21. How else is it to be explained that they would go to such efforts to eliminate a garda informant to protect the IRA? I have put in a separate chapter to address this question.

22. See the StakeKnife book op cit.

23. Phoenix May 9 2004.
Colonel Kerr is also said to have attempted to get the UDA to launch a bombing campaign in the South. This is from the diary of Brian Nelson seen by Paul Larkin a BBC journalist and mentioned by him at the above mentioned Justice for the Forgotten meeting. There he also stated that the Loyalist paramilitaries were very much protected by "an unaccountable cabal" who always "walk away without any scrutiny". The system he feels were "using paramilitaries for their own ends". He pointed out that a large number of the loyalists who helped him in his research ended up killed or intimidated. This is mentioned at http://www.michael.donegan.care4free.net/sunday_business_post290603.htm .

24. Phoenix Sept 13 2002 p.20: "...the tradition which has grown up since the Special Branch took control of Garda HQ some years ago."
Sunday Times March 20 2005 p.17: "Involvement with the Crime and Security branch is seen by many gardai as the quickest way to promotion. And the best way to impress C and S is apparently, through the regular dispatch of C77's,

top secret forms with information provided by informers."

25. Phoenix March 28 2003 p.9.

26. Phoenix Feb 14 2003 p.14.

27. Quote from Phoenix Feb 11 2005 p.14 and also Dec 6 2002 p.9 .

28. Phoenix March 12 2004 p.6 .

29. Karen McGlinchey, *Charades* (Dublin, 2005), and also see Chapter 1 above.

30. http://archives.tcm.ie/businesspost/2003/03/30/story567756159.asp .

31. http://www.sbpost.ie/web/Home/Document%20View%20Business/did-489357560-pageUrl--2FBusiness-2FNews-Features-2FAll-New-Features.asp .

32. http://wwa.rte.ie/news/2000/1009/abbeylara.html .

33. http://britishcollusion.com/news11.html .

34. www.fergalquinn.ie/NB-Report.pdf p.37 which is a good report by Brian Harvey called "Rights and Justice work in Ireland: A New Baseline."

35. http://web.archive.org/web/20040611082658/http://www.usafa.af.mil/inss/OCP/ocp15.pdf .

36. http://www.indymedia.ie/newswire.php?story_id=64499 .

37. http://www.indymedia.ie/newswire.php?story_id=69997 .

38. http://www.indymedia.ie/newswire.php?story_id=63056. An example of bureaucratic harassment, including motoring issues, of an activist can be seen I think in the experiences of Adrian Nally, who has campaigned on the Rossport issue: http://www.indymedia.ie/article/84299 and http://www.indymedia.ie/article/84446.
His comments here would I think be echoed by a lot of people:
"The media fail to air citizen's grievances. The distain for those marginalized is extraordinary. Politicians should show enough respect for people's lives to reply to their letters, especially those that plead to government to uphold its responsibilities. Government indifference dictates that the "small man" has no place in their realm. The blind-eye treatment rubs salt into deepening wounds. 'Friendly fire' between the main parties blankets their collective devil-may-care attitude towards people's troubles. Their sole interests revolve around

carving-up the spoils. People unfortunate enough to be sacrificed by the tiger economy are but a stain in their flourishing streetscapes. They have done all in their power to break me in mind, body and spirit. Is it right that government agents bludgeon those who question why they do not have the same rights as their neighbour? Years of anguish, copious letters, considerable expenses and no answers to boot; they've made my life a living nightmare. Everything I've received from local government seems to have a fraudulent aspect. Even my 1997 Bachelor of Engineering degree parchment, from the University of Strathclyde, seems to be a shadow of the document I forwarded to Limerick County Council on their request some years ago. It is unimaginable the depths of depravation that has been thrust upon me. Is there no end to their oppression?" (http://www.indymedia.ie/article/84688)

39. http://archives.tcm.ie/businesspost/2003/06/22/story274582202.asp and http://www.gargle.ie/gargle/arc_law_liquoract.php.

40. http://www.irish-independent.ie/irish_independent/stories.php3? ca=9&si=1267395&issue_id=11539. Irish Independent Thursday Oct 14 2004 has an account where the gardai even woke a person up who was asleep in the pub then claimed he could have fallen off his chair so he was claimed to be a danger to himself and on that basis prosecuted the pub owners.

41. http://www.rte.ie/tv/latelate/20050415.html Late Late 15 April 2005. It was related by the journalist Frank Connolly on the programme.

42. http://historical-debates.oireachtas.ie/S/0172/S.0172.200305150007.html .

43. http://web.archive.org/web/20031003172011/http://archives.tcm.ie/businesspost/2002/04/21/story318510.asp showing the debts that the McBrearty's have incurred trying to keep their business afloat in the teeth of all the false charges laid against them.

44. Phoenix March 25 2005 p.16.

45. http://www.unison.ie/irish_independent/stories.php3? ca=9&si=869631&issue_id=8339 Irish Independent Wed Nov 13 2002 and Sunday Times Nov 10 2002 p.15: "...defamatory leaflets, referring to the "murdering McBreartys", were printed and given to him by John White, a [Special Branch] detective sergeant, to be distributed in the area."

46. Fergus Finlay, *Snakes and Ladders* (Dublin, 1998), p.315. I appreciate that a long time later it was revealed that Lowry had an offshore account but it has also being revealed that many financial advisers and bank managers encouraged their clients to invest in these instruments and no doubt always claimed that they were perfectly legal.

47. That the powers that be may have something to hide over that outbreak can be surmised from the fact that the English farmer scapegoated as being the source of the disease in England has been served with the Official Secrets Act to keep him quiet. (http://www.warmwell.com/jun13osa.html)

48. http://www.flood-tribunal.ie/images/SITECONTENT_225.pdf. One way that George Redmond received corrupt payments was via bets laid on his behalf by a horse breeder called Thomas Brennan. (http://www.unison.ie/irish_independent/stories.php3? ca=9&si=185609&issue_id=1999). It must have been a very simple but effective way of disguising payments especially since you don't have to declare such winnings for tax purposes. In fact there seems to be a lot of corruption in horse racing in general with one former head of security for the Jockey Club in the UK saying:
"I wouldn't say it was bent. I would say it is institutionally corrupt." (http://news.bbc.co.uk/1/hi/programmes/panorama/2290356.stm). Whatever the truth of that certainly horse racing is very popular in Ireland among the political elite.

49. http://www.limerick-leader.ie/issues/20011117/news09.html .

50. A left over ghost footnote number, yeah yeah I know I know I should revert to a better abacus!lol.

51. The quote from Barry is from http://indymedia.ie/newswire.php? story_id=70109 .Barry mentioned this later adding some more details about the gardai and the operation of emergency legislation in the south of Ireland:
"They can quote the drugs act at you and then do pretty much anything they want. They can arrest you on the spot for non co-operation .

Another one, if you give them lip is to wait till your coming out of a pub and then abuse you, which means they can batter you as well as lift you on the spot for drunk and disorderly .

Oh dont forget, they can just get their superintendent to say your a member of an illegal organisation as well. They dont need any evidence, just his opinion. Internment by the back door .

At present there are Irish citizens in jail on 7 year sentences for possession (allegedly) of a wreath, one pensioner is in for a chair leg in his back yard (could be used for a grenade!). A number of men who met openly in a hotel bar to organise a prisoners social (which they hoped to hold in the same bar) were arrested in the bar and jailed for membership. The branch said it was an IRA meeting (in broad daylight in a busy hotel bar) so the judges (3 no less) kindly obliged and gave them seven years apiece .

The branch are a law unto themselves. Once they enter the frame you have no legal rights worth speaking of." (http://www.indymedia.ie/newswire.php?story_id=72353).

52. The McGlinchey reference is from the Late Late Show 18th March 2005.

53. Martin Ingram and Greg Harkin, *Stakeknife / Britain's Secret Agents in Ireland* (Dublin, 2005).

54. http://www.unison.ie/irish_independent/stories.php3?ca=9&si=1287844&issue_id=11694 Rodney Stich names this as the number one priority for cleaning up corruption in the US because of its use in silencing dissidents: "Eliminate the draconian prison sentences for most drug and other minor offenses" (http://www.druggingamerica.com/).

55. Phoenix Annual 2004 p.62.

56. p.9 see also http://www.esatclear.ie/~drugsense/news/garda.html .

57. Phoenix April 25 2003 p.9 and http://support.unison.ie/irish_independent/stories.php3?ca=9&si=950420&issue_id=9011 .

58 Phoenix Sept 24 2004 p.16.

59. Information from an architect's office.

60. http://www.iol.ie/~cparker/alternate.htm. His case also highlights the fact that modern day employment practices in Ireland tend to leave people with very little job security and that, as well as the seemingly arbitrary way that people secure employment, leaves people vulnerable to politically inspired harassment. From Parceir again:
"A. The reality is slightly more painful. I was offered a job on the basis of my historical knowledge and research 'expertise'. These were exploited, or rather pillaged (though I was told what was going on). When they had got enough I was told unceremoniously that I no longer had a job.

Q. Was any reason given?

A. I was warned to be 'discreet', but I was told that they no longer had enough money to pay me.

Q. Did you believe them?

A. No. There are some people here who couldn't tell the truth to save their miserable little lives. Lying becomes a habit after a while, just like picking their noses.

Q. And what has happened to the job since?

A. It was subsequently given to someone without any historical qualifications – but they're welcome to that chimp."
(http://www.iol.ie/~cparker/page1.htm)
and:
"What matters is an association with one of the quasi-criminal cliques here, combined with an ability to flatter.
...
But one doesn't realise that the exploitation is taking place – not until it's too late. My own experience was that I was so full of gratitude for having been 'given a chance' that I didn't realise the nature of the 'chance' I had been given. I was so loyal – when my superior threatened to resign because of criticism from 'on high' I stated that I would leave too. When I mentioned this to a friend she laughed, adding 'he wouldn't stick his neck out for you, you know'. But I am being unduly negative I hear you say, probably a little bitter. What type of people would do this type of thing? Evil bastards who should be ashamed to show their faces in public. I was so stupid; I never believed that human beings, my own 'fellow Cavanmen' could be such low down curs. I thought I had a contract, but instead it was a temporary work agreement not worth the paper it wasn't written on." (http://www.iol.ie/~cparker/alternate.htm)

This is Ciaran on local government in Cavan:
"I remember asking one particular [public representative in Cavan]...some weeks before the last local election whether he was gearing up for the contest. "Oh no, I haven't thought about that yet". He should have; he nearly didn't make it. No – they would prefer never to have to go crawling before the amorphous group known alternatively as "the hoors", "the whingers", "the Fuckers" and "the cunts". (By the way, these names are not made up: some people in this neck of the woods might care to dwell on the fact that my family were heavily involved in local politics in the past. I well remember hearing a county councillor remarking, as he entered the count centre where his party colleagues were having a hard time getting elected: "The hoors don't know when they're well off".) Instead of having to fulfill any public representative role, the vast majority would much prefer to cosy up to their buddies in the council executives and the building industry, feeding and drinking at the golden slop tank of local politics, and sharing the back-handers with their buddies."
(http://www.iol.ie/~cparker/Commentary.htm)

This is a curious reference of his: "'phone calls can be and are monitored by Catholic lay groups, so best to mind what you say." (http://www.iol.ie/~cparker/Tourism.htm)

This reference by Parceir to no doubt the Knights of Columbanus is included here out of interest but, frankly, is not a very believable account:
"The place preserves its sinister lustre even now, being used by a devillishly sinister, quasi-masonic grouping for their meetings. They usually use mirrors in their ceremonies which are reputed to include repulsive acts of Satanic worship and self-abuse, along with discussions of how they can "plant" members and sympathizers in strategic posts, all the better to achieve world domination and protect themselves and their friends from the forces of justice and condemnation. They are reputed to have a particular liking for young children who are strongly advised not to play in the vicinity on a Monday evening. These individuals often parade themselves as devout but they are the epitome of the wolves in sheep's clothing. No matter how lurid an individual's past is a place will always be found for them. They are powerful with their dirty tentacles reaching to most areas of Irish life – a Catholic masonic order no less. They claim to stand for high moral standards but people with the most lamentable pasts and presents are welcomed into the fold and defended like blood brothers. They inspire loathing and fear in equal measure, as even the dogs in the street know of those members who have gained promotion ahead of other more qualified and promising candidates. And then they are rumoured to maintain an informal blacklist with the names of those who have offended them. Woe betide such souls lest they come before a judge who is a member or a bureaucrat who takes an interest in their case. I for one would be ashamed to have anything to do with them."

So despite the long time and expense he has gone through becoming very well educated, he has a PhD in Medieval History and knows 13 languages, he finds it very difficult to secure employment and gets no respect from the money obsessed celtic tigers. The expensive and difficult work he does in historical research is generally completely unpaid and in Cavan he didn't even get a free copy of the journal which he contributed an article to: http://www.iol.ie/~cparker/goodbye.htm .

61. http://www.emigrant.ie/article.asp?iCategoryID=177&iArticleID=39518 note the curious references to some personnel in Roscommon here: http://www.iol.ie/~cparker/Commentary.htm .S

62. Phoenix June 20 2003 p.14.

63. Phoenix Annual 2004 p.62.

64. http://www.indymedia.ie/newswire.php?story_id=67411&topic=mayday2004 .

65. http://www.indymedia.ie/newswire.php?story_id=68196&topic=mayday2004 .

66. http://tash.gn.apc.org/watched1.htm .

67.
http://society.guardian.co.uk/crimeandpunishment/comment/0,8146,1452267,0
0.html and for their use against protesters:
https://www4.indymedia.org.uk/en/2004/08/296948.html .

68. The Asbo's quote is from:
http://society.guardian.co.uk/crimeandpunishment/comment/0,8146,1452267,0
0.html. For the use of injunctions against the farmers:
"Both sides are back in the High Court in front of Justice O'Donovan to consider the IMA's application for an interlocutory injunction. This is granted
pending a full trial of the action for trespass and damages.
However, the Justice rules that the IFA will have to pay a daily fine of
£500,000 "immediately" if it continues its blockade of the factories.
He warns that he will continue to impose fines "until it hurt". He appoints an
accountancy firm as sequestrator over the assets of IFA and directs the Association to disclose its assets within two days."
(http://www.farmersjournal.ie/2000/0122/home/home2.html),
bin tax protesters:
"Fingal County Council has gone all out to break this campaign. They got an
injunction that is so broad that you could nearly be accused of breaking it by
looking too closely at a Fingal bin truck or bin man. They have had Clare and
Joe [Higgins TD] jailed. They have intimidated residents with the police,
courts etc. In September they had nine people arrested and brought before the
courts for breaking the injunction."
(http://www.socialistworld.net/eng/2003/10/11bins.html)
and in the construction industry:
"Almost every recent strike by the Building & Allied Trades Union (BATU)
has been met with High Court injunctions against picketing."
(http://flag.blackened.net/revolt/ws99/ws56_brickies.html).

69. http://www.liamog.com/PDF%20Downloads/incameraletter2.PDF and
http://www.liamog.com/incamera.htm.
The quote from Paddy Doyle is from
http://www.paddydoyle.com/whatredress.html .

70. http://www.american-buddha.com/mike.reconosciuto.htm and
http://www.maebrussell.com/Articles%20and%20Notes/Napa%20Sentinel
%20INSLAW%20article.html .

71.
http://www.defraudingamerica.com/laws_violated_by_federal_judges.html .

72. For Mark Harris see http://www.greatbrutishjustice.org/father.htm and for
Sheenagh McMahon see Chapter 5 under Frank Connolly.

73. http://www.farmersjournal.ie/2000/0122/home/home2.html and http://www.farmersjournal.ie/2000/0311/beef/ .

74. http://www.farmersjournal.ie/2001/0113/home/home3.html .

75. http://www.farmersjournal.ie/2002/1005/news/currentedition/othernews.htm .

76. http://www.farmersjournal.ie/2003/1004/farmmanagement/crops/index.shtml .

77. Fine Gael acknowledges that this means that farmers have in practise no right to protest. http://www.finegael.ie/fine-gael-news.cfm/NewsID/21313/action/detail/year/2005/month/4/level/page/aid/186/ Here is an editorial in the Farmers Journal showing the atmosphere: "This week farmers have begun sporadic protests in supermarkets. The Competition Authority is keeping a watchful eye ready to pounce at any hint of "market interference". But as the chairman of the Authority said recently, they only take on cases they are likely to win. So they tackle soft targets, not the real issues, especially those in the professions that are strangling Irish life." (http://www.farmersjournal.ie/2003/1101/news/currentedition/editorial.shtml Farmers Journal 1 Nov 2003.)

78. http://archives.tcm.ie/irishexaminer/2001/05/23/story3675.asp .

This is a good speech that Noel Coogan of Fine Gael made in the Seanad 6 Nov 2002 again detailing the frustration that is felt at this behaviour by the state and the precarious position of the farmers:
"The Minister mentioned farm incomes in respect of which farmers are getting very angry. He failed to mention that incomes are set to fall by 17% by which amount he said they rose last year. Taking inflation into account, Teagasc advises that they will drop by 20% this year. This is a staggering drop that would be hard for any sector of society to take. This means average family farm income this year will be around €14,000 or about half the average industrial wage.

Political responsibility for the disastrous fall in incomes rests fairly and squarely with the Minister and the Government. Prices in all the main sectors of beef, lamb, milk and grain are down. Producers are subject to massive political regulation and excessive bureaucracy that is driving many farmers, particularly younger ones, away from the business. They have to put up with cost increases which are beyond the control of most.

For producing food of the highest quality, farmers are entitled to a decent price that will give them a modest income. That is all they are looking for. A farmer carried out research and found the yield from the average dairy cow will generate €1,800 for a farmer. A similar amount of milk will generate €18,800 for some of the super outlets like McDonalds. There is a huge discrepancy.

Before the present crisis, approximately 20,000 farmers were earning less than €200 per week. With the present crisis, it is estimated that another 20,000 are in danger of being forced out of farming in the very near future. Under the leadership of the Minister, if a farmer wanted to generate an income on a par with someone on the average industrial wage, he or she would require from his or her enterprise 250 head of beef stock and 165 acres of land, a suckler herd of 90 suckler units, a milk quota of 80,000 gallons, 550 sheep, 600 acres of barley or 400 acres of winter wheat. The average size farm in Ireland is 65 acres. To improve their incomes, farmers require an increase in prices for their produce and an increase in scale and productivity which requires access to more land at more favourable prices.

The Minister and the Government have stood idly by this and every other autumn as the factories force down the price of cattle by at least €70 per head, while the market remains stable in Britain. Prices have increased on the Continent. We have heard umpteen times that there is no cartel in the beef factories. It must be an extraordinary coincidence that on the same morning every week the factories quote lists for the price of cattle that read the same. For God's sake, who is codding whom?

Then we have the disgraceful behaviour of the Competition Authority which stated in response to farmers' complaints that it was understaffed and would take 12 months to reply. Yet on a whim after a phone call it could raid the homes of private individuals, the unpaid representatives of the farming community who are doing their best to ensure the survival of the farming sector. The Minister and the Tánaiste have a lot of questions to answer in that regard." (http://www.irlgov.ie/debates-02/s6Nov/Sect2.htm).

79. http://cryptome.org/echelon-be.htm .

80. It is well known that western agencies have routine access to this type of data. Like many international telephone companies Eircom uses Amdocs of Israel to handle that phone data. http://www.amdocs.com/successstories.asp?CustomerID=52&SID=402 Foxnews has reported that this company has been the subject of an FBI investigation for suspected espionage activities. An internal memo of the company has been referred to which shows that they use sophisticated algorithms to identify calling patterns (and hence relationship patterns) using the phone data. (http://www.rense.com/general18/isr2.htm) .

It is not just phone records that can be used to build up a profile of a persons relationships and movements as you can see from this report in the London 'Independent' Dec 22 2005:

"A major feature of the national surveillance centre for car numbers is the ability to trawl through records of previous sightings to build up an intelligence picture of a vehicle's precise whereabouts on the road network.
...
[Quoting Frank Whitely the Chief Constable of Hertfordshire, who refers of course to the use of this technology on presumed 'criminals':] "We can use ANPR (Automatic Number Plate Recognition surveillance cameras) on investigations or we can use it looking forward in a proactive, intelligence way. Things like building up the lifestyle of criminals – where they are going to be at certain times. We seek to link the criminal to the vehicle through intelligence. Vehicles moving on the roads are open to police scrutiny at any time. The Road Traffic Act gives us the right to stop vehicles at any time for any purpose. So criminals on public roads are vulnerable."
...
WHERE THE INFORMATION GOES
The new National ANPR Data Centre is to be based at Hendon in north London, the site of the existing Police National Computer. It is being designed to store 35 million number plate 'reads' per day, to be expanded to 100 million reads within a couple of years. The time, date and place of each vehicle sighting will be stored for at least two years, with plans to extend this period to five years. Special 'data mining' software can trawl for movements and associations.
WHO USES THE INFORMATION
Police
Every police force will have direct computer access to the National ANPR Data Centre. Intelligence officers will be able to access data on a car's movements over a number of years.
MI5
The Security Services have special exemption under the Data Protection Act to use ANPR information for purposes of national security. Anti-terrorism will be their main interest."
(http://www.prisonplanet.com/articles/december2005/221205surveillanceuk.htm)

The former NSA employee Wayne Madsen has described some of the surveillence software used by the police and FBI in the US:
"MAGLOCLEN allows police investigators to link various activist groups and members through the Link Association Analysis sub-system, a relational data base that identifies the "friends and families" of groups and individuals. The Telephone Record Analysis sub-system can call up records of phone calls of targeted groups and individuals. A suspect group's banking and other commercial data can be monitored by the Financial Analysis sub-system. And through a system that would have been the envy of J. Edgar Hoover, police and federal agents can also call up profiles that provide specific information on the composition of organizations, including their membership lists. The Justice Department has instituted a project called RISSNET II, which directly links the indi-

89

vidual databases contained within the various RISS centers." (http://www.cor-pwatch.org/article.php?id=1108)

81. http://agitprop.org.au/stopnato/20000502emailtstuk.php quoting Sunday Times 30 April 2000.

82 James Bamford, *Body of Secrets* (London, 2001), p.367-369.

83. http://www.answers.com/topic/communications-in-ireland .

84. "By 1975 the NSA had the capacity to bug undersea trunk telephone ca-bles. It is done by induction 'there is no physical penetration or damage to the cable'." Bamford op cit p.373.

85. Bamford op cit p.427.

86. So for example in 2001 it was reported that the NSA were planning to build from 2000-2005 a computer which would be 2 million times faster than any-thing the outside world was aware of. As you can read in that book they are many years in advance of unclassified technology. Since 1984 they have their own secret facility for developing classified computers and storage technology. They also have their own chip making plant on site. (Bamford op cit p.604, 607.)

87. http://www.kungfoo.com/index.php/news/1175 .

88. http://www.geek.com/news/geeknews/2005Mar/gee20050316029613.htm .

89. http://www.dynametric.com/call_saver.asp Taking from that link the num-ber of megabytes needed to store a telephone conversation we get something like: (1024 megabytes in a gigabyte X 1024 gigabytes in a terrabyte)/ (8 megabytes storing an hours conversation).

90. Bamford op cit p.578.

91. See comments added to the Stasiland article for the leak with respect to GCHQ for example.

92. The Echelon quote is from
http://www.abovetopsecret.com/pages/echelon.html quoting New Statesmen Aug12 1988 while the GCHQ reference is from
http://politics.guardian.co.uk/iraq/story/0,12956,1084994,00.html .

93. It is sometimes denied that Echelon has that capability but I am relying on the direct testimony of Mike Frost of the Canadian CSE who used Echelon and had been trained by the NSA. In a documentary entitled "Echelon: The most

Secret Spy System" (broadcast History Channel 2 April 2005) he has stated they use those keyword searches. He said the calls are routinely broken down by keyword recognition, dial number and voice recognition.

94. http://agitprop.org.au/stopnato/20000221echelbladn.php. See also http://www.yourmailinglistprovider.com/pubarchive_show_message.php? globeintel+177 on MI6 bugging of the Polish Prime Minister Leszek Miller.

95. http://cryptome.org/echelon-ie.htm from Phoenix magazine May 5 2000. I have seen no further reference to this 'Enternet' and I am not sure if that is the official name or a name that Phoenix humorously gives it.

96. http://cryptome.org/nsakey-ms-dc.htm .

97. http://www.totse.com/en/technology/computer_technology/163148.html .

98. I remember reading that some time ago but I cannot remember the exact company and I also can find no reference to it now on the internet. As regards the 'holes' mentioned see how Norton Antivirus does not detect PCAnywhere: http://www.radmin.com/support/forum/read.php? FID=19&TID=5949&MID=17858 and http://www.softpanorama.org/Antivirus/false_positives.shtml .
Here is a website that shows that in practise a person using PCAnywhere can do all the things that a big bad hacker is supposed to be able to do: http://www.radmin.com/support/forum/read.php? FID=19&TID=5949&MID=17858 .

99. Peter Wright, *Spycatcher* (Toronto, 1987) referred to here:http://homepages.caverock.net.nz/~bj/invis.htm .

100. http://www.totse.com/en/politics/green_planet/sec_act.html. The technology is nowhere described in detail and the Church Committee seemed to only refer to letters physically opened (and resealed again no doubt).

101. http://www.icdc.com/~paulwolf/cointelpro/churchfinalreportIIIh.htm .

102. http://www.transformmag.com/showArticle.jhtml?articleID=16101054 .

103. http://www.enterstageright.com/archive/articles/0200echelon.htm .

104. http://lists.stdlib.net/pipermail/e-voting/2005-January/004611.html .

105. http://cryptome.org/echelon-ie.htm from Phoenix magazine May 5 2000. Writing in 1979 Kennedy Lindsay noted that "the registry and computer at Northern Ireland Army H.Q. now have information on some 65% of the adult Ulster population." (Kennedy Lindsay, *Ambush at Tully-West / The British In-*

telligence Services in Action (Dundalk, 1979), p.254.)

106. One anonymous leak for the BND states that the Echelon throws up too many false positives like that: http://216.239.59.104/search? q=cache:2ld2Sug7iUcJ:www.mosquito-verlag.de/weblog.php%3Fid %3D9%26p%3D1+&hl=en&start=1 .

107. Mentioned by Mike Frost in the documentary op cit .

108. http://www.privacy.nb.ca/cryptography/archives/cryptography/html/1997-12/0107.html quoting the Times 29 Dec 1997 .

109. Mark Bowden, *Killing Pablo* (London, 2001), p.102. See also some leaks from the Swedish Security Services at http://www.kkrva.se/Links/Infokrig/Wik3.html .

110. http://news.bbc.co.uk/1/hi/magazine/3522137.stm. I know that contradicts the other reference where it says that the mobile does not need to be switched on but the other reference is quite specific and it seems probable that the BBC is wrong about that.

111. http://www.bugsweeps.com/info/esquire_5-66.html, which reprints an article from Esquire May 1966, a fascinating glimpse at such technology.

112. http://lists.village.virginia.edu/lists_archive/sixties-l.old/0246.html describing the type not requiring physical access to the phone, this from lawyers dealing with Dutch narcotic agents.

This link shows that it can be done anywhere on the telephone line: http://www.martykaiser.com/report~1.htm .

In a detailed description of one type of this bug, first developed in 1963 and in extensive use by the CIA at least since the early 70s, it is said that: "No entry to the subject's premises or modification to their telephone set is required." (http://yarchive.net/phone/infinity_transmitter.html).

113. Martin McGartland, *Fifty Dead Men Walking* (London, 1998), p.198.

114. Fergus Finlay, *Snakes and Ladders* (Dublin,1998), p.106.

115. http://members.aol.com/_ht_a/lillithsrealm/myhomepage/Humanity/HumanRights/STOA/ATPC_4DST.html paragraph 4.4.

116. http://www.eff.org/Privacy/printers/docucolor/ .

117. The Newsham quote is from:
http://agitprop.org.au/stopnato/20000221echelbladn.php .

Esoteric Technologies
Of course there is a lot of speculation out there about advanced technology that the western governments might have access to, speculation that is fueled by the huge funding and great secrecy put into so much military technology as opposed to the frequently under funded and obsolete civilian technology. The Sunday Times for example points out that the USSR was near developing the capacity to artificially induce earthquakes by using underground nuclear explosions (Sept 15 1996 http://veenet.value.net/~earth1/russia). The USSR also of course had advanced weather control capability and it might be thought both technologies have since been studied by the western powers. (http://www.prisonplanet.com/articles/october2005/211005weathercontrol.htm) Presumably this classified research is at least a few years ahead of our thinking in each field and while it is a mugs game trying to speculate about how technology might have advanced in these secret programmes it should nonetheless be attempted I think because its likely they are using techniques and equipment right now that we can hardly even conceptualise. Think of what it really means for some group to be say a decade ahead in their field. Look at for example the area of genetics as it unfolded between maybe 1990 and 2000. Before say 1990 the basic ideas of genetics were I think well understood by everybody and it was clear that humans and animals and plants had a very similar pattern of gene expression and inheritance but who could have really imagined that the ability to swap around those genes had developed to the point where by 1999 one study showed it as perfectly feasible to grow a Christmas tree with inbuilt biological lighting spliced into its genes from jellyfish and fireflies (http://news.bbc.-co.uk/1/hi/sci/tech/484809.stm). The basic knowledge was thrust forward by advances in computing and miniaturisation etc. to the point where anything now seems possible. Certainly we now know that the attempt by the South Africans to develop viruses or bacteria that can target particular ethnic groups is something that could now be easily accomplished. They had a huge secret programme running to try and discover this technology which we can see now was a perfectly feasible project where before people might have dismissed it as science fiction. Hence I think everybody has to keep their mind open to the possibilities of new technologies even if they remain classified for now.

As everybody knows, what has led to the new discoveries in genetics is the new map of the human genome, which together with many other animal and plant genome maps, allows scientists to mix and match genes across species to their hearts content. But imagine if a map like that had secretly already been developed in other fields? Take for example the brain. Clearly in some theoretical sense there must be specific places where we store information in the brain and also specific pathways where the different information travels and if it was possible to map all that then it presumably could be possible to manipulate or read that data. (One ex NSA member, John Akwei, alleges that the NSA has and makes use of such a map: http://www.naicr.org/aps/akwei.html) So if for example you knew how the ear transmits to the brain the information that it gathers then you could conceivably replace that stream with another, creating sounds that the person could hear but which had been artificially created and transmitted to the listener by microwave or whatever. (See http://www.raven1.net/v2succes.htm for a discussion of that area.) In fact in Japan they are exhibiting technology that can do something like that with the organs for balance that are located in the ear. (http://www.cnn.com/2005/TECH/10/25/human.remote.control.ap/ they use a special headset to transmit the artificial signals.) As regards the storage places in the brain apparently these have been investigated by researchers for many years and even in 1965 one researcher could manipulate bulls and monkeys by pressing a button on a remote control which stimulated a given area of the animal's brain via an implant operated by radio link. (http://www.wireheading.-com/matador.html). Hence its possibly not a good thing to dismiss out of hand all the speculation on the internet about intelligence agencies having access to these types of implant technologies, scary and all as that thought is. (See for example Dr. Rauni Leena Kilde formerly Chief Medical Officer for Lapland (northern Finland) at http://www.raven1.net/kilde1.htm, and see http://scrib-blguy.50megs.com/terror4.htm, for implants in general this is a good referenced article: http://216.239.59.104/search?q=cache:jg23q10qrj4J:www.geoci-ties.com/skews_me/implants.html+&hl=en) As regards reading some of the information stored in the brain notice how this has already been rolled out to a limited degree in a technology known as brain fingerprinting which decodes human brain waves (http://news.bbc.co.uk/2/hi/science/nature/3495433.stm. Also John Ginter has highlighted a number of articles that refer to research in this area like this one from the Los Angeles Times, March 20, 1976 entitled "Mind-Reading Machine Tells Secrets of the Brain" by Norman Kempster which says that: "Since 1973 a little-known Pentagon agency has been studying ways to plug a computer into an individual's brain waves... The Advanced Research Projects Agency say the $1 million a year program has passed its initial laboratory tests and is ready for determination of its military uses." Contracts with UCLA, Stanford and MIT, among others, were listed. http://www.raven1.net/ginter.htm).

One technology that is clearly in use by intelligence agencies is the famous 'Manchurian Candidate' type of mind/brain development. Effectively this is the extensive use of hypnosis, allied to drugs and other techniques, which can implant artificial memories and even personalities into targeted people. The shocking thing about this type of field is that one way they induce these altered personalities in people is by using trauma. This means that if a person, especially if very young, was hit by a terrible psychological or physical trauma then sometimes they can repress the memory of it and even develop a kind of second personality, both of which effects can be manipulated as part of this mind/brain training and conditioning.
Hypnosis can also be used for things like implanting false memories into peo-

ple   as   even   the   actor   Alan   Alda   found   out
(http://www.rense.com/general45/falsemen.htm). Knowing that some governments have this technology should I think make people look at some incidents
with a more skeptical eye. In particular the above link makes the point that this
kind of false memory might have been used on Ian Huntley who was accused
of the Soham murders. If you look at the case again with this in mind it certainly seems very suspicious. What happened was that both Huntley and his girlfriend freely gave very convincing interviews to police and even TV journalists
about the two missing girls and their (innocent) observations of them. Then
when held by the police Huntley was said to have suddenly gone insane and
was transferred to a top security mental institution and was to remain there in
the run up to the trial. His girlfriend meanwhile, it seems under heavy pressure
from the police, changed her story and implicated Huntley and was then subsequently charged with making an earlier false statement. Huntley was also
brought down from the mental hospital for the various pre-trial hearings in
what was reported to be quite a mental state with his tongue hanging out etc.
Finally he was judged to have made a miraculous recovery and sat the trial
without there being too much publicity given to this earlier supposed mental
relapse. Then incredibly in the trial he destroyed his own credibility by coming
up with this bizarre story about how one of the girls had a nose bleed in his
house, so discrediting his earlier statement in a way that no doubt got him convicted. Could this be that false memory technology in action?
(For the soham trial see these 3 articles by Joe Vialls:
http://web.archive.org/web/20041108024944/http://www.bigwig.net/software-
design/hollyjessica/who_really_murdered_holly_wells_.htm
http://web.archive.org/web/20041108084408/homepage.ntlworld.com/stevesey
mour/hollyjessica/who_really_murdered_holly_wells_2.htm
http://web.archive.org/web/20041022011220/www.joevialls.co.uk/transpositio
ns/pedophile1.html).

Here are some links on the whole question of the 'Manchurian Candidate' and
the related use of hypnosis etc by the CIA and other groups:
http://www.totse.com/en/conspiracy/mind_control/162398.html ,
http://educate-yourself.org/mc/falsememoryhoax1996.shtml
http://64.233.161.104/search?q=cache:RGz4oobPFRMJ:www.illuminati-
news.com/wheeler-interview.htm+%22+Cisco+Wheeler%22&hl=en
http://www.freedommag.org/english/vol36i2/page16.htm ,
http://www.raven1.net/anat-1.htm
http://www.whale.to/b/rappoport_i.html ,
http://groups-
beta.google.com/group/rec.arts.books/browse_thread/thread/aae33415a1fbf773
/9e6be3c36981b786 ,
http://groups-beta.google.com/group/rec.arts.books/msg/89bb59812a0a2e8f ,
http://www.mysteriouspeople.com/Candy_Jones.htm ,
http://my.dmci.net/~casey/
http://poynter.org/forum/?id=thememo

http://educate-yourself.org/mc/nwomcbturireview.shtml .
There is even speculation that some powerful cults have access to this type of technology and techniques, for which see Svali at: http://web.archive.org/web/20060116065148/www.lionlambministries.org/BC Chapter6.htm. More on these cult allegations, this time by David Marr, available at http://www.danofisrael.com/id33.html.

118. http://www.bjr.org.uk/data/1999/no2_mccrystal.htm .

As speculated on in the Stasiland article I think people should not ignore either technology that the western powers could be secretly using to harm the health of 'terrorist suspects' or dissidents. There is simply too many people out there who are claiming that their health has been harmed in this way. (http://www.-mindcontrolforums.com/victm-hm.htm)
In practise this kind of information rarely leaks out of governments until they fall like in the case of East Germany, South Africa and the USSR. There is also the case of Rhodesia which again had an extensive Chemical and Biological Weapons programme. The point is that Rhodesia was a country with very close ties to the UK which gives rise to the suspicion that the UK authorities faced with a similar 'terrorist' situation might have used the same tactics. The Selous Scouts for example was the main unit in the Rhodesian army that was using these tactics and it was led by a Lieutenant-Colonel Ron Reid-Daly who served formerly alongside the British SAS in Malaya. Here is a quote of his describing the Rhodesian SAS: "It was a thoroughly professional unit, which, in my opinion, more than lived up to the standards set by the British SAS." (http://www.-booksofzimbabwe.com/the_elite.html) So there are very close ties here and in the current UK SAS there is "notable representation from... the former Rhodesia" (wikipedia article on the SAS). A leading UK businessman Tiny Rowland, and one time owner of The Observer, is described as 'omnipresent' as an adviser to the Rhodesian government during the negotiations at the end of UDI. (David Martin and Phyllis Johnson, *The Struggle for Zimbabwe* (London,1981), p.294.) Fred Holroyd was told that MI5 were secretly backing the Rhodesian government and helping them to evade the sanctions. (Fred Holroyd and Nick Burbridge, *War without honour* (Hull, 1989), p.123.) Of course one objection that people would have here is that its all well and fine talking about what went on in some 'uncivilised' part of the world like Rhodesia but the UK forces would not use such heinous methods closer to home against the Irish. But Fred Holroyd who served in both places says that the UK forces were more ruthless and uncaring of the natives than the Rhodesians were. He gives one example to show this:

"I got Tosavepe to write a statement about all this [the beating up of his father by Rhodesian soldiers] and added one of my own and took them to my Brigadier, Brigadier Hoskins. I told him I had come from Northern Ireland where this sort of thing went on regularly, and rather than achieve anything positive, it simply damaged the credibility and morale of the soldiers asked to carry it out. Hoskins studied my reports, and immediately put out an order of the day, saying that if any of his soldiers were ever found maltreating the local people, they would have to answer personally to him. He then got hold of the two officers in charge of the unit and severely disciplined them. If I had tried anything like that in Ireland, it would have been me who ended up on a charge!"(ibid p. 128).

This treatment of the natives by the UK forces in Ireland can be seen as well in an interview given to the Sunday Times by Colin Demet formerly of the Queens Lancashire Regiment stationed in Ulster (April 3 2005 p.6 of News Review). He says that "the main tactic used by the soldiers was to provoke civilians while searching them." He talks about soldiers firing into pubs deliberately, knowing that innocent people would be killed and dragging old ladies down staircases etc. In the army he was "trapped in a living nightmare. I was watching them abusing people and obtaining a sick pleasure from their actions. The sadistic one third of the soldiers treated me and other decent soldiers in the same way they treated Irish people."

So I don't think you can say that great scruples are what would prevent the British army from using CBW in Ireland. This is a description of some Rhodesian practises:

"Faced with a deteriorating security situation as the 1970s wore on, Rhodesian authorities resorted to increasingly extreme counterinsurgency measures to resist nationalist guerrillas, including "pseudo-operations," psychological warfare, covert executions, and the deployment of ingenious booby traps and toxic substances. On the basis of insider accounts, there can be no doubt whatsoever that the Rhodesians employed 1) poisonous chemicals to impregnate clothing, canned food, drinks, and aspirin, and 2) lethal biological agents such as cholera bacteria and anthrax bacteria to contaminate water supplies and farmland. Although one former member of the Special Branch of the Rhodesian police – a force that was still designated, quaintly, as the British South African Police – claimed that he and his colleagues were aware of the use of poisons as early as 1973, the first clear evidence of this dates from 1975 or 1976, when the Rhodesian Central Intelligence Organisation (CIO) apparently asked doctors and chemists from the University of Rhodesia to identify and test a range of chemical and biological agents that could be used as a "fear factor" in the war against nationalist guerrillas. Professor Robert Symington, head of the clinical program in the university's Anatomy Department, then recruited several colleagues and students to carry out this research.

According to former Officer Commanding Counter Terrorist Operations M. J. McGuinness, the most senior Special Branch officer seconded to the CIO and the man who oversaw the CW program and other covert operations launched from the Selous Scouts fort at Bindura, 25-gallon drums of foul-smelling liquid were delivered to the base a dozen or so times in 1977. The chemicals were then poured into large sheets of tin and dried in the sun. When the liquid had dried, the leftover flakes wre scooped up and pounded in a mortar with a pestle. The resulting powder was then brushed onto stocks of denim clothing favored by the guerrillas, mixed into processed meat such as bully beef before being repacked in new cans, or injected into bottles of alcohol with a micro-needle. Moreover, several prisoners were forcibly brought to the fort and allegedly used as "human guinea pigs" to test the effects of the poisons, after which their bodies were secretly disposed of. Other accounts indicate that denim clothing was also brought to the André Rabie barracks of the Selous Scouts, where it was soaked in vats of odorless and colorless liquid chemicals. The distribution of the contaminated items was generally organized by the Projects Section of the Special Branch and delivered by uniformed policemen to agents and intermediaries willing to sell them to the guerrillas, but some bottles of poisoned alcohol were instead disseminated by the Selous Scouts. Secret Special Branch documents made available by Peter Stiff confirm the distribution of various poisoned items, and reveal that at least 800 people had died after absorbing the poison through their soft body tissues. Indeed, the CW program was terminated by police commissioner Peter Allum after the Special Branch commander learned of the deaths of innocent rural villagers to whom some of the poisoned clothes had been sold by unscrupulous local agents, agents who had been recruited by the Selous Scouts and Special Branch and been paid a 1000 Zimbabwean dollar bonus for each "confirmed" guerrilla death.

The Rhodesians also made several attempts to disseminate lethal BW agents, in particular Vibrio cholerae and Bacillus anthracis. McGuinness claimed that two unsuccessful efforts were made by the Selous Scouts to contaminate the Ruhenya River in northeastern Rhodesia with cholera bacteria. A former Rhodesian intelligence officer who remained in Zimbabwe after the country's independence stated that many other attempts to deploy cholera bacteria were made by the Rhodesian security forces, especially in order to pollute water sources close to guerrilla camps inside neighboring Mozambique. He admitted, however, that "this tactic was said to be of very limited use due to the quick dispersal of the bacteria." As for anthrax, this same source said that anthrax spores were "used in an experimental role in the Gutu, Chilimanzi, Masvingo, and Mberengwa areas...to kill off the cattle of tribesmen," harmful incidents that were then attributed by Rhodesian Army psychological operations officers to infiltrating guerrillas. For his part, McGuinness said he was surprised to learn from some of his colleagues that anthrax had been disseminated on at least one occasion. The Selous Scouts had originally been asked to carry out the task, but their commander Lieutenant-Colonel Ron Reid-Daly had refused because he thought it would be too risky for his men. In the end, members of the Rhodesian Special Air Service (SAS) regiment delivered the anthrax by dropping it from an aircraft near Plumtree, on the Botswana border. Even today, anthrax is only endemic to Matabeleland, where Plumtree is located. For this and other reasons, Dr. Meryl Nass' argument that the Zimbabwean "anthrax epizootic" of 1979 and 1980 might also be attributable to intentional hu-

man dissemination must at least be seriously considered. Finally, in 1979 the CIO allegedly activated a plan to assassinate either Zimbabwe African National Union (ZANU) leader Robert Mugabe or Zimbabwe African Peoples Union (ZAPU) leader Joshua Nkomo in London, and then recruited an expatriate former British SAS member nicknamed "Taffy" to do the job. After performing successful tests on dogs, he opted to use a rifle to shoot Mugabe with a dum dum bullet into which ricin toxin was inserted, but the operation was aborted at the last minute."
(http://www.nti.org/e_research/profiles/SAfrica/Chemical/)

Since the 70s there may have been greater research done in the electronic area. The Phoenix, for example, refers here to some microwave device that the US army is using against civilians in Iraq:

"The latest controversial cargo to transit Shannon en route to the killing fields of Iraq is a cute little number codenamed Sheriff. Carried aboard Hercules C-130 freighters of Heavy Lift Command USAF, Sheriff is a "silent ray" device which beams concentrated microwave radiation on "targets" at ranges of up to one kilometre. Its official name is an Active Denial System. Mounted on Humvee personnel carriers, Sheriff is described as a "non lethal weapon for use against insurgents using civilian crowds as cover". Since US troops to date have had no hesitation in firing at perceived insurgents, Sheriff is presumably for use against the "civilian cover" (women and children). The finely focused radiation is designed to cause "a burning sensation on the skin." Non-ionising radiation in small doses has, in many past studies, been associated with various cancers, particularly leukaemia in children. The Active Denial Systems being shipped through Shannon look like large satellite dishes of the sort seen on TV outside broadcast vehicles." (Feb 11 2005 p.8.)

CHAPTER 4

Does the British Government Control and Manipulate all Irish Paramilitary Groups?

"It is to be feared such extortions have been the causes of many disorders in Ireland. The English never knew how to govern Ireland till the reign of King John the first. They sent over hungry officers whose chief business it was by oppression and rapine to amass great fortunes. This was the cause of the loss of their dominions in France, and was many times near producing the same effect in Ireland. This should be ever in the mind of an Irish historian." – Queen Elizabeth I.

Loyalist Paramilitaries

The question of State control over the loyalist paramilitary groups needn't delay us too much with surely very few observers denying that although at the time, during the height of the troubles, any such allegations were treated as the ravings of conspiracy theorists. I will take just one killing of which there is a lot of public knowledge due to its high profile nature. This case is very likely to be characteristic of all the killings attributed to the Loyalist paramilitaries as all research that has been done on the subject suggests that they have a similar pattern, such as the many killings researched in the book 'The Committee'.

I mean of course the killing of Pat Finucane the Belfast solicitor.[1]

So the initial targeting of Finucane is attributed now to the commander of the UDA in West Belfast Tommy 'Tucker' Little who was working for RUC Special Branch.[2] He stated to a BBC journalist that it was two RUC detectives who told him first to target Finucane [3] although he stated to his son that it was in fact MI5 that set the whole thing up.[4] Obviously there is not much contradiction here since MI5 work closely with Special Branch.

Next up then is the intelligence officer who was detailed by Lyttle to prepare the intelligence necessary to kill Pat Finucane. This was Brian Nelson one of the very few non IRA agents being run by the FRU, a department of the British Army's Intelligence Corps. Nelson was considered an efficient and organised intelligence officer because in fact the British Army had arranged to put all his files on special cards and later on computers that they purchased for him.[5] Of course he was also effective because of the huge amount of information that the FRU were supplying him with. So this British Army agent passes on one of those intelligence cards on Finucane along with a photograph and his home address to one of the killers.[6]

Step three that needs looking at are the guns needed. They were supplied to the killers care of the UDA quartermaster in that area, one William Stobie who was working for RUC Special Branch.[7] And of course like all the others involved he kept his handlers fully informed of the impending murder. One week after appearing on television detailing the fact that RUC Special Branch knew all about the murder he was shot dead.[8]

Finally you have the actual gunmen who did the killing. One of them, Ken Barrett, has revealed details about the killing on a BBC Panorama programme during which he was secretly filmed.[9] There he describes a meeting with a Special Branch officer who told him that Finucane would have to be killed. The officer told him that:

"They didn't want any fucking about. They didn't want to wait for months. They wanted it done."[10]

He went on to state that this officer then assisted the killers during the murder, by inter alia removing a roadblock near the solicitor's house and freezing the area from any security force activity, and continued to give further help to the killers in the years afterwards.

This pattern is repeated as I said if you look at any of the loyalist killings. As you see the paramilitary organisation here is just a shell through which the intelligence agencies, including RUC Special Branch, conduct their clandestine operations. As one of the FRU handlers, Martin Ingram, has said:

> "Without the help specifically of the Force Research Unit and the Special Branch, then the Loyalist volunteers would not have been able to tie their shoelaces. They were probably one of the worst prepared, worst trained rabble of men that I have ever had the misfortune to ever come across. But none the less, the resources of the Force Research Unit and to a lesser extent, the Special Branch were fuelled and funneled towards Loyalism."[11]

The interesting question is how far back this state support for loyalist murder gangs and anti-catholic pogroms go in Irish history. There are a few details on that in the biography of probably the best known Loyalist paramilitary Gusty Spence. So here are a few quotes from Gusty noted in that book:

> [Information he had from old loyalist gunmen he knew named Buck Alec and Bobby Moore:] "They were an element of the UVF reconstituted in 1935 and some were covertly enlisted by the Ulster government at a fee of 10 shillings a day to promote a sectarian war, which they did do."[12]

...

[With respect to 1934:] Protestants and Catholics were coming together and men were hired to shoot Catholics to promote sectarianism and drive a wedge between them. They were paid ½ a quid a day. At least 3 old gunmen told me from their own mouths at separate times that was their role.

...

Its one of those things that the unionist /protestant/loyalist people will not admit to. The Ulster government did employ people to start a sectarian war and it was successful because the rapprochement between them [Catholics and Protestants] was quickly blown up and the IRA became involved in order to protect the Catholic community."[13]

At least we have a bit of Ulster Protestant plain speaking here after all the spin of those intelligence agencies. Of course Gusty was one of the main figures involved in the very early part of the troubles and he provides some information on that period as well:

"In fact the previous year two people had approached Gusty, one of them being a unionist party politician. He was told that the UVF was to be reformed throughout Northern Ireland and he was to be responsible for the Shankill. Gusty's staunch loyalist reputation along with his military experience, explains why he was approached."I cannot possibly say that I knew the ins and outs of the political machinations because I didn't. I was approached to join the UVF. The way the story was put to me was that there was incipient rebellion and I had taken an oath to HMQ to defend her – it seems grandiose – against enemies foreign and domestic. I saw my service in the UVF as a continuation of my British army service."'[14]

...

[Referring to an earlier work by Ed Moloney and Andy Pollak:]
Billy Spence [his brother] had formulated the UVF's strategy for 1966 – a clever plan that was designed to mislead the authorities into thinking that bombing and gun attacks carried out by the UVF were really the IRA's work. The idea was to halt O'Neill's 'bridge building' policies and maybe even cause a reaction against him from within the unionist party, which would force his resignation.[15]

...
He [Gusty] says opposition to O'Neill was basically for 'going too far, especially when he brought Lemass to the North. His overthrow was to take the shape of violent incidents in Belfast and Northern Ireland to hype up communal and political tensions.'"[16] [Gusty, who joined the UVF in 1965, and others were preparing for the anniversary year of 1966 so it is probably this period or a little later that this refers to.]

And this kind of insight is what always lies behind 'terrorist' actions IMHO.

The Small Republican groups

Probably the first and most important of the lesser known Republican groups is the Official IRA with reported links to Official Sinn Fein which later evolved into the Workers Party. The Workers Party of course was famous for infiltrating activist groups and media outlets in Ireland at least ostensibly to further a strong left wing agenda. Here is a description of the party with respect to RTE for example, taken from the Sunday Business Post:

"Many accounts of those days in RTE ascribe its failings to a take-over of RTE current affairs by the Workers Party, whose hysterical anti-provoism formed the backbone of RTE's system of self-censorship.
However, this is to miss the point. There was a peculiarly RTE alliance between the systems of media control originally devised by the two Joes (McCarthy and Stalin) at work. The conservative leaderships of the Irish political establishment were happy to see the republican viewpoint excluded, even if that meant the eventual if short-lived emergence of the Workers Party. The attempt by the Workers Party to control media coverage of the North was largely successful because it was in tune with a conservative fear of the consequences of permitting exposure of nationalist experience in the North. That conservative attitude continued to affect coverage long after the demise of Section 31 in January 1994 and of Workers Party influence. It was also not confined to RTE."

Apparently one of the most prominent of those WP members of that time is now reported to be as influential as the editor in the Sunday Independent newspaper offices. The amazing thing is that some source has leaked to the Phoenix that the Workers Party's activities were all along an intelligence operation by, it appears from this reference any-way, MI6 and the CIA:

"For 30 years the Official Movement (which includes the still extant Official IRA) was an important British in-telligence asset in the war against the Provisionals. It provided agents of political influence in trade unions, peace groups and the media. It also provided vital net-works of informants in so-called denied areas of Belfast, Derry and the Border near Newry. Traditional informers recruited through blackmail or greed were at risk of discovery and execution by the PIRA, but Sticky spies had immunity, because deportation or killing would provoke an armed feud which the Provos be-lieved the British would exploit.

Like many senior RUC Special Branch officers who took their swift post-Patten departures as acts of treachery (and wrote acrimonious books and gave re-vealing media interviews), the spooks who may have been behind the WP funding have long gone. Perhaps someone in the CIA or MI6 believes the time has come to clear the books [the context is the arrest of Sean Garland]. But there may be a dozen other reasons why the super-dollar [he was accused of forging dollars] show is back on the road.

Upheavals in the international world of secret intelli-gence following the Bush-Blair alliance against militant Islam, and changing security needs in Ireland after the peace process meant the Official Republican Move-ment, of which the WP is the above-ground component, was redundant."[17]

Piggybacking on 'Barry's valuable research on indymedia I think also that the Omagh bombing might be an appropriate place to look at who is controlling the other small splinter republican groups. In particular it might be instructive to look at the bombing, which was attributed to the Real IRA, from the point of view of seeing the various stages necessary for whoever arranged the bombing to see what kind of 'cover up' would be necessary to disguise the intelligence agencies role in it. What I mean by that is that many people would reply to any suggestion of state terrorism by saying that it would require a vast conspiracy among a large number of people for such a thing to happen, and that its impractical to talk about that kind of thing occurring and nobody coming forward to tell the truth. Personally I think that makes a lot of sense so that while the people directly involved in planning the bombing would not wish to come forward, to avoid prosecution for the crime, the chances are that surely others would have seen what was going on and could be expected to have revealed this later. What I think a number of people overlook in this regard is that maybe the facts that point to a state conspiracy have come to light but are not highlighted by the mass media, and hence most people aren't aware of them, and even in cases where people are aware of those facts they just dismiss the very idea of a state conspiracy in favor of the more familiar ground of half mad evil terrorist bombers, which is certainly the impression the general public usually gets from the mainstream media. So to look at this I divided it up into the various stages of the attack:

Preparation.
During the trial of Michael McKevitt, after a long process of haggling by the lawyers, a number of emails that were exchanged by David Ruppert and his handlers in MI5 were revealed in court. They represent so far as I know the only concrete details anywhere in the public domain on the preparation and intelligence gathering that were made before the Omagh bombing. From them it appears, incredible as it may seem, that it was David Ruppert himself that was most responsible for that initial preparation. He made videos of Omagh as part of this planning, dummy runs in a car to check the practicalities of bringing a car bomb into the town and it was he that suggested that the bombing could be made in Omagh.[18] David Ruppert was obviously working all this time as an agent of MI5 and the FBI. Hence there is no cover up here as these facts have already been revealed in open court.

The Bomb
In the House of Commons it was revealed that the bomb maker was a leading Provisional IRA figure called Patrick Joseph Blair, known as 'Mooch'. This corroborates the much earlier statement by the FRU agent 'Kevin Fulton' of Newry who all along has claimed that he met Blair before the bombing, that Blair told him there was something big on and that he smelt the fertiliser on him that indicated he was preparing a large explosive. Fulton states that he passed all this on to the RUC, the registration of the car involved etc and it was clearly a very specific warning because of the track record of Blair as a serious bomb maker and the fact that the resulting fertiliser explosive has to be used within a short space of time after this kind of preparation because it becomes unstable. The RUC denied all this initially claiming Fulton was a 'Walter Mitty' character and admit they did nothing with the warning received which they denied initially getting, but these facts seem now to be widely accepted.[19] Furthermore it appears that Fulton now claims that Blair

has been working all along for the security forces[20] and he certainly would be in a position to know that because Blair has been described as his mentor in the IRA within which the two were working together for about 15 years.[21] The Observer states that Blair is now rumoured to have been "spirited out of Northern Ireland by the British security services".[22] So we can have no complaints here about the data that is in the public domain on the subject of the bomb, much of it from a man who has taken great risks in coming forward to tell us the real facts.

The Car
It obviously being a car bomb it is normal that a car in these situations is stolen so as it can not be traced back to the bombers. We now also have pretty much all the facts on this heading. The car was stolen by an agent for Garda Special Branch known as Paddy Dixon.[23] Dixon was told that the bomb was to be used for a real 'spectacular' so his handler Garda Sergeant John White was very concerned and went to see some senior Gardai on the subject. They told him that "John, we are going to let this one go through." Even the day before as Dixon was passing all the information to White about the stolen car White was still imploring his superiors to stop it but all he got was their iron determination to let this particular car through. This presumably also involved stopping the 24-hour surveillance of the breakers yard where the car was engineered to accept the bomb. Dixon has been moved abroad and given a false name under a garda witness protection scheme and is now not available to be interviewed by the PSNI Omagh investigators.[24] Garda White was arraigned on false charges and a Nally group of senior Irish Govt officials have found no basis for his claims but they also state they weren't permitted to interview Dixon.[25] However it is stated that the PSNI ombudsman's office do accept White's testimony as being the truth. This is again the only really hard facts about the car used in the explosion AFAIK.

In the Town On the Day
Presumably if some members of the security forces were behind this explosion they would no doubt not wish to be themselves caught up in any blast and it might be thought that any suspicious acts of self preservation by the security forces that seemed to indicate advanced knowledge of the blast would be noticed and the truth would emerge. But in fact some of the relatives do find the events of that day in Omagh to be very suspicious and they simply haven't got any explanation for it. So to quote Lawrence Rush who lost his wife in the bombing and was driven to interrupt an RUC press conference in attempting to get answers to these questions:

> "My dear sir, this is a conspiracy. This will come out like the Derry Thirteen [Bloody Sunday]. This is a conspira-

cy by the British Government and by everyone involved in its administration. This is an example of administrative terrorism [using the word 'administration' earlier clarifies what he meant by this phrase]; that's what it is. Why did Sinn Fein close their office the day before the bomb? Why was the Army confined to barracks? Why sir, the RUC, why did they in actual fact have only three men on the streets of Omagh, and twenty-four men out in surrounding areas? Tell me that."[26]

He is now trying to sue the British state because of this but his case has got very little publicity.[27] At the inquest the families couldn't get to the bottom of the actions of the RUC on the day because the officers in question refused to answer questions on the subject on the grounds of not incriminating themselves.[28] Again the evidence is actually there but the media emphasis is entirely different and this is what persuades people that the state has no case to answer.

The Investigation
No doubt the intelligence agencies if they were responsible for the blast would be very keen to see the resulting investigation derailed and yet with such a major inquiry surely somebody would notice it going nowhere deliberately and would reveal this publicly. Again there is no cover up of the facts here as regards what happened to the investigation. We know that RUC Special Branch have done all they can to make sure it goes nowhere, or at least not to the real bombers, and we have all the information we need on that from the Police Ombudsman's office which has detailed the whole story on the subject.[29] Specifically the report states that Special Branch supplied the investigation team with the names of 5 suspects that clearly didn't do the bombing despite the Branch having more detailed accurate information on other parties that they withheld from the investigation. A short trawl of the intelligence by the ombudsman's team revealed relevant intelligence 78 per cent of which they withheld from being investigated. All that has come to light and there is therefore no grounds for anybody to accuse the wider RUC of covering up the facts, as opposed to Special Branch which with the same body in the South has a close relationship with MI5.

Members of the Security Services
Finally you have the point many people would make and that is that surely some of those in the security apparatus who knew what was going on would not stand for it and would stop it happening. But it now seems that that did happen. A member of RUC Special Branch telephoned in an anonymous warning to the RUC in Omagh on the 4th of August detailing the attack that was to happen in Omagh on the 15th.[30] The CID detective who took the call took it very seriously and warned

everybody who needed to know about it in the town including his superiors and Special Branch. When the bombing happened on that day a shocked detective asked the Senior Investigating Officer and his deputy what happened to the warning they had got but no explanation has been forthcoming.[31] It is said that the Sub Divisional Commander in Omagh was not told about this warning and, quoting the Ombudsman's report:

> "When he was shown the intelligence two years later on the anniversary of the explosion he said he would have set up Vehicle Check Points. When he met the Police Ombudsman's Investigator in September 2001 he said he did not remember seeing the intelligence and said that he would have taken other action and would not have set up Vehicle Check Points.
>
> The recollection of the Sub-Divisional Commander Omagh is not accepted by the Police Ombudsman."

So again we cannot really say that there was a water tight conspiracy of silence on the part of the security services. Somebody in fact did their best to stop the attack. Obviously if this person had revealed any detail other than anonymously he would be prosecuted under the Official Secrets Act which is no paper tiger when it comes to preserving secrets in Ireland.

The Subsequent Trials
Presumably whoever in the state apparatus who was responsible for the crime would be busy stitching up some innocent party to assuage the natural public alarm about the crime that must have been anticipated. We have a lot of details now from the trial of the first person charged with the crime. Suffice to say that the trial has been revealed as a saga of forgery, perjury and witnesses intimidated by the Garda Special Branch.[32]

So there is no all embracing wall of silence that might be supposed to be necessary for such a conspiracy to occur. There is if anything a wall of detail in the public domain which confirms it but this might not be what the main media organisations are putting before the public in Ireland or Britain. Most people are just not aware of those facts and those that are aware are probably quite happy with the usual explanation of bureaucratic incompetence rather than conspiracy. After all they probably know a lot about intelligence agencies and terrorists and judge that those agencies would simply never do such a thing. In other words they have seen all the James Bond films and 'Patriot Games'! So its no problem at all for people to believe the state's explanation for the conspiracy on the day. It is perfectly reasonable to believe that a small farmer or

108

electrician in South Armagh kissed his wife and young family goodbye and decided to massacre 29 people and maim 100's more of his fellow compatriots and many of his fellow religion in the neighbouring county. Apparently he thought this was going to achieve a united Ireland and living all his life among the troubles in South Armagh he couldn't have been expected to realise that the bomb would rather discredit Irish nationalism and spur strong measures on the part of the British government against 'terrorists'. This is doubtless because many of the local people in places like South Armagh and North Louth are reckoned to be crazed lunatics who kill like this almost for sport. So the tabloids have painted it anyway. He also drives in the bomb passing by without a thought all the huge security installations along that border, not wondering whether they keep track of cars passing along those roads which could trace a car back to its origin. He also chats away on his mobile phone oblivious to any notion that such signals could be traced later.

On the other hand the other 'conspiracy theory' involves parties who clearly have the inside knowledge to get around and block any security hindrance and any subsequent investigation. They would obviously, and justifiably, be quite certain that they would never be charged for the crime anyway. Their motivation is not as difficult to come by. A few weeks later draconian 'anti-terrorist' legislation was passed which on that timescale must have been prepared earlier and be just ready to be enacted. It was rushed through parliament with many M.P.'s not even reading it.[33] If all this sounds too macabre for some consider that the Offences Against The State Act, the main anti-terrorist legislation in the South, was passed amid the carnage of a 'terrorist' bombing which was later discovered to have been committed by agents of the British intelligence agencies. In dramatic circumstances at a public meeting in Dublin in 2003 the widow of one of those killed in the explosions demanded of the assembled panel, which included Patricia McKenna MEP, whether or not they thought that the bombing at that crucial moment was some kind of coincidence. Nobody thought that it was.[34]

The IRA

Of course the mother of all allegations relates to the IRA itself. A short while ago you would have been laughed out of it if you had alleged that the IRA was run by the UK and US intelligence agencies – and its still a close run thing – but the situation has I think changed after all the speculation about Stakeknife. So for example William Frazer who runs the FAIR organisation in Armagh and who's father, two uncles and two cousins were killed by the IRA says:

"For years, there have been countless allegations of

collusion involving loyalist paramilitaries and the security forces. What people don't realise, is the security services were doing exactly the same thing on the republican side as well. People might not want to believe that, but the evidence shows it happened, and on a much larger scale than people think."

Consulted by the Herald newspaper in Scotland they summarise his views as follows: "He said the officers claims reinforced his belief that the government and intelligence agencies controlled the IRA campaign, using double-agents to manage republican violence."[35] This view is corroborated by Anthony McIntyre, now an historian but formerly the IRA commander in South Belfast, who has stated that:

"At times I feel like I joined a regiment of the British Army when I thought I was joining the IRA. It is clear that there has been extensive infiltration of the IRA just as there was with the loyalists." [36]

This insight, into what I think is the real history of the troubles, as I said derives for many from the recent unmasking of British agents working at very senior levels in the IRA throughout that period. In particular we now know the true history of the IRA's crucial internal security unit who's ruthlessness can be gleaned from its popular nickname: 'the nutting squad'. It was run for much of the troubles by John Joe Magee and after his recent death it has now been revealed that he was a member of the elite SBS unit, which is the naval equivalent of the SAS in the British armed forces and in which Paddy Ashdown served.[37] In the context of these revelations its clear that most commentators now believe he was working all along for the British Government. The main source that we are getting this from is the Newry man known as Kevin Fulton who in fact also served in the security unit while in his case being a member of the British Army's FRU intelligence group.[38] Finally, and in this case famously, we know that the number 2 in the security unit worked for about two decades for the British army in the form of the FRU and it is his unmasking that has led to widespread speculation as to who really controlled the IRA during the troubles. Here are a few quotes from the newspapers when he was eventually unmasked, starting with the Irish Times:

"I met [him] over a dozen times. Material and vital intelligence were handed over to him. I never thought for one moment he was an informer. People like him were beyond suspicion."

This Tyrone IRA member, like many others all over the

country, was reeling yesterday at the disclosure that the head of the IRA's internal security was a British army agent. He is now "horrified" at the information he and others unwittingly gave Stakeknife.

He travelled regularly to west Belfast to meet the head of security. The meetings took place in the Park Centre, a shopping centre off the Falls Road, or a house in Clonard. "He was a small, stocky, swarthy-looking character. We never liked meeting him. He wasn't friendly. There was no chat. He just got right down to business. If we found a hidden Brit camera in a field, or a bug in weapon, we would bring it up to him."

...

Stakeknife had the authority to suspend IRA units from operating in any area. "We were always frightened he would close us down. He closed other areas down. We called him and his men 'the Rat Squad'.

"We resented having to come to Belfast and talk to them about Tyrone. But we never thought he was working for the Brits."

...

"On the basis of his reports, the Brits had a major advantage when negotiating with Sinn Féin. They also had substantial control over IRA operations for a very long time. Stakeknife would have been able to pass details of [so-called] dissidents, or potential [so-called] dissidents, to the Brits who could have them shot, jailed or sidelined."[39]

Ryle Dwyer in the Irish Independent: "Stakeknife would have had almost unlimited access to IRA secrets, with responsibility for finding spies within the organisation, as well as recruiting new members, and holding post mortems into failed operations."[40]

As even the Telegraph newspaper notes: "Stakeknife vetted IRA recruits and interrogated informers, giving British intelligence a direct route into controlling the Provisionals."[41]

Sunday Times: "for whatever reason the IRA kept the nucleus of this unit – John Joe Magee, an ex-British Special Boat Squadron member and Scappatici – intact for well over 20 years. With Stakeknife in place, the IRA effectively had no internal security."[42]

So it is now a truism to say that the British army ran the IRA's security unit, and as you can see many commentators now appreciate that also meant the British authorities knew everything that went on in the IRA and in the opinion of many 'controlled' that organisation. But few seem to take their logic to the next level and try to provide a proper academic analysis of what then the British government was really doing during the troubles, and instead many continue to talk about 'terrorism' in Ireland as something independent of the actions of the British government, which in fact it clearly isn't if even the IRA were controlled by the security forces.

In any case the whole Stakeknife affair is by no means the end of the revelations. It was reported in the Sunday Times, in elaborate detail, immediately after the death of Sean MacStiofain that he also was working for the authorities, in his case the Gardai.[43] He just happens to be the leading military figure in the early years of the Provisional IRA and intimately involved in the setting up of all aspects of that organisation. He was Chief of Staff of the IRA during a period when they killed about 400 people.[44] Chief of Staff is obviously the highest rank in the IRA.

In fact by looking at the whole question of agents being run by the security forces in the IRA we might get some idea of whether or not they really control it. So first to consider is the FRU which contains personnel from all arms of the British armed forces but is mainly an offshoot of the Army Intelligence Corps based earlier at Ashford in Kent and now at Chicksands, Bedfordshire. A former warrant officer in the FRU has come forward and helped to write a book and consequently we know a fair bit about its operations.[45] The FRU is a group that only operates in Ireland, North and South, and is said to have about 100 members and to be almost exclusively devoted to running agents within the IRA.[46] Bear in mind there is only said to be about 400 activists in the IRA [47] so as you can see it's likely that the FRU ran quite a high percentage of IRA members. Therefore it doesn't come as a surprise that in the case of Derry we get an estimate that about 20 per cent of the IRA in that city were FRU agents.[48]

But bear in mind that the FRU are by no means the main agent running agency in Ireland and in fact in infiltrating agents into the IRA they were hamstrung by rules on police primacy. This means that normal agent handling in the province was done by RUC Special Branch, the FRU could only employ former or present members of the British army or those who voluntarily handed themselves over to the army as opposed to the police. Stakeknife fell into the latter category while Brian Nelson and Kevin Fulton for example were approached to infiltrate the paramilitary groups while serving in the regular army. As you can easily appreciate this must have greatly hampered the FRU and so it is clear that RUC Special Branch would in contrast be the main agent runners within the IRA and all other paramilitary groups in the province. You must therefore add on another percentage to that 20 to account for agents of the RUC Special Branch in the IRA in Derry and that could be expected to be maybe the same or a higher percentage than the FRU. One constable in the Special Branch in Derry was simultaneously handling 5 agents in the paramilitaries, at least one of whom, Raymond Gilmour, seemed to know pretty much everybody in the IRA.[49]

Then you have the largest of the agencies handling agents in the Irish paramilitary groups, taking the UK and Ireland as a whole, and that is obviously MI5. They clearly run many agents independently of Special Branch. Willie Carlin, a former treasurer of Sinn Fein in Derry, was such an agent who was handled directly by Michael Bettaney of MI5.[50] The Saville Inquiry has also thrown up details of direct MI5 agents in Derry, not run through Special Branch, in particular 'Infliction' who was a senior member of the IRA and was very close to McGuinness but whether normally domiciled in Derry is not clear.[51] So throw in a few percent on top to account for MI5 agents in the Derry IRA.

Of course Derry is very near the border and in all probability the powerful Garda Special Branch in Donegal run agents in the IRA who at least some of the time live in that city. One man who has since left the country was referred to as being a Garda agent 'close to the IRA Chief of Staff then based in Derry. He provided the gardai with highly sensitive information.'[52] So again make room for a few more percent to account for those agents.

While information from that quarter is very lacking it is highly likely that the American agencies have many agents in the IRA. It is said that the guns sent to Ireland on the Valhalla ship were gathered in Boston by an FBI agent. John McIntyre who revealed some of these details has since apparently gone missing.[53] David Ruppert was also obviously an FBI agent in the IRA.[54] With their strong American connections there is little doubt that there must be quite a few CIA agents in the IRA and they will also have to be totted up in our analysis.

The various other bodies involved are worth considering as likely to be running agents in the IRA like the other RUC groups e.g. CID who it seems have agents in the paramilitaries like Ken Barrett who was an agent of Detective Sergeant Johnston Brown of the CID,[55] the RUC anti-racketeering squad who ran for a time Kevin Fulton as an agent in the IRA,[56] and also the Special Patrol Groups of which group Sergeant John Weir was a member while he ran an informant in the IRA called Robert McConnell.[57]

How quickly is it then before you end up with a figure of above 50 percent for the number of IRA personnel who are working for the security forces? Obviously at this kind of percentage you would definitely conclude that the security forces were then controlling the IRA. Note as well the very effective combination of agents in the paramilitaries and technical surveillance devices. So that once the security forces can identify a car it is probably routinely planted with a tracking device.[58] The same is true of weapons that are under the supervision of government agents.[59]

113

Apparently there was a separate unit that bugged and tracked all those that were identified by Stakeknife for example.[60] So showing an incredible amount of power the security forces would have over the IRA via this huge percentage of government agents in their ranks.

Of course you get various explanations to explain away this like inter agency rivalry and lack of communication. But in fact its quite remarkable the amount of gossip that travels around inside the intelligence community as we now know from people like Martin Ingram in the FRU [61], David Shayler from MI5,[62] Fred Holroyd of Military Intelligence [63] and even Richard Tomlinson of MI6.[64] They all reveal lots of details of actions they were not involved in and sections they weren't members of contrary to all the talk of 'need to know' etc. Its also remarkable how much the garda authorities are under the thumb of MI5 so there is not likely to be any lack of data flowing from Dublin to London.[65] Also some of these agencies like the Special Branches have been dealing with Irish 'terrorism' for over a century and its not realistic that they haven't managed to set up proper coordinating bodies. Locally the main such body, which brings all the various groups together, is the Tasking and Coordinating Groups and its clear none of the agencies will act till they get the go-ahead from that body.[66] Then in London there are various co-ordinating bodies like the Joint Intelligence Committee which advises the Prime Minister through the Secretary of the Cabinet.[67] Of course in practice any of the officials on the ground who may contemplate any 'sensitive' action are going to make very sure that they have high up political protection for what they do, and there is plenty of evidence for that. Before the trial of Brian Nelson (who of course was the UDA's intelligence officer during a time when large numbers of innocent catholics were killed by them and who was actually working for the FRU) John Major interceded personally with the trial judge.[68] The IRA agent called Stakeknife was even entertained by Margaret Thatcher at Chequers. Willie Carlin, the aforementioned MI5 agent in Derry, was flown out of Northern Ireland on Margaret Thatcher's private plane.[69] Albert 'Ginger' Baker, who was working for the British armies MRF unit while in the UDA during which his group killed c30 people, was visited in jail by a senior Northern Ireland minister who offered him a deal later reneged upon.[70] Brian Nelson had also been visited in jail by two government ministers.[71] There is simply no evidence at all for the kind of serious communication difficulties at the high level that some people might claim exists.

Sometimes it is also explained away by saying that it is difficult to get informants to openly testify against IRA members in court. But in fact from all we know of the lives of those agents, and particularly from their direct testimony, it appears that the opposite is the case and that they are usually anxious to testify in court and end up amazed that the authorities prevent this happening.

So Martin McGartland cannot figure out why he wasn't called to testify against his abductors.[72] Sean O'Callaghan is very disappointed that "for whatever reason he was not allowed to give evidence against his former colleagues."[73] Raymond Gilmour is the exception in that he was allowed to testify against the IRA. However his trial was unsuccessful in what he considers to be very suspicious circumstances. In fact he suspects a deal was made with some or other party, possibly between "the British government and the IRA."[74] This suspicion is corroborated by a separate reference from his Special Branch handler in the RUC. He was very disillusioned with the trial and states this:

> "This only turned to bitterness much later when I heard from two reliable witnesses the same explanation for the trial's disastrous climax. Both said that, in retirement, [Lord Chief Justice] Lowry had told friends including one of Northern Ireland's most senior politicians that he had thrown out Gilmour's evidence under political pressure. Lowry is now dead [assassinated by the IRA] and the politician is retired and living outside Northern Ireland. But I believe it. There can be no other rational explanation." [75]

Hence this doesn't explain either why this level of penetration of the IRA couldn't lead to an end to the IRA campaign. Incidentally if you read about the Gilmour case particularly, but also all the other informer accounts, you can see that the much vaunted cell system or 'need to know' type rules in the IRA are also quite a dead letter with each informant knowing a lot of information on a large number of people.

There are also many incidents that some would say fall under the general category of bureaucratic incompetence of one form or another but that in fact look a lot more like deliberate state support for the IRA. I thought I would attempt to detail 3 such incidents here:

1. In Fred Holroyd's book he talks about the transfer of power that went from MI6 to MI5 around 1974. When this happened a lot of informers were killed as he relates in this anecdote told to him by a Major Keith Farnes of the SAS who was working in intelligence:

> "an NCO in the Intelligence Corps who had been running 10 different sources in the IRA had seen them all murdered within a few days of MI5 taking over the operations. He had gone into a bunker and shot himself in the head."[76]

He talks a lot in the book about ruthless inter service rivalry between MI5 and MI6 and also about bad MI5 tactics in recruiting informers but that doesn't seem a sufficient explanation. It wasn't just some kind of incompetence because for example at one point MI5 sent an army unit to ambush him and his colleague in order to warn them off using a particular informer. The officer in charge of that unit, who was supposed to fire over their heads, managed to explain what he had been ordered to do to Holroyd and his colleague.[77] There does not appear to be any other rational explanation for this except that MI5 were assisting the IRA in keeping itself intact while it was on the ropes during the mid 70s.

2. In February 1997 almost the world was watching the activities of one particular sniper in South Armagh. They eventually ended up with sign-posts and T-shirts chronicling his activities. That particular time there was hardly any other paramilitary activity occurring in Ireland and yet the whole security apparatus was very much intact including a thicket of military forts etc ruling over South Armagh itself where the sniper oper-ated. In retrospect then it is not at all surprising to hear that the British Army had targeted this small sniper's team with all their array of techni-cal surveillance. So in an operation that went on for 6 months before mid February 1997 they had a tracking device in the AK47 carried by the snipers escort, a tracking device in the modified car used and a lis-tening device also in the car. This was done by the SAS's 14th Intelli-gence unit in Ireland with the listening device installed by 'another agen-cy' presumably MI5. There was also talk of one of the members of this unit passing on information to the security forces.[78] So when the sniper and his team started to move towards Bessbrook on February 12 the security forces knew all about what was going to happen. But the team that was going to intercept the sniper was ordered to stand down. They were amazed and wanted to know at least would the regular army in Bessbrook not be alerted and put off the snipers team by a show of force, but this was also refused. So the sniper then killed Stephen Restorick. The SAS themselves did not believe any of the explanations offered for this and apparently left the province shortly afterwards in dis-gust. The amazing thing is that this was repeated six weeks later with the surveillance team ordered to withdraw to allow the sniper to shoot whereupon he disabled RUC officer Ronnie Galway. And these sniping attacks were the only real activities of the IRA during this period I be-lieve.

3. One of the biggest of the IRA attacks has to be the Bishopsgate bomb in London and the MI5 dissident David Shayler has given a detal-ied account of the activities of the security forces prior to the bombing in a Punch magazine article.[79] There Shayler lays a very heavy hint that the Bishopsgate bomber was in fact under the protection of the security forces. This is doubtless why the Punch article he wrote this in is not al-lowed to be sold in the UK.[80]

One explanation that we hear again and again to explain away inci-dents like this is that somehow it is done to protect an informer in the IRA. But in fact, as above stated, it is likely that there are just so many informers that the security forces don't really need to worry about losing one. Here is a quote from Colin Wallace who worked in British Army HQ in Lisburn:

"We had literally the whole of the IRA listed. In Belfast we had them all on one board. From an intelligence point of view, they were all informing on each other. The Provos gave information to people not knowing they were part of the British system." [81]

Furthermore the idea that the security forces would go the extra mile like even killing people to protect one of their agents goes against all the accounts we now have about the treatment that agents of the security forces in the IRA receive. In fact they get harassed by the security forces surprisingly enough. They have had their characters assassinated: Martin McGartland talks about Crown agencies going to significant lengths 'to blacken his name';[82] Samuel Rosenfeld has brought a court case in which he claims a government agent "willfully and knowingly mounted black propaganda campaign against the Claimant";[83] Kevin Fulton meanwhile has had to fight a long battle against allegations of being a 'Walter Mitty' [84] character but was exonerated in the PSNI ombudsman's report on Omagh.[85]

Many have been harassed by false charges laid against them: McGartland has been stopped some 50 times in 4 years on spurious traffic offences.[86] Samuel Rosenfeld was charged with stealing a car and the bizarre court case was adjourned deliberately to facilitate him crossing the border.[87] He has attempted to sue as a lay litigant "Woodchester Finance, a judge and an RUC detective inspector for conspiracy to wrongfully charge him for theft."[88] He is reputed to have 'devastating information' against the security forces which he cannot reveal because of government legal harassment.[89] Kevin Fulton cannot easily find work because he has a criminal record resulting from a terrorist offence which he committed under instructions from his handlers and is also regularly harassed by the police.[90] In fact these agents are now nearly all described as penniless. Also these offences no doubt are on prominent display in internal government files and are useful in slandering them in the eyes of government officials who might otherwise assist. Dermot Ahern before he met Fulton and Rosenfeld was reputed to have read a Department of Foreign Affairs file that slandered them.[91]

They are in short collectively treated in the classic manner of western dissidents [92] and not at all with the kind of tender loving care that some might think the security forces look after their agents. Of course in the opinion of some the treatment they get when they aren't active agents is not the issue, the question is would the security forces go to these huge lengths to protect informants while they are still actively supplying information? But in fact the story of the informers is that many of them who were actively working for the authorities have been setup by the intelligence agencies to be murdered. That is after all the accepted facts of the Stakeknife case, where many useful serving informants and agents, like Tom Oliver, were murdered by the British army's IRA security unit with the full knowledge of their superiors.[93] This pattern is also confirmed by those that survived. Kevin Fulton "is sure that he was compromised [by the security forces], so the IRA would kill him."[94]

Martin McGartland is often described as one of the most important agents that the RUC Special Branch ever had [95] and continued to supply very useful information until his kidnapping by an IRA cell in Belfast. He now feels, based on statements given to him by one of his RUC handlers and other sources, that in fact MI5 set him up to be killed and that the IRA group that abducted him was working for RUC Special Branch.[96] At first he wrote a book which got a lot of publicity and detailed his good work in foiling IRA activities and with much praise for the security forces.[97] Then later he is to be found writing this second book perplexed at the constant harassment by the authorities and wondering what has been really going on during the troubles.[98] This book has got very little publicity but somebody seems to have read it because shortly after the book was first published he was shot and nearly killed by an unknown gunman.[99] Here is a quote from the book:

> "Menacingly, however, and more worryingly, I wondered how many other agents who had worked undercover inside the IRA had been betrayed by MI5 or any other British security or intelligence agencies; kidnaps arranged in secret deals between the Provos and MI5 officers, which ended in the most appalling beatings, tortures and deaths."[100]

In fact his handler told him that the IRA and MI5 have a surprisingly close working relationship and talk to each other all the time:

> "'We suspect that MI5 may even have arranged your kidnapping directly with the IRA.'
>
> 'What!', I said, disbelief in my voice. 'I don't believe you. That's impossible. That's fucking treachery."
>
> 'I know it is I agree with you,' replied Mike, 'but that's the way they work. MI5 have their contacts with the IRA at the highest level and they always have had.'" [101]

So the story of the agents in situ also does not show this concern for their informants that would explain the various incidents where the IRA has been assisted by the security forces. You sometimes hear other explanations like that the security forces were trying to assist the peace process. Leaving aside the bizarre Orwellian idea of sponsoring terrorism to assist peace, there does not anyway appear to be any evidence for this view. For example, it is not stated by anybody, as far as I know, that any of the people killed by Stakeknife were distinguished as hindering the peace process in the IRA.

Of course, to be fair, for a lot of people the point simply is that there seems to be no logical reason for the British government to support the IRA, it is for so many I think a conspiracy theory too far. I mean what are the whole troubles about if that was true? So to answer that question I thought I would throw in some references going back through history, and across into modern international experience, to illustrate the kind of black arts of international politics, a knowledge of which might shed some light on this question. The international references I have corralled into a separate appendix and what follows are just some loose historical episodes that show that things aren't always what they seem:

1. Recently, to this readers amazement anyway, probably Britain's most famous historian has compared the gunpowder plot to 9/11, with the Catholics involved being the early 17th century's answer to Al Qaeda.[102] But in fact Irish historians since the late 17th century[103] always assumed that the then British government engineered that plot itself to provide a pretext for cracking down on the Catholics and confiscating their lands. Here Hugh Reilly of Larah in Cavan, who was the Chancellor of Ireland (Prime Minister) in the exiled court of James II in 1693, comments that it was by no means the only such 'pretended' plot:

> "and in fine if we call to mind how wicked statesmen have used the like practices for ends of their own, as Cecil's own father the Lord Burleigh and his predecessor Walsingham [head of Elizabeth's intelligence agency] had frequently done in Queen Elizabeth's reign; even as in our own days the tyrant Cromwell contrived several such plots for ensnaring the royal cavaliers, and Cecil Rediviuu, creeping Shaftesbury, was no less dexterous in the late King's days: all these circumstances we cannot but conclude, as Osburn an inquisitive author of those times has already done, who plainly says, that the [Gun]Powder Plot was a neat device of the Treasurer, i.e. the crooked backed Cecil, who after he had done the mighty piece of service, was in a few years made Knight of the Garter, and in a few years high treasurer of England.
>
> ...Neither did his malice stop here, but being a famed professor in tricks (as Osburn describe him) and finding how well his wicked stratagem took in London, he frames a project to carry on the like design in Ireland."
> [Meaning the Flight of the Earls episode, the prelude to the plantation of Ulster.][104]

He goes on to make a passionate plea for honest open government and an end to that kind of plotting, but all this came too close to criticising his employer James II who was a leading public figure at the time of the equally suspicious popish plots and Captain Blood episodes of the 1680s, and so Hugh was promptly fired for revealing this and died shortly afterwards. But in fact his words lived on and his work passed through many editions and became one of the standard Irish Catholic histories during the difficult days of the 18th century.

2. The Catholic Encyclopedia paraphrases the policy that Pere Joseph, the famous Capuchin advisor to Cardinal Richilieu in France in the 17th century, followed at the start of the 30 years war in Germany during which they supported the protestant princes covertly in their rebellion while simultaneously overtly supported the Emperor in his attempts to put down the rebellion:
"He wished France to use the Protestants to weaken the House of Austria, and the House of Austria to weaken the Protestants." These two men were of course famous pillars of the Catholic Church in Europe as advisers to his 'Most Catholic Majesty' and for example would be expected to stand strong as defenders of the faith against the Turks then threatening Christian Europe. Pere Joseph had even written an epic poem calling for a new crusade against the Turks. In fact they frequently bankrolled the Turkish invasions of Europe.[105]

3. Irish people have had to wait about 120 years to discover that the main 'physical force people' in the whole Fenian episodes were in fact working for the British government and manipulated by that government and intelligence agencies for her own ends. This has all come out in a recent book by Christy Campbell.[106] The only thing that perplexes that author was why Michael Davitt, a genuinely heroic figure and like Parnell an MP for Meath, didn't reveal all he knew about this publicly.[107] But what could he do? The Irish were brainwashed at the time by decades of reading newspapers full of information on how concerned the British government was with catching those elusive Irish 'dynamitards'. To turn that around and say the whole thing was a fraud would have meant he would be dismissed as a lunatic and would have lost him all credibility. It was all he could do to keep the ship of the peaceful Land League movement afloat in the teeth of Coercion Acts that supposedly targeted the 'gunmen' but in fact led to the arrest of nearly all the leaders of the Land League campaign at various times and which led to that body being proscribed.[108] Meanwhile there was a constant effort to smear people like Parnell and the other leaders with being associated with the gunmen and their various genuinely horrific 'outrages'. A flavour of the times is given here by one of the leaders, Tim Healy, in his book 'Letters and Leaders of my Day':

"Tricks of Police Agents in reference to the crime [Phoenix Park Murders] are disclosed in a letter to my brother:
London,
12th May, 1882.
"I am astonished at your writing that you received a telegram from me about the Park Murders. I sent you no telegram, and am afraid the police have attempted some dodge – as if we could have had anything to do with the awful business. Have you preserved the telegram? Do you remember where it was addressed from? I cannot imagine who here could have your new Cork address.

This murder has ruined us practically as politicians, and I have, like many others, been thinking of giving up Parliament. However, we will struggle on a while longer, I suppose."
...

In the spring of 1883 the Government imagined that Parnell was caught in their coils! The Secret Inquiry Clause of the Crimes Act had been put in force to such purpose that in December, 1882, several men were arrested for the Phoenix Park murders.
...

That day in the House of Commons lobby Sir William Harcourt, Home Secretary, grew so jubilant that he boasted to Joseph Cowen, "the starch will soon be out of the boys!" Cowen interpreted this as implying that Parnell would be implicated.
...

Functionaries drifted into Ireland in 1882-3, who believed in Parnell's complicity in the Park murders. This tradition persisted until it was exploded by The Times Commission of 1888. Lord Spencer told J. A. Blake, M.P., in 1883, that gutter-pests, to earn money, offered to implicate the Lord Mayor of Dublin and the ex-Lord Mayors (C. Dawson, M.P., and E. D. Gray, H.P., of the Freeman), the most moderate of men, in the murders.

[Detective] Mallon's knowledge saved the Viceroy from availing himself of the perjury of such creatures. Yet his underlings gave permission to "Red Jim McDermott," one of their New York agents, to visit us in prison. Davitt, Quinn and I were brought down to a special room to enjoy the honour of his acquaintance. The

head warder came on duty to be regaled by his intima-
cies with us, but Davitt knew all about the fellow [and
knew he was a government agent] (whom I had never
heard of), including his trial in America for murder.

So he broke off the interview, and I told the head
warder that if "Red Jim" called again I was "not at
home." Next day Phil Callan, M.P., published the fact
that "Red Jim "had slipped an extreme Irish-American
paper into his top-coat pocket in a Dublin restaurant."[109]

In fact British government support for what the Irish people thought
were 'patriots' is maybe a kind of running joke among the Dublin castle
administrators over the years, particularly when combined with some
Irish peoples fatal attraction to money. Here is a quote from Major the
Right Honourable Robert Hobart writing from Dublin in 1788:

"The gentlemen, styled patriots in the newspapers,
availing themselves of the popular prejudices have, I
believe, to a man (except Connolly and Grattan) offered
their services to my Lord Lieutenant; but his unfortunate adherence to economy has proved incompatible to
their views, and they already begin to murmur. They
cannot desert the interests of their country gratis, and
so many are in the pay that it impossible to add to the
number.
Your Lordship's experience in this country must have
convinced you that a patriot selling his vote is like a girl
selling her maidenhead: the first deviation from virtue
can only be obtained by love or money. No man can
love the Marquis of Buckingham [the viceroy], consequently he must pay largely."[110]

So finally I guess I should stop waffling and offer my opinion on what
policy is really being pursued by the British government in its support for
all the paramilitary groups in Ireland. I have to say though, in my defence, that we don't have enough information to say definitively what
that policy is, although we can say conclusively that they certainly are
supporting all groups, including the IRA, while hypocritically telling us
the opposite. The 'why' is simply a little more obscure and complex but I
think its possible to make some stab at understanding the thinking here,
based as I say mainly on historical and international comparisons.

We do in fact have one leak from a high source that can possibly
guide us here. It comes from the surprising quarter of Enoch Powell the
classical scholar, Minister of Health, WWII Brigadier, and well known
Conservative and Unionist politician, the latter title being in his case

more than just the anachronistic title of the Tory party in Britain. His views on the subject can be seen in this extract from a book by Paul Routledge on Airey Neave, concentrating on the latter's death in 1979:

"On 18th Oct 1986 in a speech to Conservative students in Birmingham, Powell returned to his theme...says Neave ...met his death at the hands of 'high contracting parties' made up of MI6 and their friends.' Neave had to be eliminated he argued, because he (like Powell) was committed to a programme of integration of Northern Ireland within the United Kingdom. The killing of Neave was designed to shake the government into adopting a course more favourable to a 'united Ireland firmly within the NATO military alliance. The plot to destabilise Ulster had begun twenty years previously,' he said. It brought together the Foreign Office, British Intelligence and the United States, especially the CIA. None of the Prime Ministers of recent years – Heath, Wilson or Callaghan – knew what was going on. America secured from Britain an undertaking to transfer Northern Ireland out of the UK into an all-Ireland, presumably confederal state. The first objective in this grand plan was to get rid of the Ulster government at Stormont. 'MI6 and their friends proved equal to the job' he asserted. But the Americans took fright ahead of the 1979 election, fearing that Thatcher and Neave would take the process of Northern Ireland integration into the UK so far that it could not be reversed. Washington was alarmed at 'evidence or what they thought to be evidence' that the new leader Mrs Thatcher and aide Airey Neave had no intention of playing ball with the USA's long term aims. Accordingly 'the roadblock was cleared by eliminating Airey Neave on the verge of his taking office', and from then onwards events were moved ahead again along the timetabled path'.
Powell refused to answer reporters' questions as to whether he was accusing the Americans of Neave's murder. Asked if it would have made any difference if the MP had not been killed, he replied, 'Perhaps not, but those who have assassinated him believed it would have done.'
Powell offered no supporting evidence...[outrage in the Tory party etc]
It was not until the following year that Powell pointed, in his usual delphic manner, to CIA involvement in 'Cen-

tral America and Iran, for which evidence only came to light much later.'"[111]

So basically Powell was in receipt of some inside information, particularly from an RUC source who he trusted and who informed him "of the effective existence of a policy and motivation outside and above the IRA and INLA" which boiled down to the Americans, in alliance with MI6, being behind and protecting the IRA for reasons of their own. Specifically he was told that the Americans hoped that by upping the tension and getting rid of Stormont that they could in the long run play a decisive diplomatic role in the emerging Ireland, leading to American bases on the island and Irish membership of NATO. Powell used his high level contacts to try to figure this out and he asked Margaret Thatcher about it who told him that she didn't understand either why the Americans were so obsessed with the idea of setting up bases in Ireland.[112] The interesting point is that presumably his source was aware of a lot of evidence in the hands of the RUC of CIA and MI6 assistance to the IRA. In his biography Gusty Spence talks about being arrested in c1966 and being interrogated by Special Branch at the time who kept asking him about the 'plot' to destabilise O'Neill's government[113] and this seems to agree with the sort of early timeline that Powell mentions. The idea of a powerful American role in the troubles behind the scenes seems to be corroborated by this quote from a review of the book on Neave:

> "In the spring of 1981, Geoffrey Sloane, a research student at Keele University, interviewed Clive Abbott, a senior official at the Northern Ireland Office. He forecast a discreet role for the United States in a final settlement, which was likely to be a confederal Ireland in which Dublin would participate. This civil servant's briefing carries the strong suggestion that America was already secretly involved."

Further corroboration of this US involvement comes from Stephen Crittenden, a pilot and former manager of a CIA airline, and Richard Taus, of the FBI in New York, who have both stated that the CIA is one of the main arms suppliers to the IRA. The MI6 connection isn't all that surprising either because it ties in with the Littlejohn episode, where the two Littlejohn brothers were tasked by John Wyman of MI6 to attempt to "destabilise" the South with a bombing campaign.[114]
Some might say that Powell's timetable in this respect has almost come to pass with respect to American bases. But overall it seems a very long term plan and involved a huge expense in blood and treasure for very little gain, since it doesn't really seem that the US lacks military bases in Europe. But it might be felt nonetheless that the troubles should be placed in the context of US and UK unhappiness with Ireland in the late

50s to 60s, particularly for our role as a non aligned country in the UN following policies under people like Frank Aiken that did not go down too well in Washington and maybe they intended doing something about it. For it is now known that at this time the US and UK closely co-operated in destabilising many democratic countries e.g. Iran, Guyana and Indonesia and, as Powell himself remarked, this only emerged much later with the general public in the UK and US being completely unaware of the role of their own governments in these plots. Notice as well that Andrew Gilchrist was appointed UK ambassador to Ireland at this time, fresh from his secret, and successful, efforts at destabilising the democratic government in Indonesia by inter alia supporting para-military groups in places like Aceh.[115]

One effect of the troubles, that might have been intentional, was the weakening of Irish nationalism worldwide. Ireland is after all unique in that while it itself is a small, and not very strategic country, it's diaspora is huge and quite important in countries like the US, UK, Australia and Canada. Traditionally it was a quite a noisy and united group, generally opposed to whatever the big powers were cooking up, particularly the UK. The troubles have had a major impact in lessening the unity of this group and in fact almost making Irish people feel embarrassed and possibly ignorant of its interesting and by and large proud history and heritage. It is often said that whoever controls a country's view of its history controls that country, because the people then can sometimes lack the sense of independence and pride needed to oppose the big powers. So the suspicion is that the British government might have supported the IRA and its many atrocities as a kind of 'agent provocateur' attempt to embarrass and discredit the previously united and vocal Irish nationalist community, just like they had done in the 19th century, as we have only recently found out.

This may have been combined with the systematic running down of Irish history institutions over the last few decades. A Cork professor that has highlighted this does not accept that it is done for financial reasons and considers that it might in fact be a deliberate policy.[116] In fact 1966, when it is postulated that these UK and US plans were drawn up, was in retrospect the high water mark for Irish nationalism and it has been very much downhill from there. It is interesting that many of the media commentators in the South (some of whom are quite blatantly working for UK or US intelligence agencies, as you can see in the way their international views always agree with the agenda of those agencies) that are most vocal on IRA violence always seem to link it to the GAA or the Catholic Church or heroes from Ireland's past as if they were somehow responsible for the atrocities and in doing so, as I say, taint those institutions, unfairly, in the eyes of the Irish people. The same is true of criticism's of a 'Pan Nationalist Front' and sneering at Irish Americans and Ulster Catholics in the Southern media so spreading around a ruinous disunity which impairs an otherwise potentially powerful Irish block.

In fact at times through history the ability of the Irish as a race to oppose some state activities by united action and protest, I respectfully submit, can at least equal the best efforts of any other race or country. Even throughout the troubles you can see this to a small extent. Consider the case of the large numbers of Irish people wrongly convicted of IRA attacks in Britain in the 70s and 80s. At that time the British legal system was surely the most reputable in the world and the British government for many years never showed the slightest inclination to reexamine those cases that had already been decided. But to their great credit many Irish people persisted in questioning the judgement of the courts and kept up a campaign going on for years despite much ridicule in the media that they were only fellow travellers of terrorists and court judgements that mocked their conspiracy theory of 'an appalling vista' that just couldn't be true. And yet in the end the whole British judicial system had to recognise this brand new phenomenon of 'miscarriage of justice' which before was completely unheard of. This kind of campaign, in the teeth of official hostility from both governments most of that time, is very rarely successful in any country because generally the ordinary citizens have no culture of questioning official decisions which in some cases the Irish still maintained. So in any case that kind of united unofficial action, that characterised the Irish community in the past, scares governments and might have been also a target of their planning.

What may be the most important comparison we can make to the troubles in Ireland are revelations about the same type of instability in Italy in the same period. It was revealed in testimony given by then Italian Prime Minister Giulio Andreotti to the Italian Senate in the early 90s that the terrorism – attributed to both left and right – that rocked Italy in the previous two decades had been supported by the Italian security apparatus, in cooperation with western intelligence agencies and NATO, as part of what was called a 'strategy of tension'.[117] This amounted to creating conditions that led to public support for a kind of right wing security agenda that was in the interests of those bodies which were secretly supporting this strategy. This is described here by Ed Schooling who was working with the US army in Italy in an intelligence capacity:

> "Nor have I even touched on the subject of Operation GLADIO – commando operations in Europe in which the CIA (U.S. and allies) trained and financed European terrorists to kill multitudes of innocent people in bombings and shootings in order to frighten the public into crying out for more state security!"

This is corroborated by one of the right wing extremists, Vincenzo Vinciguerra, who was involved in the operations in Italy and who explained the logic of it in an interview in The Observer:

126

"You had to attack civilians, the people, women, children, innocent people, unknown people far removed from any political game. The reason was quite simple. They were supposed to force these people, the Italian public, to turn to the State to ask for greater security. This is the political logic that lies behind all the massacres and the bombings which remain unpunished, because the State cannot convict itself or declare itself responsible for what happened."

Gladio was the name of secret NATO units that were used as part of this type of operation all across Western Europe.[118] It has been the subject of parliamentary inquiries and heated public discourse in many of those countries, with the notable exception of the UK and the US itself who have not let anything break through their traditional secrecy on intelligence matters. Its not hard to postulate on how this type of strategy could lie beneath the Irish troubles. Basically the terrorism coming out of Ireland, and broadcast into every home in Britain and Ireland, could possibly have been a kind of mood music which provides the public support for the security services to get ever increasing powers and the ever willing cooperation of the general public in their activities and preserving their secrets. Behind the wall of that secrecy, and using those powers, they may be able to control the overall political situation in the UK [119] and also protect whatever kind of rackets the establishment gets up to on occasion.[120] This would more neatly explain why the troubles continued for so long and also the pattern of the conflict since it never really mattered who won it was only important to have a steady supply of media 'outrages' to influence public opinion. In fact the highest placed dissident in the security apparatus in Northern Ireland, Colin Wallace, has always said that the troubles should be placed in the context of psychological operations the British intelligence agencies are conducting against the UK population. He has stated that the British intelligence agencies were using "by proxy" "paramilitaries on both sides" because they felt the state was weak (and hence needed public support for a more right wing approach). This Italian scenario is then maybe the fundamental answer as to why all the paramilitary groups were supported by the UK government.

A related point, from what you might call this Italian model, is that the gladio operations also seem to have been designed to polarise public opinion onto a left-right axis. Some of the active participants seem to have been told that what they were doing was rescuing Italy from the forces of the left, not understanding that their superiors were simultaneously allied to these left wing groups. You can see some of this sentiment in this statement by the former head of Italian counterintelligence, General Giandelio Maletti:

"The CIA, following the directives of its government,

wanted to create an Italian nationalism capable of halt-
ing what it saw as a slide to the left, and, for this purpose, it may have made use of right-wing terrorism."
And in a BBC interview the Italian judge Felice Casson, who uncovered
a lot of the gladio story, explained that the strategy was:
"... to create tension within the country to promote conservative, reactionary social and political tendencies."
You can see that that matches a lot of what Wallace is saying about the
way the troubles were used to influence UK opinion, as he explains in
this quote:
"MI5's increased role in Northern Ireland from the early
1970's coincided with growing industrial unrest in the
rest of Britain. More extreme elements within the security service, aided by equally extreme associates in politics, industry and the media, projected the situation as
part of a worldwide communist conspiracy. The intelligence community saw the Irish situation as the front
line of the left's threat to the UK, and of a great conspiracy by the communist bloc to undermine the whole of
the UK...media operations played [and], as far as I can
judge, continue to play an important part in this psychological warfare." (Quoted in John Pilger, *Hidden Agen-
das* (London, 1998), p.516.)
These – possibly duped – intelligence agents, like Wallace, maneu-
vered the Irish troubles into a smear of the left in the UK by e.g. forging
documents that alleged that leading labour party figures were sympa-
thetic to the IRA. You can see some of those documents printed in Paul
Foot's book *Who Framed Colin Wallace?* (London, 1989). Hence again
the experiences of Italy could be the Rosetta stone in trying to understand what has been happening in Ireland during the same period.[121]
    There is another explanation if you are prepared to run with the idea
that the western intelligence agencies are very corrupt and are looking
after their own interests rather than any country's security. Of course
nobody is going to like this explanation if they think those agencies are
lovely people and are not able to conduct long term coordinated actions
nationally or internationally. Strange as it may seem there is a lot of evidence of their involvement in the international drugs trade and possibly
they like the idea of paramilitary or mafia style networks emerging in
some countries in order to assist in the distribution of the drugs.[122] As
Dennis Dayle, former chief of an elite DEA enforcement unit, remarked:
"In my 30-year history in the Drug Enforcement Administration and related agencies, the major targets of my investigations almost invariably
turned out to be working for the CIA."[123] And it stands to reason that
they would need distribution networks as Richard Brenneke of the CIA
stated once on Italian TV:

"The CIA money for the P-2 [the masonic lodge that secretly ran Italian politics and security] had several aims. One of them was terrorism. Another aim was to get P-2's help to smuggle dope into the U.S.A. from other countries. We used them to create situations favourable to the explosion of terrorism in Italy and in other European countries at the beginning of the 1970s." [124]

There is obviously no lack of rumours that all the Irish paramilitary groups are heavily involved in the drugs trade.[125] This then might also be a factor which encourages the western intelligence agencies to assist the Irish paramilitaries.

I am only too conscious that many readers will find it beyond comprehension that the British and other western intelligence agencies are the secret backers of the IRA. I can only quote John Pilger, the famous Australian journalist who has reported from many countries across the world, democracies as well as dictatorships:

"Western Stalinism is by far the most insidious variety.
In a democracy, manipulation of public perception and
opinion is, by necessity, more subtle and thorough than
in a tyranny."[126]

It isn't really that difficult to fool people. I will leave you with the thoughts of an anonymous RUC officer in Kosovo who was questioned by a Sunday Times journalist while serving there. The journalist wanted to know how is it that NATO was all along training the KLA despite denying it during the Kosovo conflict and this officer was quite happy to oblige him in getting to the bottom of this mystery: "Oh. We lied." [127]
It happens!

<u>Footnotes</u>

1. The Queen Elizabeth quote is from Analecta Hibernica no.6 (1934) p.429. A very detailed examination of the Finucane case by a number of American human rights lawyers is presented at http://www.humanrightsfirst.org/pubs/descriptions/beyond_collusion.pdf and I am just going to refer to their comprehensive and referenced book which they accurately call "Beyond Collusion".

2.ibid p.vii.

3. ibid p.vii.

4. ibid p.56.

5.ibid p.31.

6. ibid p.48 and p.89.

7 ibid p.40.

8. ibid p.68.

9. ibid p.84. He was later taken to Sussex in England and was, we are told, set up by the police there in an elaborate sting operation to get him to confess to the murder. But by this time he had already confessed easily enough to Johnston Brown of the RUC and also was very open about the killing in talking to journalists from the BBC so you would wonder about the 'sting' explanation. The setup involved Barrett in working for a reportedly fictitious drug smuggling group populated by police officers.
(http://archives.econ.utah.edu/archives/a-list/2004w37/msg00008.htm)

10. ibid p.87.

11 http://www.relativesforjustice.com/pressrelease/insight.htm quoting an Insight TV documentary called "Licensed to Kill – Inside the Force Research Unit". Martin Ingram is a pseudonym.

12. Roy Garland, *Gusty Spence* (Belfast, 2001), p.44. I think that date was 1935 but I'm not certain.

13. ibid p.45.

14. ibid p.48.

15. ibid p.52.

16 ibid p.53.

17. The quote on RTE was written by Niall Meehan the 'Head of the Journal-ism & Media faculty in Griffith College, Dublin' and is from http://cain.ulst.ac.uk/othelem/media/meehan/meehan03.htm quoting the Sun-day Business Post 20 April 2003. The Phoenix quote is from Oct 21 2005 p8 and it is from one or other of the numerous references to the Sunday Indepen-dent in the Phoenix in 2005 that I take the reference about the current influence of a prominent ex WP member.

18. Barry's research is at http://www.indymedia.ie/newswire.php? story_id=68249. For Rupert see http://members.freespeech.org/irishpows/NEWS/june_2003.htm#rupert_emails _omagh where it quotes the Sunday Business Post Jun 22 2003.

19. http://www.irlandinit-hd.de/sub_themen/fulflan.htm .

20. http://observer.guardian.co.uk/nireland/story/0,11008,640271,00.html where it claims that Fulton is the source of the 'rumours' that Blair worked for the security forces.

21. http://www.findarticles.com/p/articles/mi_qn4156/is_200206/ai_n12576952#c ontinue, from the Sunday Herald of Scotland June 2002 stating that Blair was the mentor of Kevin Fulton in the IRA .

22. From the Observer reference listed above. The spin in that newspaper is that it doesn't believe those rumours.

23. http://observer.guardian.co.uk/nireland/story/0,11008,1066293,00.html .

24. ibid, where the quote is from, and see http://irelandsown.net/News46.html quoting the Sunday Times 28 Dec 2003. Michael Gallagher, who's son died in the blast, is not impressed by these efforts to discredit White, as he relayed to the Sunday Independent (May 12 2002):
' "The enquiry set up by Mr O'Donoghue is part of that [the "cover up"]. It's to take enquiries and details out of the public domain and behind closed doors so that the people won't hear what is in the files," he said.
"Let me say that the discrediting has already begun. A garda sergeant who was so important to the intelligence gathering operation against the Real IRA that he was brought 100 miles to Dublin to meet with this informant is being por-trayed as a crank or a misfit."'
(http://www.unison.ie/irish_independent/stories.php3? ca=9&si=751032&issue_id=7395).

25. http://64.233.183.104/search?
q=cache:w9dnHEc2orcJ:saoirse32.blogsome.com/2005/03/06/ quoting the
Sunday Business Post of Mar 6 2005. Also
http://saoirse32.blogsome.com/2005/01/20/ .

26. http://members.freespeech.org/irishpows/HISTORY/omagh_cover-up.htm
from BBC footage Aug 12 2001.

27.
http://web.archive.org/web/20040604051416/http://members.freespeech.org/iri
shpows/bb3/august_2002.htm .

28. From Barry on indymedia op. cit.

29. http://www.policeombudsman.org//Publicationsuploads/omaghreport.pdf .

30. The fact that the person who made the warning was a member of special
branch I have from Barry again.

31. http://cryptome.org/psni-omagh.htm The warning was apparently very
detailed and accurate except that it didn't specify that the attack was to be a car
bomb.

32. See Chapter 1 footnote 5 which refers to
http://archives.tcm.ie/businesspost/2002/01/20/story57787728.asp .

33. http://www.infowars.com/pdfs/order_ch.PDF page 12 of chapter Paul
Joseph Johnson's book 'Order out of Chaos', where this interpretation of those
events is accepted.

34. Chapter 1 footnotes 7 and 8, that being the meeting referred to. Garda Detective Inspector Gerry O'Carroll describes here the political background to
those bombings:
"At the time the bombs went off, the government was sitting late into the evening debating a controversial piece of new legislation called the Offences
Against the State (Amendment) Act 1972. One of the major clauses of the Act
was a provision to allow the word of a Garda Chief Superintendent to be accepted as hard evidence in court that a person was a member of the IRA. When
news of the bombs reached Government Buildings, the opposition party, Fine
Gael, which had been wavering in support of the proposed legislation, immediately abstained from the vote and the Act was carried by 69 votes to 22. The
Fianna Fail government led by Jack Lynch was the sponsor of that Act.

It was later claimed in a report in the 'Evening Herald' by journalist Jim Cant-
well, dated 21 August 1973, that the Irish government had been given evidence
by the Garda Special Branch that two members of the Special Air Services of

the British Army were wanted in connection with the bombings. The two men were named in that report. It was believed in the highest echelons of our government at that time that British Intelligence was involved in undercover operations in the Republic and had infiltrated our own intelligence agencies. The two SAS suspects are, to my knowledge, still wanted for questioning in this jurisdiction in connection with the murders of George Bradshaw and Thomas Duffy, the two CIE employees killed in the blast.

It is my opinion, and many others in the country would agree, that the bombs were detonated to influence the vote of the Irish government on that Act, whose passage through the Dail had been problematic but which made it immediately following the bombings. This Act would be a major factor in the fight against the IRA and its enactment would suit the policy and aims of the British government in its own fight against terrorism." (Gerry O'Carroll, *The Sheriff / A Detective's Story* (London, 2006), p.99.)

35. http://britishcollusion.com/news16.html quoting Sunday Life 7 Nov 2004, in the context of yet another IRA hitman recently revealed as working for the security forces. The Herald references are from http://www.sundayherald.com/42752 .

36. The Sunday Times 1 Jan 2006 p1. He is not the only one who feels that way, this is from an interview with an IRA volunteer who was involved in the Sallins Train Robbery:
"He blamed the British for starting it all in 1972, when internment was introduced in the North. In so doing they "declared war", he said. He believed they did so deliberately, so their soldiers could have training in that type of warfare "and republicans fell into the trap". Otherwise he believes the Troubles would not have happened at all.
Internment led to the IRA having more recruits than it could accommodate. Such was the chaos, he said, that the Provisional IRA was "a sad f**king bunch when we started".
He dismissed outright suggestions that Fianna Fail or Charles Haughey had any part in their creation. "Not at all. They were created by the British army," he said."
(Sunday Tribune 3 Jan 2006 quoting Patsy McGarry, *While Justice Slept: The True Story of Nicky Kelly and the Sallins Train Robbery* (Dublin, 2006).)

37. http://www.sundayherald.com/29997 In that article its pretty clear that KF is Kevin Fulton and F is Samuel Jay Rosenfeld. Both are pseudonyms, as is Martin Ingram, but in fact their real names are not hard to come by.

38. ibid.

39. http://britishcollusion.com/stakeknife4.html Quoting Irish Times 12 May 2003.

40. http://britishcollusion.com/news11.html quoting Irish Independent 17 May 2003.

41. http://www.telegraph.co.uk/news/main.jhtml?
xml=/news/2003/05/13/nife13.xml .

42. Sunday Times February 6 2004. News Review p.2.

43. I think this was in fact in the Sunday Times that was published the sunday before his death, a creepy coincidence that doesn't bear thinking about. It is confirmed here by Jim Cusack of the Sunday Independent 21 Dec 2003. (http://britishcollusion.com/monaghan14.html)

44. Information on the number of people killed by the IRA during that period from Paul McGuill who has studied Irish Paramilitaries as part of an MA in UCD and whom I'd like to thank .(Incidentally as always the views I express are my own and I hope nobody blames anybody else for them.)

45. Martin Ingram and Greg Harkin *Stakeknife / Britain's Secret Agents in Ireland* (Dublin, 2005).

46. ibid Brian Nelson in the UDA is said to be very much the exception.

47. http://www.pbs.org/wgbh/pages/frontline/shows/ira/inside/org.html .

48. From the Stakeknife book's introduction by Greg Harkin. The book forms the basis for this paragraph on the FRU. The Guardian also states that "The army was running between 160 and 200 agents within the IRA during the late 1980s and early 1990s"
(http://www.guardian.co.uk/Northern_Ireland/Story/0,2763,939089,00.html). If we take it as a generous figure of 200 and match that with the equally generous figure of 800 for a combined figure for both active and non active IRA person-nel then we end up with about 25 per cent of the IRA being British army agents which is then much the same statistic as Harkin pointed out.

49. http://www.irelandsown.net/News31.html quoting The Sunday Times 3rd August 2002.

50. http://irelandsown.net/News18.html .

51. http://www.birw.org/bsireports/71_99/report90.html There is also a highly placed source in the Catholic community directly run by MI5 in Derry and very knowledgeable about IRA activities but not a member of that organization, known as Observer C. Could Infliction be Sean O'Callaghan? The only diffi-culty appears to a problem with dates, otherwise it fits the details given about

Infliction.

52. Sunday Independent Jan 12 2003 p5 .

53. Dick Lehr and Gerard O'Neill, *Black Mass the Irish mob the FBI and a devils deal* (New York, 2000), p.182.

54. See references to Ruppert under the discussion of the Omagh bomb above.

55. http://dispatches.phoblacht.net/archive/dispatch283.htm Barrett was in the UDA.

56. http://britishcollusion.com/fulton1.html quoting Sunday Times 8 June 2003.

57. http://www.seeingred.com/Copy/2.1_CODE_weiraff.html Paragraph 30.

58. http://www.irishexaminer.com/text/story.asp?
j=178430709188&p=y7843x7x95x4&n=178430709548 Also Sunday Times notes that all the cars dealt with by the Garda agent Dixon were routinely fitted with bugging/tracking devices which are then followed by the National Surveillance Unit using aircraft. See also Chapter 1 footnote 13.

59.
http://www.humanrightsfirst.org/pubs/descriptions/beyond_collusion.pdf&e=1 0141, Beyond Collusion p.55:
"Ingram told us that the quartermaster is extremely important, because the security forces can electronically tag the weapons under his or her control. Ingram said that once the weapons are tagged, they cannot be moved without the knowledge of the security forces. In interviews with the Lawyers Committee, Ingram claimed that this tagging of weapons was an invaluable tool in the prevention of paramilitary murders. He told us that if Stobie had been an Army agent, the weapons under his control would have been immediately tagged and emphasized that he could not contemplate a scenario in which Special Branch would not have done the same."

60. Sunday Times April 20 2003.

61. Martin Ingram and Greg Harkin, *Stakeknife / Britain's Secret Agents in Ireland* (Dublin, 2005).

62. http://www.five.org.uk/security/mi5org/shayler.htm .

63. Fred Holroyd and Nick Burbridge, *War Without Honour* (Hull, 1989).

64. Richard Tomlinson, *The Big Breach; From Top Secret to Maximum*

Security (Moscow, 2001).

65. See Chapter 1.

66. See the references to it in Martin McGartland's book *Dead Man Running* (Edinburgh, 1998), p.25, also see under the footnotes for the Armagh sniper account below.

67. http://www.archive.official-documents.co.uk/document/caboff/nim/0114301808.pdf .

68. http://cain.ulst.ac.uk/issues/violence/sf31398.htm

69. The Chequers reference is from Nicholas Davies, *Dead Men Talking* (Edinburgh, 2004), p.87, and the Carlin one: http://www.newsfrombabylon.com/index.php?q=node/2203 quoting the Sunday Herald Sept 1 2002.

70. Fred Holroyd and Nick Burbridge, *War Without Honour* (Hull, 1989), p.86.

71. Phoenix May 9 2003 p.7.

72. McGartland op cit p.174.

73. Sean O'Callaghan, *The Informer* (London,1998), p. 240.

74. Raymond Gilmour, *Dead Ground* (London, 1998), p.324.

75. http://www.irelandsown.net/News31.html quoting The Sunday Times 3rd August 2002.

76. Fred Holroyd and Nick Burbridge, *War without Honour* (Hull,1989), p.100.

77. ibid p.91.

78. http://britishcollusion.com/restorick.html quoting the Sunday Times 20 June 2004.

79. Punch, issue: 111, July 26 – August 8, 2000 quoted at http://groups-beta.google.com/group/uk.politics.misc/browse_thread/thread/1ad412877ef0e1 cc/c638e54323455a80 .

80. http://www.infowars.com/pdfs/order_ch.PDF page 3, in this sample chapter from Paul Joseph Watson, *Order out of Chaos.*

81. Paul Routledge, *Public Servant, Secret Agent: The elusive life and violent death of Airey Neave* (London, 2002), p.350.

82. Martin McGartland, *Dead Man Running* (Edinburgh, 1998), p.206.

83. http://cryptome.org/fru-claimant2.htm see also the slightly different http://ftp.tuniv.szczecin.pl/pub/Security/Crypto/linux/pub/mirrors/www.crypto me.org/fru-claimant.htm.

84. http://www.irlandinit-hd.de/sub_themen/fulflan.htm .

85. http://www.policeombudsman.org//Publicationsuploads/omaghreport.pdf .

86. McGartland op cit p.171.

87. Sunday Times Dec 8 2002 p.5.

88. Phoenix Annual 2003 p.66. Rosenfeld is a pseudonym. He is originally from Galway.

89. Irish Independent 13 Dec 2003 p.8.

90. http://www.sundayherald.com/13387 "I have nothing. I have a criminal record so I cannot get a job. When I move around Britain I'm constantly stopped by police who see me as a terrorist." See also http://britishcollusion.-com/monaghan5.html where he is unfortunately described as 'destitute'.

91. Phoenix Feb 25 2005 p.16.

92. See Chapter 1.

93. See Stakeknife book op cit. and http://www.birw.org/Stakeknife.html .

94. http://www.newsfrombabylon.com/index.php?q=node/2203 .

95. Martin McGartland, *Dead Man Running* (Edinburgh, 1998), p.22. Quoting one of his handlers: "Marty, you weren't some two-bit tout but one of the most successfull agents the Branch had in Northern Ireland at that time. You were a vital cog in the intelligence set-up for more than 4 years...You were someone the Branch would have done all in its power to protect. But they didn't." The same handler also refers to Ian Phoenix's, the head of one of the Tasking and Coordination Groups, description of McGartland as one of their best agents. (p.28.)

96. ibid p.175 and p.184-5.

97. Martin McGartland, *Fifty Dead Men Walking* (London, 1997).

98. Martin McGartland, *Dead Man Running* (Edinburgh, 1998).

99. ibid from the back cover of the book.

100. ibid p.208.

101. ibid p.24.

102. http://hnn.us/roundup/1.html quoting The Daily Telegraph 4/22/2005.

103. As well as the Reilly reference see Nicholas Plunkett in his history on the period (NLI MS 345) of c.1700. He also agrees that there was no attempt at rebellion on the part of Tyrone in 1607 'and thinks it a contrivance.' (p.400, quoting Carte's summary of Plunkett's views.)

104. For Hugh Reilly see Richard Hayes, *A Biographical Dictionary of Irishmen in France* (Dublin, 1949). The text is from Hugh Reilly, *Ireland's Case Briefly Stated* (London, 1768), p.15. Its sometimes known as 'The Impartial History of Ireland'.

105. http://www.newadvent.org/cathen/09108a.htm and http://www.newadvent.org/cathen/13047a.htm The Catholic Encyclopedia articles on Pere Joseph and Cardinal Richilieu respectively.

106. Christy Campbell, *Fenian Fire, The British Government Plot to Assassinate Queen Victoria* (London, 2002), passim. This is from his 'Note on Sources' pxxi:
"The computerised index at the Public Record Office...blinked frustratingly. 'Document in Use' -so the screen responded to multiple requests to see a 114-year old file. It was listed as the 'Secret Service papers of Arthur Balfour, Chief Secretary for Ireland 1887', and was marked 'open'. On a return visit a few weeks later, in the summer of 200, its classification had been changed to 'closed'.

I enquired at the busy delivery desk why that should be so. 'Does it concern the royal family, Ireland or homosexuality?' a helpful staff member responded. I could only guess – Ireland certainly; anything more would be a bonus. 'Then it is going to be secret.'

The papers were 'retained at the Home Office', it emerged. After lengthy supplication the file was partially declassified that autumn: half of it was supplanted by cardboard dummies, more letters were in photostat with certain sentences – occasionally whole paragraphs – carefully inked over. It was so diligently done, it was explained, 'to protect informers'. Anyone named was dead a century ago. Where Ireland is concerned, policy is seamless."

Here are some quotes from a review of the book in The Observer May 12 2002:
"It is a story of intrigue to equal anything by John le Carré. A new book says that the British Government colluded in an assassination attempt against Queen Victoria in order to undermine the Irish republicanism with dirty tricks.

In one of the most remarkable examples of a 'black operation' ever revealed, Fenian Fire, by Christy Campbell, says that Ministers were so concerned about the rise of 'Home Rulers' in the 1880s it used secret service agents to infiltrate and support republican terrorist organisations.

Ministers believed that the 'plot' to kill the Queen, revealed with great drama during Victoria's golden jubilee, would fatally undermine Charles Stewart Parnell, the charismatic Irish nationalist leader, in Westminster and destroy the republican movement.

It is thought to reveal one of the first examples of British 'black ops', schemes which governments use to undermine their enemies. Other examples of the dark art include the Zinoviev letter, a forged note allegedly from the Communist International backing the Labour Government 'leaked' to the Daily Mail on the day before James Ramsay MacDonald stood for re-election in 1924, and the work of Colin Wallace, the government information officer who planted stories in the press about links between Labour and IRA supporters in the 1970s.
...
The police said that the plot, as audacious in its target as the 1605 Gunpowder Plot, had been hatched in New York by the Fenian Brotherhood, Clan na Gael, an Irish-American secret society.

Campbell's book, to be published by HarperCollins next month, says that by the time it was revealed to an astonished and fearful public the Government was not only aware of it but had actively supported it.

Intelligence officials based in Dublin and London used the Fenian Brotherhood to stir up violence against British targets. Known republican sympathisers were hired by the Foreign Office to play a leading role in the attacks.
...
Government Ministers believed that the imaginary plot to assassinate Victoria would fatally undermine Charles Stewart Parnell, right, the charismatic Irish nationalist leader, and destroy the republican movement." (http://copy_bilderberg.tripod.com/infowar.htm).

107. ibid p.355.

108. See also Conor Cruise O'Brien, *Memoir: My Life and Themes* (Dublin, 1998), p.107.

109. http://www.chapters.eiretek.org/books/THealy/healy12.htm and http://www.chapters.eiretek.org/books/THealy/healy13.htm, the extracts being from Chapters 12 and 13 of the book put on the web by a guy in North Dublin who has made available the full texts of some great books on Irish history. Numerous chapters in the book indicate the incredible pressure the Land League was under from the Coercion Acts which were only supposed to be targeting 'gunmen' but were used for example to prosecute people who gave bread to evicted tenants.

110. Lothian Manuscripts HMC no.73 1905 p.433.

111. Paul Routledge, *Public Servant, Secret Agent: The elusive life and violent death of Airey Neave* (London, 2002) p.333-334. See also Simon Heffer, *Enoch the Roman* (London, 1998), from which some notes:
He kept in his files a copy of a US State Department Policy Statement of 15 Aug 1950 saying it was desirable to bring Ireland into NATO. (p.635)
Mentions an interview given by him on Channel 4, 16th Oct 1987, which was summarised by Heffer as:
"the CIA could well have 'used' the IRA which would have included funding them." (p.831) Not surprisingly then he wasn't fond of the Foreign Office for its role in these events (MI6 is a branch of the Foreign Office) saying "I refer to that nest of vipers that nursery of traitors which is known as the British Foreign Office."
Heffer refers to a report in the Daily Telegraph, 4 Jan 1980, of a speech he made at an Orange Lodge the previous day in which he claimed that "the Foreign Office was acting in Ulster as the CIA did in countries it sought to destabilise."
In the controversy that followed his remarks some, including Merlyn Rees, wanted the government to make a statement about the role of American Intelligence in Northern Ireland. (p.882)

I guess the wonder is why the decent people in the system couldn't have found this out before and tackled it. Maybe the answer is that they also can be fooled by intelligence agencies, here is Colin Wallace describing Merlyn Rees:
"Merlyn Rees (Home Secretary) was a very genuine and fair minded bloke and he wanted more intelligence traces on people before he would intern them. So we made up the information."
(http://web.archive.org/web/20021119130521/www.wakeupmag.co.uk/articles/dirty.htm .)

112. Simon Heffer, *Like the Roman, The Life of Enoch Powell* (London, 1999), p.886. The 'above the IRA' quote is from p.881 of the same book. Powell not surprisingly was very interested in Colin Wallace's story as you can see from

this reference to one file 'closed for review' among his papers at Cambridge University:
"Colin Wallace. Press cuttings, papers and correspondence on the sacking of Wallace, former Army information officer in Northern Ireland, over an alleged Intelligence conspiracy to destablise the Wilson Government, including: press cuttings; extracts from the memoirs of a Central Intelligence Agency (CIA) officer on clandestine warfare, with notes of psychological warfare sponsored by the CIA in Britain during the 1970's; letters from Colin Wallace (2) and representatives of Thomas Eggar and Son, Solicitors (2); issue of the Lobster magazine on covert operations in British politics, 1974-78; paper on Wallace's involvement in the Kincora scandal (concerning sexual assaults at a boys' home in Belfast)."
(http://janus.lib.cam.ac.uk/db/node.xsp?id=EAD%2FGBR %2F0014%2FPOLL;recurse=1)

113. Roy Garland, *Gusty Spence* (Belfast, 2001).

114. The Sloane quote is from here: http://www.mediamonitors.net/johnhiddleston1.html and the reference to Taus and Crittenden is from: http://www.druggingamerica.com/sample_chapter_drug.doc which is a sample chapter from Rodney Stich's *Drugging America*. You can read an affidavit by Crittenden at http://www.wethepeople.la/stephen.htm and a short affidavit by Taus at http://www.wethepeople.la/taus.htm. For the Littlejohn episode see the Barron report http://cain.ulst.ac.uk/events/dublin/barron191104.pdf .
The 'destabilise' quote is from an article on the Littlejohns in the Sunday Independent Life Magazine p.22 July 24th 2005. The British government deny the MI6/Wyman connection, as they always do in intelligence matters, but they admit a connection to the Ministry of Defence via Lord Carrington the future Foreign Secretary. At the Dublin meeting op. cit. Alderman Christopher Burke stated that he knew the Littlejohn brothers when he was in prsion in Dublin. He said they had told him that they felt protected in the south, despite their activities, because some important Irish politicians were in fact British agents. They told him the names of two of these people apparently. In a separate point Ald. Burke also said that it was high time that the two successive Ministers for Justice of the period, Des O'Malley and Patrick Cooney, came forward and told us what they know about these incidents and bombings and assist the families of the 'forgotten' to unravel the truth.

On the CIA/IRA link there are a few other straws in the wind. This is from C. Desmond McGrory:
"Those who were tried in New York in the 1980s with running guns to the Provos claimed at their trial that the operation was run by the CIA and was not therefore illegal. Former CIA agent Ralph McGehee tesitified to this effect. All were acquitted."
(http://www.indymedia.ie/newswire.php?story_id=72937&condense_com-

ments=false#comment127951) and at http://www.indymedia.ie/newswire.php?
story_id=72419:
"Take a look at the Timewatch programme on this shown on BBC2 in 1996.
They had witnesses who said the CIA had a meeting with the Provo high command to be and leaders of the Catholic heirarchy in Co. Fermanagh in 1970."

115. Conor Cruise O'Brien, *Memoir: My Life and Themes* (Dublin, 1998),
p.196. He served on the Irish delegation to the UN at the time and talked about
"Ireland's capacity to resist American pressure." It seems a long long time ago!
For Indonesia and Guyana see the appendix while Iran is I think a well known
episode now. See also Syria in the Appendix. For Gilchrist see
http://www.indymedia.ie/newswire.php?story_id=65047. It was after
consultations with Gilchrist that the proprietor of the Irish Times, Major
McDowell, wrote to 10 Downing St. asking for guidance on how to control the
newspapers output. (http://www.indymedia.ie/newswire.php?
story_id=64228 .)

116. He gives equal weight to the theory that it is done either by "policy or
drift". It was in a letter to the Irish Times from Donnchadh Ó Corráin of May 3
2003. (http://www.ireland.com/newspaper/letters/2003/0503/index.html) Later
this was referred to in an article in that paper by Belinda McKeon Irish Times
Jun 6 2003:
"In coming weeks, Ó Corráin's diagnosis was supported by letters to The Irish
Times from academics at universities in five countries, from Harvard to Hamburg. One letter, from the Dutch city of Utrecht, bore 11 signatures. The level
of international concern was striking. Although, since the prominence of science and technology, as subjects and as profit-generating activities, for universities in the 1980s and 1990s, chairs in every humanties subject are vulnerable
to abandonment or abolition, Ó Corráin's identification of the empty chairs in
Irish studies struck a chord. Why?"
...
"We are at the bottom of the league when it comes to national libraries," argues
Donnchadh Ó Corráin. "Ours is the smallest in Europe bar Luxembourg. Serious money is not being spent on book-buying."
...
"We have one or two HEA scholarships," says Duffy [of TCD history depart-
ment]. "But at the science end of campus, virtually every research student is lu-
cratively funded."
(http://www.ireland.com/newspaper/features/2003/0606/1481907432ATIRISH
.html)

Some people might say too that this intelligence agency idea of sponsoring
paramilitary groups to discredit communities was also applied to the Unionist
community. At least thats what Dr Kennedy Lindsay pretty much says in his
book published in 1979. He talks about the big loyalist paramilitary figures,
which he describes as gangsters, being immune from arrest while respectable

representatives of the Unionist community were 'smeared' with those type of activities when they made representations to the government. He was highly suspicious about how sincere the government was in its tackling of paramilitary activities e.g. writing here in the context of government refusal to set up an RUC fraud squad in 1976:

"It was one more indication that the government had its own vested interest in allowing Ulster to stew indefinitely in its crime and racketeering misery...Racketeering and syndicate crime have been invaluable to the government in that persons and organisations involved develop the characteristics of legitimate businessmen. They have employees, profits, overheads and customers to be supplied on a regular basis. Their political interests, if any, evaporate and, like business men elsewhere, they are concerned most of all to have the status quo maintained and to grant where useful, co-operation to the authorities...A government which condones and orchestrates crime, racketeering and violence as a means of alienating and isolating terrorist or political opponents from their host populations will, in the long run, pay the price of alienating itself from the general public." (Kennedy Lindsay, *Ambush at Tully-West / The British Intelligence Services in Action* (Dundalk, 1979), p.159-163.)

117. See under Italy and Western Europe in the Appendix. Here is an article from Phoenix May 20 1994 p.14 on P-2 which is mixed up in this, its also on Silvio Berlusconi:
"Berlusconi Silvio, Milan,
Industrialist.
Membership card: 1816;
Code E 19 78; Date 26/1/78; Group 17; File 0625
Fees: 100,000 lire
THESE ARE the details on Silvio Berlusconi that were found in the files of Licio Gelli, the fascist "grand puppet master", when police raided Gelli's villa in March 1981 and opened the continuing scandal of the secret Propaganda Due (P2) masonic lodge. Now Berlusconi, the former P2 member who thinks his destiny is to save Italy from communism is the prime minister of Italy. But who is Berlusconi? Is he an independent force or is there more to the man known as "the cavalier" or "the knight"?
Berlusconi, the son of a Milan bank clerk, graduated with a law degree in 1961. A few years later he decided to enter the world of business. His decision was given the personal blessing of Cardinal Giuseppe Siri, a family friend and fierce enemy of the left in Milan.
Berlusconi's first position was with the construction firm Edilnord. He soon established his own company, Milan 2, using the experience he had gained at Edilnord. But he found the complexities of construction needed more than just industrial experience. Above all, he needed contacts, contacts in the city's bureaucratic labyrinth who knew their way around the complicated zoning regulations and who could not only detect legal loopholes but create new ones.
During this period (the early 1970s) Milan was the personal fiefdom of one man: Bettino Craxi of the Partito Socialista Italiano (PSI). The ambitious

Berlusconi was quickly admitted to Craxi's inner circle, a relationship that grew over the years while, at the same time, he kept the doors open to the conservative Christian Democrats just in case.

Soon Berlusconi was to make another very important contact, Licio Gelli, a former Mussolini Blackshirt and Waffen SS man, and a fascist conspirator extraordinary. Gelli was impressed by Berlusconi's ruthlessness and invited him into Gelli's personal masonic lodge, the now illegal P2, which he joined on 26 January 1978.

Soon after being admitted to this nest of masons, whose membership reached into the heart of Italy's industrial, financial, media, military, secret service, police and criminal establishments, Berlusconi was put into P2's Group 17. Group 17 was the communications, information and media sector that had responsibility for-"subversive destabilisation". This was part of Gelli's "Plan for a Democratic Rebirth", his 1976 blueprint for a peaceful right-wing takeover of Italy.

At that time, there was no government regulation of communications. With the help of the Monte Dei Paschi Bank, a P2 front, Berlusconi set himself up in television. He became the operative arm of the Gelli plan in which his effective function was to be the co-ordinator of an "agency to link the local press and television in a national chain that can affect public opinion on the daily running of the country"."

118. The Schooling quote is from:
http://www.conspiracyplanet.com/channel.cfm?
channelid=93&contentid=355&page=2 and the Vinciguerra quote is from The Observer, 7 June 1992, quoted in
http://www.buergerwelle.de/pdf/secret_warfare_and_natos_stay_behind_armie s.htm.

The latter website is written by Swiss researcher Daniele Ganser and it details much of the gladio activities in Europe. They contained some pretty ruthless people as you can see from this quote from the commander of the Portuguese gladio group, Yves Guerin Serac, which was taken from a document found during the 1974 revolution:

"In the first phase of our political activity we must create chaos in all structures of the regime. Two forms of terrorism can provoke such a situation: The blind terrorism (committing massacres indiscriminately which cause a large number of victims), and the selective terrorism (eliminate chosen persons). This destruction of the state must be carried out as much as possible under the cover of 'communist activities' ... After that, we must intervene at the heart of the military, the juridical power and the church, in order to influence popular opinion, suggest a solution, and clearly demonstrate the weakness of the present legal apparatus ... Popular opinion must be polarised in such a way, that we are being presented as the only instrument capable of saving the nation. It is obvious that we will need considerable financial resources to carry out such operations."

119. A lot of evidence has emerged for example in Europe of the intelligence agencies funding and therefore no doubt controlling political parties in Europe (see some of the later comments in the stasiland article). Thomas Deflo Bende of the Belgium Green party (http://lists.indymedia.org/pipermail/imc-uk-reports/2004-November/1129-jn.html) states that that those agencies are now heavily involved in electoral fraud. Of course famously the CIA was involved in rigging Italian elections and also in trying to block Allende by those means in Chile. Certainly the recent UK election (2005) has brought to the fore many serious allegations of widespread fraud involving absentee ballots while in the US many details are emerging of how computer balloting is rigged with the assistance of some people in NASA (http://www.onlinejournal.com/Special_Reports/120604Madsen/120604madsen.html). Also see http://www.votefraud.org/Archive/Write/greatest.htm for accounts of earlier fraud in Cincinnati involving software supplied by the FBI. This is the definitive book on the subject: http://www.votescam.com/home1.php by two Collier brothers in Florida.

120. Colin Wallace, for example, at the Justice for the Forgotten meeting in Dublin in June 27th 2003 stated that the same unit that was responsible for the Dublin and Monaghan bombings were also behind the paedophile ring known as Kincora, which is maybe an indication of the type of activity that they would very much like to keep secret. Some think that among the Kincora abusers were 'top civil servants': http://www.rumormillnews.com/cgi-bin/archive.cgi?noframes;read=6548 .

121. The first Wallace quotes are from the 'Justice for the Forgotten' meeting held in Dublin on the 27th June 2003. See also: http://www.american-buddha.com/cia.psyops.htm. The quotes from Maletti and Casson are from http://www.isn.ethz.ch/php/documents/collection_gladio/Terrorism_Western_Europe.pdf .

122. Links on the drug question:
'A brief history of CIA involvement in the Drug Trade' by William Blum formerly of the US State department:
http://www.serendipity.li/cia/blum1.html

There is also the famous 'Dark Alliance' articles by Gary Webb in the local San Jose newspaper, which showed that the main drug suppliers on the US west coast were CIA contract agents (see http://www.copi.com/articles/darker.html). It created a big sensation and sparked off federal enquiries. The journalist was recently shot dead in suspicious circumstances.

"Murder and Drug Running in Montana / Local Residents Allege FBI and State Government Complicity" http://www.freerepublic.com/forum/a104653.htm .

Again in reference to Montana: http://www.aci.net/kalliste/tatumint.htm .

On Kosovo and Afghanistan:
http://english.pravda.ru/world/2003/03/14/44441.html&e=10141 .

On Turkey: http://www.blythe.org/nytransfer-subs/97cov/Turkey's_Web_of_Covert_Killers-CAQ .

A long discussion mentioning the Christic Institute:
http://www.geocities.com/knoxvillegreenparty/iran_contra_christic_institute/c
hristicinstitute.html .

"Information on the CIA drug smuggling operations listed above was provided by the following CIA and ONI (Office of Naval Intelligence) operatives:
Trenton Parker, Gunther Russbacher, Michael Maholy, Robert Hunt.
Documentation confirming the intelligence status of each of these men is attached. This documentation was taken from Rodney Stich's seminal work, Defrauding America.
The information provided by these men, often at great personal risk to themselves and their families, as well as information provided by CIA agents and contract agents such as Richard Brenneke, Stephen Crittenden, Gene Tatum, and Terry Reed, can leave no doubt that the CIA has been involved in drug trafficking on a massive scale and over an extended period of time."
This also lists CIA codewords for its drug smuggling operations:
http://www.wethepeople.la/drugs1.htm .

"The following facts are from the Associated Press and Washington Post stories published in April 2000 on the Hiett case.
Colonel James Hiett was stationed at the US Embassy in Colombia. There, he was the commander of 200 US military advisors and "anti-drug" agents: the Embassy's drug czar.
His wife, Laurie, has already pled guilty to smuggling $700,000 US dollars worth of heroin – she was so, ahem, confused that she thought it was cocaine – from Colómbia into the United States. One report says she used "diplomatic pouches" from the US Embassy to evade inspection by Customs Officials."
(from Narconews at http://www.narconews.com/nmonth0400.html).

"As voters in the Dominican Republic went to the polls on May 17, 2000, their fate was already sealed: Electoral fraud and drug corruption, directed by the United States ...
At stake was not only the presidency of the Dominican Republic, but which United States political party will control Caribbean drug trafficking in the years to come."
(also from narconews: http://www.narconews.com/USDominican1.html) .

This is the deposition of Desiree A. Ferdinand, the daughter of the late Colonel

Albert Carone of New York, who provides a link between the CIA and DIA and mafia groups involved in the distribution of drugs: http://www.tpromo.-com/gk/stacey/ferd.doc .

Discussing involvement by leading political figures: http://web.archive.org/web/20031203024445/http://www.madcowprod.com/3r dIssue/PuppetMaster.htm .

Extracts by a book by a retired DEA agent Cellerino Castillo called 'Powder Burns':
http://web.archive.org/web/20000816021508/http://www.riseup.com/Books/Po wderburns.html
. See also http://www.websitetoolbox.com/tool/post/whosarat/vpost? id=163286&trail=50 and http://spot.acorn.net/jfkplace/03/RM/drugs-cia .

123. http://www.thirdworldtraveler.com/Blum/CIADrugs_WBlum.html .

124. http://www.skepticfiles.org/socialis/cosiga3a.htm .

125. It would strike you as a well established fact in the case of most of the paramilitary groups. In the case of the IRA here are some comments by Kevin Sheehy, former head of the RUC drugs squad, being interviewed by Jim Mc-Dowell of the Sunday World:

"Question: While the Provos were taking money through the back door on drugs, then, for public image, and for the Irish/American image, they were pre-pared to shoot people dead with the DAAD organization, and, in instances like the 'night of the long guns'?

Answer: [after describing how their image in the catholic communities is im-portant] So their policy has always been, that they oversee major drugs traf-ficking on an international basis, millions of pounds worth, but that their peo-ple who have done time in jail are still not, officially, allowed to be involved in that.

Question: So why would the Provos go for the 'independents' -Mickey Mooney, Speedy Fagan, Brendan Campbell, more recently Ed McCoy? Be-cause they refused to play ball with the Provos?

Answer: Yes..." (Jim McDowell, *Godfathers: Inside Northern Ireland's Drug Racket* (Dublin, 2001), p.218.)

What follows are a few quotes from a book by Howard Marks describing his activities in the international drug trade. He frequently hints that he was work-ing for MI6 and here he is in conversation with Jim McCann, a leading figure in the Official IRA. It was conversations that Vincent Browne was having with the latter, I think, that caused the government to tap Browne's phone.

"McCann now using the name James Kennedy and claiming he was a close relative of the late President Kennedy was doing very well for himself. He had an office floor in the Guinness tower in Vancouver, oil interests in Venezuela and had partially financed the film Equus. He had a warm friendship with James Coburn and his wife, Beverly. Marty declined comment on the source of McCann's wealth. I gave Marty my new name and room number in the Seaporter and told him to give it to McCann, who rang the next morning."[dated about 3 days before the death of Elvis I think.]

Jim: "How's British Intelligence?"
Howard: "Slightly better than the Irish, Jim."
Jim: "Welsh ass ...smarmy as ever ..."
[they arrange to meet]...
Jim: "Are you still dope dealing Howard?"
Howard: "When I can, yes."
Jim: "Those days are f__ing over man. Dope dealers are history. High finance is where its at."
Howard: "Whats that?"
Jim: "Revolving letters of credit, shell companies and offshore banks. I'm spending money hand over f__ing fist, and its all other peoples."
Howard: "So whats different?"
Jim: "Whats different, you stupid Welsh prick, is that I'm living in the fast lane and I'm legit."
Howard: "I take it you are no longer a revolutionary?"
Jim: "I'm a revolutionary until I die. Since when was selling dope on Brighton pier a revolutionary act for f__cks sake?"
Howard: "It is a bit closer than all this upwardly mobile stuff you are into Jim."
Jim: "Is it f___? Howard doing this business I meet the people who matter, the high rollers. You understand me don't you? There is only 500 people in the world who control everything worth a f__k and I have met them all every f__ing one of them."
Howard: "Wheres Graham, Jim?"
Jim: "He's become a poof. He's living in San Francisco or some other poof place. He's probably still dope dealing, like you."
Howard: "Did you do any more Shannon deals, after I got busted?"
Jim: "I'm not telling you Howard. Graham never could control those egits in Kabul. I found out who they are and their address in Kabul. I've got them when I want them. But those days are gone Howard. You need to wise up, but we'll keep in touch. If you ever get a real problem you can ask for the Kid."
(Howard Marks, *Mr.Nice / An Autobiography* (London, 1997), p.148. On p.169 another drug deal is described, set up by Marks and McCann, the drugs to travel from Kabul to Dublin.)

126. John Pilger, *Distant Voices* (London, 1994), p.194.

127. http://emperors-clothes.com/docs/train.htm, you can see the quote in the heading of the webpage. I remember from reading the article that it was an RUC officer that said it but I cannot check that with the original. This edition is missing among those in the National Library.

CHAPTER 5

Only the Rivers Run Free: The Irish State in Donegal and Elsewhere.

This is just a rundown of some recent revelations in Ireland that came to light during the summer of 2005.

More details have now emerged about the McBrearty case, particularly from a speech that Frank McBrearty junr. gave in Dublin on July 29th. Clearly the state had put them under a lot of financial preassure with for example many people suggesting that the large number of licensing charges were designed to bankrupt his fathers business. Also "...the Minister and the Morris Tribunal have used legal costs to sanction us and, we now fully understand that this is the instrument by which he has tried to use to coerce us into subdued silence..."[1]

He talked at length about the ongoing campaign of slander and the related false charges that were thrown at them:

> "...the venomous whispers placed in the ears of government ministers and other state officials, which formed a key component of a campaign of damaging innuendo directed against us by his [McDowell's] Garda friends."

You can see this in the summary of the Carty report that was sent to the Minister of Justice by the gardai. The Minister says that the gardai refused point blank to allow the government to see the full Carty report but they did get to see this summary which talked about a 'manipulative' Frank McBrearty senior.[2] The list of false charges goes to over 300 in the District and Circuit courts and includes:

> "public order offences, dangerous driving, assaults that never happened. They also accused us of giving money to the Provisional IRA, blackmailing witnesses, intimidating witnesses and threatening Gardai and state witnesses who were Garda informers."[3]

This slander campaign also involved dividing the local community and Frank says that the gardai basically "brainwashed" the Barron family against them for example. One point that Frank has also repeatedly tried to get across is that the Irish police force are not an ordinary police force but rather are "basically run by Special Branch". He points out that unknown to most people all the senior gardai ("every single one of them") are members of this secret police force which is a circumstance surely unique in any democracy. He feels that this means that the circumstances in the South are very like that of the North with the securocrats running the show. We also now know more about the use of torture by the gardai from this case because an edited video of Frank's experience in Letterkenny Garda Station has now come to light.[4] Frank has described how he prayed he would die during it [5] and how he had to receive psychiatric help in the years following the torture, a thing common to many of those 'interviewed' in garda stations in Donegal and elsewhere.[6] Frank has since found out that the video was edited before being given to his legal team and that the parts which were deleted showed the gardai walking on his head and burning him with cigarettes.

In fact torture and the gardai have been a lot in the news lately particularly with the Rossiter case which many people think is an example of garda brutality gone to a tragic extreme. Obviously this is where the teenager Brian Rossiter was arrested with a friend in 2002 and imprisoned in Clonmel garda station after which he was found in a coma which led to his death. The gardai have their own explanation for his death but both his friend Anthony O'Sullivan and Tony Burke, who were in the garda station, say he was beaten up by the gardai.[7] He also had injuries consistent with being repeatedly struck in the groin.[8] This witness, Tony Burke, has recently had his house thrashed by the gardai supposedly looking for a gun but he is certain it is actually to keep him quiet about the Rossiter case.[9] Anthony O'Sullivan's mother meanwhile decided to withdraw a complaint she had against the gardai about the injuries to her son because she was terrified of garda retaliation against him.[10] This appears to be a well grounded fear, as an indymedia editor has pointed out:

"... the legal advice that I have heard is to refrain from making complaints to the gardai. People who make complaints and who look like having a good case for a civil action often get given extra criminal charges in order to discredit them in advance of the civil case. The gardai have the freedom to add extra charges to cases where they see fit due to evidence from their 'investigations' (like their investigations into the police complaints book)."[11]

This is an account from Oly who was beaten up by the gardai during the mayday protest in 2002:

"Warning to other people who have made complaints, that they may be under surveillance and may face intimidation.

I was hospitalised on May 6th and required stitches to my head. I made a complaint the following day and found legal representation. Last Thursday, my solicitor warned me that the Gardai have also set up a group of detectives in Dublin Castle who don't seem to be concentrating on 'complaints', as they may pretend to be, but damage limitation. They may be involved in logging or receiving records of dialed and received numbers on your phone, possibly text messages etc. and that these records could go back a few months. So if you think this information may concern you, take note.

...

It is ridiculous how we get beaten, complain and end up under investigation."[12]

What makes the Rossiter case such a sad one is the way that father and son were separated just before Brian's death. The gardai are actually not permitted to hold overnight a person of Brian's age so they called his father but when he got there they took him aside and gave him a long spiel about how his son was out of control, causing trouble taking ecstasy etc and his father believed this and wanted him kept in the station to teach him a lesson.[13] It was only afterwards, as he found out from the hospital that in fact they had found no trace of drugs in his son's system, that he began to realise that the gardai had lied to him and had set father and son apart at that crucial moment. This kind of thing is not an isolated phenomenon involving the gardai, for example when the gardai came for Frank McBrearty at the beginning of his ordeal they screamed at his children that their father was a murderer[14] and Rosin McConnell was told that her husband was having an affair when she was arrested as part of the Barron saga.[15] As Karen McGlinchey, the Donegal nurse, has pointed out:

"Gardai have perfected the art of manipulating people and the unfortunate circumstances of their families over many decades. The high profile of the McGlinchey family and their semi-publicised marital separation was consistently used by various gardai to peddle to one side of the family or the other the lies orchestrated by Lennon, McMahon and the other members."[16]

Depressingly the Rossiter case has now being added to by other examples of people killed in garda custody, in particular Terence Wheelock in Dublin.[17] Terence's case involves Store street garda station which you might wonder must harbour a strange kind of policeman when you consider the mysterious urine spraying case. This is where a number of homeless youths were drenched in urine that was thrown on top of them from an upper floor of the garda station. [18] Their case was taken up by a social worker who was also hit. This worker is convinced the gardai didn't realise there were social workers there which presumably means she feels this practice was a deliberate and presumably common enough treatment of homeless people. She was determined to pursue the matter vigorously through the courts but she eventually settled for a small sum because:
"I was told that if I didn't settle I could be liable for other side's costs, so

I couldn't take the risk."[19]

Its obviously not news that the gardai would treat homeless people like this as you can see from the reply that David got when he asked a garda why he had kicked him in the ribs:

"I can't be arsed bending down and I don't like touching shit with my hands!"[20].

Fr Peter McVerry SJ who works with the homeless is trying to highlight the ongoing problem of "young homeless persons being ..bashed up in garda stations." He says that currently its completely hopeless for a homeless person to take legal action because it comes down to his word against the gardai and he has found that the powers that be always choose to disbelieve the homeless guy. He compares the situation in garda stations to the famous Castlereagh Interrogation Centre in the north pointing out that torture there was stamped out by insisting on the presence of medical personnel which he hopes will be done in the south. He thinks as well that the situation with the gardai is very like what had happened in the Magdalen laundries, where the local people knew at least a little about what was going on but lacked a "sense of outrage" which is needed to stop it happening. Its his opinion that there is "no accountability [over the gardai] and the guards know it and they can do what they like." [21]

Torture in Ireland was also the theme of a recent showing on TG4 of the documentary "Faoi Lámha an Stáit" which featured Osgur Breatnach who was tortured and framed by the gardai as part of the Sallins Train robbery case. He described his ordeal and the psychological problems that he continues to suffer from as a result and which has unfortunately ruined his life. Many other details were given about these practices of the gardai but as well there was some revealing facts about garda special branch. Íte Ní Chionnaith, a lecturer in Irish in DIT, was interviewed and she outlined how in some four instances the special branch intervened to deny her employment even though she has never been convicted nor even charged with a terrorist offense. She managed to find out about a letter that was sent to her prospective employer mentioning her presence on some secret blacklist that is kept by special branch. She has unfortunately been unable to get a copy of this letter. The program also talked about harassment of activists mainly in the 70s. The impression was given that the state was not so much after real terrorists but was more intent on going after Irish language enthusiasts and historians as if, according to the program, the authorities were at war with their own culture.[22]

Another case was highlighted recently on Indymedia where the gardai 'ransacked' a house in Tallaght and systematically beat up some members of Na Fianna that were gathered there. There are even reports that one member with Cerebral Palsy was violently assaulted. The interesting thing I think about this case is this reference:

"A caller who identified himself as a member of the

Special Branch rang the landlord of the rented accom-
modation and informed him that the tenants partner
was a member of the I.R.A.
Whether this call was made with the consent of the
branchmans superiors or not is unknown. The branch-
man also claimed that they had been searching for explosives and firearms when they raided the house. The
caller then made a read between the lines comment
which hinted at further raids – "That man is under constant surveillance and it is continuing surveillanc." This
phonecall was obviously intended to bully the landlord
into canceling the Fians partners lease." [23]

Clearly the landlord will have had an opportunity to look over his
wrecked house and will be wondering what repeated raids will mean for
his property. I think you can see how this kind of quiet phone call and
the above secret list can really impact on the lives of people who never
get a chance to have any charges against them aired in open court.

The ongoing drama about the death of Sophie du Plantier in Cork is
also rarely far from the headlines.[24] This is where an investigative news
reporter called Iain Bailey, who had reported on the case and "who had
been very critical of the local Garda bungling of the investigation"[25], has
subsequently been hung drawn and quartered for the crime in the Irish
media, even though the garda file on the case which was sent to the
DPP is admitted not to contain enough evidence to charge anyone for
the murder. The main evidence against him rests supposedly on a local
woman who claims she saw him in the distance as she drove around
the area at 3.30 am on the night in question. She says also that Bailey
has tried to intimidate her whereas he claimed in court that she approached him to complain about the duress the gardai were putting her
under to make a false claim against him. Meanwhile the media job on
Bailey has been relentless and involves the use of extracts from his diary that were seized from him by the gardai. He doesn't now have the
diary and wasn't even allowed access to it to prepare his case during
the libel trial. The main claim in the media against Bailey is that he assaults women but the only evidence for this relates to a number of domestic incidents involving his partner Jules Thomas. What is interesting
is that she is adamant that he is not a violent man and that those incidents are wildly exaggerated. Here is some of what Thomas was saying
during the libel case:

"What is extraordinary about these and other claims is
that Jules Thomas flatly refutes them, as does her partner. She has claimed that, while under arrest, the gardai pressured her into making and signing statements
about Bailey having "duped" her.

154

The Welsh-born artist denied that Bailey was a violent man, and suggested that reports about the brutal beatings were "completely out of proportion for a domestic".

...

Jules Thomas denied that she had ever contacted Farrell or that she had told the shopkeeper: "We must do everything in our power to protect Ian."

Thomas declined to speculate on the reported sighting of Bailey at Kealfadda Bridge. However, she was convinced that Bailey was writing in her kitchen that morning. She denied that she had told gardai that her partner had a "raw, fresh and big bloody cut" on his forehead that morning.

Asked about differences in her statements to gardaí and her account in court, she said: "They kept putting words in my mouth.""[26]

So in fact it is said now that the community is divided between some who believe the garda/media story and some who believe Bailey is being framed. One person who has given the latter version of events describes the atmosphere:

"In a flurry of hysteria and fear the insular local population were quick to agree with Gardai that Mr Bailey was "guilty", although no evidence existed to condemn him. Rumour upon rumour was circulated until, like Tony Blair with the weapons of mass destruction lies about Iraq, everyone "knew" Mr Bailey was guilty. They just "knew". Some locals who had themselves been previously ostracised by the herd came forward to say how Mr Bailey had "confessed to them". This solved their problems and eased their way in the community and with Gardai."[27]

The garda/media story has been that the witnesses against Bailey have been intimidated but this source states that the opposite is happening:

"As for local gangs of vigilantes who have been hounding Mr Bailey for their personal pleasure and to ingratiate themselves with local Gardai, well, they are what they are."

Meanwhile a local anti-war activist who has taken Bailey's side has himself been raided by the gardai and faced false charges which he feels are designed to discredit him. Overall you would have to say that it looks like Raphoe on tour.

Just recently Maria Farrell has now come forward to say that she made those statements against Bailey because the gardai told her to. She states that she lied for them partly because she was frightened of the gardai ('she was in fear of her life of them') and partly because she was blackmailed over a non sexual relationship that the gardai knew about and which she didn't want publicised. She has also explained how she was coached in how to give her false testimony in the libel trial by an 'associate' of the gardai. Meanwhile the local activist who has highlighted the case relates more of what is going on in Schull:

> "Local vigilantes who tied nooses and threw petrol onto Baileys property have also been busy following, framing and spreading rumours about myself. I was called a "supporter of Bailey" when I wrote the article below and have had a busy time of it with Garda stop and searches of my person, my car and home."

The gardai incidentally refer to these new statements by Mrs Farrell as a 'joke' and insist that the investigation followed "the highest professional standards."[28]

More details have also emerged on the shooting incident at an attempted armed robbery at Lusk where the media's initial reports seem now to be quite inaccurate. According to a detailed report by Ken Foxe in Ireland on Sunday one of the raiders was shot dead while completely unarmed and the other armed raider was killed by a shot to the back of the head after he had been disabled by an earlier bullet. This is in contrast to initial statements placed in the media which referred to an "exchange of gunfire" which is now shown to be impossible because the one gun held by the raiders was never fired. That this is nothing new you can see from a case that Amnesty International are investigating, that of Rónán MacLochlain, who was also unarmed when shot dead by the gardai and where again initial reports talked of a gunfight. It turns out as well that the families of the two men killed in Lusk are mystified at the:

> "constant stream of rumour and innuendo about the two men since their deaths...[involving everything from the Russian mafia to feuds between the two families which is completely untrue]..
> Colm Griffin's sister, Sandra, said: 'They made it out as if Colm was the biggest drug dealer in the whole country but he generally didn't have a penny.
> Two weeks before he died, he'd had to give his car

back because he couldn't afford to keep up the repayments on it.

We're not trying to make him out as a saint. He had been on heroin when he was younger but he had got his life back together.

He was working on the building sites for more than six years until the Criminal Assets Bureau went to his place of work and said he was a major drug dealer. Colm had to leave his work after that because he was so embarrassed. He had been working six days a week and loved that job.

From that time on he was continually harassed by the gardai. I don't know how many times he went to the Garda Complaints Board.

He was followed 24 hours a day, searched sometimes six or seven times in the one day, even when he had his kids with him.

Not long before he died, two gardai drove up beside him and said "Griffin, we'll get you, dead or alive". This went on for years. They gave him a dogs life.

He was never up on drugs charges in his life and neither was Eric, yet they were made out to be big-time dealers.'"

Their only contact with the gardai since the killing was at a meeting where they were asked so many questions that they felt "it was as if they were investigating us." They are hoping they might get somewhere if they take the case to the European Court of Human Rights, having given up on the system in Ireland.[29]

This type of garda/media alliance that is so evident in many cases can be seen working in the North Dublin area on a 'suspect' for the brutal murder of Rachel O'Reilly and is deplored by at least one journalist, Brendan Morley of the Meath Weekender (Oct 22 2005 p.27):

"I don't know who murdered Rachel O'Reilly at her home in Naul, north Co. Dublin just over a year ago. I genuinely have no idea who battered the 30-year-old mother of two to death.

Yet anybody who has followed the coverage of this case in national newspapers since last October could be forgiven for thinking that they 'know' who killed Rachel.

Nobody has been charged with her murder, still less convicted. But the press has been continuously full of the drip-drip of heavy hints about the identity of a person who gardai view as the main suspect.

Clearly writing on the basis of off-the-record briefings from within An Garda Síochána, newspapers have been able to predict arrests with quite remarkable accuracy and have routinely deployed those by now well-worn, nudge-nudge, wink-wink euphemisms that Rachel's assailant was 'known to her' and 'lives in Naul'.

Despite what seems by now to be an almost routinely accepted consensus within sections of the media as to who was responsible for the brutal murder, the gardai seem no closer to bringing charges.

The press coverage and the incestuous relationship that has arisen between An Garda Síochána and elements of the media in this case are profoundly disturbing. Sections of the national press have uncritically accepted the word of gardai that they 'know' who did it and have reported each development in the investigation accordingly.

If charges are ever brought against the individual at the centre of this litany of innuendo, it is practically impossible to conceive of a situation in which that person will be able to receive a fair trial in the presence of a jury unblemished by the media's relentless coverage of a case which has captured public attention more than any murder of recent times.

Have we really learned nothing from the litany of miscarriages of justice that we have witnessed over the years?

Whenever police officers claim that they 'know' who committed a crime – but somehow can't quite manage to find sufficient evidence to uphold this alleged 'knowledge' in a court of law – we, especially journalists, whose function it is to scrutinise those in positions of power, including the police, should have alarm bells ringing loudly...

...trial by public smear and innuendo is the currency of vigilantism and is no substitute for the principles of equality before the law and 'innocent until proven guilty' (in a court of law), principles which are there to protect us all and are the hallmarks of a civilised society."

One person who's reputation was very successfully destroyed in the media even before her conviction is Catherine Nevin who was convicted of killing her husband in the pub they jointly owned in Co. Wicklow. Her story started in 1992 when she and her husband made some serious complaints against two local gardai, at that time:

"Mrs Catherine Nevin made a number of complaints against Garda Murphy and Garda Whelan. In March 1992 she first complained that Garda Murphy had corruptly obtained two payments of £1,000 each in connection with applications to the District Court for a restaurant certificate and its renewal. Between the 13th July 1992 and the 11th February 1993 she made a series of written statements to the Gardai containing allegations of corruption, perjury, sexual assaults and other related activities against Garda Michael Murphy and allegations of corruption against Garda Vincent Whelan."

The sexual assault allegation was for an assault against her and a 15 year old relative. Then a few years later her husband is murdered, she is convicted of it, and one of the written statements by the young girl was claimed to be a forgery, so hence with their accusers dead or discredited the two gardai were reinstated after long suspensions. Though it hasn't been plain sailing for one of the those gardai because after Nevin was convicted, and discredited, a different court case heard him accused of pushing:

"the proprietor's wife, Anne Mulcahy, and threatened her. He also threatened to plant drugs on Mrs Mulcahy's son. 'He said he'd done it before and would do it again', David Mulcahy informed the court."

Her trial anyway was against such a background of media hostility that you would have to wonder if that was orchestrated in some way. For example just before one of her appeals the media was full of lurid details about her life in Mountjoy prison, details that proved to be a pack of lies, so much so that the governor of Mountjoy, John Lonergan, came out in the media to refute them. The question is who could have been behind the planting of such erroneous information in the media? And if you think it was the usual suspects then the question is could they not rely on the facts of the case rather than this trial by media tactic? Maybe it is because the case against her was actually very weak? In fact her trial was very like the Bailey libel trial in that there was very little evidence given about the actual murder, in Bailey's case it was a litany of witnesses who claimed that he had confessed to them and in Nevin's case she had supposedly asked numerous total strangers to murder her husband for her. The obvious question is the degree to which these witnesses might have had the same experiences as Marie Farrell.[30]

Rossport has obviously been rumbling along too and there are shades of that in the case of William Finnerty and the other members of a "very small, demoralised, dejected and bewildered community" in Kilconnell, Galway, who have been trying to oppose a super dump. It has snowballed for them from a simple planning matter to one where it seems they have to fight for "genuine democracy" against an "elected dictatorship". They are shocked at the realities of the Irish media for example where there is little (if any?) coverage of an attempted bribe of 50,000 euro made by the developing company (which is owned by National Toll Roads) to the chairman of the protest group. Mr Finnerty has had to fight an ongoing expensive legal fight against charges that he shouted at a County Council employee and for which he faces a possible 18 month jail sentence.[31]

There are quite a few other cases that have come to light in the media in Ireland over the last few months that might repay noting down. There is the shocking case of what appears to be Serial Ritual Abuse of children in the Murphy household in Dalkey that stretches over a few decades. It was first mentioned in a long article in the magazine of the Sunday Independent in April last year but left out of that account was the statement that one of the victims has made of the involvement of at least one garda in this abuse. In particular the victim claims now, in a recent Sunday Independent article, that it was the relationship her father had with this garda which has caused all the delay and loss of evidence in her case.[32] As far as I know all the other news media have shied away from mentioning this garda angle except the Evening Herald which made the amazing statement that this garda abuser was in fact a "top garda".[33] It is also stated that 'Niamh' (Cynthia Owen), one of the victims, is having a lot of trouble with slander of her in the media. Specifically there is a lot of discussion of the merits of Regression therapy while in fact she never received that therapy, her testimony being entirely from her own unaided memory. In this long favourable article by Brigid McLaughlin it is clear that the victims are perplexed as to what party would have the power in the media to spread such a false story.[34] This story of a 'top garda' and SRA abuse carries with it echoes of the many cases like this which have occurred around the world where it seems that paedophile rings often need some kind of high up political or police protection to survive. This has proved true in Australia,[35] the US,[36] Belgium,[37] France,[38] Chile,[39] Latvia,[40] Portugal,[41] and even some rumours about the UK.[42] In fact there have always been stories like that circling in Ireland as well, for example this was the front page story in the Sunday Independent Sept 1 2002:

"MALCOLM Macarthur, prior to his trial for the murder of young nurse Bridie Gargan, may have been about to make sensational claims that an organised paedophile ring existed within the institutions of the State.
...
A senior garda involved in the investigation into Macarthur's murders has told the Sunday Independent that he believes Macarthur had sensational information which would have rocked the foundations of the State.
This information, he said, related to the alleged paedophile activities of politicians, members of the legal

160

profession and civil servants. Other senior Garda officers have corroborated the investigating garda's suspicions, although they all believe Macarthur was not himself a paedophile."[43]

I guess whatever the truth of the Macarthur case the chances are that the powers that be in Ireland know a lot more about it than the rest of us, bearing in mind that the garda who arrested Macarthur was Commissioner Noel Conroy and Michael McDowell was one of his barristers.[44]

A few other cases that have come up in the High Court recently are of interest I think. Firstly there is the case of Margaret McGreal of Castlebar Co.Mayo who was arrested in Oct. 2002 and accused of stealing money from her employers shop. She was strip searched and humiliated according to her affidavit and her solicitor decided to contact the husband of the owner of the shop who happened to be Superintendent Patrick Doyle. Her solicitor claims that in the garda station the Superintendent demanded 30,000 euro from her which if she didn't pay would result in her being "hung" in court for the alleged theft. He claimed this was the amount that was stolen but when the case actually came to court the defendant was only charged with the theft of 582 euro. She was charged with this even though under this pressure she gave the 30,000 to the Superintendent. The High Court found that the garda authorities were not liable for any damages as a result of this because it was held to be a private matter between the employee and the shop owner.[45]

The High Court has also been dealing with some interesting revelations by Tom Gilmartin, the Sligo businessman who is the star of the Mahon tribunal. It turns out that he had given the tribunal a lot of very revealing information which the tribunal in its wisdom decided not to pursue when he was questioned in open session. This strange reluctance of the tribunal to explore this topic has not gone without comment by the High Court:

> "The precise circumstances of this interaction are far
> from clear, because Mr. Gilmartin has said nothing rele-
> vant and the tribunal has observed a studied and at
> times Delphic economy of disclosure on the topic."[46]

In particular Mr Gilmartin relayed the substance of some conversations that he had with the Cork businessman Owen O'Callaghan during which Mr O'Callaghan apparently said that he gave offshore payments of 100,000 pounds to Bertie Ahern and 150,000 to Albert Reynolds. Gilmartin had also been told it seems that both of them had offshore accounts in Jersey, Liechtenstein and the Dutch Antilles while Ahern "also has deposits in England".[47]

The McBreartys anyway have been snowed under with phone calls and messages from people similarly treated by the gardai and the state and this led them to hold some public meetings where these victims could air their experiences. What follows is a short report on one of the meetings in Raphoe on 3rd Sept:[48]

Senator Jim Higgins MEP of Fine Gael
He described how the McBreartys had come to his clinic in Ballyhaunis and he persuaded Frank senior to draw up a statement of his experiences and armed with that he fought in the Dail [along with Brendan Howlin] to get the Morris tribunal set up. He has dealt with many cases as the former Justice spokesman for Fine Gael and building on that knowledge he described the gardai as the "so-called enforcers of law and order". He points out that the McBreartys have "let the genie out of the bottle" and in his opinion "this momentum is not going to go away". He also particularly wanted to point out that this culture in the gardai is not confined to Donegal but is "endemic" across Ireland.

Frank Connolly who broke some of these stories as a journalist with the Sunday Business Post
He came to Donegal first to inquire about planning corruption and was led to investigate the McBreartys from a lead he got from a solicitor and it snowballed from there. He followed the case of Hugh Diver and his brother where poitin was planted by the gardai. He describes meeting Sheenagh McMahon who described her horrific experiences at the hands of the gardai, especially her husband. She also stated that the gardai conspired with the Health Board to harass her and attempt to separate her from her children. Frank also spoke to the Gallagher family who in fact didn't want any publicity about the raids in St. Johnston because at that time they were simply too terrified of the gardai. In these cases the state never of course responded to help these families. The media also didn't respond and this he found particularly ominous. The local media were as silent as the national organs although they later showed some interest. In fact he found that some of the security correspondents working for the national media actually went to some trouble to rubbish this story coming out of Donegal. "Given the scale of corruption in Irish life" he doesn't think that an ombudsman by himself would fix very much.[49]

Dan Boyle TD of the Green Party
He describes himself as a frustrated member of the Dail lamenting the "failure of our national parliament" to hold the gardai accountable. In fact he feels that "people of this country should demand a democracy that works." He points out that in fact the police are simply not answerable to the elected representatives bearing in mind that the gardai have "no legal obligation to come before the Dail." Dail questions on police matters are always "creatively misinterpreted" so they aren't much use.

PJ Brogan from Inver Co Donegal

Many people wondered as well about the quality of the Gardai's investigation of many cases including car accidents etc, alleging that simple information and clues are frequently ignored. Here is possibly the best example of complaints on that front which is so bad it proved to be funny and at the meeting had the audience rolling around in laughter despite its seriousness.

A close relative of PJ rang the garda station at 9.30 one morning threatening to shoot PJ and his family. The Gardai informed this person that it was nothing to do with them unless he actually carried out an attack. One hour later PJ was shot through the eye by this person. The perpetrator then walked into the garda station placed the fired unregistered illegal sawn-off-shotgun onto the counter and said "I shot the f__ker". Then he simply walked out with the gardai making no attempt at all to apprehend him. Despite these facts and the fact that he admitted the crime in court, where the gardai also admitted the above facts, he was still acquitted and continues to commit many serious crimes. PJ later found out that some members of the jury were linked to the defendant and put on the jury for that reason. He also contacted the Minister for Justice outlining the above facts who wrote back assuring him that the gardai "went by the book" conducting a "thorough" and "professional" job. The person referred to is in fact well known to have a close 'relationship' with the gardai.[50]

PJ in trying to get justice in this case has been through the same experiences as all these families all over Ireland. They write or visit TDs who sometimes don't reply or just lie to them. They rarely get replies from media outlets or journalists. PJ was in fact told by a reporter on a local newspaper in the area that yes they knew about the case etc but they simply aren't going to publish his story because it would show the gardai in a bad light.[51] He tried to to take a civil action and one local solicitor did agree to take the case on a no foal no fee basis. The case went on for many years and eventually he confronted the solicitor who informed him that he had decided to drop the case for reasons that he was not prepared to go into. PJ is now certain that he was threatened early on and that the subsequent proceedings were only designed to string him along maybe even in the hope that he would die in the meantime. Needless to say he is also continually harassed by the gardai who constantly drag him through the courts on trumped up charges. In fact he was even jailed for a short time in Mountjoy for non payment of a dog license. He has found out about many other cases of injustice and even interviewed in jail Francis Nolan from Kilkenny who was convicted of rape and whom PJ is convinced is totally innocent. Francis' wife Helen is reported to be afraid to leave her house in Kilkenny without an escort because of the frequency of harassment she suffers from the gardai there.

Rose Doherty

She is originally from Dublin now living in Roscommon and was seriously assaulted, nearly strangled, in Roscommon by a group of two men
and a woman. So she was admitted to hospital in Galway and after
about 5 days she was visited by the gardai who assured her that they
were going to pursue the matter noting that they 'never lost a case on
the medical evidence.' Back home sometime later she was amazed to
discover she had been served with a summons, and so she rang the
gardai to know what was happening and got a ton of vitriol poured over
the phone to her. It then turned out that the 3 people were going to
prosecute her! Meanwhile the gardai claimed they never met her in hospital and denied all the facts that had occurred. It dawned on her that in
fact the 3 people and the gardai had a close relationship and which she
feels now she can prove. Meanwhile she managed to get her medical
records under the Freedom of Information Act and in there the doctor
had recorded the gardai's visit while she was in hospital. In any case
when the trial came around she found that she was convicted because
of the way that the gardai were able to withhold evidence from the case.
Her conviction was also smoothed along its way by a powerful amount
of slander that was directed at her mainly by the judge who accused her
of being a drug addict and a martial arts expert which was completely
untrue. I think she said as well that this was widely reported in the local
media destroying her reputation. In her own words she referred to this
as being painted as 'mad, bad and dangerous to know'. (Modesty for-
bids further comment!) She also suffers continual harassment which
forced her to move house etc.

Susan Grey of Donegal.

8 years ago her husband had been killed in a car accident on Boxing
Night and subsequently to that "the agony the guards have put me
through is unbelievable". I think this is the case that Eamonn McCann
refers to in this quote:

> "'It was then I realised that this man [the Superinten-
> dent] wasn't here to help me," Susan says.
> "But he wanted to find something damaging or intimi-
> dating, to keep me quiet." She suspects senior guards
> involved in the case were in a close relationship with an
> insurance company.'

Eamonn McCann further notes that:

> "It would resonate right across society. There is a wide-
> spread understanding that the cases which have come
> to light don't represent a deviation from the norm, a dis-
> tortion of the way things generally are done. They are
> typical of the way society works."[52]

Mary Kelly

Famous nurse not beloved of war mongering neocons! She described that in fact she had a long 5 year struggle while living in Donegal trying to retain access to her child from totally false charges pursued by the Health Board there. She has some interesting things to say about her own court cases. Her legal team abandoned her on the the steps of the court and after the case was adjourned her main task was simply to get her file back from her solicitor. When she asked for it from him he promptly told her he would shoot her. These facts didn't disturb the Law Society when she complained about it and in fact she now feels they are only interested in protecting the lawyers. Anyway when she eventually got the files back after 14 months she discovered numerous documents missing and some forged. Its her experience that the government does not have much power in Ireland, rather the gardai and the media are the big elements.[53] She doesn't feel that an Ombudsman would make much difference since in her opinion the state is so corrupt that they would handle an ombudsman somehow.

A Teacher (I think a Mrs Farrell)
Her story starts when she, and another person, were arrested by gardai at the time of the Punchestown Races. There they were badly assaulted. They managed to interest Joe Higgins in their plight and she feels that it was the threat of bad publicity that his involvement could generate which caused to gardai to take their next step. They accused these 2 people of assaulting the gardai. (Obviously this tactic is a kind of early slander where most people's impressions of an event are formed by the first story they hear and in this case its a lurid one of 'hooligans' etc assaulting hard working gardai. Its hard for people later to get across their 'conspiracy theory' that the opposite had occurred.) They decided to try and fight the case anyway and had to remortgage their home to pay the legal fees. Unfortunately to their amazement the state was able to call on 11 gardai and 2 other witnesses to this mythical assault. Their only witness was a doctor who in testifying to their injuries received in garda custody found himself insulted by the judge. Her experience is sadly that the "vast majority of them [gardai] are rotten to the core" and that there is a widespread "culture of cover up".

A former activist talking about his experiences in the Dublin anti drugs movement of the 80s and 90s.
Obviously this movement started with a group of people very frustrated with the garda response to the huge drug epidemic in Dublin. He didn't get time to describe the history of this movement in detail but basically he said it was crushed ruthlessly by the gardai. The main tactic they used was fabricated evidence against the activists. I believe he said that some people are still in jail on this bogus evidence. They also charged the children of the campaigners to put pressure on the parents. Although he didn't say this presumably the gardai were also careful to

slander the movement in the public eye as being just a front for paramilitaries which it seems they were not. What this activist really wanted to point out though was that while the gardai acted with such haste against this movement they didn't seem to be able to catch drug dealers who were openly selling their wares in broad daylight within a few yards of police stations. It may be that he has figured out this mystery when he pointed out that one of the gardai involved in the McBrearty case is well known in Dublin as being "as much a drug dealer as a guard".[54]

Eugene from Castlerea
He has been fighting a long case against the gardai who were trying to frame him in a complicated story involving guns and ammunition. It apparently derives from a number of people trying to seize his lands.[55] He has found that his only defence is a video camera that has recorded much valuable evidence and he advised everybody else to invest in one.

Owen Smith from Co.Monaghan
In 1991 he was the Vice Chair of Monaghan Co. Council and on the day that Margaret Thatcher resigned he was celebrating the event in his pub along with many people representing the 'cream' of Monaghan society when he was arrested by gardai. He told everybody as he was being arrested, and during his detention, that he did not intend making any written or verbal admissions which I must say is very believable in a Sinn Fein activist being arrested in the 90s. Yet despite this he was sure enough subsequently charged, in great publicity, with an IRA attack the main evidence against him being verbal and written admissions supposedly made in custody. He managed to avoid being convicted only because he had no less than 27 witnesses testifying to him being elsewhere at the time. To draw attention to his plight at the time he wrote to all the various bodies and never got any reply. Many speakers noted that Sinn Fein are going to start highlighting many long standing garda practices that they feel the public should know more about.

Brian McDonnell
A psychiatric nurse, he was trying to investigate money laundering and theft of possessions from patients in his care as a result of which his superiors started to raise problems with his performance to get him sacked. In his opinion the practice of stealing land etc from patients and stealing from their small allowances is pretty widespread. One of his patient's bank accounts actually rose in value in suspicious circumstances which caused him to suspect money laundering. For his pains he was known as an "effing loose cannon" and victimised at work.

Frank Shortt
Of course he was jailed for two and half years while in his 60s by the

gardai and for which he has subsequently been awarded a miscarriage of justice certificate by the Court of Criminal Appeal.[56] Incredibly despite the high profile nature of his case and all that he has already gone through he finds that he is still under crushing harassment from the gardai. The knowledge that this is continuing to happen is clearly hitting him very hard and his voice was breaking as he describes his astonishment at their arrogance. In new court proceedings he now finds garda after garda trooping in and he says perjuring themselves one after another. It is his experiences of many of his local gardai that they are "serial perjurers". He cannot say much about his own new case because of the sub iudice rule which he now feels is just used to gag him.

James Smith and Joe Doherty
They have spent 20 years trying to highlight corruption in Ireland and for their pains they (or at least one of them) were served with some kind of lifelong legal injunction preventing them pursuing the cases they were dealing with. (I know that will sound bizarre to some people but the fact is that many people had stories to tell about injunctions they had received, where not only the court proceedings were held in secret, but even the fact that they had been served with far reaching injunctions like this was also something they were legally forbidden to inform people about. Its obviously no surprise then that few people are aware of that practice.) Anyway they found that the legal profession is "so rotten its unbelievable". Meanwhile the garda were slandering them as being members of the IRA. Numerous people approached them talking about being battered by the gardai and also about the very corrupt banks and even the land registry. Its their experience that the high up gardai are all corrupt.[57]

Donal O'Siochain from Kerry.
He has been helping many Irish people caught up with the gardai and the legal system and has emerged as quite an expert on the Irish justice (or he might say injustice) system. He has also seen the kind of isolation that so many victims are going through and hence he is very keen on seeing a national movement begin which might bring a bit of much needed solidarity. He gave as an example the case of two people who picket Abbeyfeale police station every two weeks to try to highlight what they are going through at the hands of the gardai, and this kind of lonely struggle is what he feels should be replaced by a vibrant national organisation. He clearly has a font of anecdotes about the many senior corrupt judges including those whose name the public would readily recognise. He related particularly the story of a joyrider killed unlawfully by the gardai in Cork. They were able to cover up that case only by systematic perjury by up to 60 gardai and by jailing witnesses on false charges in order to "bury them inside the justice system".

Peter Preston from Dublin
He has been in a long struggle trying to get justice for his daughter who was assaulted by having a glass pushed into her face in a private lounge pub in Dublin. The upshot is that he feels he can prove through court transcripts that there was a conspiracy in this case involving two police stations and a High Court judge. In trying to get action he has unfortunately had to even go on hunger strike outside the Dail. In any case he gave this evidence to some senior members of the Labour Party in the hope they would pursue it but found out that they weren't really interested and he even states that some documents were changed and some missing when he got them back. He does not absolve these senior TDs from suspicion of being involved in this tampering. His saga of course involves the usual threats and intimidation that are always made against people caught up in these cases.

Finian Fallon from Dublin
This case highlights that even where the gardai are the victims people should still be wary of following the media's interpretation of events. Finian is the son of Garda Richard Fallon who is often given as the first garda victim of the troubles. He was gunned down by members of Saor Eire when he tried to stop a bank robbery in Arran Quay in Dublin in 1970. It is Finian's view now that in fact the gun used in the attack was imported by the state and paid for out of garda funds. He is even quoted in a newspaper article as saying that one of the killers escaped in a Cabinet Minister's car.[58] He talks about "physical and psychological violence" perpetuated by the state.

Ciaran Donnelly from Co.Kildare
It all started for him when his young child was made homeless during a family law case and he is determined to bring to book the people who did that. So he has been involved in this family law case since 1997 and he has been amazed at the practices of the Irish justice system. For example after painstakingly trying to piece together the history of some decisions he found that some were written up by the court clerk or judge's secretary rather than by the judge who was ill and who's signature was therefore forged. His persistence brought down upon him the usual harassment, he is now stopped regularly by the gardai, he has received threatening phone calls that his son will be hurt if he doesn't back down, and the upshot is that at times he has been too terrified to go outside his front door never mind speak publicly about his case. He also points out the practical realities of the family courts. For example the legal aid centres are supposed to aid those who cannot pay for their legal costs but he discovered in his case that a senior executive of the legal aid board had actually contacted all the centres in order to ensure that they wouldn't assist in bringing the type of legal challenge that he was planning to take. He found he had no choice but to try and repre-

sent himself only to find that you can be greeted by open laughter and sniggering when you try to do that in the family (in camera) courts. When he tried to contact one politician about his case he was actually threatened with an injunction if he didn't stop contacting him.

Jim Gallagher from Dunloe Co.Donegal
In 1980 his brother was arrested and taken to Letterkenny Garda station where he was beaten up for two solid days and nights. More harassment came from the Special Branch especially since 1996. He has found that this constant harassment from the gardai gets worse any time they try and bring a complaint. He has tried to tackle this legally but generally he has found that no solicitor is prepared to take it up.

Catherine the aunt of Tim McGarry who was found decapitated in the training centre of Mountjoy Jail.
Her nephew was supposed to have committed suicide but she cannot get any satisfactory answers about what happened to him from anybody. Since 1992 she has been contacting the President, the gardai, TD's etc and never got any real answer from any of them. In fact she now says that she has "absolutely no hope of finding out what happened to my nephew."

Jim Gallagher Donegal [59]
His view of Ireland's policing and judicial system were completely shattered when his farm was raided in March of 1997 by the gardai supposedly looking for explosives. His family were held prisoners by the gardai for 5 days and its the experiences of this physical and psychological abuse that the family suffered during that time that has started his family on yet another long and generally fruitless search for justice. About the only bright spot was when Jim Higgins raised his case in the Dail and for which he is very grateful. He also talks about the psychological trauma suffered by his family especially at the beginning, when his family were "an emotional wreck" and before the McBrearty case allowed people to come forward because only then did anybody believe or accept these cases of state harassment. In fact he talks about the whole mindset and education of the Irish people as ill fitting them to cope with this reality. He said that too many people, including himself, were brought up with a "legacy of asking no questions of the gardai." In fact he feels now that people have "no idea whats going on in the background" in Ireland. "Whats called a democracy and [the image of] 'lovely Ireland'" in fact hides "a cesspit of corruption". He says that if people only knew what his family and the McBrearty families have had to go through they would realise that "its rotten right through". In fact in trying to get answers he has begun to wonder who actually runs the country and feels a lot of the institutions are actually "such a sham". But his family have been living in his locality for 300 years and they are not go-

ing away any time soon and not till they get answers to these questions.

Pat Culhane
He has had a long struggle dealing with the state arising, I think, from the famous case in the Shannon Estuary where a number of families and livestock suffered serious illnesses arising, in all probability, from air pollution caused by some large local industrial plants. Anyhow his dealings with various state bodies has led him to the conclusion that Ireland is an "elected dictatorship of crooks".
The state agencies for example skewed the environmental surveys by deliberately selecting unusual control areas to compare the data with. Unfortunately the legal profession he found to be just as corrupt and he ended up on a hunger strike outside Blackhall Place. They are "rotten to the core" and are mostly "freemasons".[60] He particularly detected collusion between a solicitor and an insurance company. He also feels that they would be able to get around small changes like the provision of an Ombudsman.

Padraig Reilly of Belmullet Co Mayo, a psychiatric nurse.
On the 7 September 1992 he was assisting with a psychiatric patient who was held in the custody of the gardai. The patient died because he was given 2 drugs which were contraindicated for this patient. It appears that the gardai had deliberately given him these drugs because Padraig publicly at the meeting accused them of (quote) "murder". This has started him on the usual long struggle against the gardai and during which he was falsely imprisoned, the local community were shown leaked garda documents (falsely) accusing him of IRA membership in order to slander him etc etc. He is hoping his case will come up now in the High Court (I think) in December this year. His family are actually island people from Iniskea and he feels strongly that those communities are very fortunate to be free of a garda presence.

Some people also feel that a garda murder may have occurred in the case of Shaun Duffy who was found dead near Dunloe in Donegal earlier this year. It has been reported in the local media in Donegal that in fact two gardai have been called into questioning with respect to this murder. The Phoenix is so far as I know the only national media outlet to mention this case although it was also mentioned for a time on indymedia.[61] Otherwise the Irish media has reverted to its traditional silence when it comes to garda misdeeds. The point about the media here I think can be seen clearly when you consider that Duffy's murder occurred around the same time as the McCartney murder in Belfast. Both cases have of course not come to trial, and as such hard evidence can be hard to come by, but the media is only too anxious to speculate about who killed McCartney while as I say the informed views of the local people in Donegal in their opinion as to what happened to Duffy are not considered worthy of comment. It is particularly said that Duffy tried to get some incriminating information on senior gardai in order to protect himself from the gardai taking cases against him. The Phoenix reported that he had told friends shortly before he died that he had information on the gardai which was much more damaging than the McBrearty case. Rumours circulating locally allege that he even had incriminating photographs of a high ranking local garda.

Apart from that its been a great summer...[62]

Footnotes

1. http://www.indymedia.ie/newswire.php?story_id=71227. Many thanks to R.isible for transcribing this and "Citizen" for recording it.

2. http://debates.oireachtas.ie/DDebate.aspx?
F=DAL20050617.xml&Node=281.
Here is a sample of this from that report which was no doubt widely distributed and known, unlike the hard facts which would point to an opposite conclusion: "Frank McBrearty snr is a forceful individual who likes his own way.

"He is a manipulative person who has tried to manipulate the initial investigation with Billy Flynn, and it is also believed that he tried to manipulate the conduct and direction of the present investigation by other means."

Conroy's report went on: "It is evident from the behaviour of Mr Flynn that he was endeavouring to manipulate the garda investigation to the purpose of his employer.

"The initial investigation was disrupted by the behaviour of the private investigator, Billy Flynn, who re-visited witnesses who had given statements to the gardai and tried to get them to change their evidence.

"Those with evidence which could be interpreted as casting suspicion in the direction of the McBrearty family were particular targets for Billy Flynn.

"In some cases, inducements to alter statements were offered and refused." (from http://archives.tcm.ie/businesspost/2005/07/24/story6654.asp)

3. The Dublin meeting op cit.

4. http://indymedia.ie/newswire.php?story_id=70553 .

5. http://breakingnews.iol.ie/news/iestory.asp?
j=34385286606&p=34385z86793&n=34385286852 .

6. See Chapter 3 footnote 31.

7. Village magazine 16-22 Sept 2005 p.9 .To his credit Vincent Browne has championed this case both on his radio show and in repeated editions of this magazine.

8. http://www.sluggerotoole.com/archives/2005/06/irish_corruptio.php. See also the Vincent Browne Show 22 June 2005 RTE Radio 1.

9. The Village op cit.

10. I'm pretty sure I read this in the Irish Independent but I cannot find the reference now.

11. By Badman at http://www.indymedia.ie/newswire.php?story_id=5102 .

12. http://www.indymedia.ie/newswire.php?story_id=5311 .

13. This website details a lot of the media coverage of the case: http://www.irishcorruption.com/?cat=18 .

14. http://breaking.tcm.ie/2005/09/21/story221859.html and see the McBrearty video op cit.

15. http://web.archive.org/web/20031005165716/http://www.sbpost.ie/web/Home/Document+View+Business/did-489357560-pageUrl--2FBusiness-2FNews-Features-2FAll-New-Features.asp The article is By Barry O' Kelly and here are some quotes from it:
"She claimed Sergeant White talked about taking her child off her and putting him into care, and that she would do seven years in jail if she didn't tell him what happened that night.
...
She alleged she was shown photographs of Richard Barron's dead body and offered a detailed description of them. She said the photographs were shoved into her face and the officers began to switch the lights on and off.
Sergeant White was calling her Satan and the devil and said she would never see her father in heaven and that she would go to hell for what she was doing.
...
The tribunal lawyer said McConnell alleged Sergeant White said her husband was having an affair. She was made bless herself and pray to her dead father. Sergeant White allegedly then turned to her and asked her what her father had said and she replied he had told her she was telling the truth.
...
McConnell's solicitors say that as a result of her ordeal, she was admitted to St Conal's Hospital for psychiatric treatment.

McConnell is still deeply traumatised and has been unable to work ever since." Sergeant White claims that any role he had in this was entirely at the direction of his senior garda superiors which in all probability is true.

16 Karen McGlinchey, *Charades: Adrienne McGlinchey and the Donegal Gardai* (Dublin, 2005), p.267.
Karen has commented on this "strategy of isolation" tactic in an earlier article of mine at http://www.indymedia.ie/newswire.php?story_id=69044 and I would just like to thank her for her kind words and to take her correction as re-

gards her sister's finances. I think she has taken the right course too in writing a good book which I hope is an example that will be widely copied. Hopefully some day the people of Ireland will really rise up and stop this kind of thing from happening to her family and all the other families which we now know about.

17. He has recently died having been in a coma for 3 months, see Ireland on Sunday Sept 18 2005 p.34 article by Ken Foxe. There it is described how the family are getting the usual runaround e.g. being denied access to any of the evidence which is being withheld from them by the gardai, also the cell he was held in was renovated the day after he left it removing the wall fixture that he was supposed to have hung himself from. It is now being said locally that the family is being harassed by the gardai and that a witness to the assault on Terence has been charged with assault to silence him. (The wall fixture was the rectangular plaque surrounding a panic button, this is from an interview by Eamonn Dunphy with the family's solicitor Yvonne Banbury on Newstalk 105 Oct 31 2005 "The Best of the Breakfast Show" see also http://www.indymedia.ie/newswire.php?story_id=72587&condense_comments=false#comment126450) .There is also the case of John Maloney (http://www.unison.ie/irish_independent/stories.php3?ca=9&si=968880&issue_id=9157 and http://www.unison.ie/irish_independent/stories.php3?ca=9&si=1141837&issue_id=10557) which is very much part of the same pattern, this time involving Rathfarnham garda station.

18. http://www.unison.ie/irish_independent/stories.php3?ca=9&si=1329452&issue_id=12013.

19. http://www.unison.ie/irish_independent/stories.php3?ca=9&si=1338794&issue_id=12075 Sunday Independent Feb 13 2005 .

20. http://www.indymedia.ie/newswire.php?id=48598 .

21. Vincent Browne Show as above 22 June 2005 RTE Radio 1.

22. This good documentary was produced by Scun Scan of the Rathcairn Gaeltacht in Co. Meath and was also broadcast on TG4 on Feb 21 2004.

23. http://www.indymedia.ie/newswire.php?story_id=70224 .

24. Mentioning the defence claim that Marie Farrell had told Bailey that she herself was put under duress by the gardai to make a false statement http://www.unison.ie/irish_independent/stories.php3?ca=9&si=1095581&issue_id=10185. This is elaborated on in another article at the time, here it is just mentioned at the end in passing. See also http://www.sbpost.ie/web/DocumentView/did-84313623-pageUrl--2FMisc-2FEzine.asp .

25. http://www.indymedia.ie/newswire.php?story_id=66736 .

26. http://archives.tcm.ie/businesspost/2003/12/21/story80610139.asp .

27. http://www.indymedia.ie/newswire.php?story_id=66736 .

28. The earlier article on indymedia:http://www.indymedia.ie/newswire.php?
story_id=68471, for the later quote from the local person which refers to a TV3
interview by Maria Farrell: http://www.indymedia.ie/newswire.php?
story_id=72449. The gardai reference is from
http://www.unison.ie/irish_independent/stories.php3?
ca=9&si=1488012&issue_id=13138 and the blackmail allegations are
mentioned at http://unison.ie/irish_independent/stories.php3?
ca=9&si=1489102&issue_id=13145. From Village Magazine:
http://www.villagemagazine.ie/article.asp?sid=1&sud=10&aid=628 .

29. Ireland on Sunday October 16 2005 p12 and it is from that article that I got
the quotations. The 'exchange of gunfire' quote is from
http://www.breakingnews.ie/2005/05/26/story204324.html. The Ronan
McLoghlin reference is from
http://archives.tcm.ie/irishexaminer/2000/04/10/current/i_text.htm and as you
can see it seems remarkably similar circumstances:
"Solicitor James MacGuill, who is acting for the MacLoughlain family, has
commenced legal actions for wrongful death against the State on behalf of the
family. He said they will argue that Rónán MacLoughlain was unarmed and
was attempting to flee the scene of the crime when shot.
He says the ERU had the men under surveillance and could have, and should
have, in the interest of public safety, the safety of garda members and the men
under surveillance, arrested the gang before they commenced the robbery.
An Amnesty International report on the killings said: "Rónán MacLochlain
was killed by officers of the Garda Síochána on May 1, 1998, in Co Wicklow
in disputed circumstances. Amnesty International is disturbed that the police issued contradictory, and indeed incorrect, statements shortly after the killing; in
particular, it was stated that Rónán MacLochlain had been shot in a shoot out
when in fact only police officers fired their guns."

30. For the allegations against the gardai made by Nevin:
http://archives.tcm.ie/businesspost/2000/10/08/story823582138.asp
http://www.sbpost.ie/web/DocumentView/did-875549546-pageUrl--2FThe-
Newspaper-2FSundays-Paper-2FNews-2FIreland-2FAll-Ireland.asp and the
quote is from: http://www.ireland.com/newspaper/special/2000/obuachalla/.
This link refers to the fact that it was both she and her husband that were
making the complaints: http://www.unison.ie/new_ross_standard/stories.php3?
ca=34&si=188338&issue_id=2021. The later court case involving Garda
Murphy: http://www.unison.ie/wicklow_people/stories.php3?

ca=34&si=618848&issue_id=6190. The garda lost the case in the district court, won it on appeal to the High Court, but the state has appealed that decision to the Supreme Court. John Lonergan's intervention was mentioned in the media at the time and it is alluded to (indirectly) at this site: http://www.ireland.com/newspaper/ireland/2000/0706/archive.00070600013.ht ml .

31. The dictatorship quote is from http://www.finnachta.com/Hotmail17Oct2004/LongWalkToFreedom.htm, see also http://web.archive.org/web/20040623174433/http://newswire.indymedia.org/en /newswire/2004/03/801052.shtml and http://www.finnachta.com/PoliceLetter31March2004.htm. The bribe attempt mentioned in the Dail: http://www.gov.ie/debates-03/1Jul/Sect4.htm. The legal case is from: http://www.constitutionofireland.com/EuropeanCommunityAndOtherLeaders/ Email.htm where he points out:
"Please also note that the criminal offense I am being charged with is for shouting at a Galway County Council enforcement-officer, AFTER, and for no good reason that I know of, he unconditionally refused to look at an unlawful sewage discharge: which was within yards of where he was standing at the time...
...I would also like to take this opportunity to point out that the very long and ongoing abusive legal nightmare I am being subjected to..."

32. Sunday Independent July 3 2005 http://www.unison.ie/irish_independent/stories.php3? ca=36&si=1427193&issue_id=12701. From the article, which is by Jim Cusack and titled "A decade-long quest for justice after a childhood of unimaginable horror":
"Her most regular client, she says, was a garda who paid a pound or two to have sex with her in her grandmother's house on a regular basis in the years around 1974-1975. She says she was also abused by another garda who did not have intercourse with her.
Her quest for justice has led her on a seemingly interminable round of let-ter-writing and petitioning of the Taoiseach, Ministers for Justice, Garda Com-missioners, politicians and official bodies dealing with abuse. The quest, she wrote after eight years of pleading, was "killing" her. She had met what she be-lieves was a wall of official indifference and incompetence.
...
The night that she and her mother walked into Dun Laoghaire, Niamh says they met and spoke to two gardai who knew her mother and family. She says it is incredible that the gardai had not noted that her mother was carrying a shop-ping bag similar to the bag in which the body of a baby was found the follow-ing day. She asks to this day why the Garda investigation of 1973 had not im-mediately centred on her family and on her. She was never medically examined

176

and neither of her parents arrested.

...

Niamh says she was told by gardai that half of the original file into the murder of her daughter disappeared. No blood or tissue samples were kept and she has never received an adequate explanation for this.

...

Niamh has become deeply exasperated by what she perceives as a failure to gather evidence. She has complained to Ministers for Justice, the Taoiseach and Garda Commissioner's office that it was no surprise there has been no prosecution if the files being sent to DPP contain insufficient evidence.

Disturbingly, Niamh has complained that throughout the process of the "investigation" of her father, she gained the impression that one garda was openly showing signs of friendliness to her father.

Privately, some gardai are known to have expressed skepticism about aspects of Niamh's story. At least one senior figure is known to have had doubts about her story, pointing to the fact that certain therapy used to treat abuse victims has resulted in 'false memories' emerging."

33. Evening Herald Monday of July 4th 2005.

34 http://www.unison.ie/irish_independent/stories.php3?
ca=36&si=1438454&issue_id=12779 "A beautiful life lost to utter hell" some quotes from the article which was written by Brighid McLaughlin:
"She was increasingly convinced that gardai and some local people had covered up the abuse.

...

The uncle who abused him was a convicted paedophile sent home from the UK on licence and allowed to live freely in the community of Dalkey. He was just one of a known group of paedophiles living there.

...

"I remember the parents were drinking in the town hall the night that Martin hung himself in the house. The father, being the caretaker, had several sets of keys for the town hall, as had his friends. God knows what went on there. One source has told me that when Niamh [a pseudonym for Cynthia Owen] made allegations to the gardai in 1995, her father was seen taking two 'small friends' of the family to the Town Hall every Saturday morning."

...

Theresa's friends have lost faith in the gardai and the DPP who rejected Niamh's case for the fifth time, citing "the length of time and the difficulty of securing a conviction as a result". The DPP decided not to prosecute Niamh and Theresa's parents either for murder or sex abuse. Other reasons included "the lack of independent evidence and any admission of guilt".

I, like many others, find it incredible that no prosecution of any nature had

been deemed appropriate.
...

I know Niamh personally, I know that she has never had regression therapy and has willingly handed over her medical notes to gardai. I know that gardai are also aware that she has never had regression therapy and I know that the recent coverage in the media, reporting that she has had regression therapy, is a huge effort to discredit her. It is also a huge lie. ...The gardai need to do a bit of regression therapy and get their facts right.
...

It is a known fact that some members of the gardai in Dalkey were friends of Peter Murphy, who had told them years previously that Theresa and Niamh were mad. They believed him and liked him. They drank with him in the Queen's bar and the town hall several times a week for years. These victims have not received justice."

In 2002 Jimmy Guerin wrote about a paedophile ring in Blanchardstown where "both social workers and parents of those who have been abused have constantly complained about garda inaction on this case."
(Sunday Independent Dec 8 2002
http://www.unison.ie/irish_independent/stories.php3?
ca=9&si=885680&issue_id=8471 .)

Another article by Jimmy Guerin in the same paper (28 April 2002) reported that a FG councillor Garry O'Halloran resigned from the party because he was fed up at the inaction in investigating an alleged "paedophile ring" in the Kilkenny/Carlow area. He also circulated the information to other political parties but got nowhere, he stated that:
"I was a member of the South Eastern Health Board for a number of years and raised the issues referred to in Deputy Hogan's statement [to the Dail on the paedophile ring] on a monthly basis. However, these allegations were denied every time.

We were always assured there was no basis to the allegations and the affairs of the institutions mentioned were in order. When I brought this to the attention of my colleagues at a Health Board meeting, Deputy Hogan said: 'Kilkenny's good name should not be dragged through the mire by allegations which are not substantiated.'

"The then-chairman of the board, Cllr Tom Ambrose,[of FF] added: 'These allegations are very hurtful to the vast majority of people in the area to which you refer, and neither I nor your board colleagues are prepared to listen to them.'"
(http://www.unison.ie/irish_independent/stories.php3?ca=9&si=741739&issue_id=7309).

The Phoenix refers to this on Oct 21 2005 p.3:

"During the period [c.1995-1997, Garry] O'Halloran was the subject of loud, abusive denunciation at a series of SEHB meetings by politicians, officials and doctors alike because he kept raising the issue of clerical child abuse in the diocese...OHalloran received support from just one member, Labour Councillor, Michael Meaney, in this two year period from 1995 to 1997."

The article goes on to say that he was helped by Billy Mooney, Sean Clooney and also Veronica Guerin. As regards the government, it states that he was treated with disrespect by Michael Noonan as Minister for Health and dismissed as 'irresponsible' by the junior Minister Austin Currie. In the end:

"O'Halloran has since left FG in disgust, citing its refusal to stand up to abuse of various kinds."

35. http://www.gaiaguys.net/vic.introduction.htm and from The Sun-Herald June 1 2003
http://www.prisonplanet.com/anatomy_of_a_political_smear.html .

36. See James M.Rothstein, Ret. NYCPD Detective "Confidential Report on Organized Pedophilia and the Criminal Exploitation of Children" at
http://www.johnnygosch.com/,
http://www.ftrbooks.net/psych/cia_mind_control/franklin.htm and
http://www.rense.com/general68/whatthen.htm and
http://www.raven1.net/pedexample.htm .

37. http://news.bbc.co.uk/1/hi/programmes/correspondent_europe/1962244.stm and http://observer.guardian.co.uk/review/story/0,6903,710090,00.html .

38.
http://www.prisonplanet.com/tales_of_orgies_and_murder_rock_france.html,
http://www.prisonplanet.com/toulouse_officials_ordered_murder_says_serial_killer.html and
http://www.crimelibrary.com/serial_killers/predators/auxerre/3.html?sect=2 .

39.
http://www.boston.com/news/world/articles/2004/01/10/sex_scandal_divides_c
onservative_allies_in_chiles_congress/ .

40. http://archive.salon.com/health/sex/urge/world/2000/04/19/latvia/print.html
.

41. http://www.wsws.org/articles/2004/jan2004/port-j20.shtml and
http://www.dailymail.co.uk/pages/live/articles/news/news.html?
in_article_id=488654&in_page_id=1770, see also this on Montenegro:
http://www.prisonplanet.com/government_officials_in_sex_trafficking_ring_ar
rested.html .

42. http://groups.google.com/group/uk.politics.misc/msg/2553eaffedd873ab?

and the amazing if it were true:
http://www.offmsg.connectfree.co.uk/OffBEAT/britton.htm. At
http://pebpr.blogspot.com/ there is a reference to a 'Scallywag' and Guardian
(October 15th, 1997) article on shocking revalations at the North Wales Child
Abuse Tribunal .

43. http://unison.ie/irish_independent/frontpagepdfs/2002/7971.pdf .
It might also be relevant to note that Colin Wallace stated at the above
mentioned Dublin meeting that Kincora was run as a vice ring by the same
intelligence unit behind the Dublin and Monagahan bombings with the purpose
being to blackmail politicians, civil servants etc. He noted that the same person
who prosecuted him on false charges, Sir George Terry Chief Constable of
Sussex, was also asked to investigate the Kincora claims.
For Kincora see http://www.missingpersons-ireland.freepress-
freespeech.com/archive-kincorascandal.htm and
http://www.indymedia.ie/newswire.php?
story_id=20885&condense_comments=false#comment133662 .

44. http://en.wikipedia.org/wiki/Michael_McDowell and
http://www.examiner.ie/pport/web/ireland/Full_Story/did-
sg3fP9rRXRqnc.asp .

45. http://216.239.59.104/search?
q=cache:Sa5n4KT7KnoJ:home.eircom.net/content/irelandcom/topstories/2508
853%3Fview%3DPrinter+&hl=en
 and http://www.rte.ie/news/2004/0209/mcGrealm.html .

46.
http://www.courts.ie/judgments.nsf/bce24a8184816f1580256ef30048ca50/67a
96b8ced1d7f3980256fbf004c496d?OpenDocument .

47. http://archives.tcm.ie/irishexaminer/2005/06/01/story124928085.asp
Tom Gilmartin particularly gave details of a meeting in Leinster House that involved nearly all the senior figures in Fianna Fail and after which he claims
that he was effectively asked for an extortion payment of 5 million pounds.
Most of the politicians said to have been at the meeting had a bad case of am-
nesia about it when quizzed by the Flood tribunal but Mary O'Rourke has now
largely confirmed Gilmartin's account albeit she, and maybe some of the other
politicians,   did   not   know   about   the   extortion   demand.
(http://home.eircom.net/content/unison/national/2963174?view=Eircomnet)
Liam Lawlor was obviously his main nemesis. Incidentally Lawlor was a
senior Irish politician on the international stage since he had been, since the
70s, a member of the Trilateral Commission
(http://www.namebase.org/xlat/Liam-Lawlor.html) alongwith luminaries like
Garret Fitzgerald (http://www.apfn.net/TC3.htm), Mary Robinson and Michael
O'Kennedy (both listed for 1975 at

http://users.cyberone.com.au/myers/huntington.html).
This is an example of Tom Gilmartin's experiences of the Irish Justice system which is remarkably similar to what the Donegal and other families are saying:
"Q 258   If you didn't trust Allied Irish Banks, if you didn't trust Mr. O'-Callaghan, if you didn't trust Mr. O'Callaghan's solicitor Mr. Deane, why not write into the Law Society and complain about Mr. Deane being involved in the falsification of an agreement?
A   Well, as I seen it, I'd get the same justice as I got in Cavan.
Q 259   Why not write into the Law Society?
A   Why would I write into the Law Society? What would they do for me.
Q 260   Did you not know that the Law Society –
A   It's well-known that the Law Society here – most of the complaints that I've heard about being written into the Law Society are never seen to or taken care of. That would be a waste of time, in my opinion.
Q 261   Well, are you saying you considered the possibility of making a complaint to the Law Society?
A   No, I never thought of the Law Society until you mentioned it. They are not the people – I have made complaints to numerous people and all that but I got no satisfaction.
Q 262   Why didn't you complain to the Gardai?
A   Well, I did go to the Gardai and I was told "f*** off" back to England".
Q 263   Who told you that?
A   A man claiming to be a Mr. Garda Burns, and he was quoting back to me the statement I'd made to Mr. Sreenan.
Q 264   Surely now, Mr. Gilmartin, that's a grotesque distortion of the facts?
A   That is a fact, a fact, an absolute fact, and I'm under oath. I don't take an oath lightly.
...
Q 270   And did you not think that he [a Chief Superintendent Sreenan] would be legitimately interested in finding out that a member or somebody purporting to be a member of An Garda Siochana had telephoned you up, after his first telephone conversation with you to threaten you and had apparently you say been privy to what you told him?
A   I couldn't see the point.
Q 271   What do you mean you couldn't see the point?
A   I couldn't see the point.
Q 272   You were the one who made complaints about payments to politicians –
A   I had been in court. I had been unjustly robbed in Cavan. I had a Judge Sheehy threaten to do me for contempt if I even attempted to defend myself.
Q 273   And you didn't tell Chief Superintendent Sreenan about any of this.
A   And then, to add to that, he had – he made comments which were totally derogatory and outside of the court would have been libellous. It was printed in the Cavan paper, which Mr. Maguire here pointed out, so why would I trust anybody in this country."
(http://www.flood-tribunal.ie/images/SITECONTENT_257.pdf)

48. You can also see a long report in the Village 9-15 Sept 2005 p.18. Here is a short report on another meeting organised by Frank McBrearty et alios at the Mansion House Dublin 20 Nov 2005:

Frank McBrearty

Condemned "crime correspondents who try to brainwash people every week" with their hyping of gangland and other crimes. As he sees it they are just basically working for the garda press office. He also outlined that most of the posters they tried to put up to advertise the meeting were immediately pulled down by Dublin city council. As well as this in the regular media there was an organised campaign to mislead people into thinking the meeting had been cancelled. He was pleased at the attendance therefore in the light of this campaign.

Eamonn McCann

He started by relating a story about his long time friend Nicky Kelly. He said that as luck would have it during the 80s he was for a time political correspondent of the Sunday World and when invited to dinner with the then Tanaiste Michael O'Leary he decided to challenge him on the question of Nicky Kelly. The only reply he got though was that the garda commissioner had assured him that Kelly was guilty and after all, as O'Leary explained, you "don't question the word of a guard". But as Eamonn sees it it goes deeper than that. In practise "politicians are frightened of the guards because the guards know where the bodies are buried." As regards the anti-corruption campaign, he feels that political, financial and garda corruption are all mixed up together and its no good tackling it via individual cases. For example if you look to tribunals or public inquiries to solve your problem don't forget that they are run by the same judiciary that many are accusing of being corrupt. He wants a much broader political campaign and in fact he called for a slate of candidates that could be endorsed by this movement in time for the next election. The candidates could still be members of other parties, just affiliated to this movement in some way.

Sean Crowe TD

He explained that he comes from the real world and growing up in Dublin he knew the garda stations where you'd be routinely beaten up by the gardai even over small things like not having a lamp on a bicycle. But at the time "society said this didn't happen." Allegations were just dismissed claiming that "this was just the words of subversives or criminals. Many of the people who were beaten up in the garda stations ended up in institutions" and now we know what happened to them there. "If you want to see justice don't go to any of the courts in this country." He stated that when people take a case against the gardai it is routine for false charges to be served on the person making the claim and then they will offer to drop that charge if the claimant drops their (real) charge against the gardai. He himself was assaulted in a garda station by the heavy gang for putting up anti-EU posters. He personally experienced the physical and mental abuse that people suffer in garda stations. He stated that it was "not a handful of corrupt gardai" that was the problem rather it was "down

182

to a police force with unimpeded power" but now there was "a few cracks in the wall" of this corruption in the justice system.

Frank Connolly (The well known and highly respected journalist, has little cause to be thankful to the Minister for Justice in recent months.)
He is struck when he attends these meetings at the "vast number of people deeply hurt by agencies of the state...and the avalanche of allegations against the judiciary, the gardai etc.." His group, the Centre for Public Inquiry, is actually inundated with so many cases that he now realises that they simply don't have the resources to deal with them. Instead of talking further about the "so called Irish justice system" he outlined his history of digging up corruption in the planning system and highlighted the story of Tom Gilmartin. Gilmartin has alledged that his life was ruined by a combination of some powerful Irish businessmen, Ireland's largest bank, the UK inland revenue and, Connolly pointed out, there are even allegations about two Taoisigh and "a [sic!] serving Taoiseach".

Aisling Reidy of the Irish Council for Civil Liberties
She has highlighted the fact that over the course of the life of the ICCL the gardai and state agencies are actually getting more and more draconian powers despite all the evidence that has emerged since the Sallins case of the gardai abusing those powers. This she feels is because the majority of people still need to be persuaded that this abuse of power is the main problem. They in fact are heavily influenced by the media highlighting of things like gang warfare, which is what happens when the "government constantly plays the politics of fear". So to address this she feels its very important for people to build as broad an alliance as possible.

Osgur Breatnach
He "bears witness to torture...conspiracy to kidnap"...that was conducted in this state. He traces the origin of the heavy gang to Ned Garvey who was later discovered to have worked for British Intelligence. Garvey apparently recruited that group as a "systematic torture system". He was obviously arrested, on false charges, as part of a roundup of 40 people taken into custody as part of the Sallins Train robbery saga. Over 10 of those arrested were subsequently tortured and Osgur described the screams that he heard in the Bridewell before his turn came to be tortured. During his ordeal he contemplated hanging himself and eventually was driven to sign a false statement. This was done during the FG-Lab coalition and when they were succeeded by the incoming FF govt. Garvey was sacked but all the rest of the gardai involved were promoted by that govt. In any case the subsequent legal proceedings went on for a long time during which he and his family were constantly harassed and received intimidating phonecalls etc. He also found himself black listed so he couldn't get normal employment. The late Mary Reid was involved in trying to highlight his case incidentally and he would like to join with her family in pressing for a proper investigation into her death in Donegal. Eventually he had to settle out

of court under threat of financial ruin. So the outcome in fact was that tax pay-ers money was used to just cover it up, he never really got justice, the gardai were never held accountable for what they did to him and so he feels that histo-ry is repeating itself with all these new cases. It was inevitable it would only get worse if no justice was done then and "that is the relevance of the past to the present"."Deaths in custody have increased" and the situation has only con-tinued to deteriorate. He feels "the whole barrel" of the gardai is rotten not just a few bad apples. On an ominous note he found out in the course of the docu-mentary he narrated (on TG4) that the Department of Justice have "active files on 1 in 5 adult males" in this state.

Nicky Kelly (of the famous miscarriage of justice etc)
He feels there are "thousands and thousands of people.. citizens of this coun-try..who get no redress [only a] stone wall" when they seek justice. He has been "inundated by ordinary people" looking for his help in seeking justice. Unfortunately he feels that most of the politicians are looking for an easy life and "don't really care" about these cases. In fact he is very pessimistic about most of these cases ever getting justice in Ireland. He thinks they could only hope to get "justice under their [Dept. and Minister of Justice etc] conditions" which is not real justice at all. He doesn't think contacting councillors or TDs does much good. In fact, in his experience, you will "never ever get your issue dealt with" you will only find yourself in a "correspondence course". In a clearly very sincere and blunt speech he simply said "look at the nature of our country and people at the moment". Most of the politicians in Leinster House just perceive the people at this meeting as "cranks" and clearly it is going to be a long struggle if people hope to get justice.

Joe Higgins TD
Like so many indigent workers he finds himself on a payment plan as he tries to pay back his debts to Fingal Co. Council. He owes them 15,000 euro for 5 hours work put in by a barrister employed by the council when they successful-ly took legal action against him over the bin tax protests for which he was jailed. He made the point that there are large numbers of people out there that are completely unable to pay sums like that and that this makes constitutional rights a bit of a dead letter for a large swathe of the Irish population. There is also in practice no way that a TD can hold judges to account, since any criti-cism at all of judges are ruled out of order by the Cahoirleach in the Dail.

Dan Boyle TD
He talked about the difficulties of holding the system to account and he offered his services to help out a new independent movement that would challenge the corruption.

A former inter county ladies GAA player
She was sexually assaulted by a garda who was working as a coach of the local Ladies GAA club. She made a complaint to the Garda Complaints Board but

that got nowhere until another person made a similar complaint against the same person. This time the garda in question was tipped off and intimidated the potential witnesses and the victim. Now she finds herself constantly harassed, intimidated and ostracised in her local community while the garda has risen in the ranks of the GAA. It is, she feels, a complete and blatant coverup by gardai and the Ladies GAA.

Phillip Flood
He was beaten unconscious by the gardai and it was his efforts to get justice over that which has led to him being harassed by them."Taken into custody several times but never found guilty of anything." Nobody would help...solicitors ..politicians...even doctors and unfortunately he has been left mentally and physically damaged. As far as he is concerned 90% of the gardai and politicians are "all evil".

Eugene Bradley from Armagh
He has been living a life these last few years like a "James Bond movie". It has arisen from the actions of a corrupt solicitor who seems to be able to marshal the forces of the PSNI against him. He gave just one example of the way in which his phone is constantly cut off. As regards the anti-corruption campaign his message was "unite unite" and don't fall out with one another whatever happens. Meanwhile "he is working 24/7 to stay alive." He wished to point out to everybody at the meeting that he is clearly in good health (for the obvious reason that if he should not be alive in the near future that people would be skeptical of the explanation given).

John Clery
Speaking on behalf of a relative who was raped. His nephew and this relative get nothing but a litany of obscene verbal abuse from the gardai in Kilkenny when they try to get it investigated.

Kathleen Twomey
The mother of 8 children (and shows it in her unflappability and determination). She has been 13 years trying to get justice over a property dispute in Mallow. She is a professional florist and with her husband purchased a property in Mallow for, I think, 117,000 pounds in c.1990. She purchased the property with the help of a family solicitor. What she didn't realise was that this solicitor had been secretary of the company that owned the property before her. In any case various problems started to arise two years into paying off the loan they took out to purchase the property. The upshot is that she was deprived of the property for non payment of the loan despite the fact that at the time that happened the property was worth many times what was outstanding on the loan. This story descended into a long argument between a pressed-for-time Frank McBrearty and-a-determined-to-have-her-say Mrs Twomey.

On behalf of the late John Maloney junior

A friend of this person's family outlined his case. He had been arrested as part of a drugs search and taken to Rathfarnham garda station, I believe. No drugs were found but he was reported to have been held on an existing warrant over car insurance. He was found in a coma outside but near the garda station the next day and died 13 days later in hospital. The State pathologist stated that it was a drugs overdose but the hospital test done on him showed only minute traces of cocaine. The family feel that the statements given by the gardai to the inquest are very "choreographed" but they have run out of options in trying to get justice because don't have enough money to take any legal action. Meanwhile they now face "cruel vicious and organised harassment" from their local gardai. A relative had an arm broken over this and their house is raided regularly including twice this week as part of the so called crack down on gangs. Since the family have no hope of getting justice in the Irish courts, particularly because of the cost, this friend made the point that maybe the TD's on the panel might like to conduct some kind of inquiry into it so that somehow the family can get their case heard.

Larry Wheelock (brother of Terence)
He outlined how the cell where his brother was alleged to have committed 'suicide' was renovated immediately after the incident, effectively ruining it as a potential crime scene from the point of view of gathering evidence. He also stated that custody records have been doctored. Meanwhile (yet again) this family are also facing intimidation by the gardai.

Joe Mooney (on behalf of the Mulhall family of Dublin city)
Jimmy and the rest of this family were prominent anti-drugs campaigners and for this reason they have faced 10 years of constant harassment from the gardai. They were constantly stopped, strip searched etc (to look for drugs on a family that was campaigning against them). Jimmy was beaten up in garda stations ("unrecognisable when he came out") and incredibly his 10 year old son Wayne was stopped and searched. Wayne has now had non stop harassment as well since this time, for example he was beaten up at one point by the gardai repetitively banging a car door against him. The family are at their wits end. All the local politicians know all about this harassment, but still it doesn't stop, and this family know of this kind of thing happening to other families all over the city.

Helen
Representing her husband who has been wrongfully imprisoned for 5 years now. (I think this is from Kilkenny.)

Dan McCaffrey from Omagh
Involves fraud, blackmail and extortion in the Republic from 1981. Couldn't even get a solicitor to take his case despite huge efforts to get one. Amazingly, and tellingly, the only politician who has tried to help this proud Irish Republican is one Dr. Ian Paisley. He was serious and will be relaying the content of

the meeting back to the Dr and his son.

Padraig O'Reilly the psychiatric nurse from Mayo
He has been trying for many years to highlight what was done to a psychiatric patient who died while in garda custody. He elaborated on the sustained campaign of slander waged against him since he started making these complaints. Posters were put up, forged documents on garda notepaper were distributed in the locality in a slander campaign very similar to that which hit the McBreartys and involved the usual Special Branch Detectives. Because of this campaign and black listing he, and his family, has been 13 years without a steady wage which as you appreciate must make it very difficult to stay the legal course that is unfolding.

Peter Preston from Dublin
He explained that it was his idea to invite Joe Costello TD to the meeting and the reason he wanted to do this was to challenge him face to face with certain allegations... At which point he was cut off by Frank McBrearty who explained that Joe Costello was a friend of his who had always helped him and his family and he would not tolerate allegations like that being aired at the meeting. After much argument Peter resumed his story on the basis that he would relate the facts about his daughter only. So he stated that his daughter had been assaulted with a broken glass in a drinking club and he had established proof of a conspiracy to cover it up involving gardai and judges and for which he had even been on hunger strike outside the Dail. At which point he outlined his allegations against Costello. Basically he said that he had given important documents (transcripts of a court case) on his case to Costello and when he got them back some were missing and some changed...whereupon...

Joe Costello TD
...the Labour spokesman on Justice took the microphone in order to respond to these allegations. He said that he had tried to help Mr Preston with the case involving his daughter and as part of that he gave the documents to two lawyers in turn to look over and see was there any legal avenue that Mr Preston could go down to get justice. One of these lawyers is a legal adviser to the Labour party. While the second lawyer had the documents Mr Preston had told him that he wasn't interested in pursuing it with that lawyer and that he just wanted his documents back. At that he got the documents back from this lawyer and gave them to Mr.Preston in, as far as he is concerned, as complete a manner as he received them. Joe had spoken earlier in praise of the meeting and had also added the information that there is some hold up in the appointment of the three man gardai ombudsman commission because apparently there is a problem with one of them not related to any scandal or anything. (Presumably one of the candidates doesn't want the job?).

Thomas McManus a native of Co.Leitrim
He launched into what seemed like a very involved philosophical discourse

187

which threatened to stretch into a detailed critique of the celtic race...At which point some in the crowd began to debate the merits of listening to all this as the clock ticked on relentlessly and ruinously for those other victims who were trying to get in. I regret to say that it may have even been felt in some quarters that this particular clock conundrum was not unrelated to the reason why he was speaking. So the upshot was that McBrearty was bawling 'time' and much of the rest of the crowd were demanding the microphone while Thomas manfully soldiered on... getting as far as the Vikings ...before eventually some not overly patient Dub laid a hand on his jacket ...the mic was recovered and the meeting rumbled on.

Eileen
Her son was murdered by a police informant who had 20 plus warrants out for his arrest but still met with his garda handler on the day of the murder without being arrested. The informant in fact advised that garda on that date that there was going to be a killing but no effort was made to stop it. This happened to her son as he coming back from his fathers funeral. She has not got one positive answer back from any of the political parties.

Jim Cairns from Antrim later of Kilkenny
Jim has written and campaigned on the question of gardai (and politicians) being involved in the missing persons cases in the Midlands. He stated simply that there is a group in Ireland abducting people and that the guards are covering this up.
(http://www.missingpersons-ireland.freepress-freespeech.com/newbook.htm)
(http://www.indymedia.ie/newswire.php?story_id=73090)

49. This is one of his articles:
http://archives.tcm.ie/businesspost/2002/02/17/story609156728.asp .

50. Information from PJ, whom I would like to thank.

51. You can read about the sort of coverage the local media in Donegal gave to the McGlinchey case in the book 'Charades' op cit, which amounted to trying to discredit the garda victims. For example the local media made great play of a description by one garda of two of the victims as K and P, meaning that they were nut cases, while ignoring all the serious allegations as they were being played out in the Morris tribunal.
Eamonn McCann, who is working with the McBreatys in trying to highlight these cases, pointed out at the Dublin meeting that many of the security or crime correspondents in Dublin are little more than conduits for certain gardai. Clearly Eamonn has a lot of experience of working in the Irish media.

52. http://www.swp.ie/socialistworker/2005/sw246/sw-246-12.htm .

53. And one other group that I have forgotten, it might have been the legal

188

profession or the judiciary.

54. Although there was connection to the IRA on occasion according to this link: http://www.indymedia.ie/newswire.php?story_id=72781. Here is a quote from it:
"The police were always highly hostile to the anti-drugs campaigners, many of whom faced serious intimidation; they were stopped in the street, they were brought in for questioning, their houses were raided, they were beaten. It was widely suspected that some police were very close to major dealers, it is not mentioned in the book, but there were rumours that heroin appeared on the streets in police evidence bags."
See also http://www.indymedia.ie/newswire.php?story_id=9940 .

55. If you think that couldn't happen you might like to note that Tom Gilmartin has also described how a solicitor and judge conspired to take his lands in Cavan. He says "It was an absolute scandal, typical of this country."
(http://archives.tcm.ie/irishexaminer/2004/03/17/story272090874.asp).

56. AFAIK there is no prospect of any charges been brought over this, or any of the other cases, against the gardai in Donegal. Here for example is a very serious allegation about Barron's death made at the Morris Tribunal:
http://www.emigrant.ie/article.asp?iCategoryID=177&iArticleID=9831 .

57.http://archives.tcm.ie/businesspost/2005/04/03/story3695.asp and http://archives.tcm.ie/irishexaminer/2005/02/09/story187395849.asp .

58. I am not clear to what extent this account is meant to refer to James Smith alone or to Joe Doherty as well.

59. I believe that this is two different Jim Gallagher's alright but I apologise that this could be an error on my part. You must appreciate that it was a very harrowing meeting with many people trying to explain in 5 minutes decades of harassment at the hands of the state and it was difficult to follow the facts precisely. This is Jim Higgin's statement to the Dail on the Gallaghers: http://www.gov.ie/debates-02/22march/sect2.htm. Jim's brother Feargal, whom I'd like to thank, has pointed out this interview with his brother: http://www.rte.ie/radio1/story/1051235.html .

60. For allegations of masonic influence over the judiciary in the UK see: http://www.prisonplanet.com/archive_freemasonry.html .

61. http://lists.indymedia.org/pipermail/imc-ireland-newswire/2005-April/0424-w2.html. From the Phoenix May 6 2005 p.16:
"He [Duffy] had threatened to spill the beans on what he said was a conspiracy in the Garda. Faced with a court appearance in respect of criminal, non-political matters, the undertaker said he would not go down without revealing a

scandal of bigger proportions than that which provoked the Morris Tribunal. The fatal crossbow attack on Duffy underlines the ancient axiom: dead men tell no tales. Or, put another way, the courtroom privilege of free speech in front of a media audience does not extend to the dead."

62. not:-)

CHAPTER 6

More tales from a wounded Hidden Ireland

This is just a short account, and attempted analysis, of some news stories that have arisen in the last year or so in the general area of justice and intelligence agency activity in Ireland. I have tried particularly to tie some of the stories together in order to attempt to trace some of the major trends in this otherwise miscellaneous data. Unfortunately it isn't a pretty picture.

I might as well begin by pointing out that a number of human rights campaigners who have investigated abuses by the security forces et al in the UK and Northern Ireland are now, shockingly, saying that the security/justice apparatus in the South of Ireland is almost on a par with the worst examples of tyranny in Eastern Europe.[1] They are basing this on the experiences of Michael McKevitt and his family, which have been described in a small book by Marcella Sands. It is a long catalogue of security forces intimidating people, throwing people over the bonnets of cars, shining lights to keep people awake, broadcasting obscenities through loudhailers to disorientate them, and brainwashing the local people with media stories based on no evidence at all. (Michael McKevitt has been long ago branded with the Omagh bombing which he hasn't even been charged with.) Fr. Des Wilson, one of these distinguished campaigners, was at his trial and is lost for words to describe what he saw:

> "Some of us who attended the Green St. court any time during the hearing of his trial will always remember the grip of cold fear we felt at how similar this trial was to what we had read about years ago, the show trials of the dictatorships...In the past however, news media and church and universities and all kinds of people had condemned what was happening in those countries which they described as under dictatorship or communist rule. Now we were witnessing in our own people's courts the misuse of a system which we believed was so superior, so basically just, so presided over by people of such integrity that it would always be found better to set the guilty free than to convict even one innocent. This trial has been one of the most frightening and revealing of the past forty years in Ireland's courts north and south...We who are already shocked need not feel helpless. Michael McKevitt and his family need our help and that help should be given

for the sake of justice for all of us."[2]

The book also details how the lead party in McKevitt's prosecution appears to be in fact MI5, so much so that at one point Bernadette Sands McKevitt personally challenged the Taoiseach to explain on what basis MI5 were now operating openly in the south of Ireland. For example some documents given to the defence appear to show Garda Ass. Comm. Dermot Jennings, in practice the head of Irish Intelligence, helping MI5 in their preparation of the case, rather than the other way around:

"The MI5 document further states that Jennings was worried about the mistakes in Rupert's statement and that he proposed to send the MI5 agent a copy of the statement but the agent said not to send it."[3] Remember this is the prosecution in an Irish court, of an Irish person living in Ireland, for offences committed in Ireland – again he wasn't charged with the Omagh bombing. This idea that the Irish intelligence agencies are growing in influence in Ireland as part of mysterious relationships with other foreign agencies is confirmed by this from the Phoenix which states that the Crime and Security Branch:

> "has in fact increased its influence...mainly the result of globalisation and a great expansion in international intelligence cooperation, through the European Schengen agreement and joint links with British and American agencies. These working bilateral alliances have remained largely secret, only occasionally being glimpsed – as in the Real IRA McKevitt trial, where the Special Criminal Court was packed with British and American intelligence operatives from MI5, the FBI and the CIA involved in the Rupert sting operation."[4]

There is also a growing awareness that the four people convicted on long sentences for offences surrounding the murder of Veronica Guerin might also be victims of a massive miscarriage of justice. You can see this in a number of Village articles for example which have used headlines like "Veronica's murder investigation a fiasco"[5] and "Charles Bowden: The Lying Supergrass".[6] But the implications of this are huge because a number of powerful entities seemed to quickly decide on their guilt in a way that, if they are in fact innocent, comes across as a deliberate coverup. If you break it down into three areas:

(a) *The Department of Justice and the Justice system*. The Department created a whole new witness protection programme to protect a supergrass, and former top Irish army marksman, Charles Bowden. They also gave him a secret lucrative deal in return for his testimony. Yet now judges are describing him as a serial 'self-serving liar'[7] and serious questions are being asked about the true nature of the secret arrangements that were made with the Department of Justice.[8] It is even felt by observers like Jimmy Guerin that it was Bowden himself who killed his sister.[9] These four have also received massive sentences for crimes that sometimes don't attract such draconian punishments. This includes an initial – somewhat reduced on appeal – 28 year sentence for cannabis smuggling handed down to Gilligan as well as a large sentence for allegedly saying he would harm a prison officer. Holland's lawyer, the colourful Giovanni Di Stefano, even claims that there is a conspiracy involving "the judiciary, members of the Irish legal profession, Irish senior counsel, and possibly even politicians" to stop him defending his client:

> "He said that both counsels and solicitors who had taken up cases for his clients subsequently withdrew from the cases under "strange circumstances", having cited new edicts from the Bar Council. He even suggested that three solicitors his company had asked to act for Limerick criminals Wayne Dundon, Desmond Dundon and Anthony McCarthy all withdrew from the cases the day after agreeing to act."[10]

by the way the government at the time of the murder then introduced the Criminal Assets Bureau and at least one solicitor, John Devane from Limerick, is now saying that this body is also being used to intimidate solicitors who cross swords with the gardai.[11]

(b) *The media*, were clearly very quick to finger the Gilligan gang as being responsible for the murder. In fact on the same day as the murder the Evening Herald was already pointing to John Gilligan as being the culprit,[12] and the Sunday Independent followed that up a few days later with a picture of him.[13] How could they have discovered all this so quickly? If John Gilligan is innocent then doesn't it look like somebody was trying to set him up? Obviously then throughout the whole trial process elements in the media kept up the pressure as this anecdote related by Brenda Power indicates:

> "As [Dutchy Holland] stood for what seemed an eternity to await his sentence, a well-known crime reporter sitting next to me barracked him with abusive comments,"...
>
> "Even though his remarks could be heard clearly ('You're going to get yours, Dutchy, you're going down for a long time; you'll never shoot anybody else'), neither the judges nor the gardaí seemed to notice... When the sentence of 20 years was passed, Holland looked shocked. My vocal colleague went into overdrive and his taunting grew louder. As Holland was being led away he looked down at the media benches and made a remark that another reporter and I heard clearly.

The ranter on my other side didn't quite catch what Holland said, which didn't stop him repeating what he thought he heard. 'Did you hear what he said?' he asked everybody excitedly. 'He said it was just another job!'

Those words have since become part of journalistic and crimeland legend. Whenever they are repeated they are used as evidence of Holland's callousness... But that's not what Holland said. 'Youse done your job,' are the actual words he used." [14]

John Byrne in Village magazine has described this as "a telling insight into the workings of Irish crime journalism" because I guess those – strangely misheard – words by Holland then were repeated ad infinitum across the media, possibly to reinforce public support for his conviction. Brenda Power didn't name the journalist but Holland in his Sky News interview named him as Paul Williams.

(c) *The Gardai*, also went the extra mile to secure these convictions which included resorting to tactics like arresting Holland's solicitor simultaneously with his arrest which ensured that he didn't have legal representation during a crucial moment in his dealings with the gardai. This has been described as "a blatant abuse of the legal rights of both men".[15]

So the pattern is that these three entities seemed to have coincidentally come together to bring about the prosecution of what some claim now to be four innocent men, in a way that surely must cause some disquiet. Incidentally to be fair to the judges it should be pointed out that there is only one judicial decision now on record that links any of these four to the killing of Veronica Guerin, which is the recent lost Appeal by Brian Meehan. John Gilligan was actually acquitted of the crime, Patrick Holland was never even charged with it, and Paul Ward had his conviction overturned.[16] Then of course the question is who did kill Veronica Guerin and why? She certainly must have ruffled feathers among those who run the Irish drug trade and I think also that it was in the months before her death that she was assisting Councillor Gary O'Halloran in his attempts to unearth a paedophile ring in the south east.[17]

As it happens many of the gardai involved in the Veronica Guerin inquiry were also the subject of some of the very serious allegations that arose out of Donegal, so much so that Patrick Holland tried to get his case added to those which are being examined by the Morris Tribunal.[18] This tribunal, which has just issued another of its reports is now facing some very serious criticism from the various Donegal families who had originally called for it to be set up. It appears that there is almost a consensus among them that the tribunal is not genuine in its attempts to unearth the corruption in Donegal. A member of the Divers family, for example, called the tribunal something of a sham[19]; Karen McGlinchey notes with frustration that the public reports seem to be some kind of subsection of a wider secret report that the families and the public are not permitted to see;[20] Mark McConnell and Michael Peoples ("we've been obstructed at every stage. I won't be going back through the door of that tribunal again. I've had my fill") [21] are now I think joining the boycott of the tribunal which was started by the; McBreartys, whose opinion that the tribunal is only interested in covering up abuses is obviously well known.

There is also then the Barr Tribunal which reported recently on the death of John Carthy. In it Justice Barr is very critical of the senior Gardai at the scene, regarding them as ultimately 'responsible' for the death of John Carthy. The report is also notable for the unbroken record that Superintendent Joe Shelly has maintained by being mentioned in, I think, all the tribunals that have examined the gardai since the beginning of the state. He played a starring role in the Kerry babies affair where he was accused of assaulting Joanne Hayes's brother, at the Morris Tribunal he was a senior garda in Donegal at that time and is regularly criticised there, and now in the Barr Tribunal he has been castigated for his role as intelligence coordinator at the scene at Abbeylara. Mind you I think all these reports throw up more questions than answers, after all even in Kerry there is still the unsolved murder of a baby stabbed to death on a lonely beach in Dingle Bay.[22] The Barr Tribunal also throws up its fair share of questions rather than conclusions. There is one section called simply "A cover-up?"[23] which raises the prospect of the senior gardai organising a systematic coverup to disguise an earlier shot fired at John Carthy when he was leaving the house (and while his gun was probably still in the broken position). There is another interesting part to his report which is where he investigated a newspaper article that seemed designed to discredit and divide the Carthy family and possibly derail the tribunal. After much sleuthing he forms the opinion that it was in fact elements in the gardai, allied to the Sunday Independent journalist, and some party within the workings of the tribunal which was responsible for the article. He is pretty openly accusing some in the gardai of this, he is very critical of the Independent group, and he actually leaves a very broad hint that it was John Rogers, the former Labour Party Attorney General, who was the mole within the Tribunal structure. (John Rogers was appearing as counsel for some of the gardai.)[24]

One person who is also no great fan of some in the Labour Party is Peter Preston who has obviously accused a former Justice spokesman for the Labour party of being involved in covering up corruption in the legal profession. His experiences of tangling with the powers that be in Ireland has left him saying that:

"I never thought for one moment that I would have to

tell my children to be wary of the gardai, solicitors, barristers, judges and politicians. I believed that the Garda Siochana were there to uphold the law. There is nobody from an ordinary family that has destroyed my family, but only the so called 'cream' of society has...This is of major public interest because it could happen to any person."[25]

Peter Preston received serious criticism on indymedia because some felt that the idea that such independent bodies as the judiciary and an opposition politician would conspire against a person seeking justice was considered to be too outlandish.[26] But if you read the experiences of community activists across Ireland you can see that they too emerge unimpressed by the independence of many of these bodies. The Rossport 5, for example, I don't think have too many kind words to say about the President of the High Court, a leading judicial figure who effectively threatened them with losing their houses, or now about Peter Cassels, a leading Labour party and trade union official who Rossport supporters are saying now is just a government (and Shell) lackey.[27] They seem just as depressed about the state of Ireland as you can read in one of their statements:

"Initially we were jubilant and excited for Mayo and the country when we heard of the Corrib gas find. When we learned that the route would traverse Rossport we became concerned and as we looked closer and sought advice we became alarmed. As Irish citizens and mainly traditional second and third generation Fine Gael and Fianna Fail voters we instinctively sought reassurance and support from state agencies and our local politicians and as farmers from the IFA. We were initially fobbed off, then ignored and finally marginalized. As our awareness of the lethal danger to our families grew our concerns turned into resistance.
...
We have been betrayed by our government, marginalized by sections of the media and ignored by the "alternative" government. Instead it has been the people of Ireland who have sustained us during this time of crisis and personal trauma and who have rallied and continue to rally to our aid – thank you."[28]

As you can see this criticism does extent to questioning the sincerity of opposition parties as Martin Collins from Derrybrien, a small community in Galway fighting against a wind farm developer, indicates: "Our experience in this case has been that politicians from all parties ... turned their back and walked away" with the exception of some MEPs particularly Patricia McKenna.[29] He had further serious criticism to make of the many 'independent' – his quotation marks – bodies designed to deal with complaints and planning in Ireland, as you can see from this summary of a speech he made in solidarity with the Rossport families:

"The politicians are losing the run of themselves and putting profit before people. Businesses, planners, State companies and politicians are acting against the people. They have no respect for the dignity of communities and their areas. Many so-called "independent" arms of the state – which pretend to be separate – work as one going forward with regard to unsustainable developments. The politicians and public servants, our employees, feed in to this when they should be doing the bidding of the people."[30]

William Finnerty, an activist from Kilconnell also in Galway, has come away with much the same impression based on his many dealings with these various bodies:

"...it is becoming more and more clear to me that organisations such as the Irish Council for Civil Liberties, the several Ombudsmen's' Offices, the Human Rights Commissioners, The European Court of Human Rights, The Law Societies and so on, are, it seems, just "window dressing" – which are actually designed to slyly support all of very worst of the political, legal and corporate corruption that I am battling with: while fraudulently pretending to be providing a sound defence against it. In other words, and all taken together, they are nothing more (at the present time) than a very shoddy and very mean confidence trick – in so far as I can judge from my direct dealings with them.

"Go here, go there, go somewhere else; but, wherever you go we will always make sure the very serious problems you raise will NEVER be addressed in a way which threatens the core of the political, legal and corporate corruption we wish to hold on to, and to keep control over."" [31]

It is interesting that he would include one of the European bodies that others, like Michael McKevitt, are pinning their faith in. Maybe W. Finnerty is right if this speech by the English MEP Ashley Mote is anything to go by:

"Mr President, I wish to draw your attention to the Global Security Fund, set up in the early 1990s under the auspices of Jacob Rothschild. This is a Brussels-based fund and it is no ordinary fund: it does not trade, it is not listed and it has a totally different purpose. It is being used for geopolitical engineering purposes, apparently under the guidance of the intelligence services. I have previously asked about the alleged involvement of the European Union's own intelligence resources in the management of slush funds in offshore accounts, and I still await a reply. To that question I now add another: what are the European Union's connections to the Global Security Fund and what relationship does it have with European Union institutions?"[32]

Apparently its a huge EU slush fund used to bribe politicians and others within the member states in order to get the various EU treaties passed.[33] Three dissident MEPs from the EU's Budget Control Committee, Mote alongwith Hans Peter Martin MEP from Austria [34] and Paul van Buitenen from the Netherlands [35], are now trying to investigate the relationship between the EU and this fund and another shady fund/clearing bank called Clearstream which was said to have been involved in handling bribes to the French Justice Minister among many others.[36] The sums of money involved are quoted in trillions.

Back in Ireland we have found out more details about the somewhat lower scale of corruption in Dublin County Council. Bill O'Herlihy, the RTE soccer presenter, has given details to the Mahon tribunal of a conversation he had with an employee of one of the land developers in Dublin in 1992. Over coffee while they were waiting for a vote of Dublin County Council, as Bill innocently expressed the hope that the councillors could see the merit in the development, his companion, a former Dundalk Town clerk, guffawed at his incredible naivety and replied:

"the councillors never recognise quality and merit, it has nothing whatever to do with it, he said if you want to get a planning change or a material contravention through, you have to buy it and he said that planning changes and material contraventions were worth, in his judgement, about 50,000 a year into the back pocket of the councillors, if they cooperated with the developers."[37]

He went on to explain how this was done, to a shocked O'Herlihy, by getting a lead councillor, possibly one in each of the political parties, to handle the bribery arrangements among the councillors until they had the required majority for the developments. Doesn't this highlight one of the unfortunate aspects of Irish corruption in that it is much more hidden than it is in modern day Eastern Europe for example. The fact is that at that time anyway the general public had no idea that it was all corrupt like this. Hence they would have spent a huge amount of time and energy debating these planning issues thinking that at least the councillors would consider the issues on their merits. For example many people on both sides of the debate on Carrickmines Castle must be feeling like proper mugs when it was later revealed that the road was diverted to go through Carrickmines in order to enrich some corrupt people who owned the land around the castle.[38] So picture the scene among the dining tables of the well heeled citizens of south Dublin as some argued that the historic castle should be saved (the good guys INMO) and others talked about the traffic gridlock etc. In retrospect both were completely wasting their breath even debating the subject which had already being decided for them by the big power and money brokers in Ireland, and they had decided on a route which was not the best from a traffic point of view nor for the conservations of course. The merits of both arguments were just irrelevant to the real – corrupt – decision making process. Maybe the lesson is that people should insist on having genuinely uncorrupt and democratic institutions before they get bogged down in the minutiae of political debate in Ireland. It maybe worth bearing in mind as well that the leaders of three political parties, which represent two thirds of the current Dail, were all members of Dublin County Council at this time and some would say were undistinguished in stamping out this corruption.[39]

If anything the atmosphere surrounding planning, and allegations of corruption, seem to have worsened since the 90s if this account by Colum McCann in the Village is anything to go by:

"For five short days I travelled the length of the Galway and Mayo coasts and talked to a good few locals who felt outraged by what had happened to their countryside.

They had tried to rescue old ruins but could not. They had tried to fit houses into the landscape but planning permission had been denied. They tried to block certain developments but they were threatened with being burned out. A peculiar resignation had settled in on some of them, like ash. They shrugged and said how terrible it was but that nothing could be done, the politicians, developers and the planners were in it together, covered in the steamy bedsheets of the euro."[40]

Why so much apathy in the face of these kind of threats and practises? Maybe what is happening is that the vast majority of people trust implicitly the headline news they receive and yet those news bulletins seem frequently to play down some stories and blunt the edge of a maybe justifiable outrage. This is what I think Barry McConville is saying with respect to some police shootings in the North for example:

"After his [Neil McConville's] death, as in the case of Pearse Jordan, the media quickly regurgitated the PSNI press releases. Checkpoints were being rammed,

199

guns were being brandished, drugs were being ferried and finally dissident republican links were being investigated, all false and – as in the case of Pearse Jordan – these events were later accepted by the police as being false. There was no checkpoint in Neil McConville's killing, his car was rammed from behind and then he was shot by PSNI personnel at point blank range while his car was stationary. The Police Ombudsman was slow to attend the scene that night but they were quick to recount the PSNI version of events on live TV, giving credence to a story which they later embarrassingly discovered had no resemblance to actual events that night.

Last week another young man, Steven Colwell, was killed because he drove through an alleged roadblock, only he didn't, he turned the car he was driving before the roadblock and was shot at point blank range by PSNI personnel...
They [the PSNI in these cases] close ranks, intimidate witnesses, concoct a story and use black propaganda in the media to blacken the name of the person they unlawfully killed."[41]

But is it really true that if you cross the powers that be that you will be "threatened with being burned out" as described above? Surely that is going too far? That certainly didn't get mentioned on any news bulletin but I'm afraid that doesn't make it untrue, here is a startling story like that from Limerick highlighted on indymedia:
"News from Tournafulla Today is that the remote Home of a Dutch Lady was the subject of a arson attack. It has [been] noted over the recent Weeks that this may occur, as a few individuals in the area have shown interest in the Property. This Lady has been the victim of much harassment over a long period of time by a variety of People. One of the interested Parties in the Property was in fact a Solicitor 'acting' for this Lady in a Land dispute. A few Days ago, on leaving 'her' Solicitor's Office, 'her' Solicitor remarked,' I will give you 30,000 euros for your House and 3 acres, less of course 5000euros for my Fee to date. When she declined this 'offer', he remarked, 'you know your House is not insured'. 'It could burn down you know.'"[42]
And yet even this story is depressingly believable because it matches so many other sagas that are tumbling out of the woodwork from the hidden Ireland, another account on indymedia:

"Exactly the same happened to us in Limerick after a local garda wanted to purchase our family home for near to nothing and told me a woman without man would be vulnerable and I should expect getting robbed and awful things could happen to me. They did and the gardai were always at the house shining lights in and pissing on the windows and everywhere else in a later stage. I was beaten up so badly on one occasion that 70% of my body was black and blue. If they were outside I would be in a corner hiding and waiting for them [to] gain access to the house and beat me up. I would call the womans refuge and they heard them laugh and talk and they would not even care to be silent as they knew the womens refuge would not back me up. I moved but am a poor person now in every way. I still cannot sleep at night." [43]

This is reported to be quite a common complaint against some in the legal profession and gardai in Ireland as you can read: (a) in the testimony of Tom Gilmartin to the Mahon tribunal where he states that an alliance between, inter alios, his land agent, a solicitor and a judge attempted to steal his land near Virginia in Co.Cavan;[44] (b) in a fully documented case from Belfast where it is claimed that a group including Belfast's largest firm of solicitors, allied to powerful people in the RUC, and Official Solicitors, conspired to rob the family of a mentally handicapped man of many valuable properties in downtown Belfast;[45] (c) and in another detailed account of a property 'stolen' by a number of solicitor firms that were supposed to be acting for the Bland family in Laois.[46]

Other people like Eugene in Castlerea have reported the kind of pressure they are under to 'sell' lands to this kind of corrupt clique.[47]

One organisation that a lot of these families, which face injustice and corruption, pinned their hopes on was the Centre for Public Inquiry. This was obviously set up in Ireland by the distinguished journalist Frank Connolly, with funding from Atlantic Philanthropies and headed by a blue ribbon board of directors, with a goal of tackling corruption in Ireland. As everybody knows it was crushed by the Minister for Justice who leaked a passport application which he said proved that Frank Connolly had gone to Colombia where his brother was arrested for alleged paramilitary activities. This allegedly inaccurate passport application, the only evidence proffered against Connolly, was not even the subject of a prosecution by the DPP, which obviously works closely with the Minister's office, some would say in order to prevent the documents from being discussed in open court. Feargus Flood, a former High Court judge, has called attention to this anomaly saying that "despite the DPP's decision in March 2003 not to prosecute Mr

Connolly, a private and public blackening of his character has been unleashed by the Minister."[48] In fact a constant wave of slander seems to have dogged Frank Connolly throughout his career as he attempted to unearth some of the corruption in the planning process in Dublin and in the gardai in Donegal. In 2002 "he was not fired by the Sunday Business Post but management made him aware he should seek alternative employment", as a result of this same will o the wisp Colombia story printed against him in some Irish newspapers.[49] This campaign of slander apparently dates from as long ago as 1997 when Dermot Ahern was reported to have claimed he was linked to the INLA, again giving no evidence but fuelling whispering campaigns that have now twice cost him his job.[50]

I wonder if even his brother has been misrepresented with respect to Colombia. According to the official story three people linked to the IRA, James Monaghan, Martin McCauley, and Neil Connolly are supposed to have been instrumental in rearming and retraining the FARC, a left wing paramilitary group, in preparation for a fresh offensive in Colombia. They in fact have been acquitted of the charge in the lower courts in Colombia and very little hard evidence has emerged as to how they could have done this in the light of the huge surveillance that was clearly focused on them. But one wonders if it suited some intelligence agencies to disguise their own hand in arming the FARC by putting forward these three as patsies. There is, in contrast to the other story, compelling evidence that the CIA has supplied the FARC with a huge arms shipment in order to assist them in their campaign against the Colombian government. The allegation is that they are doing this in order to keep pressure on that government which in turn leads to the Colombians seeking US military assistance (a 'Plan Colombia') which has effectively allowed the US to take over that country. There is a lot of data out there in the public domain about all this although of course not a whisper has been allowed on it in the Irish media. The story revolves around Vladimir Montesinos, the former Peruvian intelligence chief who effectively ran a nominally democratic Peru throughout the 90s – on behalf of the CIA in the opinion of most observers.[51] He is now on trial in Lima and there they are discussing an operation he organised where he purchased 10,000 assault rifles in Jordan and, using Ukrainian mercenaries, dropped them by air to the FARC in Colombia. The fact that this was all authorised by the CIA is even confirmed by the Jordanian government:

> "According to Atef Halasa, the head of protocol at the Jordanian Foreign Ministry, his country would not have released the weapons without informing US authorities. Halasa was reported as saying that the American government not only knew of the deal, but that it was authorised by the CIA."[52]

One concept that emerged from the CPI drama was that the government seemed annoyed that any independent group had the right to set up a body to tackle corruption.[53] It appears they are only happy with government funded official entities and it is no wonder when you consider the difficulties they put in the way of whistleblowers in the state apparatus. As an example of that atmosphere one commentator, writing about a homeless charity that receives funding from the state, described in detail how a FF councillor and a Minister tried to hunt down members of the charity that were accused of aiding a homeless protest. This was felt to be part of determined government policy "to silence all opposition to it's policies."[54] It seems that anybody who tries to speak out while within any part, even a nominally independent part, of the state apparatus is sure to be bullied into silence. I will give three examples:

(a) Dr Joan Power, the Munster regional director of the Blood Transfusion Service, was the main whistleblower to highlight the use of contaminated blood products in the health system for which a senior official in the Department of Health threatened to "bury her" professionally. In due course her professional life became "an absolute nightmare".[55]

(b) In 2004 the same department was accused by three orthodontists of organising "a fairly strong bullying campaign against us...We are paralysed in our lives. I have been in bad health and people attribute that to the stresses imposed upon us by what has happened. It is political bullying." They tried to get some help in their plight from a Dail Committee but all they got was advise to use 'honey' rather than vinegar in their dealings with the department. That is except for Michael Ring TD who condemned this intimidation: "They should not be intimidated, but should be protected...This country is turning into a dictatorship."[56]

(c) Justice Dermot Kinlen, the Inspector of Prisons, is supposed to head an independent office to visit and report on the state of the prisons but he has found that the Department of Justice have successfully stopped any attempt he has made to highlight the terrible state of the prison system. When he tried to say this in his second annual report it was held up by the Dept. of Justice for a year "claiming it was libelous (of them), and the AG agreed." He even offered to publish it himself, where he would carry the liability for any court proceedings, but that wasn't accepted. Eventually they just sent a copy of the report to him by car and told him that was the finished report whether he liked it or not. Before that in trying to setup his office he had to face Department of Justice officials (as he wrote in his first report) whose "smarminess was replaced by ignorant arrogance". Having been through all that he is now taken to referring to the Department of Justice and the Minister as "frightening and fascist".[57]

One person who has had many dealings with the Minister for Justice, and who is also now questioning his integrity, is Billy Flynn, a Private Investigator from Enfield who has helped many of the families in Donegal. He has been through the usual experiences, harassed by the gardai, false charges laid against him and he now states that he was slandered by a Circuit Court judge, I think with the 'mad' (he had a nervous breakdown as a result of all the harassment) as opposed to the 'bad' slander although he is getting that too. In particular he was accused of all sorts of shady dealings in the way that he helped expose, via phone logs, one of the tormentors of the Donegal families. The present Commissioner, it states in an account of his story in Village magazine, was more interested in investigating how he got the phone data than he was in the fact that the threatening phonecalls came from the home of a garda. Much the same happened when he tried to expose "massive corruption" in the Navan area. The powers that be responded by, unsuccessfully, trying to prosecute him (in a 'premeditated' manner) over the alleged theft of a file rather than addressing the corruption. It all started for him when he tried to survive as a small business person:

> "I put a lot of money into the central heating business
> and it was a con. I couldn't get anyone to do anything
> about it and I started looking. It lifted from there. I was
> telling a couple of other people (of what happened and
> of the investigation) who had also suffered injustice. I
> sorted out their cases, although I couldn't sort out my
> own, and just went on from there."

Incidentally he is very clear on the fact that Minister McDowell knew everything about what was going on in Donegal from the very beginning, when he was still Attorney General, but did nothing about it.[58]

Billy Flynn in describing what happened in Raphoe has also described, briefly, a kind of mysterious vigilante group that was involved in harassing the Donegal families in cooperation with certain gardai. Maybe it might be similar to what Dr Les Dove describes in his account of what dissidents go through in the UK and the US:

> "The police and intelligence agencies in many countries
> often use goon-squads. Their job is to harass and try to
> intimidate their 'targets' at every possible opportunity.
> They also try to provoke their targets into fights and
> other bad situations so that they will incriminate
> themselves. Goon-squads are also used to denigrate
> victims and damage their character through spreading
> lies and false rumours about them and their families.
> This character assassination inevitably causes many
> targets to loose their jobs and quickly become alienated
> from their friends and families."[59]

There are other accounts of such groups in Ireland e.g. in Schull "Local vigilantes ... have also been busy following, framing and spreading rumours about myself"[60], which I guess sums up what the same type of group were up to in Raphoe. Rose Doherty has also given an account of a group like that harassing her in Roscommon in exactly the same manner and which has been linked to senior local gardai.[61]

One other person who has stated that he is under "McBrearty style" harassment is Jerry Beade, a Dublin building contractor, who won a High Court action that proves at least some kind of conspiracy against him within the planning offices of Dublin City Council. Despite this judgement they have taken 15 prosecutions against him which he feels is similar to what has happened in Donegal.[62] One other interesting aspect about his case is that simultaneously with this harassment, his bank, ACC, managed to 'lose' the title deeds to a €14 million property of his which needless to say threatened him with bankruptcy. ACC, wondrously, managed to find the deeds only after he picketed their parent head offices in the Netherlands. I wonder if he is suspicious that he may be under harassment from a wider group than just DCC. After all Tom Gilmartin is on record as saying he was harassed, in a coordinated fashion, by AIB, a Dublin County Council and Councillors, and of course senior politicians.

Another person who is being targeted by an organ of the state is Det. Sgt. John White, the Garda Special Branch whistleblower. He is the only garda that the state has been trying to prosecute over the events in Donegal and this is hardly a coincidence considering that he is so outspoken about abuses in the gardai. He says himself that he was targeted for prosecution, twice unsuccessfully, because
(a) he questioned the validity of McBrearty's confession,
(b) because he complained of the bugging of Letterkenny garda station,
(c) "because of his persistent claim that 'top class intelligence'" was ignored by the gardai with respect to the Omagh bombing. Michael Gallagher, whose son died at Omagh, supports the view that that might be behind the prosecution, saying after the verdict that: "They [the garda authorities] hoped to bury him [White], but the people of Donegal have vindicated John White not for the first time."[63]

Sgt. White has also revealed a lot about the kind of widespread surveillance that is practised in secret by Garda Special Branch. He has said that on a massive nationwide scale the state has been bugging "Garda stations...houses, cars and apartments and phones, and it was done totally illegally and the senior Garda authorities know."[64] That of course refers to the bugs and hidden cameras that we don't know about, while Damien Corless has written in the Irish Independent about the blanket surveillance that we do – kinda – know about in Ireland now. This includes Dublin Bus where each bus is now fitted with up to 8 digital cameras feeding data real time to the Gardai. He described how Michael McDowell has pioneered the storage of phone and internet data in Europe giving rise to a situation where "Irish citizens now live under the most far-reaching regime of state-surveillance in Europe." He also quotes a submission from a US law firm which states that "The Irish law [now in force on data collection] would [create] a regime far more intrusive that anything previously known in the EU or even in comparable democratic societies."[65]

This dovetails with recent leaks from America on the kind of huge surveillance apparatus that the state uses to keep its citizens in line. A member of the NSA has come forward to talk about an enormous programme that watches up to millions of Americans using sources like phone call data from the phone companies which has been continuing without any other legal basis than a secret Presidential Order. This whistleblower, Russell Tice, has hinted that all this is only a tiny part of what he found out about NSA activities:

> "..what has been disclosed so far is only the tip of the iceberg...
> "I think the people I talk to next week [in the US Congress] are going to be shocked when I tell them what I have to tell them. It's pretty hard to believe..
> Tice said his information is different from the Terrorist Surveillance Program that Bush acknowledged in December and from news accounts this week that the NSA has been secretly collecting phone call records of millions of Americans. "It's an angle that you haven't heard about yet," he said. ... He would not discuss with a reporter the details of his allegations, saying doing so would compromise classified information and put him at risk of going to jail. He said he "will not confirm or deny" if his allegations involve the illegal use of space systems and satellites."[66]

So it seems we have a long ways to go to try to figure out what kind of surveillance the NSA really practises. This hint at a much more elaborate surveillance capability is echoed by Margaret Newsham who was also trained by the NSA who said that "it is almost impossible to imagine how all-encompassing the system must be today...If only I could tell you everything, then you would understand that Echelon is so big, its immensity almost defies comprehension." She cannot tell us because of the danger she is under, she sleeps with a loaded pistol under her pillow etc.[67] So what is this new concept of surveillance probably using satellites? Believe it or not there are actually persistent allegations out there that it is now possible to even effect a persons health via surveillance by satellite. Whatever is the answer I think we are bound to be surprised by their capability considering the huge sums of money that those organisations like NSA and NRO have to conduct their projects and research.[68]

One curious point, I think, about all this is the way Tice's insights came across in the media. What happened is that just before Tice came forward the whole media and political establishment seemed to do a sudden 'mea culpa' on the use of unauthorised bugging as part of the war on terror. Instead of any coverup there was blanket coverage given to the administration's negligence in 'cutting through red tape' and 'not going through the proper channels' in the war on terror. In a sense they cheerfully admitted in advance all of the stuff that Tice later accused the government of doing. With one difference. They talked endlessly about a 'few thousand' cases of unauthorised bugging of US citizens, while Tice talked about a million! Of course that small 'error' makes all the difference. A lot of Americans are going to accept that these thousand or so 'mistakes' are sometimes necessary to catch the terrorists but of course if we are talking about a million people then we are into the realm of a police state and not just some police action against a few suspects. But because early impressions of an issue are everything when Tice later came out with his story most people didn't catch the difference in what he was actually saying from the impression they had already formed about the surveillance scandal. This I respectfully submit is no accident, it is standard intelligence agency news management.[69]

The US intelligence agencies, for example, invest a lot of time and effort influencing the media not only in the US but also in countries like Ireland. The Phoenix has recently written an article on this describing a big meeting held in Texas where various military heavyweights formulated a policy of using 'Influence Operations' against some target countries. These are basically psychological warfare operations which were explained in the documents discussed at the meeting: "IO offers the use of influence operations (in) capturing and maintaining the support of indigenous subcultures and populations, and keeping targeted governments off-balance and on the defensive." One person who is involved in forwarding this policy has been named as Major Gen. Paul J. Lebras, Commander, Air Intelligence Agency, who also "has the job of monitoring those trying to spy on US military flights at Shannon and Baldonnel." The article then went on to link this operation to an 11 day conference held at the State Department in Washington where a large Irish delegation received training on how to be better "media spokespersons". The Irish delegation (a "bevy of official and party political spokespersons") was led by Supt. Kevin Donohue of the Garda Press Office and included FG Press officer Mike Miley and PD policy director Seamus Mulconry.[70]

I guess it would be fascinating to see if one could detect that kind of news management in Ireland. One case that I think comes across very strongly was what happened to Peter Preston where he was charicatured as wanting harsher sentencing for the people who assaulted his daughter, entirely different from what he was actually saying.[71] In fact he had been briefly in jail as part of his ongoing case and he thought the conditions in the prisons were terrible so he is unlikely to be so keen on anybody going in there. The cry for harsher sentences, and for more and more gardai, are standard themes pumped out constantly in the Irish media and you would wonder to what extent that is being pushed by elements in the media rather than genuine reporting, as it really wasn't in this case. When you look at the Irish media right now I think you have to conclude that some issues are given blanket coverage and others none at all. For example I think that before the poster ban came in there were frequent complaints broadcast in the media about the terrible litter problem caused by political postering. Supposedly it was the number one environmental problem plaguing the country. So of course the government responded to widespread public disquiet (in happy media land) with some draconian legislation regulating the putting up of posters. Then what happened was that the poster ban was used to squeeze political activists, from outside the main parties, all across the country, to the undoubted glee of the powers that be.[72] The disquiet felt among these activists then gets almost no publicity in the media. I know most people don't feel that its possible for a measure like that to be proceeded by a long term orchestrated media campaign but I am suspicious nonetheless!

One issue that has got a lot of publicity about a year ago, which could be part of that pattern, is the complaints made about the state of the electoral register. Everybody seemed to agree that there were large numbers of people on the register who shouldn't be on it and so in response a group has been set up within the Department of the Environment which so far has succeeded in eliminating about 200,000 of those.[73] But in fact Mary O'Rourke contends that the main problem with the register is that many people are not on it who should be, she estimates that "out of 500 houses, 200 people were not on the register."[74]

This 'cleaning up' of the register is motivated I think by a similar step that has been taken in the North but there some people are even claiming "120,000 people were disenfranchised". While that is denied by the government, it is admitted that large numbers of "young people, students, people with learning disabilities and those living in poorer areas" have been disenfranchised by the new rules they introduced.[75] At least one commentator is suspicious that the way this is being done now in the South will similarly cause a lot of young voters to be struck off, and he feels that this is "no accident ... For these young voters are the very ones who cannot be trusted to vote for the existing establishment parties."[76] Which gives rise to the suspicion that the strategic and important electoral register could be undergoing some quiet underhand editing, and one wonders then if the earlier media stories about the register were somehow orchestrated?

Of course until very recently the media's main punchbag – and still is to a certain extent – was one Charles J Haughey who could probably have walked to the moon and back with the amount of critical newsprint that had built up against him in Ireland over some 40 years. Maybe now that he is gone it might be worth while figuring out how much of this criticism was justified. Three major issues were held against him:

(a) The Arms Trial. Obviously the accusation was that he was heavily involved in trying to import arms for the IRA in 1969 and lied about all that during the trial and throughout his career. But of course what happened after he left politics was that the original statement made by Col. Heffernan, the then head of Irish Military Intelligence, turned up in the Irish archives under the 30 year rule.[77] And that document seemed to show that the then Minister for Justice, Des O'Malley, supposedly the white knight at this time as opposed to Haughey's dark prince, had suppressed the real truth of his evidence which would have exonerated Capt James Kelly at least. In response to this new information Justin Keating, who in 1970 was a Labour member of the Dail Committee that investigated the payments made through Haughey, confirmed that in his opinion "Haughey, Blaney, Luukxs and the two Kellys were unjustly accused. Putting them on trial was a dreadful injustice."[78]

(b) Also he was always subject to rumours, and later accusations and tribunal hearings, into the source of his wealth, in particular how he could afford to purchase Kinsealy. But amazingly Vincent Browne, who most people interpret I think as the main authority on this, now claims that Haughey had always answered questions on his wealth perfectly truthfully, and that in fact he had no dark secret to hide on that subject at all.[79] The tribunals meanwhile have trawled exhaustively, and there are allegations aggressively,[80] through his finances and found what seems to be very little evidence of corruption.

(c) Then there is the allegation of secretly instructing Sean Doherty to bug certain journalists and of personally reading the transcripts. He obviously denied doing that and now it appears that a third party has come forward to back up his, rather than Doherty's, version of events.[81] Don't get me wrong I am not denying some of the allegations, particularly the serious statements by Tom Gilmartin, which touch Haughey although not nearly to the same extent as they do certain other FF politicians, but you cannot help wondering if the media has got some issues here spectacularly wrong over a long number of years. Haughey himself seemed to feel that some of his media, and other, troubles could have been orchestrated by some outside party. In fact at one time he accused Garret Fitzgerald of meeting a trained British spy which is probably an indication of who he thought was behind this, especially at the time when he opposed EEC and UK policy over the Falklands War. There is I think some evidence to show that some party, with a lot of money, was pulling a few strings against him.[82] Anyway he had obviously many a colourful phrase to encapsulate these woes one of which he delivered to the editor of the Irish Independent in 1982, as he recounts here:

> "After the usual pleasantries from John [Meagher], saying how well the company was and the papers were doing, he turned to Charles Haughey and said: "Now Deputy Haughey have you any questions you would like to ask us?"
>
> I don't know if it was the "deputy" that did it but Haughey's mood visibly darkened. The hooded eyes swivelled around in my direction and Haughey growled: "Yes, as a matter of fact I do have a question."
> "We have just come through a bruising four weeks election campaign and every time myself or the other Fellow were mentioned in the main headline he was always Garret and I was Haughey. Do you consider that fair and reasonable?"
>
> Lamely I explained that the typography and layout format we were using at the time only allowed us to use seven to eight letters in each line of our four deck headline. The name FitzGerald was impossible to fit, even more so as Garret insisted on spelling his name with a middle G as a capital, whereas Haughey fitted just perfectly.
>
> That, I said, is the explanation.
> "Well that," thundered Haughey, "takes the f****** biscuit."
> The lunch went downhill from there."[83]

And on the bright side ...eh ...well...at least the GAA still works...

Footnotes

1. e.g. Fr Raymond Murray http://www.indymedia.ie/article/77899 .

2. http://homepage.eircom.net/~michaelmckevitt/index_files/foreword.htm see further reading at http://www.indymedia.ie/article/78167 for more from this book.

3. See under Further Reading at http://www.indymedia.ie/article/78167 .

4. The Phoenix 23 Sept 2005 p.16.

5. Village 22 June 2006 p.13.

6. Village 13 April 2006 p.7-11.

7. http://furnacemagazine.com/life/witness_protection_in_a_shambles.html and Sunday Business Post 2 January 2005 http://archives.tcm.ie/businesspost/2005/01/02/story1277.asp .

8. From Sunday Business Post ibid: "While the suspected hitman is now enjoying life under a new identity, questions are being asked about the secret deal he obtained from the Department of Justice...Details of Bowden's immunity deal are still shrouded in secrecy."

9. ibid.

10. Irish Independent 16 March 2006 p.9.

11. http://archives.tcm.ie/irishexaminer/2006/02/18/story958889612.asp .

12. Village 29 June 2006 http://www.villagemagazine.ie/article.asp? aid=2037&iid=105&sud=10 .

13. Sunday Independent 30 June 1996 page 4.

14. Village 13 April 2006 p.7-11 by John Byrne quoting Brenda Power in the Sunday Times of 26 March 2006 http://www.villagemagazine.ie/article.asp? aid=1611&iid=94&sud=10 .

15. The Phoenix 7 April 2006.

16. Sunday Business Post 2 January 2005 http://archives.tcm.ie/businesspost/2005/01/02/story1277.asp. There is some more detail on the case available at these links:

http://archives.tcm.ie/businesspost/2005/01/02/story1277.asp and
http://archives.tcm.ie/businesspost/2001/05/20/story656032928.asp on Ward's
sentence:http://news.bbc.co.uk/1/hi/world/europe/1887529.stm; Gilligan:
http://www.rte.ie/news/2002/0627/print/gilligan.html and
http://archives.tcm.ie/breakingnews/2002/06/25/story57136.asp .

17. The Phoenix Oct 21 2005p.3 quoted above at chapter 5 footnote 34.

18. The Phoenix 13 Sept 2002 p.20.

19. In an RTE Prime Time interview in 2006. I cannot remember the exact
words I'm afraid but they certainly were along those lines.

20. Village 13 October 2005 p.27 letter from Karen McGlinchey. She also says
that "it beggars belief that one of those officers [involved in the scandal] remains on normal duties in Letterkenny." The Phoenix 17 June 2005 p.8 also
mentions a second Morris Report "kept from the public" by the Official Secrets
Act.

21. Sunday Times 20 Aug 2006 p.1.

22. http://www.siobhandowd.co.uk/stories/ and for a description of
Superintendant Shelley's role during the controversy see Irish Examiner 3 June
2005 by Seán McCárthaigh at
http://archives.tcm.ie/irishexaminer/2005/06/03/story57830747.asp .

23. http://www.eire.com/photos/Barr_Tribunal.pdf p.434.

24. See further reading http://www.indymedia.ie/article/78167 for some quotes
from the report which illustrate this.

25. http://www.indymedia.ie/article/76572.

26. Debate on Peter Preston is at http://www.indymedia.ie/article/77433 .

27. http://www.indymedia.ie/article/77806 and
http://www.indymedia.ie/article/77621 .

28. http://www.corribsos.com/index.php?id=205 .

29. See further reading http://www.indymedia.ie/article/78167 .

30. http://www.corribsos.com/index.php?id=32&type=event .

31.
http://www.indymedia.ie/article/77437&comment_limit=0&condense_comme

nts=false#comment161339 .

32. 11 April 2005 http://www.ashleymote.co.uk/news2.php?
subaction=showfull&id=1113911900&archive=&start_from=&ucat=14&TB=
home47 .

33. See further reading under the EU at
http://www.indymedia.ie/article/78167 .

34. http://www.hpmartin.net/The_European_Transparency_Initiative-lang-
en.html .

35. http://www.europatransparant.nl/?pag=145&siteid=145 .

36. http://www.ashleymote.co.uk/search.php?
misc=search&subaction=showfull&id=1117110516&archive=&cnshow=news
&start_from=&%5C%22to_date_day%5C%22=&TB=home5 .

37. See further reading at http://www.indymedia.ie/article/78167 .

38. "The entire Carrickmines Castle controversey could have been avoided,
and the castle saved, if the original route of the South Eastern Motorway leg of
the M50 had been picked, as it avoided the castle remains. But that route was
inexplicably changed, to go through both the castle site and the lands owned by
Jackson Way, that became the subject of an investigation by the Mahon
(Flood) Planning Tribunal."(http://tarawatch.org/?cat=10)

39. Bertie Aherne FF, Mary Harney PD, and Pat Rabitte Labour.

40. Village 27 April 2006 p.25.

41. Village 27 April 2006 p.45. Another letter from the McConville family of
Lurgan Co.Armagh whose son was shot dead 2 and half years ago by the PSNI
has this to say about "The Ombudsman's office has continually given us and
our solicitor Kevin Winters the run around. Their obstinacy is incredible. The
psychological mind games the Ombudsman is playing with our family is as
cruel and unjust as the shooting dead of innocents."(Village 23 Sept 2005 p.31)

42. http://www.indymedia.ie/article/76927.

43. http://www.indymedia.ie/article/77022.

44. "Yes, in Cavan, I bought a piece of land, four acres – I was intending to
build a house on because at the time we were thinking of returning. I had a sis-
ter-in-law living in the area and my wife liked the spot. I'll just tell you the
story of it so that Mr. Maguire doesn't go away with any misapprehension of

my character. I bought the piece of land. We had it and I was planning to build a house on it. A gentleman from next door wanted to – sorry, an agent approached me to see if I'd let the meadow on it, so I did. I told him go ahead – I told him actually I didn't want any money for it, they could have the meadow, so he said "You can't do that because they may get a claim to your land". So I charged some minimal figure. Some time later that same agent rung me to see if I'd sell it, and I says no, I was not selling it. A few days later I got a contract from a solicitor agreeing to the sale of my land. I refused to go along with it because I had not sold it and I had stated categorically, and had witnesses, that I was not selling that piece of land. But I was sued for specific performance on the grounds that if an agent proved that he acted for me, he could sell my land. He sold the land for a pittance, an absolute pittance, to a cousin of his. So I was sued for specific performance. I went to court. That Mr. Judge Sheehy wouldn't hear my evidence or any witness on my behalf. As it happened, I was there sullying the names of decent local people. That's right, I was a shifty person alright [the Anglo Celt 5/5/1978 reprinted comments from the judge very critical of Gilmartin. The last two sentences refer to what the judge said about him.], and he didn't even hear my evidence! He didn't allow me to talk in the box. That is a fact and I will prove it, and Gerald Scallon and O'Brien acted for me in that case. It was an absolute scandal, typical of this country. (Members of the gallery applaud)"
(Thomas Gilmartin at the Mahon tribunal 16 March 2004 http://www.flood-tribunal.ie/images/SITECONTENT_255.pdf).

45. http://www.justbelfast.com/sitemap.html. The site is written by this handicapped person's elderly sister who has found herself on the receiving end of all kinds of slander for attempting to pursue justice in this case:
"I have a copy document, dated 23rd September 1985 written by the then Official Solicitor to senior consultant Dr A Lyons. In this document I am referred to as, quote, "bitter and frustrated". How many more people have been subjected to these diabolical untruths in order to pervert the course of Justice. Every opportunity appears to have been taken to destroy my character."
(http://www.justbelfast.com/to.bar.council.18.9.90.html) and: "The Court spent more time trying to undermine my credibility than protecting Freddie's rights."
(http://www.justbelfast.com/letter_to_john.html)

46. http://www.indymedia.ie/article/77697 .

47. http://www.indymedia.ie/article/72186 .

48. http://www.publicinquiry.ie/ .

49. Village 15 Dec 2005 p.14.

50. http://wwa.rte.ie/news/1999/0506/flood.html. I wonder if he would relate to this description of the life of dissidents in the west which was written by Dr

Les Dove, the author of a Phd thesis on the role of MI5 in the UK:
"Dissidents will in all probability loose their jobs. If they are self-employed they will very quickly find that their customer base rapidly declines. Business "problems" will erupt and increase at every turn. Friends once considered "the best of" might suddenly turn against them as MI5's smear machine goes into full gear. This "character assassination" by MI5's psychological warfare department will apply not only to the dissident but also to their families. No one is spared."
(http://www.mindcontrolforums.com/pro-freedom.co.uk/l_dove.html he provides links on this subject here:
http://www.mindcontrolforums.com/v/dove.doc .)

51. "Any sort of problem Americans had in Peru, the embassy could call Montesinos and the problem would be solved," says Stanford professor Mc-Millan. "He was a fixer."...
U.S. Senators Patrick Leahy and Christopher Dodd had written letters to the head of the CIA in 1996 questioning the agency's connections to Montesinos.

A former U.S. intelligence agent who spoke to FRONTLINE/World on the condition of anonymity, and who interacted with Montesinos on a regular basis, said that during the mid-1990s, the CIA was getting feedback from the State Department that "the U.S. government should not deal with him or meet with him." This intelligence agent still thought that Montesinos was a valuable asset.
..."Maybe Mr. Montesinos didn't need to be influenced," said former French ambassador to Peru Antoine Blanca, who was representing French government interests in the case at the time. "He knew exactly where his interests were ... he worked for the CIA.""
(http://www.pbs.org/frontlineworld/stories/peru404/pmontesinos.html)
"Montgomery: Bruce Goslin is retired CIA field agent. In the mid-1990s, Goslin was assigned to Peru where he worked as an agency liaison to Montesinos. Goslin says for years, U.S. intelligence agencies maintained close ties to Montesinos despite concerns about his possible links to death squads and drug traffickers.

Goslin: We used to call him the dark prince. I think he fancied modeling himself after Machiavelli. He enjoyed being behind the scenes and pulling the strings of power.

Montgomery: Goslin says the relationship with Montesinos was closely controlled by officials in Washington. The CIA declined to comment, but Goslin says the agency passed millions of dollars to Peruvian intelligence units in the 1990s.
...
Some of the videos [the famous 'vladivideos'] reveal not just Montesinos's deals with Peruvians, but his warm relations with the CIA. In one video,

215

Montesinos throws a party for the departing CIA department chief."
(http://americanradioworks.publicradio.org/features/corruption/transcript.html)

52. http://news.scotsman.com/international.cfm?id=182602004 there is also a couple more links in the Appendix under Colombia.

53. http://www.publicinquiry.eu/2005/12/10/victory-for-corruption/ .

54. http://www.indymedia.ie/article/73559 .

55. http://archives.tcm.ie/irishexaminer/2002/08/10/story869827139.asp .

56. See further reading at http://www.indymedia.ie/article/78167 .

57. The Phoenix 8 April 2005 p.4 and a number of other Phoenix articles around that time. The 'fascist quote is from http://www.politics.ie/news_index.php?topic_id=13650 .

58. Village 4 May 2006 p.13-19 and The Phoenix 19 May 2006 p.5.

59. http://newswire.indymedia.org/fr/2005/10/825979.shtml. He goes on to say that these groups might deliberately harm the health of their targets, based on his experiences in South Africa, Rhodesia, the UK and the US. I thought this bit from the same author was worth retelling in the light of recent incidents:
"The 'frame-up' or 'set-up' has long been used to neutralize dissidents and may well be tried along with some of the other drastic measures mentioned earlier. For instance, a targeted dissident may by various means be introduced to 'Agents Provocateurs'(16). These could be male or female. MI-5 uses both sexes in their efforts to 'entrap' and 'criminalise' dissidents. Whatever, these provocateurs will attempt to integrate themselves into the dissidents company and gain their confidence, after which the dissident will then be introduced to other undercover agents who will in their turn invite the dissident to a 'party.' During this 'party' – and unknown to the dissident, drugs will be used and pho-tographs will be taken that shows the dissident 'in the close company of drug dealers.'"
(http://www.mindcontrolforums.com/v/les-dove1.htm)

60. http://www.indymedia.ie/newswire.php?story_id=72449 .

61. See Chapter 5 under Rose Doherty. There was more details on this given at the McBrearty meeting at the Mansion House where a friend of hers in Roscommon named senior gardai that were involved in this systematic harass-ment and frame up.

62. Sunday Independent 30 April 2006 p.4 and see also under Further Reading at http://www.indymedia.ie/article/78167 to see some quotes from the High

Court Judgement in his favour. Its under Dublin City Council.

63. Irish Independent 28 July 2006 p.16. From an early date Sgt White was trying to help the Donegal families: http://archives.tcm.ie/businesspost/2003/03/30/story567756159.asp, although obviously they had no reason to like him much before that. For the Omagh bombing and White's revelations see above Chapter 4 between footnotes 23-25.

64. http://www.publicinquiry.eu/2006/04/09/bugging-claims-widen-inquiry/ quoting Christine Newman in the Irish Times. See also under further reading at http://www.indymedia.ie/article/78167.

65. Irish Independent 30 July 2005 Review p.6.

66. http://www.prisonplanet.com/articles/may2006/130506Whistleblower.htm see also Further reading at http://www.indymedia.ie/article/78167 under 'Surveillence and Satellite capabilities available to the US'

67. http://www.mindcontrolforums.com/outting-bigbrother.htm .

68. Paul Baird presents some of the allegations of this kind of use of satellites at his site: http://www.surveillanceissues.com/default.htm. It seems that some of the information he presents was leaked to him by senior police and ex-intelligence agency personnel in Australia: http://www.surveillanceissues.com/case.htm .
Also an article by Dr.Rauni-Leena Luukanen-Kilde, the former Chief Medical Officer of Northern Finland, maybe relevant and is available here: http://houston.craigslist.org/pol/197423613.html, and originally published in the 36th-year edition of the Finnish-language journal SPEKULA (3rd Quarter, 1999). SPEKULA (circulation 6500) is a publication of Northern Finland medical students and doctors of Oulu University OLK (Oulun Laaketieteellinen Kilta). It is mailed to all medical students of Finland and all Northern Finland medical doctors: http://houston.craigslist.org/pol/197423613.html .
Also see John Akwei's article, reportedly an ex-NSA whistleblower: http://www.naicr.org/aps/akwei.html; an interview with Julianne McKinney a former "Area Intelligence Case Officer" in the DIA http://mp3.rbnlive.com/Greg/0604/20060419_Wed_Greg1.mp3 and her detailed account which is at http://www.mindcontrolforums.com/mck-clsc.htm .

69. For intelligence agencies and the media in general see Chapter 3 under the list of agencies.

70. The Phoenix 27 Jan 2006 p.6.

71. http://www.indymedia.ie/article/77294#comment159593 .

72. http://www.indymedia.ie/article/73552#comment133628 .

73. http://talk-ireland.com/article.php?sid=2284 .

74. http://debates.oireachtas.ie/DDebate.aspx?
F=SEN20060503.xml&Dail=29&Ex=All&Page=3 .

75. http://news.bbc.co.uk/2/hi/uk_news/northern_ireland/3302319.stm .

76. Eoin Ó Murchu: "The practise being adopted to change this [electoral re-gister] is even more undemocratic than the problem it is meant to address...What is being done now, however, is that if you're not in when the re-gister checkers call, your name is struck off.
Young people in particular are especially vulnerable to this way of putting the register together...[feels that using PPS numbers would be better] but it is no accident that this is not being done. For these young voters are the very ones who cannot be trusted to vote for the existing establishment parties."(Village 27 July 2006 p.14).

77. http://wwa.rte.ie/news/2001/0413/arms.html .

78. http://www.coiste.ie/articles/ella/splitnew.htm .

79. Vincent Browne: "With a mutual friend I visited him in his first grand home, Grangemore, in 1968. I remember very little about the visit but he later recalled I asked him then where he got the money to afford such a fine house. I asked him the same question again and again over the years and one time in 1979, a few months before he became Taoiseach, he told me the truth but I did-n't believe him. He said he was able to borrow money on the asset of his man-sion and estate at Kinsealy and that was precisely what emerged later at the McCracken and Moriarty Tribunals." He elaborated on this in his radio pro-gramme where he said that he consulted his old notes some time ago and he feels now that Haughey was all along completely truthful and honest in his an-swers about his personal finances. He added that he felt the banks and the rev-enue commissions were, in the long run, not in anyway short changed in their dealings with Haughey.
(http://www.villagemagazine.ie/article.asp?sid=1&sud=39&aid=1970).

80. Catherine Butler, Haughey's secretary:
"I felt the Tribunal lawyers didn't want to hear anything positive about Mr Haughey, though I answered each and every question regardless of the conse-quences or how painful or difficult it was. I had two very heated meetings with them. Highly unpleasant. I think I met them four or five times in private.

Even before I had been contacted by the Moriarty Tribunal, a senior Fianna Fáil official telephoned me at my office expressing his great pleasure in informing me that Fianna Fáil had given my name to the Tribunal as "someone of interest". He laughed as he said it. Certain political interests tried to influence what evidence I would give to the Tribunal. At one stage I could not answer my home telephone or mobile phone; in the end I had to obtain an ex-directory telephone number."
(Village 29 June 2006 http://www.villagemagazine.ie/article.asp?
aid=2041&iid=105&sud=10)

81. Catherine Butler at http://www.villagemagazine.ie/article.asp?
sid=1&sud=40&aid=1959 .

82. Some data that may point to a mysteriously organised opposition to Haughey, beginning with a Transcript made by Intelligence and Security Branch at Garda HQ of a conversation between the then FF Government Ministers Ray MacSharry and Martin O'Donoghue on 21st Oct 1982, which was taped by MacSharry.
MacSharry: "...[even] if I was to go around with the arse out of my trousers I would not take a brown penny from anyone...but I was a bit surprised to hear that there was some talk of money and where such money would be coming from."
O'Donoghue: "...What was being said was if there was any suggestion of somebody being compromised financially that it would be sorted out."
...
O'Donoghue: "There is a lot of money around alright but not for CJ not for him to stay."
MacSharry: "That kind of money, you could never have a situation develop where there would be money around to move a political party in any kind of situation."
O'Donoghue: "That is why I am not going after that aspect, I am concentrating on what is the ...for and against and how you would read the situation and that is why I came to talk to you."
...
MacSharry: "I was glad when you rang this morning because that was still on about what Brennan ahd [presumably 'had'] said about and you may not be in as good a financial state as rest of us and that there would be 100,000 pound to put that right, that was said."
(Joe Joyce and Peter Murtagh, *The Boss, Charles J Haughey in Government* (Dublin, 1983), p.376-82.)

Other bits and pieces from the 'Boss' book that maybe relevant:
"MacSharry maintained that O'Donoghue was simply telling him that a bribe was available for him."(p.326)
"Haughey asked that "Britain should stop interfering in the Irish election cam-

paign.""(p.326)

"He also accused FitzGerald of having lunch with a trained English spy [Duke of Norfolk]."(p.300)

"Haughey's advisers had been telling him for some time that the British were behind many of the disclosures that were emerging in public. The collapse of Anglo-Irish relations over the Falklands War and the ill feeling over James Prior's Northern Assembly helped to encourage that belief."(p.297)

Also there is this revealing information on Sean Doherty from the Phoenix:

"In contrast to all the personal hand wringing and political manoeuvring that Doherty was engaged in during the successful heave against Haughey, Doherty's financial situation miraculously went from critical to very successful in a matter of months.

...

Yet an amazing transformation of Doherty's financial fortunes then proceeded, more or less in tandem with the political cruxifixion of Haughey. Despite the litany of financial woes described above [including the threat of eviction from his home], Doherty then managed to apply for planning permission to add a twelve-bedroom extension onto his Cootehall Yacht and Country Club. At the same time, Doherty was also involved in an even more ambitious development of a marina...estimated at the time (1992) to cost £500,000."

(The Phoenix 17 June 2005 p.3)

83. "Irish Independent / 100 Years in the News 1905-2005" p.9, an article by Dr. Vincent Doyle.

CHAPTER 7

The real government policies being pursued in modern Ireland

"I could honestly say that I regretted having wasted my time contributing all my life to this awful system, to this denial, to this con democracy, this cod democracy, that was being administered by cod civil servants, cod public servants. Because that is all I would call them. I mean contributing both as a teacher and even in just living here. In a way I had wasted 40 years functioning in an environment that I found out didn't exist."- Micháel O'Sheighin[1]

Those strong words are by one of the most prominent of the Rossport campaigners and unfortunately I think they reflect quite well the experiences of some Irish people who have seen the modern Irish state at close quarters. We are told we live in a democracy and then sure its supposed to be the case that the policies pursued by the state are the ones freely chosen by the people and all that but you'd wonder if that is what really happens right now. Anyway in this chapter I attempt to trace the threads of five 'real' government policies that I think are being pursued in modern Ireland with the aim of controlling dissent by subtle long term social engineering techniques. I hope I'm wrong and that these policies are not being pursued but if you get fed up enough about what is going on in Ireland right now then you might be inclined to believe me. I know this is a mouthful, but in deference to some well known policies from the troubles I call them bureaucratisation, indebtedisation, securitisation, cosmopolitanisation and isolationisation:

1. Bureaucratisation
It is I think perfectly obvious that any properly functioning police state, like famously the former East Germany, always tries to get centralised government control over all economic and social activities within the state. In that type of society you have to get permission from the state to do virtually anything e.g. East Germany compelled all businesses to get centralised licenses to be allowed to exist etc etc. This brought with it certain advantages of political control, for example:

(a) It created a vast intelligence database that the domestic intelligence agencies used to keep tabs on the population. Whenever a person would register for anything they would have to supply a huge amount of personal – they might have felt irrelevant – data which unknown to the populace was systematically indexed and used by the huge secret police apparatus.

I respectfully submit that many people in Ireland right now, especially Social Welfare recipients and the self employed, spend an enormous amount of time informing the state about all aspects of their lives via hugely complex and rigorously enforced state regulations. Also nearly all the self employed have quietly become subservient to state licensing schemes, like even recently private security personnel and driving instructors. It has also become much more necessary to have tax clearance certificates and P.P.S numbers which might point to the way that the Irish intelligence agencies are indexing this data hoard.

(b) In countries like East Germany sometimes 'bureaucratic' problems would start to arise whenever the citizens fell foul of the state for some reason. Dissidents in the Eastern Bloc countries found that the state regulations, that controlled their lives so much, discriminated against them making their lives a misery.

Obviously there is great potential in Ireland for the state to act like this against citizens who offend it. Drawing again on the experiences of Rossport I notice that Micháel O'Sheighin says this about some of that community's dealings with Mayo Co. Council:

> "At various times, they were refused photocopies. Other times they'd get them but be held up all day. There was all this petty bureaucracy nonsense trying to frighten people, trying to intimidate them."[2]

There are also some very serious examples of state agencies turning on Irish citizens and seeking to put them out of business using various 'bureaucratic' regulations like in the case of the Department of Agriculture and its dealings with John Fleury [3] in Offaly and the Hanrahan family in Tipperary.[4] I personally think that Michael Lowry should be looked upon as an Irish dissident because of his attempts to root out corruption in the semi state sector which in turn drew harassment on him by state agencies:

> "Here is one of the things I want to get off my chest: I was disappointed that a system in any democracy would download to such an extent on any individual or citizen. I have felt a sense of State oppression against me. I got a sense of the power of the State's institutions, how domineering and controlling they are when they turn their sights on you."[5]

Of course like all dissidents, East and West, they are always assailed by whispering/slander campaigns against them and this is as true in Ireland as elsewhere. Michael Lowry has obviously had his character assassinated in the media over pretty minor tax matters while the Hanrahan family have been able to identify Frank Dunlop, the former government press spokesman, as one of their tormentors in the usual whispering campaigns.[6]

(c) It has a useful psychological effect on both the population in general and on state employees in particular. What happens is that as people get used to just filling out forms and spend half their lives abiding by all kinds of regulations they then start to lose their independent character and common sense. For a lot of people abiding by the regulations – and the laws that underpin them – becomes a kind of a religion and they begin to dehumanise and lose touch with the 'common sense' aspect of the regulations.

I will give one example of that type of psychological wearing down of people's intelligence and 'common sense'. In rural areas in Meath it is extremely difficult for anybody to get planning permission for any type of building with e.g. structures like two storey houses – as opposed to dormers – being pretty much banned completely on the grounds of being visually intrusive. This is especially true of any building that would be visible from Tara because we are told that the Council takes particular care to preserve the view from that historic hill. Also any ordinary house, or any kind of development, being built within any of the historic areas of Meath – like near Tara – has to undergo an archaeological dig to determine if there is anything historic there and if so the house is of course never built. (All these regulations by the way cost the ordinary people of Meath enormous sums of time and money to abide by.) But then the same Council makes no objection when a six lane motorway comes crashing through that landscape that they claim to be so keen on preserving! And in fact even many of the ordinary people see no contradiction here, after all the motorway comes under a different bureaucratic heading and I'm sure they have all the forms filled out. So as you can see, I hope, the government employees, and to an extent the ordinary people, start acting like intellectless bureaucrats after a while under this overly bureaucratic type of atmosphere. That is how the famous 'nomenclatura' was created in the Soviet Union, an army of unthinking and heartless state employees that can afflict all kinds of inhumanity on the citizens in the name of state regulations and laws.

So if you think about it maybe you can see that this wave of bureaucracy, which is crashing over the heads of Irish citizens right now, has 'good' qualities to it from a corrupt state's point of view. Hence maybe it is not an accident that the Irish state is developing along these lines right now.

2. Indebtedisation
It is obvious now that the economic boom in Ireland is by and large caused by individuals and families borrowing large sums of money, in many cases taking on huge 40 year mortgages to pay for astronomic-

ally expensive housing. Imho what is happening is that capital flowed into Ireland under large scale government borrowing from the mid 70s to the mid 90s and that has been replaced by this large scale personal borrowing. Just like in the case of that state borrowing, this boom has to be followed by a corresponding bust because people inevitably have to tighten their belts to try and pay back the huge debts.

I think it is fair to say that the state has encouraged this effect by, for example, sponsoring 'social and affordable' housing schemes that actually just involve encouraging poor people to borrow heavily. This is in total contrast to the past where social housing meant building houses at the expense of the state and giving them to people at a nominal rent. So why would the state want to sponsor this splurge of personal borrowing? I can think of two reasons. Firstly maybe the banking institutions (and international banks?) have huge sway over the Irish political system and can simply force this policy through. This policy after all is obviously in their interests, making, as they do, huge profits out of it in wide interest rate differentials and extortionate banking charges.

The other point is that this process of indebtedness brings with it useful social control aspects. I think a person tied to a huge mortgage often becomes obsessed with money, unlike the more footloose rent paying person, and might trim his/her political or rebellious instincts in order not to scare off the next paycheck. I'm convinced anyway that if you ever have some grand war crimes tribunal in Ireland in the future asking why government employees didn't speak out you'd be told that they had the mortgage to consider. This 'had to pay the mortgage' might turn out to be the Irish equivalent of the German 'only following orders'.

I think therefore that this indebtedness has a subtle but definite social control aspect to it.

3. Securitisation

I don't mean that in the financial sense, I am just referring to the increased security measures rolled out since 9/11, at airports etc. It seems to this observer that the powers that be know perfectly well that your average 70 year old with a nail clippers or a bottle of water is no threat to anybody and that they have other reasons for these changes. Maybe they are copying the type of measures that were pioneered by the British army in Malaya, high visibility security procedures that have a subtle psychological effect on the people policed like this. Basically it was felt that the mass of the population could be slightly intimidated by the state when it acted this way, with a consequent drop in rebellious activities. Of course this didn't have much effect on the Malayan insurgents themselves, it was more a question of scaring the people around them, employers, parents etc. If you think about the current atmosphere picture a parent worrying about whether or not their children will be able to go on that holiday to America, through the increased security procedures, if they go on that Shannon protest or whatever. When Major Fred Holroyd – and remember he was actually taught by General Kitson, widely considered the foremost British expert in this area – was asked about the enhanced airport security measures, at the Justice for the Forgotten meeting in Dublin, he called it "all part of the intimidation system."

In any case it is obvious that this has become quite a characteristic of modern Ireland, with enhanced security at the Four Courts, the Dail, not to mention enormous security changes, and delays, at the Irish airports. Not only that but many Irish businesses, hostels and nightclubs seem to have become almost a Celtic version of the Big Brother house with their many cameras and personnel employed to spy and stare at people walking in and out. I wonder too if the artificial and almost tense atmosphere that these measures create might also add to the isolationism discussed below. It just seems to me anyway that it creates an unrelaxed type of atmosphere which is very evident I think if you walk around places like Temple Bar. A lot of the time there are more bouncers and gardai policing the area than there are members of the public. And this over the top security makes it difficult for ordinary people to really relax and for social outlets to properly fulfil their role.

4. Cosmopolitanisation.

I use that phrase as meaning the same thing as de-nationalisation, a kind of process of changing a country in order to make a nation lose its sense of unique identity. I think the best example of that type of policy can be seen in the history of the Soviet Union. The Soviets always felt that it was easier to control their Union if they could de-nationalise (and incidentally de-Christianise) the various peoples they controlled. They did this firstly through a myriad of complicated migration policies e.g. by encouraging Russians to migrate to the Baltic States in order to dilute their sense of identity and by various forced migrations of races like the Chechens. And secondly they used the media and education systems to play down the historic and separate identities of the various races, including even the Russians themselves as Alexander Solzhenitsyn relates:

> "During the 20's the very understanding of Russian history was changed—there was none! And the understanding of what a Russian is was changed—there was no such thing! And what was most painful, we Russians ourselves willingly walked along this suicidal path. The period of the 20's was considered the dawn of liberation...I recall from my school days that even the word 'Russian', such as 'I am a Russian' sounded like a call to counter-revolution...But everywhere was heard and printed the term 'Russopyati'." [a curse word for 'Russian'].

225

The Russian national character and sense of solidarity then broke down under this pressure, which left them more vulnerable in the gulags:

"All nations in the Gulag crawled in order to survive and the lower to the ground they got, the better the chances of survival. But Russians in 'their own Russian' camps were the lowest order."

Based on these experiences Solzhenitsyn feels that nationalism is very important for everybody:

"Before the camps, I regarded the existence of nationality as something that shouldn't be noticed—nationality did not really exist, only humanity. But in the camps one learns: if you belong to a successful nation you are protected and you survive. If you are part of universal humanity – too bad for you."[7]

So that process of encouraging people to feel as if they are just one atomised member of 'universal humanity' as opposed to feeling as an integral part of a unique nation is what I am calling 'cosmopolitanisation'. As we stand today I think that a wave of cosmopolitanisation – particularly the large immigration inflow – is hacking away at the intellectual and emotional roots of Irish nationalism:

Intellectual
In some ways what we are seeing now is a sort of race for the intellectual high moral ground on this issue, with the winner being able to throw down 'racist' and 'fascist' insults at the loser coming up the hill! As I see it the modern roots of Irish nationalism derive from the period 1890-1910 say when our ancestors rebelled against the bland uniformity of the British Empire and sought Irish independence in order to protect and foster what were seen to be the unique characteristics of the Irish race. At that time they obviously emphasised things like the Irish language, folklore, music, Gaelic games, the struggles of the Catholic Church in a Protestant country, and Irish genealogy and modern Irish nationalism grew from this into a feeling that we needed Irish Independence in order to protect this heritage and these characteristics. This feeling culminated maybe in the various Irish Race Conventions held at that time, like in Dublin in 1896 and New York in 1916, and in expressions of people like Pearse saying that Ireland should become 'not free merely but Gaelic as well' etc. Sometimes this is known simply as the 'Irish Ireland' movement and I think you can see that there is now a faint whiff of 'racism' and 'fascism' beginning to attach itself to phrases like that in the intellectual atmosphere now in Ireland. Its obvious to me anyway that the new thinking about 'inclusiveness' for the new immigrant population is in fact intended to have the effect of casting aspersions on what is, I suggest, the intellectual underpinnings of Irish nationalism. Again I'm suggesting that this is no accident, this imho is one of the

reasons why huge immigration inflows are being sponsored by Irish government agencies,[8] it is quite consciously intended to weaken Irish nationalism and identity. One might think looking at this that there is no reason why Irish identity couldn't coexist quite happily with the increasing immigrant population, and maybe it can but that is not what our government has in store for us in my opinion.

Just look at the church for an example of this kind of thinking. According to the recent census 87 per cent of Irish people are Catholics and the proportion in some areas, like Mayo, is probably a lot higher. Yet despite that background when a group of nurses wanted to set up a crib in Castlebar hospital recently they were told that they couldn't because to do so would be "racist" and uninclusive of other faiths.[9] The management of the hospital explained that a crib would be the thin end of the wedge, if they allowed that they might have to allow a crucifix! As you can see this is quite a change from a few years ago and clearly 'inclusiveness' is in fact being used to crush the faith of the majority. I'm convinced that the same thing is going to happen to Irish culture. Already it is the case that the Irish language requirement in the Gardai and for some university courses has been dropped "in the context of an increasingly multicultural Ireland."[10]

Emotional

What seems to be happening on an emotional level now in Ireland is that Irish people are beginning to feel like strangers in their home localities. They are beginning to tune out of really caring about what happens here because they don't identify with the country anymore, it just doesn't feel like home. This is being noticed by some recent visitors to Ireland:

"There was such manifest sadness in the eyes of the few "old Irish" we encountered. Their homeland is becoming unrecognizable to them."[11]

It doesn't feel like their homeland because most, or very many, of the people they meet as they walk down the street don't seem like people of their own ethnicity, and don't use the familiar accents and even language that Irish people are used to. So Irish people are starting to feel rootless, and are beginning to lose their identity in their own country.[12]

One other point, which I think ties in with this, are the wholesale changes being made to the Irish landscape. Clearly Ireland has become a concrete jungle of motorways and anonymous housing estates which makes the whole country look indistinguishable from California or Germany or wherever, which again weakens the sense of a unique Irish identity. One person writing to the Irish Independent has mentioned how people feel anonymous in this landscape:

"Urban sprawl increases traffic, congestion and related problems. It also creates an anonymous society which leads to social isolation and related ills, such as crime, violence, drugs and the culture of death."[13]

I think again that this is a deliberate planned effect pushing the ever expanding motorway network, they want people to feel like nobodies in a bland world, they are easier to control that way.

Anyway like cutting Samson's hair, when a people lose confidence in their right to a separate national identity, which is what happens when those intellectual roots are cut off, and when they psychologically lose the sense of an Irish homeland then Irish nationalism weakens making it easier for supra national organisations, particularly the EU, to control us. This I think is the reason why these policies are deliberately pursued like this. It also has the effect of helping to control internal dissent in Ireland. Just look at Rossport as an example and ask yourself why has that protest proven to have infinitely more teeth than any other recent protest in modern Ireland. I think you'd have to admit that the people out there amidst an heroic landscape, steeped in Irish folklore, language, music and historical traditions – maybe even with strong religious traditions as well – simply put up a much better fight than protests which are based in transient communities situated in bland housing estates off some motorway or other.[14] The powers that be in Europe know this perfectly well, they know that peoples and communities with a strong cultural and ethnic identity are more of a threat to them than the cosmopolitan or multicultural type. So in fact I think they are quite deliberately destroying that unifying and enriching sense of identity among the Irish people.

5. Isolationisation

(That's a perfectly good word by the way, you just have to keep going when you get lost in the middle!) According to Julianne McKinney, who served as a US intelligence agent in Berlin during the Cold War, the Soviet Union had a policy of trying to "divide and isolate the populace" in order to maintain its control over the subject peoples of the Soviet Union.[15] The thinking here was that strong community structures made it difficult for the KGB to isolate those dissidents that they wished to harass, so where possible they would prefer to break down those communities everywhere.

Again if you look at Rossport you can see why a government might feel threatened by communities and groups much more than by individuals. What started there was that about two people initially dug their heels in and opposed the pipeline, then in court about five people were prepared to go to jail rather than be bullied by the system, then after they were jailed maybe about 1,000 people in the same community rose up and challenged the authorities. Its obvious that when you have a strong community that sticks together like this then the government has much more problems than in those parts of Ireland where people have been jailed in almost total community silence and anonymity. Its the existence of a tight knit community itself that causes problems for the state, it would be much better from their point of view if people didn't have wide circles of friends, family or neighbours that will defend each other. You need to isolate people to crush them.

I believe that governments at a high level know this very well and maybe you can see some of that thinking in events like the crushing of the mining communities in England in the 80s. They were probably the most close knit and rebellious communities in Britain before they were wiped off the map, some would say on the basis of exaggerated economic problems.

As well as the question of communities like this being able to sustain long strikes and protests against the state I think there are two other specific reasons why governments prefer to break up community structures. One reason is that the flow of information in tight knit communities is often directly by word of mouth from some primary source e.g. there is a good chance that somebody might personally know a guy in the Gardai say and will pass the information along to everybody else whereas when people are isolated their only source is the, typically government controlled, mass media.

Another reason is that when people are not used to knowing a wide circle of friends etc. they start to lose the capacity to judge people properly. In other words they find it hard to accurately assess a person's integrity and even sanity and stuff like that. In the Soviet Union this then allowed the KGB to go around claiming that such a such a dissident was 'mad' or an 'enemy of the state' and the general public just believed the state agencies when they said this about a person because they themselves had become such poor judges of character. Don't think for a second that this issue is only relevant to the former Soviet Union! If you follow the Irish media with respect to intelligence whistleblowers you will be amazed at how many of them are called 'Walter Mittys' by the media and the state. In fact even Frank McBrearty has been fighting a lonely battle trying to testify in the courts in the teeth of "sinister" government attempts to compel him to go for repeated psychiatric examinations.[16]

So anyway I think it is a cardinal rule of political control that the state would like to destroy any sense of community or comradeship that may be developing, in so far as it can. Hence I think people should be a bit suspicious of any changes that they observe in that line in Ireland today, and should ask themselves if some of those changes are deliberate. A simple example might be all those complaints about tight knit Dublin communities being transported out of the city into anonymous housing estates where no facilities were provided – even shops – which would have allowed them to develop a community atmosphere. That might have been the whole idea. Another example might be where community facilities are run down in rural areas, like Post Offices, Garda Stations, banks etc, using what maybe over hyped economic excuses to crush the community atmosphere? I personally think you could make a case that all the current social outlets in Ireland seem to be under siege from government regulations and suspiciously unremedied transport problems. Think of over the top security procedures – necessary to comply with government drug laws – hyped up drink driving campaigns, the smoking ban, and shorter opening hours for nightclubs, all leading to a situation where many people no longer go out and meet people and instead stay in and become slaves to the mass media. This again might not be far from what the government actually wanted to achieve with things like the smoking ban. A few other specific areas might be worth looking at in the same vein:

(a) Some of the older companies in Ireland are home to a staff with a strong sense of community and solidarity. I would suggest companies like Aer Lingus, the Irish Sugar Company and Irish Ferries, all of them under various stages of siege or abolition, and maybe not accidentally.

(b) Believe it or not I would include boarding schools under this heading. They tend to be characterised these days as very expensive and exclusive but in the past many poor people went there, especially to get around transport problems in rural areas. Anyway they fostered a very deep sense of community and are now in various stages of collapse, supposedly from random problems like insurance costs.

(c) I actually think that Bebo and internet chat sites are seen by the powers that be to be a threat in that they can build up quite a few friendships and a community atmosphere. (I think as well that is why some sites discourage idle chat making among their users, anything to stop strong trust and groups forming.) Its obvious when you follow the Irish media that the powers that be don't like those sites and are hyping paedophile stuff to discredit them. (Which is not to denigrate the seriousness of that problem outside of the internet.) As well as this Irish second and third level institutions have been encouraged to introduce special rules designed to block Bebo and the other social networking chat sites.[17]

(d) It seems to me as well that some of the new community policing and ASBO type rules that are being rolled out are now being used to stop communities forming in some areas. It seems to me anyway that three people at a street corner doing absolutely nothing but chatting are now being accused of 'anti-social behaviour' – ironically enough – and are being asked to move on by the community police.

(e) Maybe some of the planning and local authority rules are deliberately designed to break up communities e.g. in rural areas by denying the locals housing, and in small towns by introducing draconian parking arrangements that drive people out of those towns into more soulless out of town shopping centres.

I know most people reading this are saying "yeah right, there is no deliberate long term plan here" but I think people ought to be a little more suspicious, and unfortunately, maybe a little less naive about the workings of the modern EU controlled Irish state. I think we have to get away from this idea that the Irish state is run by morans who don't know what they are doing, it could be that the people are the foolish ones who are not scrutinising properly what the state is really doing? Because if you look again at some of these drifts you might feel that this 'isolationism' policy is a better way to explain what is really happening than what we are usually told. I think even if you look at what has happened to the close knit community of Ballymun you might wonder if this type of "social engineering" is what is happening there rather than a genuine effort to regenerate that community.[18]

So I think we should stop criticising the powers that be in Ireland as incompetent or unintelligent, their project Ireland is progressing very well thank you very much!

Footnotes

1. The Rossport 5, *Our Story* (Magheramore Co.Wicklow, 2006), p.75.

2. Ibid p.74.

3. For references to John Fleury see Chapter 1 footnote 19.

4. For the Hanrahan family see the Irish Independent 3 Feb 2007. Another example of this type of harassment can be seen I think in the experiences of Ashley Mote MEP:
"Over the last three years I have become one of the fiercest critic of the EU inside the parliament. I have made a lot of powerful enemies, especially those concerned with the misappropriation of public funds (uncovered with the help of a team of brilliant analytical accountants). Silencing me would be a huge relief to many in Brussels and inside the present British government. See elsewhere on this website for details.

The publication of my book Vigilance – A Defence of British Liberty in 2001 was followed within four months by the original action by Chichester District Council to stop housing benefit without notice. Publication of my book Over-Crowded Britain in 2002 was followed within two months by the Ministry for Work and Pensions joining in the hunt. Acceleration of matters to a court case followed less than one month after it became known that I had been elected high on the electoral list for the June 2004 elections to the European Parliament. I don't believe in that many coincidences.
...
The law was once championed as a shield for the protection of the common man. In the hands of today's ruling elite it has become a weapon of the state. It is now much to be feared. It is used ruthlessly to destroy opposition, however modest, wherever it is perceived." (http://www.ashleymote.co.uk/topics.php?filter=&sec=article&art_id=474)

5. Sunday Independent 1 April 2007 p.33.

6. Irish Independent 20 May 2000.

7. Alexander Solzhenitsyn, *200 Years Together* (2001-2002), quoted at http://www.vdare.com/allen/070427_solzhenitsyn.htm.

8. For which see http://www.indymedia.ie/article/78897. These quotes by Daniel Sheehan, an Irish MP of the period, show I think how the atmosphere in Ireland was transformed by the activities of the Gaelic League and by this new national consciousness and strengthened identity. He describes first how that identity was deliberately eroded by the British authorities:
"Through the whole of the nineteenth century it had been the malign purpose

of England to destroy the spirit of nationality through its control of the schools. Just as in the previous century it sought to reduce Ireland to a state of servitude through the operations of the Penal Laws, so it now sought to continue its malefic purpose by a system of education "so bad that if England had wished to kill Ireland's soul when she imposed it on the Sister Isle she could not have discovered a better means of doing so" (M. Paul Dubois). And the same authority ascribes the fatalism, the lethargy, the moral inertia and intellectual passivity, the general absence of energy and character which prevailed in Ireland ten or twelve years ago to the fact that England struck at Ireland through her brain and sought to demoralise and ruin the national mind."

Then the atmosphere after the Irish Ireland movement started:

"In giving to the young especially a new pride in their country and in their own, great and distinctive national heritage, it did a great deal to strengthen the national character and to make it more independent and self-reliant. It started the great work of rooting out the slavery which centuries of dependency and subjection had bred into the marrow of the race. Mr Arthur Griffith has admitted that the present generation could never have effected this work had not Parnell and his generation done their brave labour before them, but considered in themselves the achievements of the Gaelic League can only be described as mighty both in the actual revolution it wrought in the moral, intellectual and spiritual sphere, in the reaction it created against the coarser materialism of imported modes and manners, and in the new spirit which it breathed into the entire people."

(Daniel Sheehan, *Ireland since Parnell* (London, 1921), available at http://www.gutenberg.org/files/13963/13963.txt .)

It is felt by some that we are in danger of losing that strong identity in the current era, like for example in this letter by Pauline Bleach:

"The Irish like to party, we always will and cocaine is a dreadful drug.

In travelling, I noticed that Irish people tend to get less messed up than most, possibly because we were brought up with a strong cultural core. We knew who we were, from a local to a national to a historical and a mythological core.

Back in Ireland, that core is being eroded in the name of prosperity, a nice house, a shopping mall and a motorway. When we have nothing left in this core, all dismissed as irrelevant as long as we can get to work easily, what have the proportion of our population who value the spirit of Ireland left to belong to?

And how would I have reacted if this had been the case when I was 15? All the money in the world cannot fill your soul. And an empty soul will be filled whether with shopping, drugs or thoughts of suicide." (Irish Independent Sept 4 2007)

9. "The crib is very symbolic and while you wouldn't describe it as offensive we don't want to set a precedent that is difficult to move away from. It could easily lead to a crucifix..."
(http://archives.tcm.ie/westernpeople/2005/12/20/story28622.asp). The 'racism' reference is from the Irish Family Press newspaper at the time of this controversy. A discussion on the controversy can be read here: http://www.castlebar.ie/board/2006/jul06/133189.htm. It became a big issue in Mayo and the HSE eventually had to give in.

10. A report on the Department of Irish Folklore in UCD:
"While recognising the major importance of the Irish language material in the Department's teaching and research programmes, the PRG recommends that in the context of an increasingly multicultural Ireland, where deemed appropriate, the Irish language requirement for entry to year 2 and 3 be relaxed."
(http://www.ucd.ie/quality/reports/summaryirishfolklorereport.doc.doc)

This letter was written in response to the dropping of the Irish language requirement for the Gardai:
"However, by changing the rules on Irish, admittedly for all applicants, the Government is making the kind of error made by British and Dutch governments. That is to say, they are downgrading the norms and culture of the State in the vain hope that this will somehow make the State seem more tolerant. In reality, however, immigrants, as in Europe, will take this as a signal that integration is not required and full participation is not expected.
Furthermore, what signal does this action send to the many who speak Irish and are proud that their language is an official language of the State? Is Irish to be official only for native-born Irish and not for others? What other norms will be dropped in the near future to make us more inclusive? Lowering standards has been shown to be a failed concept and once that particular Rubicon has been crossed other ideas, standards and norms cherished by the Irish people will surely fall on the altar of multiculturalism.- Yours, etc,
TREVOR TROY,
Connaught Place,
Athboy,
Co Meath."
(http://www.gaelport.com/index.php?page=clippings&id=509&viewby=date).

Also its now apparently forbidden for people to register their addresses in Irish with An Post because:
"Tá go leor inimirceach ag obair linn agus ní bheadh siad in ann Gaeilge a léamh."(http://www.politics.ie/viewtopic.php?t=20260).

11. http://www.remnantnewspaper.com/Archives/archives-2006-0630-pilgrimage06.htm .

12. Here are just a few references that show how some Irish people are begin-

ning to feel that their culture is being threatened by the extent of the immigration inflow:
"And what was once a wonderful urban village neighbourhood in Dublin, complete with artisanal shops of long tradition and history, has long since had those shops removed and replaced with call centres operated by ... [various immigrant groups.]...That's the erosion of culture at work and it has led to an erosion of values, as neighbours no longer know or care for each other..."
(http://www.politics.ie/viewtopic.php?
t=18768&postdays=0&postorder=asc&start=24)
"Our Identity, Culture Language are under threat like never before.What we have witnessed over the past 10yrs regarding Mass Immigration to our Country beggars belief!!
... Social engineering thats what it is!!" (http://www.politics.ie/viewtopic.php?
t=17946&start=576&sid=c907709f19ca3c0d5f44534f1cd747b5). More from these heated debates at politics.ie:

"In contrast, I have often been struck by the number of people who oppose Mass Immgration who have lived for extended periods abroad and/or who are married to foreigners or have non-Irish lovers. In my case my non-Irish cohabitant expresses incomprehension that so many Irish people willingly set out to destroy the ancient Irish nation by fomenting Mass Immigration. As she says, when she agreed to live in Ireland it was Ireland, it no longer is. If she wanted to live in Poland or Bangladesh she's go there. She doesn't."

(http://www.politics.ie/viewtopic.php?
t=24963&postdays=0&postorder=asc&start=96).

I guess some feel that maybe Ireland is not learning from the mistakes of many other countries, where immigration has become a very big issue, as you can see from these assorted references:

Germany

"Helmut Schmidt, the former German chancellor, has inflamed the country's debate on immigration by saying that multiculturalism can only work under authoritarian regimes, and that bringing millions of Turkish guest workers to Germany was a mistake.
"The concept of multiculturalism is difficult to make fit with a democratic society," he told the Hamburger Abendblatt newspaper.
He added that it had been a mistake that during "the early 1960s we brought guest workers from foreign cultures into the country".
Mr Schmidt, 85, who was the Social Democratic chancellor from 1974 until 1982, said that the problems resulting from the influx of mostly Turkish Gastarbeiter, or guest workers, had been neglected in Germany and the rest of Europe. They could be overcome only by authoritarian governments, he added, naming Singapore as an example."
(The Telegraph 25/11/2004 http://www.rense.com/general60/fidid.htm)

Netherlands
"Liberal Holland hits the cultural panic button
The Dutch are backing out of multiculturalism after two high-profile murders.
As Britain, too, gets jumpy about its social mix, Ian Buruma suggests a way
out.

Until a few years ago the Dutch prided themselves on being the most tolerant,
most progressive people on earth. If multiculturalism was going to work
anywhere, it would be in Holland. That was the view, at any rate, of the
intellectual elite which was by and large of a leftist disposition.
...
[After a famous murder in Holland] a consensus rose among a section of the
Dutch commentariat: multiculturalism had been a disaster;
...
In the beginning people barely noticed these shadowy figures cleaning trains
and the like. It was only once their families arrived a decade or so later and
children were born that old working-class neighbourhoods began to fill up with
halal butchers, mosques and satellite dishes tuned to Arab and north African
television stations. This happened after the economic boom was pretty much
over.

The views of most Moroccan villagers and Turkish men who settled with their
families in the shabbier parts of Amsterdam or central Rotterdam had little in
common with those of the newly secularised and sexually liberated Dutch. But
the progressive multicultural view was that this did not matter. Each to his
own. We may not like the way Muslim men treat their wives and daughters,
but who are we to say that our ways are better? High crime rates and
unemployment in immigrant areas were rarely discussed and those who tried to
were frequently dismissed as racists.
...
The reaction to the multicultural ideal in the 1990s came from two sides. The
fatwa against Salman Rushdie mobilised metropolitan progressives, most of
whom had been multiculturalists before, against Islamic intolerance. Further
down the social scale people began to feel they had been betrayed by the elites
who had, especially in Holland, put European idealism above national pride
and taken no notice when people no longer felt at home in the streets they grew
up in.
...
Immigrants, especially Muslim immigrants, became the main focus of a
discontent that was rooted in deeper anxieties. A combination of global
capitalism, European bureaucracy and excessive individualism made many
people feel dislocated and powerless. Resentment of Muslim immigrants and
the rejection, in Holland and France, of the European constitution were aspects
of the same attack on multiculturalists, Eurocrats and the bien pensants
metropolitans who ignored the common man."

(The Sunday Times November 19, 2006 Review Section
http://www.timesonline.co.uk/section/0,,2092,00.html .)

England
"From the 1950s onwards there were incessant waves of immigration, with the white working class forced to share what were already cramped quarters with a huge influx of immigrants.

When they complained, they were dismissed by the chattering classes as Little Englanders and racists. The incessant attempts to accommodate an increasingly dense population scattered the white working class out of their original habitat. Many moved out to the suburbs, geographically fracturing the strong family networks and communities.

Before that the working class were born and bred in the place they would live for the rest of their lives. Existing cheek by jowl with family, friends and neighbours meant that everybody knew everybody else and their business. A lack of respect or a stepping out of line could haunt you for life; there was an incentive to keep your nose clean and do as you would be done by. That enforced morality and standard of behaviour began to unravel in the anonymity of the new estates.
...

The culture of political correctness and the widespread (and often accurate) view among many working-class people that every other social and ethnic group's needs came above theirs when it came to government resources bred resentment. From the 1980s the multiculturalists formed part of a breed within civic bodies, keen to erase evidence of the local heritage of the white working class and emphasise the historical presence of every other creed and colour. Had all this been done to any other ethnic or social group, its problems would not have remained so hidden.
...

I would argue that divorcing today's young working-class lads from a sense of their own history and belonging has played a large part in their underperformance. When the poor academic performance of black boys became an issue, experts were quick to point to the causes: a lack of positive male role models, racism and history.

The poor performance of black boys at school first became an issue in the 1970s. Nobody then mentioned what was happening to the likes of us. I left a comprehensive school with one CSE. Only a handful of my white working-class contemporaries went on to further education. Now, 30 years on, it is depressing to say the least that things have got even worse."
(The Sunday Times Review Section Nov 19 2006.
http://www.timesonline.co.uk/newspaper/0,,2766-2459733,00.html .)

US

The Harvard political scientist Robert Putnam has conducted a study on the level of 'social capital' – the sort of things that flourish in strong and thriving communities, like volunteering and political engagement etc – in the US:

"The study, the largest ever on civic engagement in America, found that virtually all measures of civic health are lower in more diverse settings.

[By which he meant ethnically mixed communities. He spent many years trying to find if there was some other explanation for this finding but has now ruled out any other factor:]

"But even after statistically taking them all into account, the connection remained strong: Higher diversity meant lower social capital. In his findings, Putnam writes that those in more diverse communities tend to "distrust their neighbors, regardless of the color of their skin, to withdraw even from close friends, to expect the worst from their community and its leaders, to volunteer less, give less to charity and work on community projects less often, to register to vote less, to agitate for social reform more but have less faith that they can actually make a difference, and to huddle unhappily in front of the television."

"People living in ethnically diverse settings appear to 'hunker down' – that is, to pull in like a turtle," Putnam writes.

In documenting that hunkering down, Putnam challenged the two dominant schools of thought on ethnic and racial diversity, the "contact" theory and the "conflict" theory. Under the contact theory, more time spent with those of other backgrounds leads to greater understanding and harmony between groups. Under the conflict theory, that proximity produces tension and discord.

Putnam's findings reject both theories. In more diverse communities, he says, there were neither great bonds formed across group lines nor heightened ethnic tensions, but a general civic malaise. And in perhaps the most surprising result of all, levels of trust were not only lower between groups in more diverse settings, but even among members of the same group. "Diversity, at least in the short run," he writes, "seems to bring out the turtle in all of us.""
(http://www.thetruthseeker.co.uk/article.asp?ID=6974)

13. Letter by William A Thomas in the Irish Independent 30 April 2007 p.33. I think the actor Edward Norton touches on this type of atmosphere in a recent interview. He seems to suggest that the banality of the modern globalised and motorway intersected landscape has this demoralising effect on people:

"But I had a very similar feeling doing that to the feeling I had doing the 'Fight Club' in that it's totally about people seeking authenticity, and having absolutely no idea how to find it; the way that the modern world has encased us in such a way that makes psychic desperation the only route out. Literally, insanity is the only escape from the banality of it all.

California, he says, throws these contradictions into particularly vivid relief, with its 'remnants of this Steinbeck-like agricultural landscape, almost like paradise', flickering like dying embers in a sea of bland uniformity.' A friend of mine had a film testing out in Burbank at a multiplex, and I was driving around looking for a place to park, and it was staggering – there was nothing but franchises. Starbuck's, Radioshack, McDonald's. That is the entire reality. And it went on forever. There were kids walking around, and I was thinking, where do you get your identity from when it all becomes the same – when the textures are completely the same everywhere? How do you have any sense of yourself?'" (7 April 2007 Telegraph Magazine p.24.)

14. To see the way that these factors have strengthened and inspired the Rossport community see The Rossport 5, *Our Story* (Magheramore Co.Wicklow, 2006), p.59-61, and this from p.96:
"People will tell you locally that the last battle from some prophecy or other will be the battle of Ballinaboy. To me this is an echo of the awareness of people back to the Bronze Age time. An awareness that having a grip on a place is tenuous and can be destroyed."

15. See Chapter 1 footnote 16 of this work.

16. "McBrearty Jnr has branded the move as "sinister" because the proposed psychiatric and psychological assessment will be carried out by practitioners nominated by the tribunal...The tribunal is obviously intent on not allowing me to get on with my life even though the state has examined me three times." (Sunday Tribune 12/11/2006 http://www.tribune.ie/article.tvt? _scope=TribuneFTF&id=79032&SUBCAT=&SUBCATNAME=&DT=12/11/ 2006%2000:00:00&keywords=McBrearty%20psychiatric&FC=).

17. http://www.tomrafteryit.net/irish-schools-being-blocked-from-accessing-social-networks/.

18. The Craig Gardner Report of August 1993 stated that the authors initially looked upon Ballymun as a 'community in crisis' but instead concluded that "Ballymun is an estate with a very strong sense of a community identity, and a level of community activity which is very high."(http://www.brl.ie/pdf/Ballymun_A_History_1600_1997_Synopsis.pdf p.63.) (Its obvious when you read that account that the Ballymun residents were very active opponents of Dublin Corporation and the powers that be.) From indymedia in the same vein: "For all its problems, Ballymun has always had a strong sense of social identity." (http://www.indymedia.ie/article/73355).

Imho this sort of thing is always bad news from a corrupt governments point of view so I am suspicious about the way they moved in to demolish the flats in the teeth of resistance from many local residents, one survey that was undertaken "included 539 face to face interviews and demonstrated that 86% of the residents of the flats preferred partial or full refurbishment to the demolition of their homes." (http://web.archive.org/web/20030717231324/ourworld.compuserve.com/homepages/tonylowes/itlet2.htm).

After the flats had been mostly knocked the government unveiled surprising new Social Welfare rules which seem, to this observer anyway, to be designed to disperse the community atmosphere that developed in the flats. See http://www.oneparent.ie/pdfs/1_Rent%20Supplement%20Campaign.pdf and http://www.indymedia.ie/article/66799. From comments on the latter article: "City planning out in Ballymun is beginning to look more like some form of "social cleansing"." And this by John:
"This has been happening for some time.

I would ask anyone to point out a single area of Dublin city that has been "re-generated" and where after five years anyone on a salary similar to the original occupants could afford to live there.

Smithfield, Temple Bar, in fact, the entire city centre looks like going this way over the next few decades and the children of families that have lived there for generations can, as far as the government is concerned, make do with a 2-bed semi in Clonee and a three hour commute to work / family."

This is the current view of some local activists about the 'regeneration' process: "By involving as many people as possible in its activities they [the local BPBP activist group] plan to turn around the disastrous effects that "regeneration" is having on the social fabric of Ballymun."
(http://www.indymedia.ie/article/73355). Is this by accident or design?

APPENDIX

The Strategy of Tension Worldwide

These are just some international links that show that intelligence agencies sometimes secretly support paramilitary groups that they publicly are opposed to. There are in fact many different reasons why some parties who overtly oppose terrorism actually support it, and hopefully some insight into this practice can be gained from reading the following links. I guess the simplest way to understand it is that intelligence agencies support terrorists in the same way that police forces run agent provocateurs, and presumably it took many years for political dissidents and protesters to realise that this tactic was being used. I have provided a few quotations, or at least a set of keywords, that could help anybody searching for these links later. The phrase 'Strategy of Tension' refers to the Italian Prime Minister's description of the Italian state's covert assistance in the creation of left and right wing terrorism in Italy in the 70s and 80s.

Afghanistan

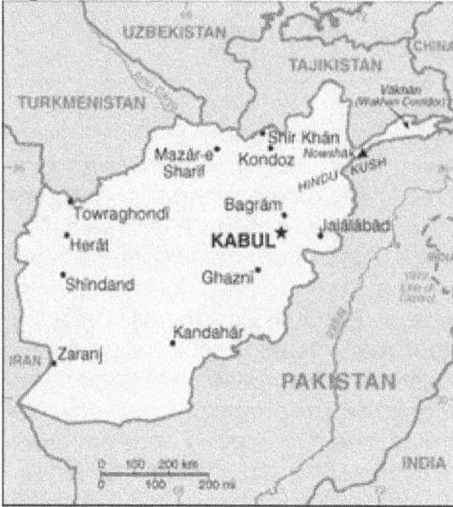

http://www.prisonplanet.com/news_alert_032402_terror.html

"Britain was accused last night of falsely claiming that al-Qaeda terror-ists had built a 'biological and chemical weapons' laboratory in Afghanistan to justify the deployment of 1,700 Royal Marines to fight there."

http://www.pbs.org/now/printable/transcript208_full_print.html

Seymour Hersh talking in an interview about a battle in Afghanistan:
"Okay, the cream of the crop of Al Qaeda caught in a town called Kon-duz which is near ... it's one little village and it's a couple hundred kilo-meters, 150 miles from the border of Pakistan. And I learned this story frankly-- through very, very clandestine operatives we have in the Delta Force and other very..

...

There was about a three or four nights in which I can tell you maybe six, eight, 10, maybe 12 more-- or more heavily weighted-- Pakistani military planes flew out with an estimated-- no less than 2,500 maybe 3,000, maybe more. I've heard as many as four or 5,000. They were not only-- Al Qaeda but they were also-- you see the Pakistani ISI was-- the mili-tary advised us to the Taliban and Al Qaeda. There were dozens of se-nior Pakistani military officers including two generals who flew out.

And I also learned after I wrote this story that maybe even some of Bin Laden's immediate family were flown out on the those evacuations. We

242

allowed them to evacuate. We had an evacuation."

Algeria

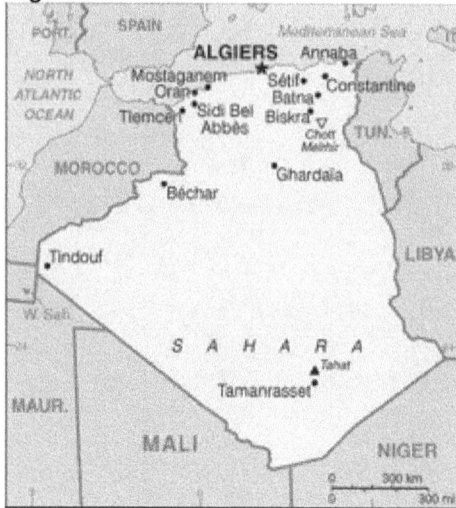

http://www.algeria-watch.de/mrv/mrvtort/torturesirish.htm

This link includes this statement from a defector called Inspector Abdessalam:
"Europe and the US are equipping the security forces in Algeria's dirty war."

http://eatthestate.org/06-07/AlgerianConnection.htm

Giving the wider background, refers to a book which says GIA is indeed under the control of the Algerian government.
"In Algeria, the government-supported GIA has sought to disrupt and discredit any Islamic opposition though deadly infighting and the indiscriminate massacring of civilians in the name of Allah. The military regime's monster is thought to be the most vicious player in the unending cycle of violence that is tearing Algeria apart."

http://www.muslimedia.com/archives/book00/algmassacbk.htm

A more detailed review of that book (which is 1473 pages long and has a forward by Noam Chomsky).
"Few readers will be able to avoid the conclusion that the GIA is indeed a part of the Algerian regime's counter-insurgency strategy rather than an anti-government movement."

http://www.larouchepub.com/other/1995/2241_gia.html

"Following the December 1991 elections, which were won by the FIS, the Algerian government moved to outlaw the FIS, annul the elections, preventing the second round from taking place. The FIS, 9,000 of whose members were rounded up and jailed, maintained its commitment to the democratic process. Numerous government-instigated provocations aimed at eliciting a violent response, were rejected by Abdelkader Hashani and other FIS leaders.
...
In the Algerian war, it is said that "there are three kinds of Islamists: the 'honest' Islamists, the 'SM'[Algerian Intelligence] Islamists, and the Islamists on the 'other' [foreign] intelligence services.'"

http://www.pegmusic.com/terrorism-really.html

"Living in exile in Germany, after he served as military attache at the Algerian Embassy in Bonn, Samraoui wrote that "the terror groups in the underground were bred and manipulated by the secret service of Algeria."

According to Samraoui's insider knowledge, the state-run terrorists were recruited from existing Algerian opposition Islamists, who were turned around after arrest, and then run by such entities as the CPO operations department of the secret services. Ostensibly, this was supposed to be for infiltrating Islamist movements, but in reality, the waves of terror over the next years were set up by that operation. On one night in July 1991, the first artificial Islamist terror base was set up some 50 kilometers from Algiers, Samraoui found out, and the first pro-extremist leaflet of "Islamist terrorists" was printed at the "military Antar barracks in Ben-Aknoum, the headquarters of the most important CPO center for illegal operations."
...
Also the alleged blacklists with civilian targets of the "terrorists," Samraoui found out, were produced at the Centre Ghermoul, where the HQ of the counterespionage DCE was located. All the so-called "emirs" of the Armed Islamic Group (GIA) terrorists were run as puppets of the secret services, and the terrorists were always activated with special brutality whenever the Algerian government made attempts to reach a conciliation deal with the non-terrorist Islamist movement."

245

Angola

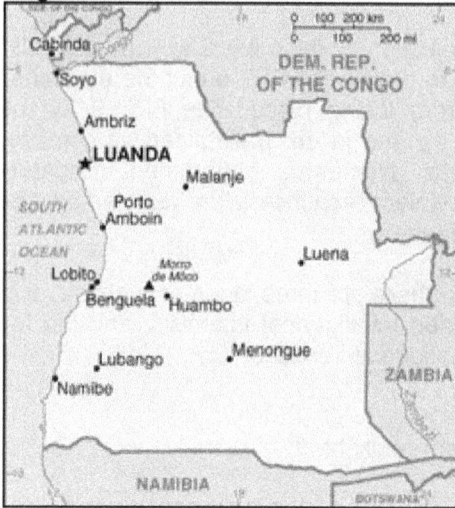

http://www.fpif.org/commentary/2002/0202savimbi_body.html

A good biography of Savimbi. Allied to not only the CIA (receiving support especially from their man Mobutu in Zaire) and apartheid South Africa but even the Portuguese secret police pre- independence:
"Savimbi is widely seen as responsible for a nearly non-stop war that has taken nearly one million lives and as the principal spoiler of the Angolan elections and United Nations-backed peace plans in the early 1990s. As the Namibian government said in announcing his death, "Savimbi chose the way of terrorism and turned Angola into a land of many killing fields."
...
The United States bears some blame for Angola's brutal civil war because Savimbi was long the darling of American right-wing, conservative politicians and the CIA.
...
Since the start of the Angolan liberation struggle, Savimbi had touted himself as a nationalist fighting for independence from Portuguese colonialism. However, Savimbi showed more hostility toward the other indigenous freedom parties and forged a clandestine alliance with the Portuguese colonial government and its secret police, PIDE, according to University of Southern California professor Gerald Bender and a series of subsequently released documents. As part of this alliance, code-named 'Operation Timber,...'"

http://groups.google.com/groups?q=Theo-

Ben+Gurirab+namibia+savimbi+cia&hl=en&ie=ISO-8859-1&oe=ISO-8859-1&selm=0.1300003960.502906807-1463792126-1015157608%40topica.com&rnum=1

Some good links, including the above article, listed here on the occasion of his death not long ago.

William Blum, *Killing Hope* (London, 2003), p.250.

"The origin of our story dates back to the beginning of the 1960s when two political movements in Angola began to oppose by force the Portuguese colonial government: the MPLA, led by Agostinho Neto, and the FNLA, led by Holden Roberto. (The latter group was known by various names in the early years, but for simplicity will be referred to here only as FNLA.)

The US, not normally in the business of supporting 'liberation' movements, decided that inasmuch as Portugal would probably be unable to hold on to its colony forever, establishing contact with a possible successor regime might prove beneficial. For reasons lost in the mists of history, the United States, or at least someone in the CIA, decided that Roberto was their man and during 1961 and 1962 onto the Agency payroll he went.(New York Times, 25 September 1975; 19 December 1975.)

At the same time and during the ensuing years, Washington provided their NATO ally, the Salazar dictatorship in Lisbon, with the military aid and counter-insurgency training needed to suppress the rebellion."

Bangladesh

http://www.scoop.co.nz/stories/HL0509/S00082.htm

"Who let loose their tentacles to start guerrilla war to segregate one-tenth of our territory?

Who provide them weapon, training, money and shelter?

From which country arms, explosives and ammunition come to Bangladesh? Is there any person who can term India as a friend of Bangladesh after learning all these information? Lets the Indians come forward to challenge the genuineness of even one these allegations mentioned above.

...

Let us come to the latest incident of August 17. Though the Industries Minister passively pointed his fingers to the involvement of India in that serial bombings (of August 17), but the opinions of print media, observers and analysts were more open concrete. RAW [Indian intelligence agency] connection of Shaiyakh Abdur Rahman is now well-known to all. Above all, the pattern of the explosives that were used in the bombs of August 17, were detained and recovered earlier repeatedly when they were being smuggled to Bangladesh through Benapole, Bhomra and bordering routes. Same type of bombs, explosives and technology are not available in Bangladesh. Indian attitude and behaviour and ground situation and reality indicate that no other country, except India, is the supplier of these materials and technology. Moreover, some of the arrestees in their confessional statements have already admitted that the bombs and their raw materials were brought from India.

248

Considering circumstantial reality, it is neither impractical nor unnatural to blame and accuse India for the bomb blasts of August 17.

The responsibility of changing this trend inclusively lies with India. It cannot be an acceptable and logical argument that India couldn't be blamed for the bomb blast, though she provides shelter and training to the Bangladeshi terrorists in her soil. It is India to prove that she is not our foe, but friend. India herself stated to show inimical attitude and un-friendly behaviour against Bangladesh. The Foreign Minister or the In-dustries Minister only reacted to those (inimical attitude and unfriendly behaviour) through their mild comments. It is known to all that India, has been endeavouring to brand Bangladesh as a terrorist-infested country. For that reason, it is logical if one blames India for the bomb blasts of August 17. The grievance of the Bangladeshi people was just simply ventilated through the comments of the Industries Minister."

http://usa.mediamonitors.net/headlines/raw_and_bangladesh_one,
http://usa.mediamonitors.net/content/view/full/23249 and
http://usa.mediamonitors.net/headlines/raw_and_bangladesh_final.

This is a full book online here called "RAW [the Indian government's main intelligence agency] and Bangladesh" by the author of the above article, journalist and researcher Mohammad Zainal Abedin. He clearly feels that the independence of a small country can be completely un-dermined by the activities of the intelligence agency of the neighbouring large country:
"RAW is not accountable to the Indian parliament i.e. Lok Sabha and Rajya Sabha. Both Lok Sabha and Rajya Sabha have no legal right to question its activities. Neither the Public Service Commission nor the Staff Commission has any role in appointing the officers and staff of RAW. As a matter of fact RAW is one of the few organisations in India which is absolutely sovereign. It also has the power to carry out supervi-sory functions on othey organisations.
...
Tasks assigned to RAW agents include:

a. To supply secret and sensitive information particularly about national defence and national policies.

b. To further Indian economic and other interests.

c. To mount malicious propaganda about founding principles and ideo-logical basis of the country and create favourable public opinion for merger with India.

d. To create political unrest, promote terrorism and lawlessness and impede economic growth of the country by resorting to hartals, bandhs, blockades etc. These are done to ensure that Bangladesh remains dependent and shackled to poverty and hence unable to follow sovereign policies.

e. To spread communal and religious disharmony.

f. To create disturbances in educational institutions to encourage more Bangladeshi students to opt for admission in Indian educational institutions.

g. To encourage and promote separatist and subversive movements in the country.

...

Now to over run a country an aggressor cripples its citizens psychologically...Though the country seems to be independent outwardly but psychologically and culturally its people are made subservient. They become imitative. Their cultural identity and exclusiveness and their spirit of nationalism gradually die down. A day then comes when they fail to perceive the significance and necessity of protecting independence and sovereignty. RAW relentlessly has been endeavouring to create such a situation in Bangladesh.

...

RAW is pushing various narcotics through its agents, traders and smugglers into Bangladesh. Under RAW's instructions, Indian border authorities connive with smugglers and help them in trafficking of narcotics into Bangladesh.

...

RAW has been smuggling arms, ammunition and explosives in Bangladesh to supplement terrorism. Their primary targets are universities and other educational institutions, trade unions and political parties. Due to unabated smuggling of weapons by RAW agents, the country is witnessing unparalleled proliferation of arms. The frequency of armed clashes between various student groups, trade union activists and cagres of political parties has increased manifold. Only in ((Dhaka university 55 students were killed in armed clashes during the last 24 years.

...

The Daily Inqilab reported that Railway police arrested a RAW agent named Ganesh Biswas from compartment No. 3599 of Khulna-Goalando mail train with arms and ammunition on January 6, 1995. Ganesh was smuggling arms and ammunition on behalf of Dilip Boshak of Nadia District, India and was to deliver it to an individual affiliated to a political party. Ganesh told police that he has been involved in trafficking of illegal arms inside Bangladesh for the past many years.

250

...

RAW's safe houses serve as virtural sex houses where carnal desires of its agents are taken care of Of course such compromising moments are also preserved in the cameras for future black mailing in case the agent shows signs of wavering or slackening. It may be mentioned that such practices are resorted to by other intelligence agencies as well at limited scale.

...

RAW uses terrorists of Shantibahinf not to allow any oil exploration in the Chittagong Hill Tracts region including Samutang. Understandably no foreign firm will risk an exploration work in the region as long as violence persists in the area.

...

designs. According to a press report published in the 'Daily Inqilab' during January 1993, Deputy Director Habibur Rahman of Geological Survey Directorate Bangladesh was paid cash money, expenses for travel to India and a phd. degree in exchange for secret survey reports regarding mineral resources of Bangladesh.

Besides creating strong impediments in the way of exploring oil reservers, RAW has been creating hindrances in exploratory work of other mineral resurces as well.

...

Ninety percent of the officers of BTV [state owned bangladesh TV] have close links with RAW. These officers receive regular monthly allowance from RAW (Weekly Sainik: July 17, 1991).

...

Besides pressurizing Bangladesh through political and economic measures including water blockade RAW has been instigating and promoting separatist movements to completely destabilize and disintegrate the country. RAW has been providing training and arms to various separatist movements to create anarchy in Bangladesh. One such organisation is named Shanti Bahini. It is fighting for creating an independent state named Jhumland in Chittagong Hill Tracts region.

The details of RAW's covert acions and involvement in Chittagong Hill Tracts insurgency have been exposed by many Chakma leaders themselves. Mr. Shamiron Dewan,Chairman of Khagrachari Local Council disclosed in a press conference that Indian Government is helping Shanti Bahini by giving shelter, money, arms and training. He added that the Chakmas have no genuine eco-political cause. They are being used by RAW for achieving India's geo-political interests."

Belgium

http://www.conspiracyplanet.com/channel.cfm?
channelid=93&contentid=355&page=2

There is just one short reference to Belgium but it is from a former LAPD detective, Ed Schooling, who was stationed with the US army in Italy with a top secret clearance.

You can see part one of his story from the link at the bottom. He is clearly in some danger for speaking out, and knows it.

"Nor have I even touched on the subject of Operation GLADIO – commando operations in Europe in which the CIA (U.S. and allies) trained and financed European terrorists to kill multitudes of innocent people in bombings and shootings in order to frighten the public into crying out for more state security! In the words of one Belgian terrorist whose leader reported to the CIA, "we were told to kill mostly just women and children..." Read – machine gunning innocent women and children in supermarkets and while they were fleeing outside the market!

This was in a city in Belgium."

http://lists.indymedia.org/pipermail/imc-uk-reports/2004-
November/1129-jn.html

"The CIA, with the help of the Belgian State Security, had organized state terror, in the form of so-called communist bombings by the terrorist CCC and in the form of senseless super market killings by the Bende van Nijvel. This was done in order to push the Belgian government to accept American nuclear missiles on Belgian territory (completely against public opinion), in order to further strengthen the grip of the State Security on domestic affairs, and in order to shift the public opinion towards the right. This strategy, known as the Strategy of Tension, is now replaced by a strategy of vote fraud."

(Startling account of the Belgian Green party being hit by electoral fraud by intelligence agencies.)

Bhutan

http://www.himalmag.com/dec97/features.htm

By Subir Bhaumik, Eastern India correspondent for the BBC:
"When Bodo militants attacked a Bhutanese police post at Nanglam in Southern Bhutan one morning in September, the totally unexpected had happened. The attack defied logic, for why should Bodo rebel groups, who have used Bhutan as their main transborder refuge, attack Bhutanese policemen and invite retribution from the kingdom's administration?
...

Meanwhile, ULFA's chief of military wing Paresh Barua claimed that the Indian secret agency, the Research and Analysis Wing (RAW), was behind the attack. In a telephone interview from an undisclosed hideout, Barua said that RAW maintains close links with the BLT, which is being used to undercut the NDFB's influence amongst the Bodos. According to Barua, New Delhi finds the BLT's objectives more acceptable than the NDFB's fullscale secessionist designs.

The RAW would have goaded the BLT to carry out the attack on Nanglam, says Barua, in order to agitate the Bhutanese and persuade them to act against the rebels along the southern border. The attack, he said, could also help India build up necessary pressure on Bhutan to allow the Indian army to launch a sustained transborder military operation. There was no response to these charges from RAW or the Indian government, even after Barua's interview was broadcast on the BBC."

Bosnia

http://www.btinternet.com/~nlpwessex/Documents/WATamericanjihady
ugoslavia.htm

Al Qaeda and the Bosnian and Kosovo conflicts. A former Canadian ambassador to Yugoslavia, James Bisset, agrees with Milosevic's claim that Al Qaeda were in these conflicts in force and supported by the Americans. Milosevic has quoted from an FBI statement that was given to congress in December of 2001 stating that as well. Many interesting quotes on this website.

Brazil

http://www.aci.net/kalliste/rhayes.htm

From the Affidavit of Robert M. Hayes:
"In March or April of that year, I received a call from Frank Ryan, an official at the U.S. consulate in Sao Paulo. He asked me to come to the consulate to update some paperwork. When I arrived at the consulate, Ryan escorted me to an office within the consulate, where Sibley was seated at a desk.

After Ryan left the room, Sibley informed me that his "real" name was John Joseph Michaels and produced corroborating identification that I recognized from previous experience as genuine CIA credentials. He then recited in great detail and accuracy my previous connections with and service for various U.S. intelligence organizations, including the agency. He also recited details of my work for Israeli and West German intelligence.

Michaels then requested my assistance in illegal clandestine operations that he referred to as "projects." He said these operations were targeted against communist agents in Latin America, primarily those working for or under the control of Cuban intelligence operatives.

I agreed to work for Michaels and subsequently accepted several operations in which the identity and loyalty of the targets was established to my satisfaction. These operations occurred between 1974 and 1976 and ranged from routine intelligence gathering to kidnapping, interrogation and assassination.

I accepted these operations in the belief that I was serving the best interests of the American government and was operating with the sanction of that government. I received no payment for conducting these operations and frequently spent large sums of my personal funds to accomplish them.

My relationship with Michaels ended abruptly [in] 1976 after Michaels proposed an operation that I considered not only absurd, but also contrary to the best interests of the U.S. government.

In the spring of 1976, Michaels proposed that I arrange to "simulate terrorism." I responded that there was no way to "simulate" terrorism. I insisted that an act is either terrorist or not, and anyone knowingly engaging in a violent act against civilians is in fact a terrorist and beyond sanction.

Despite my objection, Michaels continued to endorse the concept, explaining that evidence would be planted in such a manner to ensure that the operation would be blamed on Cuban agents.

When I asked what the target of this "simulated" act was to be, he proposed three: A large Catholic cathedral in Sao Paulo, a twin theatre complex near the U.S. consulate in Sao Paulo and the U.S. consulate itself."

Burma

San Francisco Chronicle 16 Oct 1970 p.22 summarised in Blum op.cit.p.414.

"...when the US military aided the Burmese air force to mount strikes against Burmese rebels, while the CIA was assisting the rebels from its operations in Laos."

Cambodia

http://web.archive.org/web/20050301162956/http://www.druggingameric
a.com/Tatum_pegasus.html

From the memoirs of 'Chip' Tatum, a US Special Forces operative:
"A plan had been drawn up at the highest levels of Nixon's administration. Team Red Rock were to secretly enter Cambodia's capital, Phnom
Penh, and attack the airport, military and civil installations – wrecking as
much havoc as possible. The plan called for the team to parachute into
the outskirts of Phnom Penh carrying with them captured NVA "Sappers." Taken in unarmed and alive, the Sappers would be "sacrificed"
and their bodies left to be discovered by Cambodian forces. A furious,
Lon Nol would assume North Vietnam was to blame. Such an act
would, it was hoped, stiffen Lon Nol's backbone. With nowhere else to
turn, the US puppet would urgently seek US hardware to strengthen his
forces and continue the battle."

http://web.archive.org/web/20010504042638/http://www.camnet.com.kh
/ngoforum/aboutcambodia/Resource_Files/Tribunal/butcher_of_cambod
ia_set_to_expos.htm

SAS support for rebels in this country in the 80s. You might have heard
of them. The Khymer Rouge. (From The Observer Jan 9 2000.)

http://web.archive.org/web/20040513032101/http://csf.colorado.edu/bca

s/sample/karma-ng.htm

More detailed analysis of western support to the Kymer
Rouge...strategic realities you understand.

http://english.pravda.ru/main/2001/09/25/16153.html

This writer is very critical of the western powers, the article includes details of the new tribunal that is revealing:
"Guerilla leaders Prince Norodom Sihanouk and Son Sann joined the
Khmer Rouge in forming a Coalition Government of Democratic Kampuchea, which at Western insistence, represented Cambodia at the
United Nations in place of the government of Cambodia. This provided
a fig leaf of legitimacy for Western support of a movement dominated by
the Khmer Rouge. American and British advisors and arms shipments
aided Sihanouk-s and Sann-s forces, which carried out coordinated mili-
tary operations with Khmer Rouge troops and were often commanded
by Khmer Rouge officers. Western arms frequently found their way into
Khmer Rouge arsenals as many members of Sihanouk-s and Sann-s
organizations belonged to the Khmer Rouge.
...
During the peace negotiations, American officials insisted that the
Khmer Rouge be given a prominent role in the new governing coalition.
As one U.S. negotiator explained, "No Khmer Rouge, no deal."
...
As Cambodian government troops closed in on the last remnants of
Khmer Rouge forces in March 1998, Khmer Rouge warlord Ta Mok
communicated an offer through Thai military channels to turn the Khmer
Rouge leader, Pol Pot, over to the United States. Taken by surprise,
U.S. officials turned down the offer. No desire for a tribunal here. They
didn-t want him. But Cambodia wanted him, so the U.S. had to act to
prevent that eventuality. The U.S. needed time to structure proceedings, presumably in order to ensure that the American role in support of
Pol Pot would not surface during a trial. While U.S. officials worked on
arrangements for a trial on their terms, Pol Pot committed suicide.
Following the final defeat of the Khmer Rouge, the Cambodian government announced that Khmer Rouge leaders would be tried for crimes
against humanity. Without delay, the U.S. responded by demanding that
any trial be conducted solely under United Nations auspices, in other
words, under terms dictated by the U.S. After lengthy wrangling, Western threats and pressure forced Cambodia to relent and seek a compromise in which the trials would be conducted in Cambodia, but with a mix
of Cambodian and Western prosecutors and judges. A major sticking
point is whether the controlling majority will be Cambodian or Western.
In response to a hostile letter sent from UN Secretary General Kofi An-

nan in April 2000, Hun Sen announced that the Khmer Rouge trials would not be limited to the years in which it held power, but would cover the entire period of 1970 to 1999. This touched directly on the worst fears of U.S. officials, spanning events from the CIA-backed military coup in Cambodia in 1970 through the final years of Western support for the Khmer Rouge. Only a hastily drawn American plan for evenly divided prosecution and judicial teams brought an agreement on the trial, ensuring that only the events of Khmer Rouge power would be considered... Clearly the U.S. motivation is to steer any trials in a direction favorable to its interests."

http://www.fromthewilderness.com/free/hall/Mac.html

KHMER SEREI mccarthy proj. CHERRY
"Their missions included the conduct of BLACK TERROR against the civilian population of Cambodia, while leaving evidence of their atrocities blaming Cambodian forces for their actions. The purpose of these activities was to create CIVIL UNREST and a rebellion against the Cambodian Regime. It worked. Similar operations utilizing KHMER SEREI were also directed from the United States Embassy in Bangkok, Thailand."

http://www.worldnetdaily.com/news/article.asp?ARTICLE_ID=19063

'...alleged British SAS involvement in training the Khmer Rouge.
...
"The SAS were there doing training in Cambodia all right," [Nina] Morrison [a former pilot with the CIA's Air America] told WorldNetDaily. "Just like they were involved recently in East Timor."
"The world in general has become a lot more complicated. As such, journalism must also adapt and become more thorough and complex to put all of the missing pieces together. In regard to the Khmer Rouge, this is dangerous work indeed," said Morrison. "True history has a way of disappearing into the night." '

http://www.waynemadsenreport.com/2007_03010314.php

From Wayne Madsen 2 March 2007:
"Israel has been a major, albeit covert, player in Southeast Asia since Israeli multi-billionaire tycoon Shaul Eisenberg began supplying weapons to Cambodia's genocidal Khmer Rouge regime in the 1970s. Eisenberg, a close business partner of China's military, was also an early arms supplier to Khmer Rouge leader Pol Pot...

He [Eisenberg] began selling weapons from his new business partner – China – to the Cambodian forces of Khmer Rouge leader Pol Pot. After the defeat of the U.S.-backed military government of General Lon Nol, installed after Richard Nixon's National Security Adviser Henry Kissinger, a close friend of Eisenberg, ordered the CIA to overthrow Cambodian head of state Prince Norodom Sihanouk, Cambodia fell victim to a bloody civil war between Vietnamese troops backing Pol Pot's one-time ally Hun Sen and the Chinese-backed "Democratic Kampuchea" government of Khmer Rouge leader Pol Pot.

It was no mistake that the Gerald Ford administration and Secretary of State Kissinger backed the Khmer Rouge. Kissinger and Ford's long-time Michigan financial backer, industrialist Max Fisher were both financially and ideologically linked to Eisenberg. Ford's supposed "grand moment" – the repatriation in 1975 of the crew of the U.S. "merchant" (spy) ship, the SS Mayaguez, from Khmer Rouge forces was a Kissinger- and Eisenberg-designed ruse designed to build up Ford's support in the face of the American military defeat in Southeast Asia. That ruse came at the cost of 41 Marines and countless Cambodian military forces and civilians.

Kissinger authorized Eisenberg to begin a discreet program to modernize China's armed forces with $10 billion in Israeli and U.S.-designed weapons, re-exported through Israel. The reason – neoconservative to its roots – was to have China counteract Soviet military power in Asia and beyond.

As a result of Eisenberg's Israel-China military alliance, Pol Pot's Khmer Rouge forces were amply supplied by Israel and China. Logistics were no problem since Eisenberg's Israel Corporation owned a 49 percent share in Zim Shipping, the world's third largest shipping company. Although Eisenberg died from a sudden heart attack in Beijing in 1997, the weapons smuggling activities of his friends in Mossad and Zim Shipping continue to plague Southeast and South Asia.

...

The suspicions about Israeli involvement in smuggling stored Khmer Rouge and other weapons were heightened in 1999 after a mysterious fire destroyed the Cambodian military weapons storage facility at the Ream Naval Base near Sihanoukville. According to a New Zealand intelligence officer in Cambodia, the depot was destroyed by an Israeli squad after it was revealed they were smuggling weapons from the facility to guerrilla groups throughout Southeast Asia, including the small "Free Vietnam Movement" battling Vietnam's central government and Hmong guerrillas battling Laotian government forces. The Vietnamese became even more suspicious about the role of the depot after weapons from the Ream warehouse were seized by Cambodian and Vietnamese police at the Bavet border checkpoint. The weapons were destined for guerrillas of the Free Vietnam Movement.

WMR [Wayne Madsen] visited Phnom Penh, Cambodia and discovered that the Mossad and Cambodian criminal syndicate allies continue to obtain bought-back Cambodian weapons from Cambodian government warehouses and are selling them to guerrilla groups throughout Asia, including Sri Lanka's Tamil Tigers, anti-Laotian Hmongs, the small anti-communist Free Vietnam Movement, and Burmese tribal guerrilla groups.

WMR photographed a number of Zim shipping containers portside along the Mekong River in Phnom Penh. From this and other port facilities, including the port of Sihanoukville, bought-back Cambodian weapons, some originally provided to the Khmer Rouge by Eisenberg and the Chinese, are making their way to insurgent groups around Asia, possibly including Iraqi guerrillas battling U.S. forces in Iraq.

Not far from Zim's Mekong port facilities in Phnom Penh sits a quiet and unassuming Mossad surveillance station. From this vantage point, Israeli operatives keep a close eye on Mekong river traffic and any "new players" who arrive into town. With new oil deposits being discovered in contested waters of the Gulf of Thailand, border skirmishes in the region are likely to increase, driving up the demand for small arms in the region. The cached weapons in Cambodia stand to make Israeli intelligence a handsome profit.

...

Although Israel has been supplying weapons and training to Sri Lanka's government to be used against the Tamil Tigers, it has been playing a double game in also supplying Cambodian weapons to the Tamils.

...

If Cambodia is any measure of Israel's true intentions, it is clear that Israel's double game seeks to destabilize world and regional peace by selling to adversarial sides in civil and other wars and reaping huge profits as a result."

Canada

Charles M. Byers, employee of a specialised military explosives company in Arizona: "Their mission included surreptitiously transporting and detonating a small, man-portable nuclear backpack bomb at an Iraqi nuclear weapons development facility to make it seem like an Iraqi nuclear accident.

...

Orders were given by U S Government personnel that this plane be destroyed before it reached the United States of America."

Chile

http://groups.google.ie/group/flora.mai-
not/browse_thread/thread/efc8400144f97ffe/32b9cfb4beaf60b2

"According to recently de-classified files, the U.S. aided and facilitated Condor operations as a matter of secret but routine policy.

...

Condor [at least nominally run by General Pinochet] was a covert intelligence and operations system that enabled the Latin American military states to hunt down, seize, and execute political opponents across borders.

...

The regimes hunted down dissidents and leftists, union and peasant leaders, priests and nuns, intellectuals, students and teachers--not only guerrillas"

(See also
http://web.archive.org/web/20010818144246/http://www.guardian.co.uk/
Pinochet_on_trial/Story/0,2763,194697,00.html,
http://www.wsws.org/news/1998/oct1998/pino-o31.shtml and
http://free.freespeech.org/americanstateterrorism/usgenocide/CrbnCnSt
hAmrc.html on the wider question of the US in South America.)

Colombia

http://www.alternet.org/story.html?StoryID=11131

Some notes on the story of Montesinos in Peru and particularly the CIA connection, the article points out where some of the CIA's money went to fund the FARC across the border, of course the CIA never realized this could happen!

"Three separate Peruvian military intelligence sources told ICIJ that surveillance equipment provided by the CIA for use in the drug war was instead used by the SIN to intercept the conversations of opposition political figures, journalists, businessmen and military officers suspected of disloyalty to the Fujimori regime. "Intelligence services" were sold to wealthy individuals, corporations or influential officers. A buyer could pay $1,000 to $2,500 per week to receive intercepts from the tapping of a single phone. Or, the military intelligence sources said, the wealthy buyers could pay spies to gather other information about individuals of their choosing."

http://www.narconews.com/peralta2.html

More on the same story with the CIA/drug cartels effectively controlling Peru through blackmail bribery etc...the usual pretty picture.

http://www.narconews.com/montyspies.html

This simply shows how much Montesinos cooperated with the US authorities in Colombia. He had his own 120 man intelligence network in Colombia and at all times cooperated with the US govt. which makes it very hard to see how the CIA did not know about his support for the FARC.

http://groups.google.com/groups?
q=montesinos+farc+cia&hl=en&selm=3B1F0C84.A62891C9%40ucs.or
st.edu&rnum=5

Further details referring to testimony put before the US senate:
"New allegations concerning the CIA's alleged connection with cocaine dealing in Latin America are bubbling to the surface in the wake of fresh elements in the investigation into the so-called Jordan-Latina Connection, a traffic in arms to Peru and Colombia by Jordan go-betweens. The traffic is said to involve CIA agents in both Latin America and the Middle East
and government officials in Peru and Jordan.

As Intelligence Newsletter revealed last September (IN 389), the trade consisted of delivering weapons to the Revolutionary Armed Forces of Colombia (FARC) guerillas and to the Medelin cartel in exchange for cocaine.
...
What could have led the CIA to turn a blind eye to the traffic? According to legislators who testified before the Senate's intelligence committee, the CIA might have reckoned the weapons delivery to FARC would help continue the spiral of violence in Colombia and thus justify Washington's Plan Colombia, a program aimed at gaining more military and intelligence influence in the entire Andes region."

http://www.narconews.com/miamiterror.html

Meanwhile we are all shocked to discover that the right wing paramilitaries and a US bank are getting along famously:
"The Colombian press – the daily El Tiempo, on Saturday, October 20th – has now reported the identity of the United States banking institution whose checks funded the AUC – defined by the U.S. government as a "terrorist organization." The bank was Barnett Bank, and the checks were reportedly cut in 1995, before Barnett was purchased by Nations-Bank in 1998."

http://www.dailystar.com.lb/article.asp?
edition_ID=1&article_ID=165&categ_id=13

From a Lebanese newspaper: "...10,000 assault rifles bought from Jordan were parachuted to anti-US Colombian guerrillas by Ukrainian mercenaries, an operation allegedly masterminded by Peru's former intelligence chief, Vladimiro Montesinos, who's now on trial in Lima. Soghanalian, one of 36 co-defendants, is being tried in absentia.

...

Montesinos, widely feared during his years as the eminence grise of now-disgraced President Alberto Fujimoro, was on the payroll of the CIA, and that has led to speculation that the agency may have been involved in the Colombian business as well.

...

The most popular conspiracy theory is that the CIA wanted to escalate violence in Colombia to justify Plan Colombia, a controversial $2.5 billion US military aid program to the Bogota government to crush drug trafficking, which went into effect months after the Jordanian rifles were delivered to FARC. The US government has denied any CIA role in the gunrunning."

Costa Rica

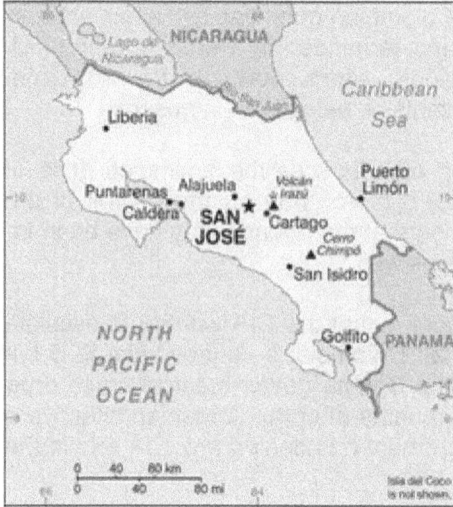

Charles D. Ameringer, *Don Pepe, A Political Biography of José Figueres of Costa Rica* (University of New Mexico Press, 1978), pp.124-5 quoted in Blum op.cit.p.83.

The head of state of Costa Rica José "Figueres accused the US Central Intelligence Agency of aiding the Somoza movement against him. He claimed that the CIA felt indebted to Somoza for the help he had given in overthrowing the Arbenz regime. He asserted that the same pilots and planes (the F-47) that had participated in the attack upon Guatemala, afterwards came from Nicaragua and machine-gunned eleven defenceless towns in our territory." According to Figueres at the same time that the US Department of State arranged the sale of fighter planes for Costa Rica's defence, CIA planes and pilots were flying sorties for the rebels."

Cuba

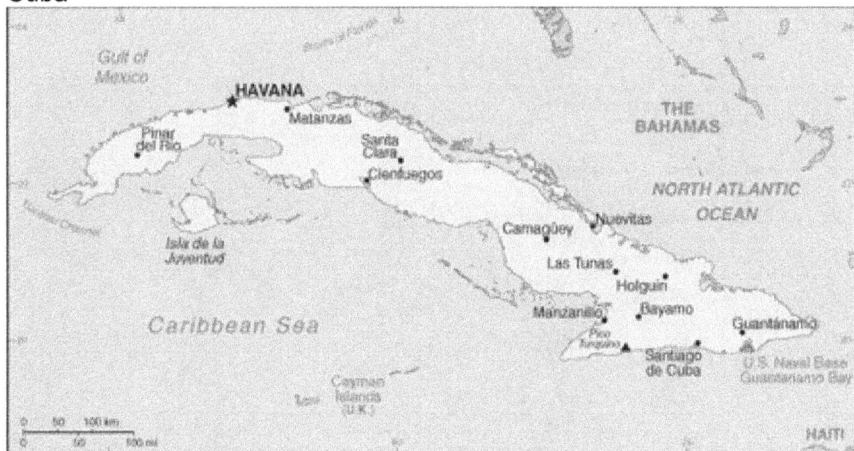

http://en.wikipedia.org/wiki/Frank_Sturgis and
http://www.ajweberman.com/nodules/nodule6.htm .

Frank Sturgis had a Top Secret clearance with the US army in Germany, arrived back in the US, changed his name, and then was to be
found trading in guns for Castro's forces in Cuba. The guns were
sourced from a US arms company, Interarmco, which was associated
with the CIA.

William Blum, *Killing Hope* (London, 2003), p.192.

"To add to the irony [of the Communist Party's support for the Batista
government and its hostility to Castro] during 1957-8 the CIA was chan-
neling funds to Castro's movement; this while the US continued to support Batista with weapons to counter the rebels; in all likelihood, another example of the Agency hedging its bets."
(Sourced from Tad Szulc, *Fidel, A Critical Portrait* (New York, 1986),
pp.427-8.)

Ecuador

Former US State Department official William Blum in *Killing Hope* (London, 2003), p.154:

"CIA agents would bomb churches or right-wing organisations and make it appear to be the work of leftists. They would march in left-wing parades displaying signs and shouting slogans of a very provocative anti-military nature, designed to antagonise the armed forces and hasten a coup."
(Blum's source is mainly Philip Agee who worked for the CIA in Ecuador.)

Egypt

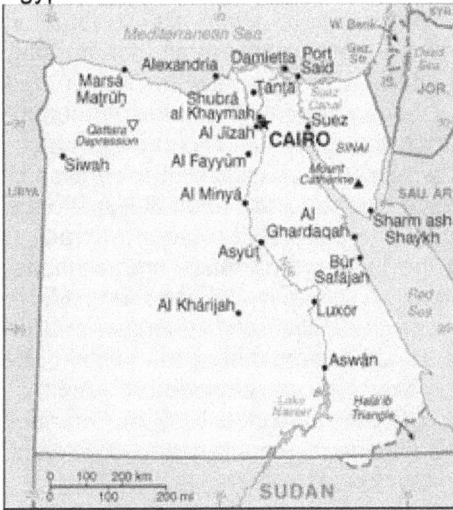

The Lavon affair...Also see under Israel and Britain.
"In July 1954 Egypt was plagued by a series of bomb outrages directed mainly against American and British property in Cairo and Alexandria. It was generally assumed that they were the work of the Moslem Brothers, then the most dangerous challenge to the still uncertain authority of Colonel (later President) Nasser and his two-year-old revolution. Nasser was negotiating with Britain over the evacuation of its giant military bases in the Suez Canal Zone, and, the Moslem Brothers, as zealous nationalists, were vigorously opposed to any Egyptian compromises.

It therefore came as a shock to world, and particularly Jewish opinion, when on 5 October the Egyptian Minister of the Interior, Zakaria Muhieddin, announced the break-up of a thirteen-man Israeli sabotage network. An 'anti-Semitic' frame-up was suspected."

Kennedy Lindsay, *Ambush at Tully-West / The British Intelligence Services in Action* (Dundalk, 1979), p.242.

This was written by Prof. Kennedy Lindsay, a member of the Northern Ireland Assembly in 1973 he also had a doctorate in modern history and was for a time on the staff of the Royal Military College of Canada: "A most dangerous possibility is that a number of like-minded men may conspire together in one or more intelligence organisations to use the

contacts and facilities under their control to achieve an agreed objective, political or non-political, without reference to or interference from
director-general or anyone else. The so-called Lavon affair in Israel in
1954 is an example. The British and American governments (including
the relevant section of the CIA) had swung to the view that Britain had
to withdraw from the Suez Canal Zone in order to secure permanent
Egyptian goodwill and to strengthen the Egyptian strong-man, Lieut.-
Colonel Gamal Abdel Nasser, as a bulwark against Soviet expansion in
the Mediterranean. Israeli observers realised that, once British troops
would withdraw, Egypt would occupy the canal and close it to Israel. A
number of key individuals within the Israeli intelligence organisations,
Mossad and Shin Beth (equivalent of DI6 and DI5 [MI5 and MI6]),
hatched a covert operation to harden the British and American publics
against Egypt and to sew doubts as to Nasser's ability to maintain law
and order. Several small bombs were to be exploded in Americ-
an-owned buildings such as the US Information Office. An informer
tipped off the Egyptians. Eleven Israeli agents were arrested. Two were
executed and the remainder given long prison sentences.

In the recriminations that followed the plot, Phinhas Lavon, the Israeli
minister of defence, was accused of having been responsible, but six
years later a cabinet committee concluded he had neither known that it
was to be implemented nor had he authorised it. The truth was that
there had been a conspiracy by persons in Mossad and Shin Beth who
were confident that they knew best what action should be taken and assumed that they would "get away with it". It was the kind of internal intelligence conspiracy for which parallels are likely to be found when the
day comes for Ulster covert happenings to be scrutinised."

France

http://www.buergerwelle.de/pdf/secret_warfare_and_natos_stay_behind
_armies.htm

"Admiral Pierre Lacoste, director of the French military secret DGSE from 1982 to 1985 under President Francois Mitterand, confirmed after the discovery of the secret NATO armies in 1990 that some "terrorist actions" against de Gaulle and his Algerian peace plan were carried out by groups that included "a limited number of people" from the French stay-behind network."

Germany

http://www.wsws.org/news/1998/aug1998/bomb1-a27.shtml

Story of the bombing attack that was the pretext for bombing Libya has taken a long time to come out, and the truth is...
"A documentary broadcast August 25 by German public television [ZDF] presents compelling evidence that some of the main suspects in the 1986 Berlin disco bombing, the event that provided the pretext for a US air assault on Libya, worked for American and Israeli intelligence."

http://groups.google.com/groups?
q=Von+Buelow+cia+bnd+mossad&hl=en&selm=UwWMijA8gk44IAx9%
40lastings.softnet.co.uk&rnum=3

A discussion involving earlier attacks in Germany, quoting the Guardian March 26 2000:
"Black September, the Palestinian terror group that killed 11 Israeli athletes at the 1972 Munich Olympics, was allowed by the German government to hijack a passenger jet two months later to provide a 'cover story' for the release of the three gunmen captured at the scene."

Greece

http://www.buergerwelle.de/pdf/secret_warfare_and_natos_stay_behind
_armies.htm

"According to former CIA agent Philipp Agee the Greek stay-behind
army LOK (Lochos Oreinon Katadromon) was a paramilitary unit used
to influence domestic politics in Greece: "In the eyes of senior CIA officials, the groups under the direction of the paramilitary branch are seen
as long term 'insurance' for the interests of the United States in Greece,
to be used to assist or to direct the possible overthrow of an 'unsympathetic' Greek government. 'Unsympathetic' of course to American manipulation."

...

In arguably the best know terrorist attack during this period the Gor-
gopotamos railway bridge was blown apart by a bomb in 1965 precisely
at the moment when the Greek political left and right united on the
bridge to commemorate their resistance to the Nazi occupation, and
specifically their successful resistance to the German blowing up of the
bridge during the occupation period. The massacre left five dead and almost 100 wounded, many gravely. "Well, we were officially trained terrorists", an officer involved in the secret operations declared years later
in a Gladio [the secret NATO armies] interview, highlighting that they
had enjoyed powerful support."
(Extracts from a detailed book by Daniele Ganser on Gladio operations
in Europe.)

Guatemala

A former US special forces member Stan Goff speaks in a moving intro-
spective account. Also good for El Salvador and Colombia and the drug
trade.
"Zumwalt [of the US embassy] told me at a bar once that he was training the finest right-wing death squads in the world.
...
They [the poor people there] have to be invisible so they can be ignored. They have to be sub-human so they can be killed.
...
This July, Commander of the Colombian Army, Jorge Enrique Mora
Rangel intervened in the Colombian judicial process to protect the most
powerful paramilitary chief in Colombia, Carlos Castano, from prosecution for a series of massacres. Castano's organization is networked for
intelligence and operations directly with the security forces.
That network was organized and trained in 1991, under the tutelage of
the U.S. Defense Department and the CIA. This was accomplished under a Colombian military intelligence integration plan called Order 200-
05/91.
...
I was in Guatemala in 1983 for the last coup. In 1985, I was in El Salvador; 1991, Peru; 1992, Colombia.

People don't generally hear from retired Special Forces soldiers. But
people need to hear the facts from someone who can't be called an ef-

278

fete liberal who never "served" his country.

A liberal will tell you the system isn't working properly. I will tell you that the system is working exactly the way it's supposed to.

As an insider on active duty in the armed forces, I saw the deep dissonance between the official explanations for our policies and our actual practices: the murder of schoolteachers and nuns by our surrogates; decimations; systematic rape; the cultivation of terror.

I have concluded that the billions in profit and interest to be made in Colombia and neighboring nations has much more to do with the itch for stability than any concern about democracy or cocaine. After reflection on my two decades plus of service, I am convinced that I only served the richest one percent of my country.
...[Quoting General Smedley Butler:]
"I spent 33 years and four months in active military service in the Marines. I helped make Tampico, Mexico, safe for the American oil interests in 1914; Cuba and Haiti safe for the National City Bank boys to collect revenue; helped purify Nicaragua for the International banking house of Baron Broches in 1909-1912; helped save the sugar interests in the Dominican Republic; and in China helped to see that Standard Oil went its way unmolested. War is a racket."

Like Gen. Butler, I came to my conclusions through years of personal experience and through the gradual absorption of hard evidence that I saw all around me, not just in one country, but in country after country.

I am finally really serving my country, right now, telling you this. You do not want some things done in your name."

Guyana

http://www.jagan.org/articles5i.htm

This was written by the ousted Premiere of Guyana, Cheddi Jagan. Very interesting in the context of the last UK elections.
"In 1961, the PNC lost the elections.

After losing the election, the PNC leader LFS Burnham made a deal with the US government. This was exposed by Arthur Schlesinger Jr., Special Assistant to President Kennedy in his book, A Thousand Day, John F. Kennedy in the White House, when he wrote:

"Thus far our policy was based on assumption that Forbes Burnham was, as the British described him, an opportunist, racist and dema-gogue intent only on personal power ..... Then in May 1962, Burnham came to Washington ..... Burnham's visit left the feeling, as I reported to the President, that 'an independent British Guiana under Burnham (if Burnham will commit himself to a multi-racial policy) would cause us many fewer problems than an independent British Guiana under Jagan'. And the way was open to bring it about, because Jagan's parliamentary strength was larger than his popular strength: he had won 57 per cent of the seats on the basis 42.7% per cent of the vote. An obvious solu-tion would be to establish a system of proportional representation."

The American columnist, Drew Pearson, in a syndicated article pointed out that the late President Kennedy applied pressure on the Macmillan government to withhold independence and to change our electoral sys-tem.

280

The British government could not easily succumb to this pressure. This was because of its commitment made at the Constitutional Conference held in London in 1960. Then Burnham's demand for proportional representation and my demand for independence were rejected on the understanding, however, that whichever party won the 1961 elections would lead the country to independence.

Consequently, the strife and violence, fomented and financed by the Central Intelligence Agency (CIA) to provide the British Government with an excuse.

All of this is now public knowledge. The New York Times, on February 23, 1967 headlined a story by Neil Sheehan: "CIA is linked to strikes that helped oust Jagan". The London Sunday Times on April 16 and 23, 1967 carried two stored by the Insight Team, headed "How the CIA got rid of Jagan" and "Macmillian, Sandys backed CIA's anti-Jagan Plot". In the first story it is said: "As coups go, it was not expensive: over five years the CIA paid out something over £250,000. For the colony, British Guiana, the result was about 170 dead, untold hundreds wounded, roughly £10 million worth of damage to the economy and a legacy of racial bitterness."

The second story said: "Although known at first only to Macmillan, Sandys and the two top security men in Britain, it inevitably become known to a similar number of British officials in Guiana." The latter no doubt included the British Governor, the Commissioner of Police and the Head of Security Branch, and explains why my government could not get the full backing and support from them, and the army and police which they controlled.

Incidentally, the Times story also stated: "The CIA insured one ex-Jagan supported for $30,000 in 1964."

Clearly, violence was the result of the conspiracy of the UK and US governments and the Guyana political and trade union leaders to overthrow the legally-constituted PPP government."

http://www.thirdworldtraveler.com/Insurgency_Revolution/Subversion_l AR.html

"According to the London Times, which in 1967 conducted an investigation of happenings in British Guiana four years earlier, the account that Jagan gives in his book The West on Trial is essentially correct. The British government agreed to a campaign of subversion to unseat Ja-

gan.
...

According to a secret report of the British police superintendent in British Guiana to the British commissioner, written on September 1l, 1963, which came to light in a debate in the House of Commons in 1966, the violence was instigated by a terrorist group which included British agents. The document states that O'Keefe, the CIA agent, financed these operations through "monetary transactions" with Ishmael.
...

While Jagan's rule was being undermined through these illegal means, the United States was working to change the election law so as to make possible the defeat of Jagan by the constitutional process. Having concluded that Forbes Burnham, a former Jagan associate and now his arch political rival, "would cause us many fewer problems than an independent British Guiana under Jagan," Schlesinger reported to the President that the "way was open to bring it about" by persuading the British to adopt an election law based on proportional representation. (In 1961 Jagan's party had won a plurality of 4z.6 percent of the popular vote and under the existing law a substantial majority of parliamentary seats.) In October, 1963, as a result of Kennedy's conversations with Prime Minister Macmillan a few weeks earlier, the British changed the law. In the elections the following year, Jagan, despite the increase in his popular vote, giving him almost six percent more than any other party, lost to Burnham, now backed by a coalition of the other two parties. The terrorism that had continued throughout 1964 came to an end. The Burnham government quickly made it clear that despite election slogans advocating nationalization, it did not intend to disturb the investments of the Aluminum Company of America in bauxite, the Texas Oil Company's oil field, or the manganese industry, also under U.S. control."

http://www.guyanaundersiege.com/Other%20single
%20pages/Subversion.htm

"After failing to wrest the leadership of the PPP from Cheddi Jagan, Forbes Burnham, with the active support of the British Colonial Office and the American CIA, split from the PPP to form his own faction of the PPP. Burnham's faction of the PPP was repeatedly trounced in elections, by Jagan's faction.

Burnham joined forces with local reactionary forces, such as the League of Colored People, to form the PNC. He then formed an illegal Security Force (comprising ex and serving military personnel), and unleashed a wave of terror which resulted in racial riots."
(This site includes the full text of the police reports from Guyana referred to the UK House of Commons.)

William Blum, *Killing Hope* (London, 2003), p.64.

"The strike period [called by CIA funded trade unions] was marked by repeated acts of violence and provocation, including attacks on Jagan's wife and some of his ministers. [Richard] Ishmael [noted in the police reports as having handled the finances on behalf of the CIA agent Gerald O'Keefe] himself was later cited in a secret British police report as having been part of a terrorist group which had carried out bombings and arson attacks against government buildings during the strike. [Which the UK government approved of as exacerbating the tensions.]
...
The British Colonial Secretary, Duncan Sandys, who had been a leading party to the British-CIA agreement concerning Jagan, cited the strike and general unrest as proof that Jagan could not run the country or offer the stability that the British government required for British Guiana to be granted its independence."

Haiti

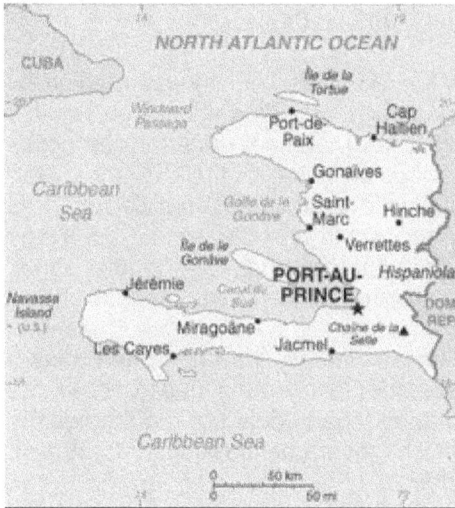

http://news.xinhuanet.com/english/2004-03/30/content_1390551.htm

"The United States armed and trained in the Dominican Republic the groups that rose against former Haitian President Jean-Bertrand Aristide, a preliminary report issued in the Dominican Republic indicated Monday.

...

Priest Luis Barrios and lawyer Briant Concannon, both members of the "independent" commission, presented the preliminary results of the investigation that contradicted the Dominican authorities which had previously considered "surrealistic and oneiric" the delivery of US guns to Haitian rebels in their national soil, as some accusations stated."

India

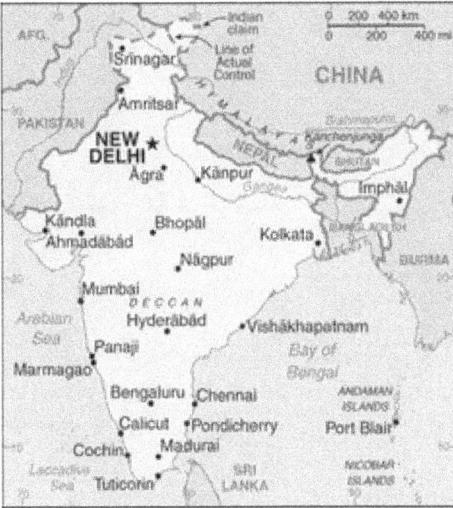

http://news.bbc.co.uk/hi/english/uk/newsid_138000/138009.stm

Allegation that the Indian government, with British help, wanted to support an insurgency in West Bengal province as an excuse for the central Indian government to intervene.
"...he continued to arrange to buy a plane from the Latvian state airline. He says this was with police approval. North Yorkshire Police's Special Branch deny this.
...Mr Bleach had expected the plane to be intercepted before the arms were dropped but this did not happen.
...
In Delhi there was a Congress government and in West Bengal there was a Communist government and the two are not the best of friends.
...
An armed insurgency in West Bengal would have allowed Delhi to have impose direct rule on the state and oust the ruling Communists."
(More information is available at
http://news.bbc.co.uk/hi/english/world/south_asia/newsid_846000/846093.stm and
http://news.bbc.co.uk/hi/english/world/south_asia/newsid_628000/628041.stm. In the Sunday Times, Dec 1 2002, it was revealed that Mr Bleach had been a member of the British Army's Intelligence Corps.)

Indonesia

http://www.ratical.org/ratville/JFK/Indo58.html

Internal rebellions in Indonesia in the 50's and 60's, inspired it seems by the usual suspects, and no I'm not talking about long bearded cave dwellers!
The author L Fletcher Prouty, one the most valuable CIA whistle blowers of the period, is here quoting a letter by Sukarno's widow:
"I must now ask you, Mr. President, in the name of freedom and justice, in the name of decency in relations between states and statesmen, between powerful nations and developing lands, in the name of the Indonesian people and the Sukarno family: did the United States of America commit these hideous crimes against Indonesia and against the founder of the nation? Will your Government be prepared to accept responsibility for these evil practices? Over one hundred million Indonesians have been brainwashed, as was the rest of the world by the present regime's propaganda to believe that the communists carried out the insurrection. My countrymen, as well as everyone else, have the right to know the truth of the historic facts."

http://www.indymedia.org.uk/en/2003/01/49902.html

Bali Robert Finnegan Joe Viallis

http://www.atimes.com/atimes/Southeast_Asia/DK07Ae02.html

'Indonesian military's links to terror' by Tom Fawthrop writing in the Asia

Times.

"The highly politicized Indonesian military, trained in waging terror during more than 30 years of General Suharto's dictatorship, are among the suspects in last month's Bali bombing, according to a respected Indonesian commentator."

http://www.insideindonesia.org/edit65/fealy.htm

"In interviews earlier in the year, however, he and his lieutenants boasted of their relationship with TNI [Indonesian army]. In one interview, Ja'-far claimed to have a hotline to TNI commander Admiral Widodo (Panji Masyarakat, 26 April 2000). Another FKAWJ leader also admitted that TNI officers have assisted in the training of Laskar Jihad [militant islamic group] (Gatra, 25 March 2000)."

http://www.theage.com.au/articles/2003/02/26/1046064102788.html

"The border between the Indonesian province of Papua and Papua New Guinea has become a no-go area for Indonesian police and human rights workers, according to human rights and independence groups.

The groups say the border is home to Indonesian army-run training camps for Islamic militants and Papuan militia groups.

They say the militant groups are being used by the Indonesian Army's special forces, Kopassus, to foment conflict between Christian Papuans and Muslim settlers from elsewhere in Indonesia."

http://www.smh.com.au/articles/2003/08/12/1060588372558.html

"'I'm sure the CIA are behind both attacks," Bashir told el-Shinta radio station. "It was to discredit Islam."
...
Bashir could be jailed for 20 years if found guilty of the treason and the church bombings. He has not been named a suspect in the Bali bombings or the Marriott attack.

He denies any wrongdoing, and claims Jemaah Islamiah does not exist.'

http://bulletin.ninemsn.com.au/bulletin/EdDesk.nsf/0/51be6a46cfa0028e ca256ccd00138341?OpenDocument

"A string of violent incidents on the border of Papua New Guinea and Indonesian Papua has thrown into the spotlight the shadowy relationship between the Islamic extremists of Laskar Jihad and the Indonesian military (TNI). Questions are also being asked about the role of Jemaah Islamiah, the group suspected of masterminding the Bali bombings."

http://www.angelfire.com/rock/hotburrito/laskar/cdi080302.html

'In this regard Laskar Jihad is no exception to Jakarta's list of predicaments, but the matter is confounded by the group's oblique but well-known link with the Indonesian military (TNI). Jakarta's hands-off policy with TNI — which is now under civilian control after decades of dictatorship ended with Suharto — has enabled generals to retain old links with radical group such as Laskar Jihad. The support the militant group continues to receive from the highest levels of the Indonesian military ensures its survival. Sympathizers within TNI are believed to provide the group with cash, and possibly arms, and to order Moluccan officials not to crack down on Laskar Jihad members. According to Western intelligence sources, Laskar Jihad was actually founded with covert backing of military hardliners who wished to destabilize the post-Suharto reformist government of Abdurrahman Wahid. Jafar branded former president Wahid as anti-Islamic, claiming that his government was "positioned to oppress Muslim interests and protect those of the infidels."'

http://www.indymedia.ie/newswire.php?story_id=65047

The (London) Independent 16 April 2000:
"Newly discovered cabinet papers show that British agencies, including MI6, had supported Islamic guerrillas and other dissident groups in an effort to destabilise Sukarno. The disorder fostered by the British led to General Suharto's takeover and dictatorship, and a wave of violence unseen since the Second World War. The massacre set the stage for almost 35 years of violent suppression, including the 1975 invasion of East Timor, which was only reversed last year.

The cabinet documents (which are separate from the revelations of Reddaway) were uncovered by David Easter, a historian at the London School of Economics. His research – which is published this week in the journal Intelligence and National Security – shows that the cabinet's defence and overseas policy committee asked the head of MI6, Dick White, to draw up plans for covert operations against Indonesia in

January 1964. According to Dr Easter, these operations began in the spring of that year and included supplying arms to separatists in the Indonesian provinces of Aceh and Sulawesi."

http://web.archive.org/web/20040109231439/http://mail2.factsoft.de/pip ermail/national/2002-November/010303.html

"The American ambassador here, Ralph L. Boyce, does not have to venture far from his heavily fortified embassy to be challenged about who was responsible for the Bali bombings that killed more than 180 people. The perception among many of the educated elite in this largely moderate Muslim country is that it was not, as the United States has suggested, a radical Islamic group with links to Al Qaeda. Instead, they blame the Central Intelligence Agency."

http://observer.guardian.co.uk/print/0,3858,4532601-110490.html

Sidney Jones in The Observer Oct27 2002: "In the aftermath of the 12 October bombing in Bali, Indonesians are convinced they have terrorists in their midst. They're just not sure who they are. Absurd, as it may seem, if talk shows and media commentaries are any indication, the most likely candidates in most Indonesians' minds are the U.S. government and the Indonesian army. Al-Qaeda is a distant third.
Only these three, the thinking goes, have the expertise, the contacts, and the motivation to carry out an attack on the scale of the Bali attack."

http://web.archive.org/web/20040603145358/http://www.jpost.com/com/ Archive/14.Oct.1999/Books/Article-2.html

A review of Paul Lashmar and James Oliver, *Britain's Secret Propaganda War 1948-1977* (Stroud, Gloucestershire, 1998), in the Jerusalem Post 14 Oct 1999:

"Working at times in harness with the CIA to fight a secret war after World War II against the "menace of communism," the British Foreign Office's Information Research Department (IRD) spent countless millions of pounds without Parliament ever knowing what it was up to.

Its operations were clandestinely financed from the UK's Secret Intelligence Service budget. It also worked hand in hand with the MI6 security services. Its activities stretched across the world.

...

As Lashmar and Oliver explain, the vast IRD enterprise had one sole aim: To spread its ceaseless propaganda output (i.e. a mixture of outright lies and distorted facts) among top-ranking journalists who worked for major agencies, papers and magazines, including Reuters and the BBC, as well as every other available channel.

The authors clearly point a finger at IRD for laying the seeds of the ghastly massacre of the civilian population at present being carried out in East Timor by the Indonesian army and militia as a result of US and British "dirty tricks" over 20 years ago.

...

Employing their 400-strong staff at their Thameside headquarters and other secret sites all over the world, IRD mandarins plotted along with MI6 to rid themselves of Jakarta's ruler."

http://www.rantburg.com/poparticle.asp?HC=&ID=8410

"As the noose tightens on Hambali, security authorities also expect to uncover a series of links back to covert operations conducted by former intelligence czar General Ali Murtopo in the 1970s in the interests of the Suharto regime...
The source says that in the 1970s Hambali was a Special Operations (Opsus) plant into Jemaah Islamiyah. He was given the codename G-8 and tasked with building the financial structure of Jemaah Islamiyah.

Whoever Hambali is, for the incumbent government, capturing the mastermind of the Bali terrorist attack is as much a matter of disclosing the dark forces of the Suharto era rather than only a part of the US war against terrorism and al Qaeda."

http://www.prisonplanet.com/omar_al_faruq_recruited_by_the_cia.htm

"Former State Intelligence Coordinating Board (BAKIN) chief A.C. Manulang has said that Kuwaitd citizen Omar Al-Faruq, a terrorist suspect who was arrested in Bogor, West Java, on June 5, 2002 and handed over to the US three days later, is a CIA-recruited agent.

Al Faruq was assigned to infiltrate Islamic radical groups and recruit local agents within these groups.

"When Al Faruq finished his assignments, the CIA created a scenario that he had been arrested," Manulang told Tempo News Room in Jakarta on Thursday afternoon (19/9)

...

This kind of operation is aimed at starting conflicts in Indonesia and creating the image that Indonesia is a land of terrorists.

"After the CIA obtained complete data on this matter, they then made Al-Faruq disappear. It's common in intelligence world," said Manulang.
...

As for Al Faruq's testimony in Time magazine that he had masterminded the plan to murder Indonesian President Megawati and several bombings in Indonesia, Manulang considered this as an attempt to making Islamic groups the scapegoats for all terrorism incidents.

"Anti-Islam intelligence agencies committed the bombings in Indonesia. They have been trained for this and they are very organized," said Manulang."

http://www.waynemadsenreport.com

From ex-NSA intelligence officer Wayne Madsen, writing on 27 March 2007:

"Our Indonesian and American sources report that there was a significant U.S. and Israeli military-intelligence connection to the October 12, 2002 bombings of the Sari Club in Bali, Indonesia. A DeHavilland Dash-7 aircraft registered in Queensland, Australia, landed at Denpasar Airport in Bali only hours before a massive explosion ripped through the Sari Club, killing over 200 people, many of them vaporized.

Our sources claim that an Israeli military team arrived at Denpasar Hospital a after the explosion and claimed four bodies of white men in uniform and flew them out of Bali on the Dash 7. The plane took off an hour after the explosion. Our sources have revealed the plane was permitted to pass through Singapore for an unknown destination.

After the bombing and the plane's departure, the tower logs were altered at Denpasar Airport to indicate the Dash 7 had not landed there. However, in a major oversight, the apron logs were not tampered with. Our sources have revealed the Dash 8 was Israeli-owned.

Several victims of the Sari Club bombing at Kuta Beach had flash burns on their bodies – something common with people exposed to a nuclear blast. Our sources also have revealed that a CIA contract agent – an Indonesian national – was at Kuta Beach the day before the terrorist bombing. He is also known to have been involved in other terrorist attacks on behalf of the CIA since 1998.

Our sources also indicate that the then-U.S. ambassador to Indonesia, Ralph Boyce, who is now posted as ambassador to Thailand, was fully aware of U.S. intelligence pre-knowledge of the terrorist bombing in Bali. Boyce told the American managing editor of the *Jakarta Post* that it would be unhelpful if the paper pursued the U.S. angle in the Bali bombing."

Iran

http://www.antiwar.com/justin/?articleid=1798

MEK Mujahedin-e-Khalq perle

Iraq

From a book by an Iraqi immigrant to Israel, Naeim Giladi, who documents the real story behind bombings and riots that occurred in Iraq just prior to the Jewish exodus from there to Israel and for which he has first hand knowledge.

"Alexis de Tocqueville once observed that it is easier for the world to accept a simple lie than a complex truth. Certainly it has been easier for the world to accept the Zionist lie that Jews were evicted from Muslim lands because of anti-Semitism, and that Israelis, never the Arabs, were the pursuers of peace. The truth is far more discerning: bigger players on the world stage were pulling the strings.

These players, I believe, should be held accountable for their crimes, particularly when they wilfully terrorized, dispossessed and killed innocent people on the altar of some ideological imperative.

...And that is why I have written my book and this article: to set the historical record straight.

We Jews from Islamic lands did not leave our ancestral homes because of any natural enmity between Jews and Muslims. And we Arabs-I say Arab because that is the language my wife and I still speak at home-we Arabs on numerous occasions have sought peace with the State of the Jews. And finally, as a U.S. citizen and taxpayer, let me say that we Americans need to stop supporting racial discrimination in Israel and the cruel expropriation of lands in the West Bank, Gaza, South Lebanon and the Golan Heights."

294

http://www.ukar.org/orr01.htm

More details on the above incidents from Akiva Orr who served in the Israeli army in 1948:
"...emissaries from Israel who often used dirty tricks like throwing bombs into synagogues to create the impression of anti-Jewish persecution to stampede the Jews to Israel.

This answer outraged my heckler even more, and he shouted in an agitated voice: 'You are a liar, no Jew ever threw a bomb into a Jewish synagogue.' The audience weren't used to seeing someone denounce a speaker as a 'liar'. Being British, they assumed such an accusation was based on solid information capable of withstanding a libel charge. The ball was now in my court, but having encountered this charge many times before I was well prepared. I had copies of the Israeli weekly Haolam – Ha-zeh (of 20 April and 1 June 1966) with me, which published details, with photographs, of these events. Some Iraqi Jews who had become disabled as a result of the bombs thrown by Israeli agents into the Mas-uda Shemtov Synagogue in Baghdad had sued the Israeli government for damages, in Israel. The government had preferred to settle out of court and pay damages, but the legal exchanges had reached the Israeli press and had been published by some magazines. When I read out the details of the case from the Israeli magazine all eyes turned back towards my adversary. I demonstrated convincingly that I was not a liar. What would he say now?

There was a moment of silence and then he blurted out: 'You see, unlike the Arab countries Israel is a democratic state. You can publish everything in the press there.' The audience burst into laughter; I didn't."

http://www.kimsoft.com/korea/cia-kurd.htm

The CIA in Iraq since the Gulf war, sponsoring car bombs in Baghdad that killed over 100 people...From ex-CIA officer's Ralph McGehee's Ciabase quoting the Washington Post:
"Most embarrassing U.S. failure in Kurdistan is that of CIA, which backed the wrong horse. The CIA centered its covert program styled as the Iraqi National Accord, or WAFAQ in Arabic. Accords leaders were once Saddam's cronies. The leaders promised they could mount a quick coup. They failed. One of the key bomb-makers disclosed publicly that bombs financed by CIA have killed scores of Iraqi civilians in Baghdad and destroyed HQs of rival National Congress in Salahedin."

295

http://csmonitor.com/2004/0430/p11s01-woiq.html

Abdul-Latif al-Mayah Dr. Muhammad
Wide scale assassinations of intellectuals in US dominated Iraq.

http://www.rense.com/general56/chris.htm

Sam Hamod, a former adviser to the US State Department:
"With these matters in mind, it appears as if this new "attack on the Christian churches is just another attempt either by the American CIA or its operatives, or the Mossad of Israel, to paint Islam with terrorism and to split the Muslim and Christian communities in Iraq.
...
This is another sad chapter in the U.S. occupation of Iraq. Since the early days of the war, the Iraqis complained about the treatment of prisoners taken by the Americans. Unfortunately, no one would listen to the Iraqis or those of us who reported these atrocities. You all know the truth by now, how we were lied to by our government and by the U.S. media; so much for truth and "embedding." So, once again, we have to report to you, this is just another American cover-up to create more chaos in Iraq, just as America did in Viet Nam to keep us in that war, and to justify more attacks on Muslims groups in Iraq.
...
At this point, there is no telling what the U.S. or the Israeli Mossad will do in Iraq in order to foment civil war among the Iraqis and to justify the continuation of an American occupation in Iraq."

http://www.abc.net.au/news/newsitems/s1093087.htm

Reported by ABC in Australia:
'Followers of the radical Shiite cleric Moqtada al-Sadr have blamed British forces for the coordinated series of car bombs which killed 73 people in the southern Iraqi city of Basra yesterday.
...
The targets of the attacks were Iraqi police stations and a uniformed policeman who joined the protest said "the British were the ones who attacked us".'

http://www.newyorker.com/fact/content/?040628fa_fact

Seymour M. Hersh's article in the New Yorker:
"Israeli intelligence and military operatives are now quietly at work in

Kurdistan, providing training for Kurdish commando units and, most important in Israel's view, running covert operations inside Kurdish areas of Iran and Syria. Israel feels particularly threatened by Iran, whose position in the region has been strengthened by the war. The Israeli operatives include members of the Mossad, Israel's clandestine foreign-intelligence service, who work undercover in Kurdistan as businessmen and, in some cases, do not carry Israeli passports.

...

Turkish sources confidentially report that the Turks are increasingly concerned by the expanding Israeli presence in Kurdistan and alleged encouragement of Kurdish ambitions to create an independent state."

http://www.brushtail.com.au/july_04_on/zarqawi_bush.html

By Nick Possum in Sydney: "If Abu Musab al-Zarqawi, the terrorist leader credited with the beheading deaths of Nick Berg and Kim Sun-Il, did not exist it would be necessary for the United States to invent him. That may well be what the CIA has done.

What? Really? Is that credible? Would an intelligence and espionage service really murder its own people, or neutrals, or citizens of an allied country? Would it cynically kill harmless civilians with terrorist-style bombings? Would it snuff out the lives of innocents to make a political point or create a climate of fear?

The answer is Yes. For an example and we need look no further that the career of Iyad Allawi, the new, hand-picked, prime minister of Iraq. According to a New York Times report in June this year, former CIA operatives say Allawi, who ran a CIA-backed exile organization, the Iraqi National Accord (INA), organised a bombing and sabotage campaign in the early 1990s. The targets included a cinema and a school bus. At the time the CIA was trying to foment a military coup against Saddam Hussein and it is probable that the bombing campaign was intended to destabilise the regime by creating a climate of fear and instability.

In the espionage community, operations like this, for which no group claims responsibility, are known as "grey operations". If they are attributed to a source other than that which carried them out, they're called "black operations" and they're carried out by "false flag" operatives."

http://web.archive.org/web/20041013034458/http://www.libertyforum.or
g/showflat.php?
Cat=&Board=news_international&Number=865236&page=&view=&sb=
&o=&vc=1&t=-1

From the Tehran Times referring to reports in the Egyptian press relating to the the assassination of Ayatollah Mohammad Baqer al-Hakim .

http://www.fromthewilderness.com/free/ww3/030503_ansar.html

Claims of US approaches to a group they later called terrorists.

http://weekendinterviewshow.com/audio/giraldi.mp3

Interview with ex-CIA officer Philip Giraldi during which he claims that there are as many as 800 Israeli agents in Iraq keeping the country destabilised and hoping to do the same for Iran. As quoted at http://anti-war.com/horton/?articleid=6888:
"Giraldi told me he's heard reports that up to 800 Israeli agents are combing Iraq. The story is that our soldiers train together. (Remember the story about Israelis at Abu Ghraib?) According to Giraldi, however, their true purpose is to sow instability and pressure for Kurdish autonomy. This is another looming fault line in the brewing intra-Muslim conflict."

Ireland

http://ftp.die.net/mirror/cryptome/fru-ingram02.htm

An insight into the Force Research Unit, by an ex-member:
"I should have opened my mouth at the time," he says in regard to the 'running' of Nelson, "but you view things in a different perspective when you're part of the intelligence community. Now as long as I have a breath in my body, I will take up the cudgel for the truth."
(Some more details on the FRU are available at
http://ftp.die.net/mirror/cryptome/hmg-murder.htm .)

http://cryptome.org/committee.htm

Extracts from 'The Committee', stranger than fiction, but the author went on to win an important libel action in London despite such luminaries as David Trimble being in the dock against him:
"I am especially grateful to Tim Laxton who, since 1994, has helped me in countless ways to complete the investigation I began in 1991.
Tim's first career as a City accountant has left him with few illusions about what seemingly respectable people are capable of doing; so he found no difficulty in believing that the Loyalist assassination campaign was being run by affluent and well-connected individuals, including a banker, a lawyer, an accountant, a clergyman and the owners of some of the largest businesses in Northern Ireland.
...
I have come to appreciate more fully that the Committee, which ran the Loyalist assassination campaign from 1989 until late 1991, was merely

a more formal expression of a phenomenon which existed for many years. Though even now I still do not know the complete cast list of Committee members, I understand more fully than before that the RUC Inner Force was indispensable to the murder conspiracy. For, as a key source has recently explained to me, the initiative in Loyalist attacks on Republicans has always come from the RUC, which employed men such as Robin Jackson and Billy Wright as and when it suited. These two notorious Loyalist assassins, this source made clear, could not have operated as they did without official protection from the highest levels within the security forces-including Britain's domestic intelligence agency, MI5, which always worked closely with RUC Special Branch.

So it is, I think, fair to say that no-one can be said properly to understand the conflict in Northern Ireland without taking into account the following facts, which have been effectively concealed from the public in Ireland and Britain for many years.

RUC Special Branch, working with the elite RUC Special Patrol Groups [SPGs] which spearheaded the war against the IRA, employed a small number of hard-line Loyalists to assassinate Republicans and, when necessary, to attack the general Catholic population. One of these assassins, Robin Jackson, murdered more than 100 people.

British Military Intelligence and MI5, which worked closely with RUC Special Branch, fully supported this strategy. The new information presented in Chapter 13 of this paperback edition shows that this strategy of state terrorism against the Catholic population was implemented on both sides of the Irish border, with lethal effect.
...
Once the Committee's existence and murderous activities were exposed on Channel 4 Television in 1991, an elaborate propaganda exercise initiated by the RUC and championed most notably by The Sunday Times succeeded in discrediting the broadcast revelations. After Channel 4 had dropped this story, which was simply too hot to handle, no other British media organisation dared to pick it up again. Britain's largest public service broadcaster, the BBC, ignored the story for eight years before finally, in March 1999, broadcasting a small part of the truth – when it screened an interview with former terrorist Bobby Philpott, who admitted that the RUC had been indispensable to the Loyalist assassination campaign. The British press also failed to report the story, with the result that the British public has been kept in ignorance of the facts documented in this book for the first time.
...
In late 1997 I was trying to arrange meetings with some of the leading figures in the Loyalist assassination campaign in an effort to discover whatever I could about more of the Committee's "unsolved" murders. I

had made tentative arrangements to meet R.J. Kerr who, though not a member of the Committee, had helped Robin Jackson to murder William Strathearn in 1977, had participated in the attempted murder of Paschal Mulholland in 1984 and had been involved – albeit at a low level – in Loyalist sectarian killings over a period of nearly thirty years. He was in a position to fill in many gaps in my knowledge of Loyalist terrorism and had grown disenchanted by developments within the paramilitary underworld. Shortly after I had learned of his willingness to talk to me, the news reached me of his death in a mysterious explosion, reportedly an accident. I had also taken initial steps towards arranging a meeting with Billy Wright in prison where he was serving an eight-year sentence – not for murder, not even for attempted murder, but for threatening to kill a woman in his home town, Portadown. I was told he would see me but I did not really expect to make any significant breakthrough in my research from such a steely and ruthless terrorist. Before any date was fixed for the meeting, he was murdered by a Republican splinter group on December 27th, 1997. And my hopes of securing an interview with the Committee's other key assassin, Robin Jackson, were also dashed when, in January 1998, I learned that he was dying of lung cancer."

http://www.seeingred.com/Copy/2.1_CODE_weiraff.html

The affidavit by ex-RUC Sergeant John Weir prepared in connection with the legal cases involving 'The Committee':
"Some months after the Strathearn murder I was called to a meeting with the head of RUC Special Branch in Newry, Chief Inspector Brian Fitzsimmons. He confirmed what I had already been told by Chief Inspector Breen that I was to be transferred to Newtownhamilton RUC station. During this meeting Mr. Fitzsimmons let me know that he was aware that I had been involved in Loyalist terrorist activity for some time but it was clear he was not bothered by this. He told me that he knew all about my paramilitary past activities with James Mitchell and that my local connections to Loyalist paramilitaries were part of the reason why I was being placed in charge of Newtownhamilton RUC station. I understood the message of my meeting with Chief inspector Fitzsimmons to be that I had the green light to carry on with my activities. I now know that Chief Inspector Fitzsimmons rose to the rank of Assistant Chief constable and that he was killed in the Chinook helicopter crash in Scotland in 1994."
...
I drew this lesson from the death of Army Intelligence officer Captain Robert Nairac who had infiltrated both sides, Loyalist and Republican, in an attempt to intensify the conflict so that each side would wipe each other out.

...

[RUC Constable William] McCaughey had stated: "the RUC in South Armagh are the UVF."

...

He told me that Martin O'Hagan [the late assassinated journalist who assisted Sean McPhilemy, the latter being the author of 'The Committee'] lived close by and could be dealt with any time. He then asked me if, from my conversation with Sean McPhilemy I thought he would be easily scared. I told him that I had not talked enough to Sean McPhilemy to be able to answer that question but I thought as a journalist he would be obviously difficult to put off what he was working on. I understood this to mean that he and others had talked or considered putting pressure on Sean McPhilemy to make him drop the story."

http://news.bbc.co.uk/hi/english/audiovideo/programmes/panorama/new sid_2019000/2019301.stm

Here you can get the transcripts of the Panorama (the BBC's main investigative programme) screenings that have definitively established British army and RUC control over the UDA at the time of the Finucane killing.

Specifically its the story of the main UDA intelligence officer in Belfast, Brian Nelson, who also worked for the British army in the guise of the FRU. Here is a quote from the transcript:

"By our count at least 80 people listed on Nelson's targeting files were attacked. 29 were shot dead. We do not suggest Nelson had a role in all these attacks.

What is clear is that only a tiny minority of the victims were involved in terrorism."

http://www.sundayherald.com/14148

"'IT IS as simple as this," the former intelligence officer says. "The British Army took an honest soldier, paid him to become a terrorist and then fed him the information he needed to set up Catholics for assassination. We turned an ordinary man into a monster."'

http://www.sundayherald.com/29997

"However, court documents leaked to the Sunday Herald show that Magee, head of the IRA's infamous internal security unit, was trained as a member of Britain's special forces. The IRA's torturer-in-chief was in reality one of the UK's most elite soldiers."

Islamic

http://www.informationclearinghouse.info/article5943.htm

"One of al-Qaeda's most dangerous figures has been revealed as a double agent who fooled MI5, raising intense criticism from European governments who had repeatedly called for his arrest. Britain ignored warnings from friendly governments about Abu Qatada's links with terrorist groups and refused to arrest him"

http://www.larouchepub.com/other/2001/2838bin-london.html

"With the U.S. bombing of the Afghan headquarters of Osama Bin Laden, the alleged mastermind of the terrorist bombings of the U.S. embassies in Kenya and Tanzania, the American public has suddenly been hit with wildly exaggerated newspaper articles and television reports depicting Bin Laden as some new "Carlos the Jackal," a semi-mythical figure at the center of "international terrorism."
Only in the fantasy-ridden world of Hollywood do "rich" "criminal masterminds" carry on their own wars and terrorism. Outside the world of James Bond, things work quite differently."

http://prisonplanet.tv/articles/june2004/062504manufacturedfront.htm

"To kidnap, torture and execute people are terrorist actions which are in no way related to God or to Islam, and these actions are not rewarded by paradise as some ignorant Western media figures would like to believe.
The terrorist event of New York 11 September 2001, and the terror event of Madrid on 11 March 2004, and other terror events commonly connected to Islam, are clearly not related to Islam if we consider that the Al-Qaeda terror organization was established by the C.I.A in the 1980s. Al-Qaeda is nothing but a conveniently "Islamic" front which enables the C.I.A. to commit crimes in the name of Muslims. It is well known that the Mujahadeen terrorists of Afghanistan were organized, trained and funded by the C.I.A. using the Pakistani ISI as a "cut-out" in order to lure the Soviet Army into Afghanistan at the end of 1979. The Mujahedeen can be seen as C.I.A. terrorism with an islamic name and "islamic" perpetrators. Afghanistan has, for all purposes, been destroyed by these fanatics in furtherance of American interests."

http://www.prisonplanet.com/news_alert_mi5terror_2.html

"The alleged spiritual leader of the al-Qaida terrorist network is living with his wife and children in northern England, in a safe house paid for by the intelligence services, it was claimed yesterday.
Abu Qatada, a Muslim cleric believed by several European countries to be a pivotal figure in international terrorism, disappeared from his west London home in December, before a round up of alleged terrorist suspects. It was rumoured that he had fled abroad.
Time magazine's sensational but bizarre claim is attributed to senior members of European intelligence services.
The report says that Mr Qatada, claimed by some to be Osama bin Laden's right-hand man in Europe, and his wife and family are being fed and clothed by British intelligence."
(There are many other links on this subject at http://www.madcowprod.-com/ .)

http://www.prisonplanet.com/news_alert_mi5terror_8.html

"Astonishingly, despite suspicions that he was a high-level al-Qaeda operative, al-Liby was given political asylum in Britain and lived in Manchester until May of 2000 when he eluded a police raid on his house and fled abroad. The raid discovered a 180-page al-Qaeda 'manual for jihad' containing instructions for terrorist attacks."

http://www.communitycurrency.org/vital.html

Review of Richard Labeviere, *Dollars for Terror- The United States and Islam* (New York, 2000), a book that links the CIA and Bin Laden's organisation.

Israel

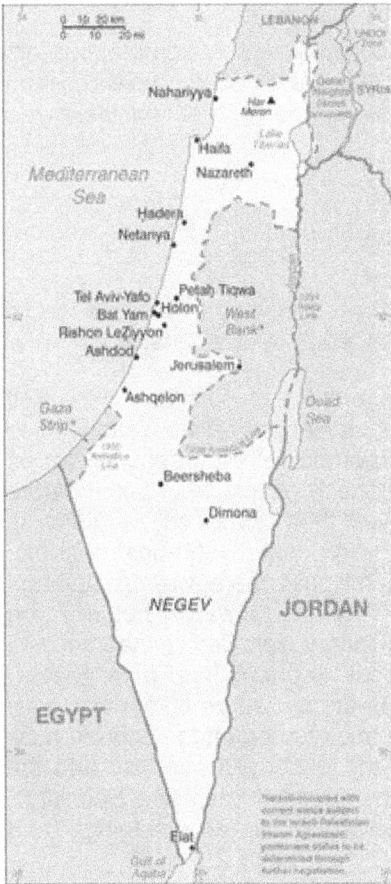

http://www.larouchepub.com/pr/2001/2850arafat_on_hamas.html

The Hamas allegations. Arafat's version of its genesis and support:
'Dec. 21, 2001 (EIRNS)-In interviews with leading Italian publications, Palestinian Authority President Yasser Arafat went into some detail regarding the genesis and operation of Hamas. To Corriere della Sera on Dec. 11, he said, "We are doing everything possible to stop the violence. But Hamas is a creature of Israel which, at the time of Prime Minister [Yitzhak] Shamir [the late 1980s, when Hamas arose], gave them money and more than 700 institutions, among them schools, universities and mosques. Even [former Israeli Prime Minister Yitzhak] Rabin ended up admitting it, when I charged him with it, in the presence of [Egyptian President Hosni] Mubarak.'"
(See also http://www.larouchepub.com/other/2002/2902isr_hamas.html

for more on these allegations. There is also this from http://www.propa-gandamatrix.com/puppet_on_a_string.html quoting United Press International:
"Israel and Hamas may currently be locked in deadly combat, but, according to several current and former U.S. intelligence officials, beginning in the late 1970s, Tel Aviv gave direct and indirect financial aid to Hamas over a period of years.")

http://www.geocities.com/jewishterrorists/black.html

"Disgusted intelligence sources in Palestine claim that the latest bombing atrocity that killed 10 and wounded 57 was an "inside job"...

The intelligence sources point to damage at the crime scene in the Beit Israel district of Jerusalem as proof of their claims that the weapon used was a car bomb rather than a suicide bomber. Photographs shown on this web site prove the claims correct. These photos were taken before the mainstream western media received their "sanitized" versions, in which there is no car and very little shrapnel visible. From the outline of the car we can tell that there was an internal explosion, with the blast shock waves radiating outwards, before being deflected upwards to atmosphere by a nearby wall. Before the truth was re-written by the Jerusalem Mayor, local reports carried a reasonably accurate account: "Burial society volunteers picked up body parts amid debris slick with motor oil and blood. A truck ferried off the charred husk of a car..." and: "Fierce flames from the destroyed car rose into the night sky on the street where the blast ripped through the Beit Israel district of the city just as worshippers were emerging from synagogues..."
But then Jerusalem police chief Mr Mickey Levy took over and said a suicide bomber with a shrapnel bomb strapped to him had walked up to a group of people and blown himself up. The bomber "got to the center of the neighborhood, approached a group of people (and detonated) a large explosive on his body," he said."

http://www.hendontimes.co.uk/archive/display.var.576507.0.0.html

David Shayler states in a local London newspaper: "I read some communication between [British MI5] officers in which a senior officer who had been looking into the Israeli Embassy bombing in 1994 said: 'I believe the Israelis did it themselves'. So this is not my ridiculous conspiracy theory. These are the words of a senior MI5 officer whose opinion is based on the investigation."

http://news.bbc.co.uk/2/hi/middle_east/2550513.stm

From the BBC: "Officials from the Palestinian Authority have accused the Israeli spy agency Mossad of setting up a fake al-Qaeda terrorist cell in Gaza.

Palestinian leader Yasser Arafat said that Israel had set up the mock cell in order to justify attacks in Palestinian areas.

...

Colonel Rashid Abu-Shbak, the Palestinian head of preventative security, said eight Palestinians had been approached from outside Gaza, and had been asked by Israeli agents to work for al-Qaeda with offers of money and weapons.

Colonel Abu-Shbak said the first approaches were made in March this year, and that all communications had been traced back to Israeli intelligence."

(There is more on that story at
http://www.federalobserver.com/archive.php?aid=5156 .)

http://www.prisonplanet.com/news_alert_hamas6.html

U.S ambassador to Israel Daniel 'Kurtzer said that the growth of the Islamic movement in the Palestinian territories in recent decades-"with the tacit support of Israel"-was "not totally unrelated" to the emergence of Hamas and Islamic Jihad and their terrorist attacks against Israel. Kurtzer explained that during the 1980s, when the Islamic movement began to flourish in the West Bank and Gaza, "Israel perceived it to be better to have people turning toward religion rather than toward a nationalistic cause [the Palestinian Liberation Organization-ed.]."'

http://www.public-action.com/911/toothfairies.html

suicide bombers Tooth Fairies

307

Italy

http://www.guardian.co.uk/Archive/Article/0,4273,4158945,00.html

Testimony of General Maletti referring to the Strategy of Tension and other matters, as reported by The Guardian:
"Among the larger western European countries, Italy has been dealt with as a sort of protectorate. I am ashamed to think that we are still subject to special supervision."

http://www.paranormalnews.com/textfiles/conspiracies/Arthur_E_Rowse _The_Secret_US_War_To_Subvert_Italian%20Democracy.txt

This is a very full article on Gladio from the respected Covert Action Quarterly no 49 summer of 1994.
"That the Red Brigades had been thoroughly infiltrated for years by both the CIA and the Italian secret services is no longer contested. The purpose of the operation was to encourage violence from extremist sectors of the left in order to discredit the left as a whole. The Red Brigades were a perfect foil. With unflinching radicalism, they considered the Italian Communist Party too moderate and Moro's opening too compromising."
(The footnotes to that article are available here in German:
http://groups.google.com/group/z-netz.datenschutz.spionage/browse_thread/thread/443891c5b66e5aaa/d bbde9ee34618950#dbbde9ee34618950 .)

http://www.spitfirelist.com/rfa.html

"According to information developed by the Pike Committee (a congressional committee investigating CIA misdeeds), P-2 member Michele Sindona was the conduit between the CIA and the architects of "the Strategy of Tension." Formalized by Italian fascist Stephano Delle Chiaie, the Strategy of Tension was a program of terror designed to discredit the Italian left and provoke a reduction of civil liberties and a broadening of police and surveillance powers. Its ultimate goal was a restoration of fascism in Italy. Epicenter of the Strategy of Tension and the coup attempts of the 70's, the so-called "Super SISMI" group functioned as an intelligence service within an intelligence service. (SISMI is one of Italy's intelligence services.) Composed of P-2 members and their allies within the SISMI, the "Super SISMI" cynically created and manipulated terrorism of both the left and the right. One of the apparent victims of the Strategy of Tension was former Italian Prime Minister Aldo Moro. Having invited the Italian Communist Party into a ruling coalition, Moro was kidnapped and murdered by the Red Brigades. (An Italian parliamentary commission investigating the activities of the P-2 lodge found that Licio Gelli had helped to found the ostensibly left-wing Red Brigades, whose program of terrorism discredited the Italian left and weakened Italian democracy.)"

http://www.skepticfiles.org/socialis/cosiga3a.htm

Ex-CIA officer Richard Breneke in a discussion on Italian TV: "The CIA money for the P-2 had several aims. One of them was terrorism. Another aim was to get P-2's help to smuggle dope into the U.S.A. from other countries. We used them to create situations favorable to the explosion of terrorism in Italy and in other European countries at the beginning of the 1970s.

Q: Excuse me, but your statements are very serious. You say that the P-2 was a creation, the financial and organizational arm of the CIA to destabilize, to run cover operations in Europe?

Breneke: There is no doubt. The P-2 since the beginning of the 1970s was used for the dope traffic, for destabilization in a covert way. It was done secretly to keep people from knowing about the involvement of the U.S. government. In many cases it was done directly through the offices of the CIA in Rome and in some other cases through CIA centers in other countries."

http://www.namebase.org/sources/UU.html

A reference to a book by Philip Willan, *Puppetmasters: The Political Use of Terrorism in Italy* (London, 1991):

"In this book Philip Willan peels back another layer of the onion and looks at the "strategy of tension." This technique – used by Licio Gelli's secret P2 lodge in collaboration with right-wing spooks and generals – sponsored ostensible left-wing terrorism in an effort to undercut the electoral position of the Italian Communist Party..."

http://www.commondreams.org/views05/0210-22.htm

"At the end of last month, Frank Cass in London released a new book by Dr. Daniele Ganser of the Center for Security Studies at the Federal Institute of Technology, Zurich called, "NATO's Secret Armies. Operation Gladio and Terrorism in Western Europe," which offers plenty of evidence that there was also a "Salvador Option" [a new Pentagon plan leaked by Seymour Hersh] in post-war Europe. It turns out that during the Cold War, European governments and secret services conspired with a NATO-backed operation to engineer attacks in their own countries in order to manipulate the population to reject socialism and communism.

It was called "the strategy of tension" and it was carried out by members of secret stay-behind armies organized by NATO and funded by the CIA in Italy, Portugal, Germany, Spain, and other European countries. The strategy apparently involved supplying right-wing terrorists with explosives to carry out terrorist acts which were then blamed on left-wing groups to keep them out of power.

Only three countries, Italy, Belgium, and Switzerland, have had a parliamentary investigation into NATO's role and a public report. The US and UK, the two nations most centrally involved, are refusing to disclose details, so crucial pieces of the story are missing. Still, Ganser's book offers some disturbing insights into a hidden aspect of the Cold War."

Libya

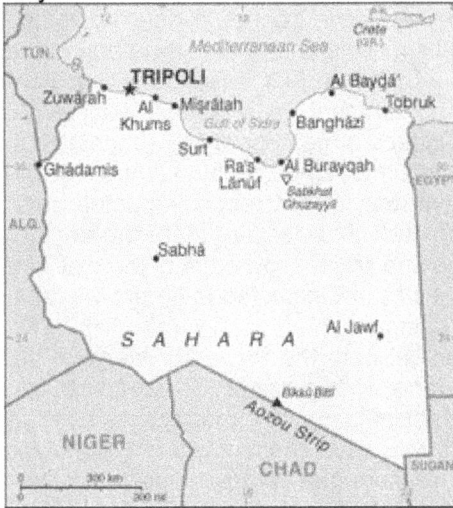

http://news.bbc.co.uk/hi/english/static/audio_video/programmes/panorama/transcripts/transcript_07_08_98.txt

This is a transcript of a BBC programme on David Shayler (MI5 dissident) outlining his allegations of MI6 support for a Libyan Islamic paramilitary group.

"It was only when I met PT16B discussing other matters with him that he mentioned this thing in a kind of note of triumph saying that yes, you know, we've done it, you know, we are the kind of intelligence service that people think we are almost, you know. My reaction was one of total shock. I mean this was kind of really against what I though I was doing in the Intelligence Services. And against what people had been telling me as well. I mean against what I'd been telling people. I mean in my job in MI5 I knew quite a few journalists because I used to be a journalist, and from time to time a conversation would come up about the work of the Intelligence Services and so on and I would say these stories are either rubbish or.. you know.. somebody has completely misunderstood what's going on. Yes, and the intelligence services don't get up to the things that were reported in the 1980s. I mean there have been some bizarre stories about them being involved in murdering Princess Diana's bodyguard and so on. And I was determined to tell these people this sort of thing didn't go on. But this was a kind of refutation of that. Suddenly it was like this sort of thing does go on and I was absolutely astounded when I heard that this was
the case..."

http://cryptome.org/shayler-gaddafi.htm

The significance of this is that we now have from an insider source an allegation that as late as 1996 British intelligence were using one of the large number of Islamic groups, who have their headquarters in London, to overthrow a middle east government. Its a credible source because we know that Shayler was indeed a member of MI5 (appointed to the Libyan section) because the British Govt. prosecuted him under the Official Secrets Act. The document, the full CX report is printed here, doesn't prove MI6 involvement of itself, Shayler had that from another source, it just proves the existence and MI6's knowledge of the plot. Notice how the projected government was not expected to be pro-western, which would further disguise MI6's hand in it.

David Shayler: "We need a statement from the Prime Minister and the Foreign Secretary clarifying the facts of this matter. In particular, we need to know how around £100,000 of taxpayers' money was used to fund the sort of Islamic Extremists who have connections to Osama Bin Laden's Al Qaeda network. Did ministers give MI6 permission for this? By the time MI6 paid the group in late 1995 or early 1996, US investigators had already established that Bin Laden was implicated in the 1993 attack on the World Trade Centre. Given the timing and the close connections between Libyan and Egyptian Islamic Extremists, it may even have been used to fund the murder of British citizens in Luxor, Egypt in 1996."

http://web.archive.org/web/20040604091339/http://www.library.cornell.e
du/colldev/mideast/libylndn.htm

More on the question of British intelligence's attitude to Libyan and other Islamic "terrorist" groups, from the Washington Post Foreign Service Oct 7 2001:

'Among the thousands of dissidents who have found refuge here are dozens of activists allegedly linked with bin Laden's al Qaeda movement or associated groups. Over the years, some dissidents suspected by foreign governments of involvement in terrorist acts have been protected by the British government for one reason or another from deportation or extradition... and could be used as a subtle means of political pressure against authoritarian regimes, from Libya to Saudi Arabia to Yemen.

...

"Britain has been playing this game in the Middle East for a very long time," said Yosri Fouda, London bureau chief for the Arab TV channel al-Jazeera, who has made a detailed study of Islamic groups in Britain. "It's a political game that can be effective as long as you know how to play it, but it can also come back to haunt you."'

http://web.archive.org/web/20041012044034/http://www.dawn.com/200
2/02/01/fea.htm

On the same subject from Dawn, the Pakistani newspaper.
"Following the Sept 11 terrorist attacks in New York, Britain has become
the news centre of the world not merely for taking part in the fight
against global terrorism but also for playing a key role in providing a logistics base for Islamic extremists and Al Qaeda itself. The recent raids
in London and other British towns and earlier arrests of the suspected
terrorists have shown that the UK does appear to be far more significant
than previously thought.
...
In Washington, Paris and capitals across the Middle East and Asia, intelligence agencies are reportedly pointing to the UK some thing more
than just a haven for Islamic dissidents and a centre for the dissemination of extremist propaganda."

http://www.larouchepub.com/lar/2000/terror_memo_2703.html

David Shayler: "We paid £100,000 to carry out the murder of a foreign
head of state. That is apart from the fact that the money was used to kill
innocent people, because the bomb exploded at the wrong time. In fact,
this is hideous funding of international terrorism."

http://web.archive.org/web/20020715075655/http://www.xs4all.nl/~ema
gs/scallywag/swg3000a.html

An article in Scallywag Magazine called "Tiny Rowland Flirtations With
Terrorism":

"On a crisp spring morning in May 1985 a private Lear jet left an British
airport bound for Cairo. On board was a small delegation with an
ambitious mission. Either to persuade the Egyption Prime Minister,
Husni Mubarak, to abandon the Camp David agreement and side with
Sudan and Libya – or to blow up Tahrir Square in the luxury Garden
City quarter with 100kgs of dynamite.

The leaders of this trecherous band were none other that the Libyan
Head of Intelligence, Ahmed Gaddaf Al Dam, Gadaffi's murdering
cousin, and Ashraf Marwan, one of the least known but most sinister
players on the London property stage, and on the international arms
dealing arena.

Just two years before, Marwan had bought in to the House of Fraser – then owned by Tiny Rowland's Lonrho, whose flagship was Harrods. By December Marwan had 3.2 million shares worth £6 million. It was not the first time he had done business with Rowland. In 1979 he had purchased 40% of a cargo airline company called Tradeswind. Lonrho owned the other 60%. Marwan had nominated in his place as director none other than the same Gaddaf al Dam.

Rowland was on the board, alongside prominent Tory, Sir Edward Du Cann. Under al Dam, Tradeswind quickly started a brisk business transporting arms from the US to the Lebanon and Libya. To get through the complicated US government embargoes, they bribed two bent CIA officers, Ed Wilson and Frank Terpil.

Using the legitimate cover of the seemingly respectable airline, Marwan and Al Dam transported an awesome amount of deadly weapons, not just to the governments of Libya and the Lebanon, but to all sorts of terrorist groups such as the Abu Nidal group, and in a wholly personal deal organised by Al Dam, to the IRA. The CIA officers were eventually arrested, and for a while the trade stopped. There is an arrest warrant waiting for Marwan and Al Dam should they ever set foot in the United States." (Its well known that this magazine was crushed by the British Prime Minister, using what most see as completely spurious libel proceedings.)

http://www.deepblacklies.co.uk/terminal_velocity_pr.htm

"A well placed and knowledgeable source has told This Writer that the fatal shot [which killed a policewoman in London] almost certainly came from the upper floors of No. 3 St. James Square – location of the secret joint MI5/CIA surveillance post. The operation was engineered to create public outrage that would have hardened the existing "soft" view of Libya by the British government. We were also told that the operation "planners" were concerned that deaths of Libyan protesters by Qaddafi's own assassin, wouldn't be enough to mobilise the govern-ment to take extreme retaliatory measures. Consequently, an additional target was chosen that was certain to inflame public opinion. Yvonne Fletcher was the sacrificial lamb." (A detailed account building on sources like a Channel 4 Despatches documentary of April 1996 and which raised questions by Tim Dalyell, and others, in the House of Commons.)

http://www.geometry.net/detail/scientists/wilson_edwin_page_no_3.html , http://www.disinfo.com/archive/pages/dossier/id334/pg1/ and this

interesting site:
http://www.bibliotecapleyades.net/sociopolitica/secretgoldtreaty/secret_t
reaty_part%202.2.htm

"In 1977, Edwin P. Wilson sold Libyan dictator Moammar Quaddaffi, 42
000 pounds (20 tons) of C-4, one of the most powerful explosives
around, and perfect for terror operations Libya was on the US list of nations sponsoring terrorists, and was therefore off limits to this kind of
business. ...Wilson was claiming that he had been working for the CIA
when he sold the C-4 to Quaddaffi."

Macedonia

http://www.emperors-clothes.com/articles/choss/washbe.htm

"Introductory note: Emperor's Clothes has published quite a selection of articles which, though there are disagreements amongst them, point to the same indictment: Washington is the key force behind the terrorist assault on Macedonia"

http://observer.guardian.co.uk/international/story/0,6903,449923,00.html

The Observer March 11 2001: "The United States secretly supported the ethnic Albanian extremists now behind insurgencies in Macedonia and southern Serbia.

The CIA encouraged former Kosovo Liberation Army fighters to launch a rebellion in southern Serbia in an effort to undermine the then Yugoslav President Slobodan Milosevic, according to senior European officers who served with the international peace-keeping force in Kosovo (K-For), as well as leading Macedonian and US sources."

http://web.archive.org/web/20040602202114/http://breaking.examiner.ie/2004/05/01/story145446.html

Reported in the Cork Examiner: "Macedonian police gunned down seven innocent Pakistani immigrants, then claimed they were terrorists, in a killing staged to show they were participating in the US-led war on terror, authorities said.

Police spokeswoman Mirjana Konteska...described a meticulous plan to promote Macedonia as a player in the fight against global terrorism that involved smuggling the Pakistanis into Macedonia from Bulgaria, housing them, and then coldly gunning them down."

Maldives

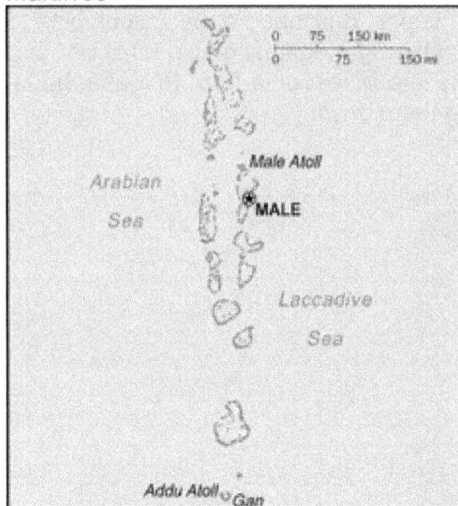

http://www.defencejournal.com/jan99/rawfacts.htm

Dr Shireen M Mazari, the Director General of the Institute of Strategic Studies in Pakistan: "Even as the Indian forces were bogged down in the Sri Lankan quagmire, RAW created a bizarre drama in The Maldives. Terrorists belonging to the RAW-funded Eelam Peoples Revolutionary Liberation Front (EPRLF) staged an attack on Male ostensibly in an effort to use The Maldives as a base for anti-Sri Lankan action. The whole drama ended when, within 24 hours, Indian troops arrived on the 'request' of Maldives' president and captured – effortlessly – the EPRLF personnel. However, no one at home or abroad was deceived by this RAW engineered drama."

Mexico

http://web.archive.org/web/20020110015306/http://www.angelfire.com/o
h2/elevatorbrewing/houston60.htm

"Army General and Head of the PGR Releases Two Israelis Arrested
With Guns and Explosives Inside the Mexican Congress."

Morocco

http://web.archive.org/web/20041012074114/http://www.news24.com/n
ews24/africa/features/0,,2-11-37_1413226,00.html

"Rabat – French national Pierre Robert, who is on trial in Morocco for allegedly leading a Muslim extremist cell involved in the May suicide attacks in Casablanca, told a court on Monday that he worked for French intelligence."

Mozambique

"When the security of the pipeline was threatened in the early 1980s, in the context of the expanding war between the Mozambican government and the South African-backed Renamo insurgents, Lonrho [a UK company owned by Tiny Rowland] entered into direct contact with Renamo to arrange a deal.

In June 1982, a Lonrho subsidiary signed a secret protection agreement with Renamo leaders covering the Beira oil pipeline. The agreement stipulated that payments of US $500,000 would be made to Renamo each month from June to August, to be continued indefinitely thereafter, unless either party gave one month's notice to terminate the arrangement."

Namibia

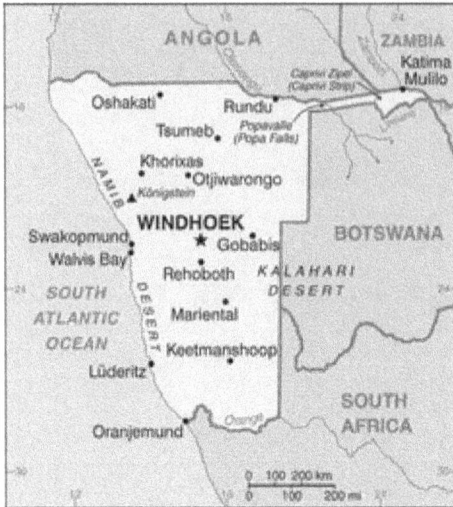

http://216.239.59.104/search?
q=cache:B1qTagzCHtkJ:www.angola.org/news/mission/august99/capri
vi.html+&hl=en&start=1

Recent attempts to destabilise a part of Namibia, this is August 1999 long after the fall of apartheid obviously. The links between UNITA, lead by Savimbi, and the CIA are too obvious to bother documenting (but I have listed some under Angola). Note that Namibia had sent troops into the Congo in support of Kabila who was being attacked by Rwanda and Uganda, for the western manipulations of the latter two countries see under Rwanda.

"Adding to its destabilizing activities in Congo Brazzaville and in the Democratic Republic of Congo, it appears that Jonas Savimbi's rebels were involved in the August 2 uprising in the Caprivi strip in northern Namibia."

http://www.christiansciencemonitor.com/2002/0320/p09s01-woaf.html

The Namibian foreign minister notes this in the context of the new US war on terrorism:

"With US help, Angolan rebel leader Jonas Savimbi not only tried to topple the Angolan government during the 1980s, but throughout the 1990s he armed rebels who undermined the newly democratic Namibia.

"They did this against our Constitution," says Gurirab, who for 27 years

322

fought South African rule of the country now called Namibia, with the South West African People's Organiztion (SWAPO). "They were attempting to dismember our country by violating the territorial integrity and sovereignty of Namibia."

Nepal

"The main purpose behind writing this book is to enhance the feeling of patriotism, make the Nepalese people happy and remove hurdles standing in the way. Nepal wants to have good, friendly relations with India. We don't have any ill-intention to hurt India or to show unfriendly behavior. It is the democratic as well as natural right of a nation to express its problems and sufferings. At this point of time, the Indo-Nepal relation is deep, bitter as well as suspicious. Nepal's formal relations are with the government of India but reality stands far removed.

...

The act of fanning out internal conflict in Nepal has gained momentum, for the purpose of which minority groups and nationalities have been incited [by Indian intelligence]. Different issues ranging from demanding independent states to reservation have been raised by inciting women, linguistic groups, indigenous peoples, nationalities and Dalits. Linguistic movement and the Maoist conflict involving the Dalits and others should be looked at from this perspective. All demands from Khambwan, Limbwan, Magarat and Tarai Liberation Front to the federal structure as demanded by the Nepal Sadbhawana Party are a part of this whole design. Many things such as shelters for them, cash amount, weapons and trainings provided by India confirm this beyond doubt. It raps terrorism outside and wears a mask of anti-terrorism but provides dynamism to terrorism and disintegration. Rallies, processions, vandalism, picketing, strikes, sit-ins, etc are funded by India. And this will lead to instability and lawlessness.

It provides money to the political parties and their leaders to contest

elections and help them win election by sending goons. To win or lose elections is in their hands. Thus it maintains its dominance over government, parties and MPs."
(For a look at CIA involvement in Nepal see http://india.indymedia.org/en/2002/09/2190.shtml .)

http://www.nepalnews.com.np/archive/2005/others/guestcolumn/jul/gue st_columns_jul05_1.php

By Jan Sharma in Nepal quoting a report from the Islamabad Policy Research Institute by Rashid Ahmad Khan and Muhammad Saleem:
"In Sri Lanka, RAW was instrumental in securing Indian support for the 1983 Tamil insurgency and then to send the Indian Peace Keeping Force to "enforce peace" in the northeast.

Both Indira Gandhi and her son Rajiv patronized LTTE so as to "prevent the Tamil struggle from becoming a challenge to the nation-state system in South Asia, and to pressurise the Sri Lankan government to recognize India as the regional super power."

India first supplied, through RAW, the Tamil guerrillas with arms, ammunitions and training "only to intervene to police a peace settlement."

Reading the reference on Sikkim in 1970s is like reading something on Nepal today. RAW prepared necessary grounds for India's direct military intervention in the former Himalayan kingdom.

RAW agents established "a close liaison with men, who, in the words of the Indians, could help in establishing a democratic government in the state." Indian military intervention came in April 1973 "to protect the Chogyal" [king of Sikkim].
...
The authors, for curious reasons, put Nepal in the same chapter as Sikkim. They see RAW hand behind the June 1985 bombings in Kathmandu and elsewhere.

However, they are conspicuously silent on its role in the Khampa insurgency smashed by the Royal Nepal Army on the eve of late King Birendra's February 1975 coronation. [The writer probably suspects the authors of not wishing to offend the US which was said to be heavily involved in the Khampa insurgency.]
...
"There is enough evidence to show that India is inciting a situation of full-scale civil war. The motive behind these actions seems to be the Indian plan to undertake a military invasion of Nepal on the pretext of re-

325

sorting peace as it had earlier done in Sri Lanka," the authors conclude.

RAW is also helping, they say, the Maoist insurgency to build pressure on Nepal. They endorse the unstated official Nepali position that the Maoist insurgency is not capable of sustaining itself without the support it gets from its sanctuaries across the border in India."

http://www.peoplesreview.com.np/2005/101105/detail/n11.html

A long paper submitted to a 2005 conference in Kathmandu by M. R. Josse Consultant Editor, The People's Review, Kathmandu, former editor-in-chief of The Rising Nepal, Kathmandu and Deputy Permanent Representative of Nepal to the United Nations, 1985-1990:
"In fact, short of an unconditional surrender by the King and the RNA [Royal Nepalese Army] to India's proxies – the Maoists and the agitating political parties – there is, in such circumstances, no realistic prospect for meaningful peace talks in my view.

Indeed, the situation has morphed into such a dangerous stage, among other reasons, precisely because of the open-ended support to India from the US and the UK (as also the EU) for the advancement of her long-standing designs on Nepal, albeit in the guise of advancing the cause of democracy in Nepal. Incidentally, why democracy in Nepal must serve India's and the West's interest, and not that of her own people, has never been explained!

At this point it will perhaps be germane to underline that such a policy – aimed, in my view, at capitalizing on the large Indian market for her products and investment, and, in the longer term, to contain a China that is fast emerging as a super power and rival – is bound to set alarm bells ringing. After all, China is extremely sensitive about protecting her borders. That, of course, includes the Sino-Nepalese one on the southern flank of Tibet, long considered in the West as China's "soft underbelly".

No doubt, that Beijing, which is cognizant of how party-governments in the past winked at the illicit anti-China activities of the Dalai Lama's followers in Nepal, has not forgotten the CIA-funded, Nepal-based Khampa operations of the 1960s.
...
Given the West's propensity for pushing the independent Tibet cause, including by American politicians active at the current "regime change" effort in Nepal, and considering the rock solid understanding presently subsisting between Kathmandu and Beijing, it would be extremely naïve to assume that a naked move to stage "a Sikkim" in Nepal will be

treated with unconcern by China.

At this juncture, when New Delhi's backing for the Maoists has been advertised to the world, it also remains to be seen whether the West, principally the United States on a self-proclaimed messianic mission to democratise the world in her own image, will continue to support New Delhi and, by doing so, endorse the brutal actions of the Maoists, which it placed on its terrorist list and declared constitute a threat to the United States.

At the external level, Nepal's continued survival as an independent monarchy or its transformation into an Indian vassal state will, ultimately, depend, among other factors, on such a policy reversal, not to mention China's response or that of the other South Asian nations or of the larger international community."

http://peacejournalism.com/ReadArticle.asp?ArticleID=4513

The above former diplomat writing in 'The Rising Nepal':
"This TRN reader, for one, would doubtless have benefited enormously from his [the UK ambassador, Bloomfield's, comments defending the Maoists from the charge of being terrorists] bottomless diplomatic wisdom and boundless guerrilla warfare expertise if he had just cared to explain how a ruthless foreign-inspired/participated/funded "people's war" against a legally constituted State can be considered wholly indigenous, even legitimate, as he seems to imply.

Let me elaborate. Does the world not know that the Nepali Maoists, who routinely employ tactics of terror as a matter of policy, are guided, aided and abetted by organisations such as the London-headquartered umbrella outfit, the Revolutionary International Movement (RIM)? Is Bloomfield, a counter-terrorism expert, totally unaware that they are joined at the hips to a variety of Indian Naxalite/Maoists groupings, including the Maoist Communist Centre (MCC) and People's War Group (PWG) which last year merged to form the Communist Party of India-Maoist (CPI-M)?

Has he forgotten his former colleague, then Indian Ambassador, Shyam Saran's disclosure at a public function in Kathmandu that two Indian terror groups, the MCC and the PWG, were going from India "to training camps in western and mid-western Nepal." (Kathmandu Post, January 11, 2003)?

Likewise, does the British envoy with his background in counter-terrorism policy formulation, not know that there is another supra-revolutionary organisation that has an important, perhaps even decisive, say in matters related to Maoist-style revolutions in South Asia? If not, let me inform him, here and now.

I refer to the Coordination Committee of Maoist Parties and Organisations in South Asia, or CCOMPOSA. Let me also recall that, as has been widely reported in the regional press, including the South Asia Tribune, that a meeting of CCOMPOSA held at Kolkata last year brokered that unity move. Another very significant decision, also reported in the non-mainstream Indian media, is the creation of a Red Zone, the so-called "Dandakaryna Desam" that "starts from Bhutan-Nepal and covers the whole region of North Bengal, Bihar, Jharkhand, Orissa, South Madhya Pradesh, and Andhra Pradesh." Furthermore, that conclave also decided that CCOMPOSA should provide shelter and training camps to Nepali Maoists.

In addition, who in Nepal today is unaware that the Maoist insurgency has continued to get solid political, media and financial support in India and safe havens on Indian territory? Has Bloomfield not read widely reported disclosures – in the Indian media among others – of how only quite recently Indian intelligence officials escorted Maoist leaders to meetings with senior Indian politicians in New Delhi, despite their being termed terrorists and against whom Interpol Red Corner notices for arrest have been issued?"
(You can read many articles by the same writer at http://peacejournalism.com/SearchArticles.asp?AuthorID=158. He describes how the 'Axis powers' of the UK-India-US squeeze Nepal as it tries to deal with an insurgency that is aided, he says, by at least some of those powers. He seems to accuse India and the UK of trying to engineer a Sikkim scenario and he wonders if the US is hoping to establish Nepal as a satellite power as part of a containment ring around China.)

http://www.nepalitimes.com/issue251/fromthenepalipress.htm

"Maoist leader Dr Baburam Bhattarai was in New Delhi in mid-May hobnobbing with the Indian leadership and officials...Bhattarai and his team met many leaders-from the newly-elected General Secretary of the CPI-M Prakash Karat to General Secretary of the CPI, AB Bardhan and former Defence Minister George Fernandez. But none of them have formally confirmed these reports. Though Karat admitted to meeting Nepali Maoist leaders in The Times of India, he immediately issued a press statement saying that he had 'met Nepali Maoists in a meeting arranged by Indian security agencies'.

The news of the meeting between the Maoists and the Indians was first broken by the Dubai-based Gulf News a week earlier. Informed sources say their relationship dates back to the 1970s when both were studying at Jawaharlal Nehru University. The Indian intelligence agency, RAW, has had its hands soiled in many political episodes in South Asia right from Sikkim's integration (into India) to the establishment of Bangladesh and Sri Lanka's Tamil rebellion. PK Hormiz Tarakan who was appointed chief of RAW early this year is reputed to have an in-depth knowledge about Nepal's politics and was the RAW station chief in Nepal until June 2001. Tarakan, who was set to retire this month, may have been promoted to make his own priorities felt. Some agree, although Bhattarai flatly denied Indian intelligence officers had a role in his Delhi mission."

http://www.nepalitimes.com/issue173/fromthenepalipress.htm

Maoist leader Baburam Bhattarai responds to what must be widespread suspicion of Indian involvement in the insurgency:
"The only surprise we have is the way these elements [obviously the Nepali government etc], who cannot survive even for one day without alms from foreigners, have been shedding crocodile tears just because we chose to meet on foreign soil. They are also harping on about how the Indian state has protected the Maoists. Moreover, some people are demonstrating their intellectual bankruptcy when they say that the meeting between Maoist and UML leaders in Siliguri two years ago and the latest one in Lucknow justifies their argument that India has been the base of the entire 'people's war'. They also made a foolish argument that the Maoist problem will not be solved until our party leaders are arrested and extradited by the Indian government."

Nicaragua

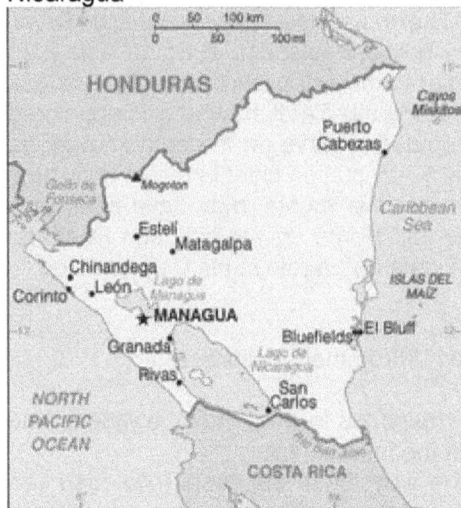

http://www.nicaliving.com/node/view/800

"All this comes in the same week that George Bush named John Negroponte as head of the US intelligence services. Negroponte, in his acceptance speech, said that his most important work in this post would be to reform the intelligence services so as to be able to fight with more efficiency in the war against terrorism.

The news was met with horror in Nicaraguan press. The headline in El Nuevo Diario's Feb. 18 edition read "State Terrorist as Supreme Chief Against Terrorism." The article went on to remind readers of the horrors that were carried out against Nicaraguan citizens by the contra forces, funded and trained by the US army in Honduras, and against El Salvador citizens by death squads also funded and trained in Honduras during Negroponte's time as US ambassador to Honduras during the 1980s."

http://www.defraudingamerica.com/sample_chapter_def.doc

"CIA-fed media releases claimed that the United States had to fund the Contras for freedom purposes and to combat communism. The real reason appeared to be the profitable drug trafficking. My CIA contacts stated the CIA was shipping arms to both sides, defending this practice in a tongue-in-cheek comment, 'How else can the CIA keep the war going!'

The CIA sought support from Congress for its Contra operation by reporting that the Sandinistas were trafficking in drugs and claimed that the Contras were not doing the same. Actually, U.S. intelligence agencies were selling arms to both the Contras and the Sandinistas and taking drugs as part payment. The drugs were then shipped back to the United States in the same aircraft used for shipping the arms."

Pakistan

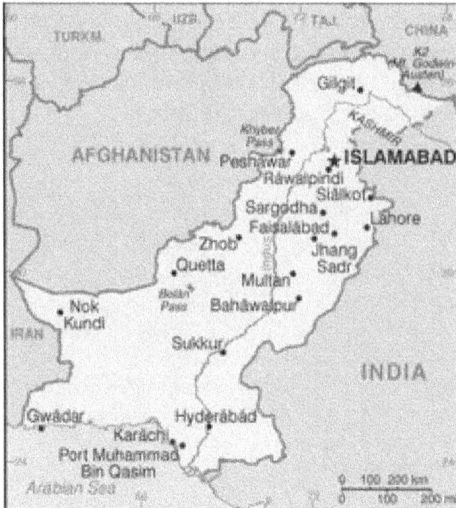

http://www.guardian.co.uk/Print/0,3858,4387811,00.html

The Guardian April 5 2002 on the kidnapping of Daniel Pearl:
"The principal kidnapper, the former LSE student Omar Saeed Sheikh –
whose trial begins in Karachi today – has added to the mystery. He
carelessly condemned himself by surrendering to the provincial home
secretary (a former ISI operative) on February 5. Sheikh is widely believed in Pakistan to be an experienced ISI "asset" with a history of operations in Kashmir. If he was extradited to Washington and decided to
talk, the entire story would unravel. His family are fearful. They think he
might be tried by a summary court and executed to prevent the identity
of his confederates being revealed.
So mysterious has this affair become that one might wonder who is
really running Pakistan."

http://www.gulfnews.com/Articles/News.asp?ArticleID=45233

More on the sort of leads that it seems Pearl was pursuing.
"It is also rumoured that Pearl was in fact especially interested in any
role played by the U.S. in training the ISI or backing it in any way, especially during the war against the Soviets in Afghanistan in the 1980s.
"Details of any U.S.-ISI cooperation would of course not be appreciated
even in Washington, especially regarding U.S. cooperation in promoting
any kind of Islamic militancy," stated a source close to the Pakistan foreign office."

332

http://www.guardian.co.uk/alqaida/story/0,12469,1028044,00.html

From The Guardian newspaper 23 Aug 2003: "Experts who have been following the attempts of the Pakistanis and the US to find the al-Qaida leader have suggested that:
 The Pakistani president, General Pervez Musharraf, struck a deal with the US not to seize Bin Laden after the Afghan war for fear of inciting trouble in his own country;"

http://www.globalresearch.ca/articles/CHO311A.html

"A recent Reuters report (11/13/03; scroll down) quoting Labeviere's book "Corridors of Terror" points to alleged "negotiations" between Osama bin Laden and the CIA, which took place two months prior to the September 11, 2001 attacks at the American Hospital in Dubai, UAE, while bin Laden was recovering from a kidney dialysis treatment."

Peru

http://web.archive.org/web/20011006112842/http://dailynews.yahoo.co
m/htx/nm/20010922/wl/attack_peru_montesinos_dc_1.html

A report from Reuters which states that among the Vladivideos, record-
ings by Peru's fallen spy chief, Lima is described as a 'rest area' for Bin
Laden's group. See Chapter 6 footnote 51 for American connections to
Montesinos.

http://www.narconews.com/whitecollarterror1.html

Long editorial from narconews which puts that fact in context.
"The Al Quaida network of Bin Laden could not have enjoyed such
refuge in Peru without the approval of Montesinos, who ran Peru with
an iron fist, and collected a fee from all whom he protected."

http://groups-
beta.google.com/group/alt.activism/browse_thread/thread/a0c58100b7c
054b4/c1ee3229708bfd21

A radio interview with a former Army CID investigator Gene Wheaton:
"Well that's the, the turning the American public's brain to cottage
cheese so they don't look at the big issues. One of the major covert operations these guys in Washington had going (and again, this is sort of
the "lunatic fringe"; it's not the mainstream people. Because the mainstream CIA and Pentagon people do not agree with what's going on.)

They set up an operation called "Operation Screw Worm", built this secret airbase down on the Mexican-Guatemalan border and were moving weaponry down to Peru, and being... ostensibly to furnish to the Peruvian government to fight "Shining Path" revolutionaries and the drug smugglers. But in fact, when the consignments would get down there, the covert operators would break 'em up, *sell* *to* *both* *sides* to *keep* agitation going and to *keep* the business of covert operations and weapons movements viable. It's the entire covert operations sub-culture, and the movement of weapons around the world. And these paramilitary, low-intensity conflict operations are *strictly* *business* with these men."

Philippines

An 8,000 strong army is chasing a group said to be no bigger than 80 on an island 20 miles by 40 and yet American special forces have to intervene, strange. This parish priest has a few theories though:
'Amid the prolonged hostage crisis in the island-province of Basilan, a Catholic parish priest decided to reveal what he knows about an alleged military conspiracy with none other than the notorious bandits themselves.

...

Dominguez, a former Western Command Chief, branded Nacorda's exposé as "the concoction of a sick mind," adding only a person with a "sick mind" would say that the military has been using the Abu Sayyaf in

336

a "vicious war game" in Basilan."

...

Army spokesman Lt. Col. Jose Mabanta, meanwhile, stressed that an internal investigation concluded, "There is no collusion between Army officers and the Abu Sayyaf." '

http://www.inq7.net/specials/inside_abusayyaf/2001/features/spy_turns
_bandit.htm

The amazing story of Angeles a Filipino intelligence agent inside the Abu Sayyaf. He says he planned some raids "to justify the signing into law of the proposed Anti-Terrorist bill pending in Congress at that time." (There is more here on the background of the Abu Sayyaf:
http://web.archive.org/web/20041014212921/http://www.bulatlat.com/ar
chive/016abu_us.htm, and their links to the military:
http://web.archive.org/web/20041014211400/http://www.bulatlat.com/ar
chive/016abu_caloy.htm. A collection of links on this subject is available here: http://www.lazamboangatimes.com/abu_sayyaf.html .)

http://web.archive.org/web/20030616110017/http://erap.com/news/marc
06_03.htm

'Sen. John Osmeña [one of 24 Senators in the powerful Senate in Ma-nila] yesterday accused Malacañang [Phillipine govt.] of fabricating the bombings and the disturbance in conflict-torn southern Philippines, say-ing the "manufactured situation" is mainly a plot hatched by the US gov-ernment and Philippine Defense Secretary Angelo Reyes.
The strategy of Washington and Reyes, Osmeña charged in a state-ment, aims "to create a situation whereby military entry by the United States in Mindanao will be justified" and "to support the increased budgetary requirement by the (Philippine) Department of National De-fense (DND) and the Armed Forces of the Philippines (AFP) consider-ing that a war in Mindanao will require a billion pesos a month of in-flows." '
(More on Philippine politics here:
http://www.larouchepub.com/other/2002/2923philippines.html).

http://www.defendsison.be/archive/pages/0303/030309Fake.html

Michael Meiring CIA By Craig Hanley & Jun Bersamin Davao City
"What is unusual about the case, The Manila Times reported, is that Meiring [Described as a terrorist by Davao Prosecutors] was: whisked out of Davao, past the Philippine National Police guarding him at the

hospital, and on to a chartered plane, accompanied by what Immigration officials described as agents of the US National Security Agency and agents of the US Federal Bureau of Investigation."

...

The Manila Times quoted a friend of Meiring who said he was: told by a Filipino in Davao, carrying a message from the US Embassy that Michael would never be charged with a crime in connection with the explosion. The investigation will end up as a stonewall. Michael will be protected and...the incident will be shortly forgotten, if you re willing to forget it.

Officials in Davao City will not forget. The suspicious blast took place during a wave of terror bombings across Mindanao as US and Philippine troops conducted anti-terror exercises. President Arroyo threatened to declare a state of emergency and demanded that lawmakers rush through her tough new anti-terror bill. Rush it through they did.

Now Prosecutor Bendico says the US-shielded terrorist was trying to blow the hotel up."

(Big story in the media in the Phillipines.)

http://www.guardian.co.uk/Print/0,3858,4733855,00.html

Naomi Klein writing in The Guardian Friday August 13 2003: "Yet the Meiring affair has never been reported in the US press. And the mutinous soldiers' incredible allegations ['that the army has fuelled terrorism in Mindanao by selling weapons and ammunition to the very rebel forces the young soldiers were sent to fight'] were no more than a one-day story. Maybe it just seemed too outlandish: an out-of-control government fanning the flames of terrorism to pump up its military budget, hold on to power and violate civil liberties. Why would Americans be interested in something like that?"

http://www.sunstar.com.ph/static/bag/2003/05/16/news/cia.may.be.behind.saudi.bombing.ka.roger.html

A spokesman for the Communist Party of the Phillipines: "He said that the CIA's Philippine station also maintains a covert terrorist cell, which includes explosives, sabotage and psy-war experts recruited and handled by the CIA.

"All indications show that the series of bombings in Davao City and Koronadal were carried out by this CIA terrorist cell," said Rosal."

http://www.hrnow.org/monitor/m2001_0727_04.htm

'U.S. military efforts to intervene in the Abu Sayyaf hostage crisis appears to be a turnaround from their reported links to the Mindanao extremists several years ago. In May last year, Senate President Aquilino Pimentel Jr. described the Abu Sayyaf ("Bearer [or Father] of the Sword" in Arabic) as a "CIA monster."
...
Pimentel also cited revelations by a police asset, Edwin Angeles, who has since died mysteriously, that the military equipped the Abu Sayyaf with vehicles, mortars and assorted firearms for its raid of Ipil in April 1995. In the raid – the group's first large-scale action – 70 people died while 50 teachers and schoolchildren were kidnapped.'

http://groups.google.ie/groups?q=%22+ZAMBOANGA+CITY+
(FaxNews+INTERNATIONAL)+---+Muslims+in+this+part+of+the
%22&hl=en&lr=&selm=33199228.32F1%40jetlink.com.ph&rnum=1

"Today, we all know that Mayor Climaco's killing was masterminded by a few ranking officers assigned at the Southern Command (SouthCom) whose main objective was to eliminate someone who was constantly interfering with their multi-million peso criminal activities at the then Barter Trade.
At the same time, the military officers who plotted the mayor's brutal murder had hoped to draw the Muslims and the Christians into a Holy War --- using a popular US military tactic called "Divide And Rule" which was widely used during the Vietnam War --- but somehow failed after Malaya exposed the plot in a series of articles.
"Who will greatly benefit from the bishop's murder?"
If one were to ask this question here, surely majority of the respondents would point to the military---since it is a widely known fact that the Muslims loved Bishop De Jesus (his internment in Jolo at the request of the Muslim populace there instead of his hometown in Bulacan can attest to that).
As to the motive why the military would profit from the bishop's death, there are many. Consider this:

* THE ABU SAYYAF MYTH --- In a situation like the one prevailing in Jolo, Sulu right now, military generals assigned in the province of Sulu stand to make no less than P2-million a day as long as the "full-red alert" status remains. The money comes from certain percentage of the hazard (battle) pay of their men in active duty and deployed in the area. Generals also
reportedly receive part of the money used to procure more armaments to be used in the make-believe military operations against Muslim groups that do not even exist such as the Abu Sayyaf. Last month,

former SouthCom Chief Lt. Gen. Edgardo Batenga told reporters in Davao City that the Abu Sayyaf Muslim extremist group never existed and that the group was merely the "creation" of the government and the military."

Russia

http://www.guardian.co.uk/Archive/Article/0,4273,3973053,00.html

The Observer on some politically convenient bombings:
"Evidence shows secret police were behind 'terrorist' bomb."
(The author of this report has published a more detailed analysis here:
http://cryptome.org/putin-bomb5.htm. More on the Ryazan incident
here:
http://web.archive.org/web/20030921232605/http://terror99.com/archive
/2000.html. This link refers to a TV program on the bombings:
http://www.cdi.org/russia/johnson/4630.html .)

"Hot Spots" a documentary on Chechnya presented by Mark Urban,
broadcast BBC2 Tuesday 10 August 2004.

"For certain the FSB...provoked and instigated the second Chechen
war." said by Boris Berezovsky.
(See http://www.guardian.co.uk/russia/article/0,2763,662476,00.html for
an account of more allegations along these lines by Berezovsky.)

http://www.bu.edu/iscip/digest/vol6/ed0614.html

This includes a summary of revelations published in a book by an FSB
dissident, extracts of which were published in a Moscow newspaper. It
claims a pattern of terrorist incidents blamed on the Chechens were in
fact caused by the FSB [Russian Security Services]. This is a chapter

and verse account of who planted the bombs.
(Scroll down to the paragraph headed Caucasus / Chechnya.)

http://eng.terror99.ru/publications/085.htm

Therein quoted: "What is then the purpose of today's FSB terrorist, according to Litvinenko, activity? In his response to that worrying question,
Litvinenko recalls the situation when police asked security agents to
form a gang to deal with unruly businessmen. In his opinion, the FSB
resorts to terrorist acts like police to security agents. Same purpose,
same tactics, but at a different level of authority. At the state level. Like
in the case with police, the state hires, or puts up with, a gang of bandits to create an atmosphere of fear. To make people live in constant
fear of terrorists so that they yield to passport checks. and sacrifice part
of their freedom space."

http://eng.terror99.ru/archive/2000.htm

References to the Baltimore Sun 14 Jan200 and this from The [London]
Independent 6 Jan 2000:
"On the video, Lieutenant [in the GRU, Alexei] Galtin said he was captured at the border between Dagestan and Chechnya while on a mine-
laying mission. "I did not take part in the explosions of the buildings in
Moscow and Dagestan but I have information about it. I know who is responsible for the bombings in Moscow (and Dagestan). It is the FSB
(Russian security service), in cooperation with the GRU, that is responsible for the explosions in Volgodonsk and Moscow." He then
named other GRU officers."

http://www.libertyforum.org/showflat.php?
Cat=&Board=news_international&Number=293475302

"MOSCOW, March 24. (RIA Novosti)-Rizvan Chitigov, who was killed in
the district center Shali in Chechnya on Wednesday and was the third
most influential warlord after Shamil Basayev and Doku Umarov, had
graduated from an elite U.S. subversion and reconnaissance school
and had served on a contract basis in a U.S. Marine battalion, Kom-
mersant reports.
Marine dog tags indicating his name, and date and place of birth, were
discovered on his body."

http://100777.com/node/view/98

342

"Mr Berezovsky, [the powerful politician and businessman] now living in London, called a press conference to produce a British explosives expert, a French documentary-maker, a former Russian agent of the FSB (successor to the KGB), and a woman who lost her mother in the blasts, to accuse the security service and demand an official inquiry. "I am sure the bombings were organised by the FSB. It's not just speculation. It's a clear conclusion", Mr Berezovsky said yesterday."

http://www.mosnews.com/news/2004/10/04/ukbeslansuspect.shtml

Beslan london Kamel Rabat Bouralha

http://www.alertnet.org/thefacts/reliefresources/227337.htm

From Reuters: 'The FSB, a successor body to the Soviet-era KGB, said in a statement: "The FSB has reliable information about the training of mine and explosives experts for armed groups of international terrorists fighting in Chechnya.
"One group which is secretly carrying out such operations inside Russia is the international non-governmental organisation, the Halo Trust."
...
'"We have information that most of them are members of various British military structures and the leader, Matthew Middlemiss, is a staff military spy," the FSB said, adding that it was holding an unspecified number of the charity's workers.'

http://www.heritage.org/Research/RussiaandEurasia/BG1339.cfm#pgfld
=1052167

Endnote 2 of that article: "Julie Corwin, "Lebed Posits Secret Agreement Between Basaev [Chechen rebel] and Russian Leadership." RFE/RL Caucasus Report, September 30, 1999. [Former Governor of Krasnoyarsk Territory, the late General Alexander] Lebed made his accusations in an interview published on September 29 in Le Figaro, which is quoted by Corwin. Also see Anna Husarska, "Copycats," The New Republic, October 25, 1999, p. 50. Allegations against tycoon Boris Berezovsky were made in Moskovsky Komsomolets, September 14, 1999, and quoted in RFE/RL Newsline, September 14, 1999. General Alexander Korzhakov, President Yelstin's former chief bodyguard, accused Berezovsky and the Russian intelligence services of instigating the bombings. See Natalya Shuyakovskaya, "Korzhakov Says Bombings Were Berezovsky's Doing," The Moscow Times, October 28, 1999,

p. 1. In addition to Lebed and Korzhakov, these charges were made repeatedly by cabinet-level figures in the "Fatherland" movement headed by former Prime Minister Evgeny Primakov and several Russian political analysts and journalists. The charges were echoed by Basaev and other representatives of the Chechen community."
(Obviously everybody is accusing everybody else of the bombings, the point is few now think it was terrorists acting without the support of someone in the Russian intelligence agencies or government.)

http://eng.terror99.ru/publications/083.htm

"'It was the FSB [Russian domestic intelligence agency] that ordered the attacks. The name of the FSB chief Nikolai Patrushev has been mentioned on several occasions," he [Krymshamkhalov charged as accomplice to the attacks] said in the letter to a Russian investigating committee and dated July 28, 2002.'

http://eng.terror99.ru/publications/096.htm

This is an interview with a Special Forces operative who was in the Moscow theatre siege posing as a Chechen terrorist. It reads like something out of Le Carre:
"So it seems, the FSB and the MVD just trying to solve and acting out someone else's scenario.

During the second Chechen war such methods were well tested by military intelligence. The leaders of the so-called "squadrons of death" were the employees of the GRU. Executions of our compatriots without court hearings – it is their work. And neither the FSB and the MVD, nor prosecutors, or the courts can do anything about their bloody leadership. Then again, a common practice of the GRU squadrons is to use the Chechen bandits. And also, – their former victims (widows – who became such after the actions of the "squadrons of death") – since this is very convenient material for reaching the goals of terrifying all people.

So – was it them? Or someone else, unknown to us?

I don't have an answer. But it is very important to get to the bottom of this. And it is also, without doubt, necessary.

... So what did the people die for? What kind of an insane price is 129 lives?

Here is what we saw, when light was shed on a tiny part of the story about an agent provocateur of our days.

People have died, but the agent provocateur is thriving. And it is exactly him, who is a part of the political inner circle. He is well fed, looks well, and, most importantly, he continues... In the next few days he leaves for Chechnya. What will he prepare this time?

"I need 24 hours to meet with Maskhadov," he says.

"Only 24 hours?"

"Well, perhaps two days."

Khanpash is condescending towards the nanve. Towards us."

http://eng.terror99.ru/publications/099.htm

"The author accuses you of an inclination towards conspiracy plots. ...How would you reply to this?

Anna Politkovskaya [the journalist on the above story]: No, I most defin- itely do not have inclination towards conspiracy plots. I can tell you quite openly – after "Nord-Ost", a large number of foreign journalists and em- bassy employees came to our newspaper's editorial office, and they kept asking the same question: "What do you think, are the Russian special forces implicated in this terrorist act? Did you, perhaps, notice anything suspicious?" Every time I answered that I saw no such possib- ility. Just because if I allowed for this possibility, it would be very difficult for me to live with it. But then, starting approximately in January, certain information has started to come to our editorial office. This information was evidence to the special forces' complicity after all. I started to check the information for one reason only – to prove to myself that it is false. And, generally speaking, all this material arose from my attempts to prove to myself, that it is not so. It seems to me that all of this is mon- strous. The reality that surrounds us is horrifying. It is horrifying that the special forces have more power than the President, than all of the au- thorities; it is horrifying, that the special forces make us jump through their hoops. I started at the opposite end – with the intent to confirm that it is not so, that the society is more powerful, that we live in a demo- cracy. And then... It was a lengthy process. Preparing this article took a long time."
[I know the feeling!]

http://eng.terror99.ru/publications/098.htm

The late Politkovskaya again: "The authorities perceive society as a burden. The further away its representatives, the more boring are their faces, whenever society raises questions that concern it...Now, in the wake of universal capitalization, we have become a problem – the public with its questions. Representatives of power understand that without us, the "millet", they cannot have their desired delicacy – power – and so they prefer somehow to coexist.
...
Having analyzed this entire collection of diverse information there is one assumption that we can make: at various times Russia's special services have been linked to various provocations that have been necessary to maintain tension in the North Caucasus. But different special services have had a different relationship to different provocations."

http://www.cdi.org/russia/169.html

'Moscow, 29 August 2001 (RFE/RL) – The weekly "Novaya gazeta" this week caused a sensation with the publication of 22 pages of excerpts from "The FSB Blows Up Russia," a new book alleging to expose government complicity in hired assassinations and other criminal dealings.
The book, which has yet to be published, is co-authored by Yurii Felshtinskii, a historian and writer who emigrated to the United States in 1978. His writing partner is former FSB Lieutenant Colonel Aleksander Litvinenko.
...
The authors also examine the still-unsolved string of 1999 apartment bombings in Moscow and other Russian cities that left more than 300 people dead. Authorities at the time blamed the blasts on Chechen terrorists, and used the incidents to justify Russian military re-engagement in Chechnya. But Litvinenko and Felshtinskii allege that it was actually the FSB, and not terrorists, who were responsible for the bombings."
...
Felshtinskii says that after traveling to Moscow and speaking with a number of FSB officials, he concluded that his suspicions were correct: "When it became clear to me that the FSB had organized the blasts, I lost my emotional block [telling me that such a thing could never happen]. The most difficult thing for us [Russians] is to believe that a branch of the state could blow up apartment houses in its own country. We all live with a sort of psychological block – that such a thing is impossible."'

http://www.guardian.co.uk/russia/article/0,2763,761551,00.html

A Chechen 'terrorist' claimed to be working for British intelligence.

Rwanda

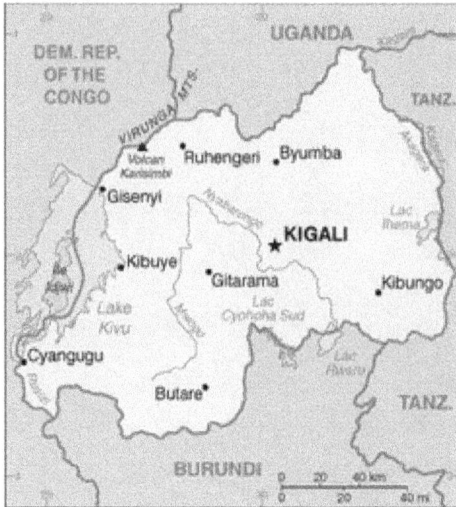

http://groups.google.com/groups?
q=wayne+madsen&hl=en&selm=9fv762%24g2o
%241%40pencil.math.missouri.edu&rnum=8

This covers the same ground as under the Congo, but includes many interesting details of US support for the RPF in this country, and on the attack on the aircraft that started the genocide. US Congresswoman Cynthia McKinney: "Western countries have incited rebellion against stable African governments by encouraging and even arming opposition parties and rebel groups to begin armed insurrection."

http://web.archive.org/web/20040213002700/http://www.africa2000.com
/indx/rwanda2.htm

"For several years before 1994, the hostility between the Hutu-run gov-ernment and the Tutsi exiles in the RPF was shaped by foreign powers. The French and Belgian governments backed the old regime to protect their interests, while the British and Americans sought to increase their influence in the region by supporting the RPF. From 1986, the RPF was openly backed by the government of neighbouring Uganda, which acted as an Anglo-American proxy. Rwandans serving in the Ugandan military received training from the British at their base at Jinja, Uganda, while the Americans began schooling the RPF leadership. RPF leader Paul Kagame, for example, attended the US army and staff college at Leavenworth, Kansas. From 1989 the USA supported joint RP-F-Ugandan attacks upon Rwanda.

348

As American and British relations with Uganda and the RPF strengthened, so hostilities between Uganda and Rwanda escalated. By 1990 the RPF was preparing to invade Rwanda with the full knowledge and approval of British intelligence. Belgium then terminated its support for Habyarimana and shifted towards the RPF, allowing it to set up office in Brussels. This left France as Habyarimana's sole Western supporter."

Saudi Arabia

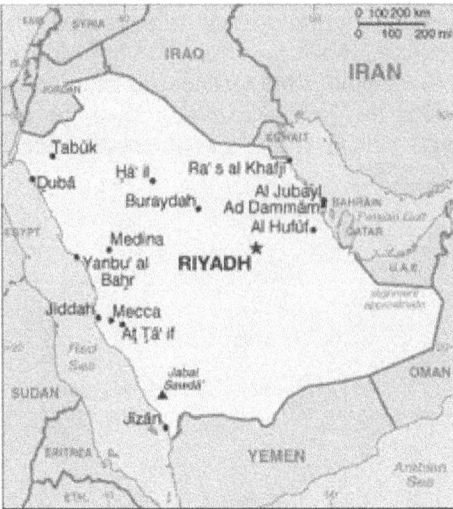

http://www.guardian.co.uk/saudi/story/0,11599,787811,00.html

"British embassy staff in Riyadh have been accused by the Saudi Arabian authorities of coordinating a campaign of anti-western terrorist bombings in the kingdom, the Guardian has learned."

Scotland

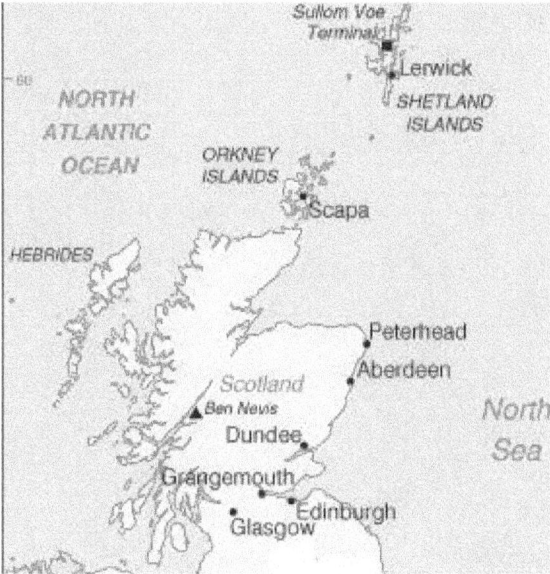

http://www.indymedia.ie/newswire.php?story_id=68750

An extract from Andrew Murray Scott and Ian MacLeay, *Britain's Secret War, Tartan Terrorism and the Anglo-American State* (Edinburgh, 1990):

"The powers of the PTA [Prevention of Terrorism Act] allow the police and Special Branch to perpetuate legalised terror campaigns against political activists. The PTA...is, of course, entirely ineffective in stopping the terrorist bombings...It is effective, however, in creating a climate of fear and mistrust in which everyone is prepared to inform on everyone else.

...

Through the use of agents and informants and the skillful treatment of "dupes" the State has thoroughly infiltrated and controlled the outbreaks of terrorism in Scotland."

Sierra Leone

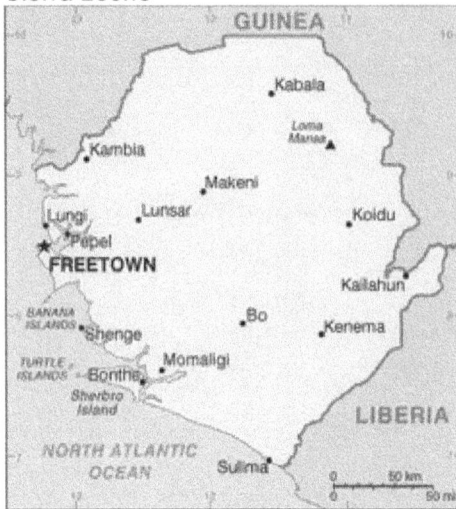

http://216.239.59.104/search?
q=cache:DN1hZWgl8ilJ:pilger.carlton.com/print/19282+&hl=en

John Pilger: "A reliable source of what Tony Blair, Geoff Hoon and Robin Cook are up to in West Africa is the Wall Street Journal, the authentic voice of American corporate power. On 22 March, reports the Journal, the US embassy in Freetown called a top-secret meeting of the multinational corporations that control Sierra Leone's diamond mines, the Freetown government and the RUF rebels, whose territory includes the mines. The US and Britain had forced the government into a coalition with the RUF and demanded that Foday Sankoh, the RUF leader, was given immunity from prosecution and made minister for natural resources, meaning diamonds. That his men were then spreading terror by amputating the limbs of children was not a consideration."

Sikkim

(Gurudongmar lake in Sikkim by Abhi182 from
http://en.wikipedia.org/wiki/Image:Gdm.jpg.)

http://orion.lib.virginia.edu/thdl/texts/reprints/nepali_times/Nepali_Times
_035.pdf

"In his book on the Indian intelligence agency, 'Inside RAW,The story of
India's secret service', Ashok Raina writes that New Delhi had taken the
decision to annex Sikkim in 1971, and that the RAW used the next two
years to create the right conditions within Sikkim to make that happen.
The key here was to use the predominantly-Hindu Sikkimese of Nepali
origin who complained of discrimination from the Buddhist king and elite
to rise up. "What we felt then was that the Chogyal [king of Sikkim] was
unjust to us," says CD Rai, editor of Gangtok Times and ex-minister.
"We thought it may be better to be Indian than to be oppressed by the
king."
(Of course in response to these troubles stirred up by RAW in Sikkim it
was only natural that the Indian army would come in "to protect the
Chogyal."
(http://www.nepalnews.com.np/archive/2005/others/guestcolumn/jul/gue
st_columns_jul05_1.php)

The Chogyal wasn't very worried about this as his former aide-de-camp Captain Sonam Yongda relates: "The Chogyal was a great believer in India. He had huge respect for Mahatma Gandhi and Jawaharlal Nehru. Not in his wildest dreams did he think India would ever swallow up his kingdom." But in fact these Indian troops stormed the palace and arrested the king in 1975 who sent off this last furious message to Indira Gandhi: "I have no words when [the] Indian army was sent today in a surprise attack on Sikkim. Guards who are less than 300 strong and were trained, equipped and officered by [the] Indian army who looked upon each other as comrades... This is a most treacherous and black day in the history of democratic India in solving the survival of our little country by use of arms."

(http://www.geocities.com/articlesonbhutan/politics_pages/bhutanesesyndrome.htm)
The takeover was sealed by a referendum that supposedly decided the fate of the monarchy but that was reportedly "'a charade," says KC Pradhan, who was then minister of agriculture. "The voting was directed by the Indian military."')

Spain

http://www.irishdemocrat.co.uk/news/2001/spains-dirty-war/

Review of a recent book on GAL.
"It has now been clearly established that the Socialist Party (PSOE) administration in the 1980s set up a series of death squads known as the GAL (Grupos Antiterroristas de Liberación – Anti-terrorist Liberation Groups). The GAL operated almost exclusively in the French Basque Country, where ETA maintained its organisational bases.

The death squads targeted leading members of ETA, but at least a third of their victims had no connection with terrorism."
(Here is a BBC article on GAL:
http://news.bbc.co.uk/hi/english/world/europe/newsid_141000/141720.stm .)

http://inn.globalfreepress.com/modules/news/article.php?storyid=467

From The Times June 21 2004: "The man accused of supplying the dynamite used in the al-Qaeda train bombings in Madrid was in possession of the private telephone number of the head of Spain's Civil Guard bomb squad, it emerged yesterday.
...
The revelation has raised fresh concerns in Madrid about links between those held responsible for the March bombings, which killed 190 people, and Spain's security services."

Sri Lanka

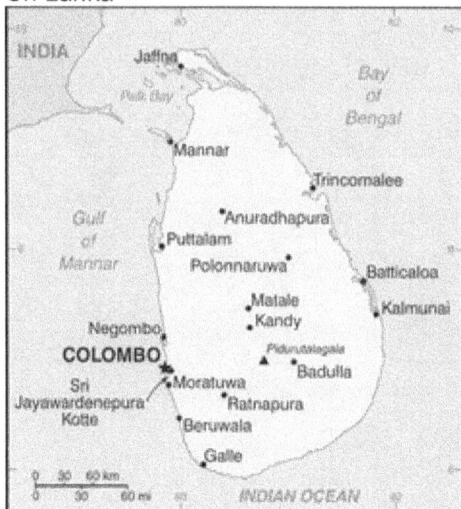

http://www.larouchepub.com/other/1995/2241_south_india_groups.html

"According to accounts by retired officials of the Israeli secret service, the Mossad, the Israelis were simultaneously training the Sri Lanka Army and the Tigers, and providing arms to each. Victor Ostrovsky, author of By Way of Deception, told Indian Abroad news service in 1991 that the Tigers were trained in Israel in 1985."

...

The British Special Air Services (SAS) firm Keenie Meenie Services, was simultaneously training the Sri Lankan Army and the LTTE."

http://groups.google.com/groups?
q=Victor+Ostrovsky+mossad+and+LTTE&hl=en&selm=901006113217.
2360116b%40AMARNA.GSFC.NASA.GOV&rnum=1

'In the case of [Sri] Lanka, a Mossad officer made a connection with the country's leader, sold him military equipment, including PT boats for coastal patrol, then turned around and supplied the rebel Tamils with anti-PT boat arms to fight the government. It then trained "elite forces for both sides, without either side knowing about the other, and helped Lanka cheat the World Bank out of millions of dollars to pay for all the arms they were buying from them."'

http://www.defencejournal.com/jan99/rawfacts.htm

By Dr Shireen M Mazari, writing from Pakistan, and citing inter alia the Jain Commission Report for the Indian Government as proof of that government's intelligence agency's (RAW) links to the Tamil Tigers: "So RAW saw a perfect opportunity to exploit within the prevailing dispute between the Sinhalese majority (74 percent) and Tamil minority (14 percent) over distribution of economic and social spoils of independence. Before the two sides could work out a compromise, India, through its RAW, managed to polarise the two sides as well as militarise this essentially political conflict. On the Mukti Bahini model, RAW built up terrorist training camps in India for a number of Tamil terrorist organisations, while India suddenly began orchestrating a public campaign feigning concern because of the links the Tamils had with the 50 million Indian Tamils of Tamil Nadu state – which was separated from Sri Lanka by the Palk Straits. It was only a matter of time before the militants trained in India began sidelining the moderate Tamils and instead demanding complete independence – Ealam. Ironically, the presence of Tamil training camps in Tamil Nadu often created a law and order situation when large arms were captured by the state police. The surprise for the state government came when New Delhi ordered that such captured material be returned.

According to Rohan Gunaratna, in his book Indian Intervention in Sri Lanka, RAW waged a secret war in India beginning 1983 so that when the Sri Lankan armed forces launched a major offensive against the Tamil militancy in 1987, the Indian government had already ensured that the Tamils were well supplied and were able to conduct terrorist acts that brought the war closer to Colombo. Tamil Nadu had become the sanctuary for the Tamil terrorists in their hit-and-run tactics. Already, a year prior to this offensive, that is by 1986, there were over 20,000 Indian trained and financed Tamils and India forced Sri Lanka through this militant pressure to alter its foreign policy. But even more crucial, India by now was systematically destabilising Sri Lanka. Being unable to resist the temptation to now intervene directly, India used the Sri Lankan offensive against the Tamil terrorists to force Sri Lanka to accept India's armed intervention ostensibly to save ' innocent Tamil civilians'."

Sudan

http://www.twf.org/News/Y2001/0614-BushSudan.html

"'For the last eight years, the U.S. has had a policy which I strongly dis-
agree with in Sudan, supporting the revolutionary movement and not
working for an overall peace settlement."--Former U.S. President Jimmy
Carter, April 2001'

http://www.iabolish.com/news/global/2002/talisman03-05-02.htm

"'America leads the civilized world in a war against terror," Jacobs said.
"Here is a Western oil company, trading its shares on the New York
Stock Exchange, instigating and funding the same jihad-terror that
struck America.'"

http://www.sudanupdate.org/REPORTS/Oil/21oc.html

"February 93: 'Tiny' Rowland, chairman of the Lonrho group and long-
time back room operator in African politics, reveals that for the last nine
years he has been a member of the SPLM/SPLA."[An insurgency army
fighting against the Sudanese government.]

http://www.libertyforum.org/showflat.php?
Cat=&Board=news_crime&Number=293254353#Post293254353

"Jordanian sources said three Israeli nationals were detained and interrogated by Jordanian authorities over charges that they supplied
weapons and ammunition to rebels in Darfour. The sources said the Israelis confessed to the charges.
The ringleader of the purported Israeli arms smuggling ring was identified as Amos Golan, the sources said. Golan operates a defense company in the Tel Aviv area and was said to provide training for militaries
in Africa, Middle East Newsline reported."

http://www.wsws.org/articles/2004/nov2004/sudn-n19.shtml

"Mounting evidence of US destabilisation of Sudan."

Switzerland

http://www.the-times.co.uk/news/pages/sti/99/08/29/stifgneur01017.html?2392

The Sunday Times August 29 1999:
"[Dino] Bellasi ["former chief accountant of the secret service"] had a series of arms caches, indicating links with the underworld and guerrilla groups. Bellasi has claimed that he was acting on orders from above in "a secret intelligence project" that might even have been designed to re-place the state secret service with an independent group."

http://news.bbc.co.uk/2/low/europe/427606.stm

"The head of Switzerland's secret service [Peter Regli] has been sus-pended as part of an investigation into a multi-million dollar fraud and the discovery of a huge cache of arms.
The scandal has led to widespread speculation of a high-level connec-tion to organised crime or even the setting up of a secret army.
...
One Sunday newspaper, Sonntagsblick, said Bellasi had links with the Serbian secret services and the arms were destined for a secret inter-vention force being created within the Swiss army."
(Incidentally Regli has been implicated in war crimes in South Africa: http://www.news24.com/News24/South_Africa/0,1113,2-7_1103738,00.html .)

360

Syria

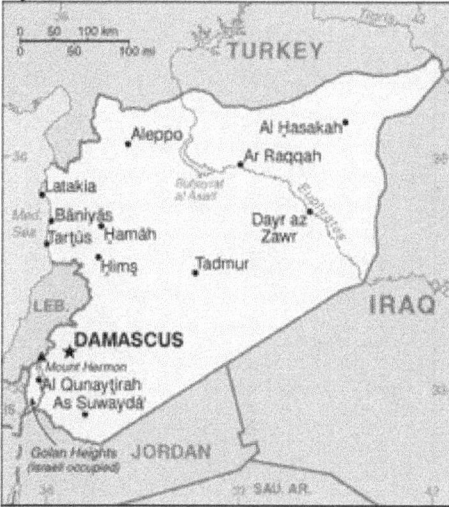

http://www.guardian.co.uk/syria/story/0,13031,1050908,00.html

A recently discovered US and UK plan to destabilise Syria in 1957, reported in The Guardian: "The report said that once the necessary degree of fear had been created, frontier incidents and border clashes would be staged to provide a pretext for Iraqi and Jordanian military intervention. Syria had to be "made to appear as the sponsor of plots, sabotage and violence directed against neighbouring governments," the report says. "CIA and SIS should use their capabilities in both the psychological and action fields to augment tension." That meant operations in Jordan, Iraq, and Lebanon, taking the form of "sabotage, national conspiracies and various strong-arm activities" to be blamed on Damascus.

The plan called for funding of a "Free Syria Committee", and the arming of "political factions with paramilitary or other actionist capabilities" within Syria."

Thailand

http://www.melbourne.indymedia.org/news/2004/07/74269.php

"A New Zealand security official says his services have uncovered an Israeli operation to create al-Qaeda cells in Thailand. The security official in Thailand said Israeli terrorist are posing as operatives of al-Qaeda."

http://sanpaworn.vissaventure.com/?id=104

A translation from the Matichon newspaper of Bangkok, April 7 2005: "Regarding Bangkok Senator Suphon Supapong's indication that the bombings in Hat Yai, Songkhla, may be a plan by the United States to interfere in Thailand's domestic affairs according to the Pentagon['s]

362

plan, Perayot Rahimmula, a Democrat party-list MP and former academic with expertise in turmoil in the three southern border provinces said that the story of foreign interference must be said to contain some truth because [he] has noticed that since [sic] the two years of violence, there have been many embassy officers from many countries in Europe and Asia traveling down to the three border provinces area. At the time [he] was still a professor at Prince of Songkhla University (Pattani campus) and therefore was always being invited to comment to these embassy officers.

...

Mr. Perayot continued that the event of bombing in Hat Yai was an attempt to make the event have similarities to international terrorism [—for example,] similar to intervention from al-Qaeda or JI [—] so as to open up the possibility for a superpower to come in and intervene in Thailand's domestic affairs. So what Mr. Sophon said [must] be considered an affirmation of the fact that took place."

(Perayot Rahimmula was the assistant professor in political science at the Prince of Songkla University in Pattani and as early as 2002 discounted the possibility of the indigenous separatist groups in the south being behind the renewed violence since "together [they] have no more than 100 fighters."

(http://www.montereyherald.com/mld/observer/2002/08/26/news/39338 13.htm))

Turkey

"On November 3, a truck crashed into a Mercedes Benz in Susurluk, 90
miles south of Istanbul, and killed three Turkish passengers: a fugitive
heroin smuggler and hitman, a former high-ranking police officer, and a
former "Miss Cinema." The lone survivor was a rightwing member of
parliament. In the car's trunk, police found a forged passport, police
identification papers, ammunition, silencers and machine guns.
...
The car carsh has created a sensation in Turkey and had led parliament
to hold hearings on the ties linking the True Path Party, the police, and
thugs like Abdullah Catli. Newspapers in Turkey are making connections between what they are calling the "state gang" and a secret paramilitary force that for decades has attacked the left.
...
"The accident unveiled the dark liaisons within the state," former prime
minister Bulent Ecevit told parliament in December. Now leader of a
small opposition social democratic party, Ecevit knows a lot about those
liaisons. He first told me about them--and the American connection--
back in 1990, when I interviewed him in his Ankara office, where he sat
in a soft, brown chair sipping a cherry drink.
...
Ecevit became prime minister in 1973. He told me he was startled the
following year when the Turkish military high command requested
money from the prime minister's secret fund to pay for a new headquarters for the Special Warfare Department. General Semih Sancar, Turkey's army commander, told him about the department. He said the

364

Americans had funded it from the start, but now they were allegedly pulling out. Sancar advised Ecevit not to look too closely at the matter. Ecevit investigated and found no such organization in the state budget.

"There are a certain number of volunteer patriots whose names are kept secret and are engaged for life in this special department," a military briefer told Ecevit. "They have hidden arms caches in various parts of the country."

At the time, Ecevit worried that these so-called lifetime patriots might have a rightist slant and would use their weaponry to advance their ideological goals. But he felt he was in no position to deny them funds. Ecevit's party was the largest, but it had won only a third of the votes. He was running a shaky coalition government. Ecevit released the funds the military wanted and never discussed the matter with the United States.

But the U.S. government surely knew about it. It set up the secret stay behind organization and funded it for more than two decades.

Working out of the Joint U.S. Military Aid Team headquarters, it was known first as the Tactical Mobilization Group and then the Special Warfare Department. In 1971, after a military coup, it was dubbed the counterguerrilla force and turned into an instrument of terror against the left."
(More detail on this group can be read at
http://www.consortiumnews.com/archive/story33.html and a Covert
Action Quarterly article on this group available here:
http://web.archive.org/web/20040428120735/http://www.ozgurluk.org/co
ntrind/caq.html, also:
http://web.archive.org/web/20040405022319/http://www.ozgurluk.org/co
ntrind/komisar.html .)

http://www.washington-report.org/backissues/0499/9904060.html

A discussion of the links between the Kurdish paramilitary groups and Israel, by a leading Mossad dissident, Victor Ostrovsky:
"In fact, because of such Mossad activities and its casual attitude to-ward the export of high tech weaponry, Israel sometimes finds itself on both sides of the same conflict. This has been the case in Sri Lanka, Cyprus and Bosnia. Such also has been the case with the Turks and the Kurds. This is further complicated by the fact that the divided Kurds themselves are sometimes on more than one side of an equation."

http://www.indymedia.ie/cgi-bin/newswire.cgi?id=5646&start=0

A sceptical view of some suicide attacks and human bombings in Turkey.

Uganda

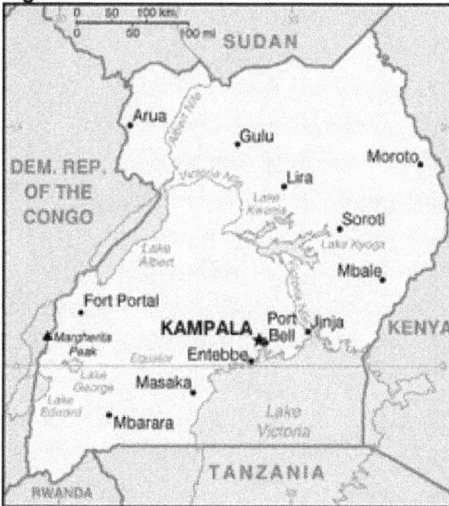

"Newly released British documents contain a claim by an unnamed contact that the Shin Bet security service collaborated with the Popular Front for the Liberation of Palestine to hijack the June 1976 flight from Israel that was diverted to Entebbe, Uganda, the BBC reported Friday.

...

"The operation was designed to torpedo the PLO's standing in France and to prevent what they see as a growing rapprochement between the PLO and the Americans," the BBC report said British diplomat D.H. Colvin wrote in the document, citing his source.

"My contact said the PFLP had attracted all sorts of wild elements, some of whom had been planted by the Israelis," Colvin reportedly wrote. "According to his information, the hijack was the work of the PFLP, with help from the Israeli Secret Service, the Shin Beit."

The document was written on June 30, 1976, three days after the hijacking and prior to the rescue operation."

United Kingdom

Qatada Hassaine MI5

Moussaoui "has persisted in naming Ahmed as both an al Qaeda con-spirator and a British double agent. Moussaoui's claims are self-serving, since his defense strategy relies on establishing that the FBI and other intelligence agencies knew all about the terror plot, and therefore must have known that he himself was not part of the "Nineteen Martyrs Team." Yet his charge that Atif Ahmed was working for British intelligence is suggestively consistent with the apparent news blackout."

http://www.aboutsudan.com/issues/terrorism/governments_worldwide_p
rotest__l.htm

"The American media have been typically remiss in their reporting of
this phenomenon, of London's safehousing of leading international terrorists; however, since November 1995, at least nine governments have
denounced London as the center for world terrorism, and each has
provided evidence to prove it. In some cases, the protests have taken
the form of official diplomatic demarches to British officials; in other
cases, the protests have taken the form of detailed expose in the official
government news agencies.
...
In April 1996, Egyptian Interior Minister Hasan Al-Alfi, told the London-
based weekly {Al-Wasat} that ``all terrorists come from London. They
exist in other European countries, but they start from London."
(Peru, France, Egypt, Israel, Saudi Arabia, Libya, Nigeria ..details
listed .)

http://web.archive.org/web/20041019164653/http://www.aboutsudan.co
m/conferences/schiller_institute/terrorism_speech.htm

Linda de Hoyos: "Naturally, British intelligence or its subcontractors will
tend to back all sides in a conflict--since the conflict, NOT the victory of
any one side--is the goal."

http://news.telegraph.co.uk/news/main.jhtml?
xml=/news/2002/07/26/wmous26.xml

Moussaoui 'plans to address the jury on his main obsession: that
September 11 was known about by the United States but was allowed
to happen in a murderous conspiracy designed to discredit the Islamic
world.
...
He named in court Atif Ahmed, "who is a British agent who has taken a
very important part of this", whom he wished to summon. "My aim in
pleading guilty was to expose the information I have."'

http://www.guardian.co.uk/afghanistan/story/0,1284,649744,00.html

Investigation in The Guardian: 'Documents compiled in Madrid, Milan,

369

Paris and Hamburg and seen by the Guardian indicate that most of the known attacks planned or executed by al-Qaida in the past four years had links to Britain.

...A senior German intelligence officer summed up the mood [in Europe with respect to Al Qaeda] when he said: "All the clues lead to London. All the roads lead to London." '

Kennedy Lindsay, *Ambush at Tully-West / The British Intelligence Services in Action* (Dundalk, 1979), p.262.

"In the Second World War it [MI5] was responsible for explosions in various places partly to convince the Germans that agents, who had been captured, were still at large and partly to alarm the British public into greater security vigilance. They included explosions at the de Havilland aircraft factory; an electricity generating station at Bury St. Edmund's; a food storage dump at Wealdstone, and army huts in Hampshire."
(Sourced from Sir John C. Masterman, *The Double-Cross System* (1972), chapters 6, 7 and 9.)

United States

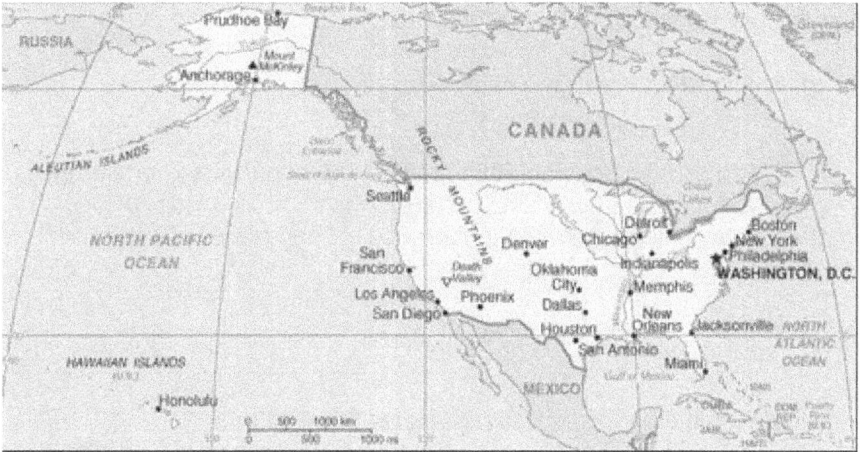

http://www.whatreallyhappened.com/RANCHO/POLITICS/OK/wtcbomb.
html

New York Times article on the first WTC bombing.

http://www.guardian.co.uk/waronterror/story/0,1361,583254,00.html

School of Americas George Monbiot

http://scribblguy.50megs.com/terror1.htm

This is a book by David Hoffman, *The Oklahoma City Bombing and the
Politics of Terror* (Venice, California, 1998). This is the definitive work
on the Oklahoma bombing, fully researched and documented. The story
that emerges bears no comparison to the public perception of the incident. The whole book is online here.

http://www.sundayherald.com/37707

Neil Mackay urban moving

http://www.whatreallyhappened.com/RANCHO/POLITICS/OK/ok.html

oklahoma PHOTO REMOVED Daily Oklahoman

http://www.counterpunch.org/floyd1101.html

super-Intelligence Support Activity

http://web.archive.org/web/20040603031559/http://www.libertyforum.or
g/showflat.php?
Cat=&Board=news_news&Number=86615&page=&view=&sb=&o=?
=1&vc=1&t=-1

tehran times npr radio newscaster 9/11

http://www.themedianews.com/news/twa800-2.htm

twa Exposing The Truth Cmdr. Donaldson

http://216.239.59.104/search?q=cache:2ld2Sug7iUcJ:www.mosquito-
verlag.de/weblog.php%3Fid%3D9%26p%3D1+&hl=en&start=1

An amazing, although anonymous, leak from a recently retired BND, German intelligence, officer: "Because of our intelligence findings, there is not one government in Europe that believes the official version hand-ed down to the American people. That includes Tony Blair, Mr Bush´s staunchest ally. Every prime minister and every president within the EU (and most not in the EU) knows that 9-11 was an internal operation, and though their intelligence services have made that fact known to their American counterparts, none dare address the US government directly. To some extent this is where Mr Rumsfeld´s "mad dog" policy had some success in the beginning. However, Germany´s foreign minister (and my last political boss) Joschka Fischer, saw off US pressure to commit German troops to Iraq by privately telling Rumsfeld that sanctions against Germany would result in his publishing these findings in the me-dia and telling the world about it. It worked, and the Bush administration backed off."
(Long detailed extraordinary account.)

http://oag.ru/views/ivashov_who.html

This is useful in corroborating the above otherwise incredible account. Many of those facts are echoed here and this is certainly not an anony-mous source. Its from General Leonid Ivashov the Kremlin's soldier in charge of relations with NATO during the Kosovo crisis, during which he met Milosevic many times, and who has attended NATO conferences: "A terrorist network whose purpose is to undermine Russia is organized and coordinated from London. There, under the wing of British intelligence, thrive the world's most radical Islamic terrorist organizations, such as the "Islamic Liberation Party", the "Worldwide Islamic Front", the "Defenders of Shariat", the "Mukhadjiri" movement, the Islamic Movement of Uzbekistan and others. I've named only those organizations which are forbidden in the majority of Islamic countries. In London also are located the nerve centers of Chechen terrorism along with the bank accounts of the terrorists.

Especially alarming is the possibility of nuclear terrorism. Let's analyze a curious chain of events which occurred recently: First, the Pentagon orders a study on the possible consequences of a portable nuclear device exploding in a Moscow-type subway system. Then information appears in the press that 'Al-Qaeda' possesses such a weapon, along with rumors that such weapons were sold by the Ukraine. And finally, the final link in the chain: on February 9th [2004] an explosion (conventional, for the time being) occurs in the Moscow underground. Was this the finale, or merely a dress rehearsal for a more serious nuclear attack yet to take place?"

The following links show that many insiders and knowledgeable commentators are articulating a different perspective on 9-11:

Andreas von Bülow former German defence minister and also for a long time head of the German parliamentary commission over their intelligence agencies.
http://web.archive.org/web/20031203160432/http://www.intellex.com/~rigs/page1/wtc/bulow.htm
http://www.prisonplanet.com/021104vonbuelow.html

General Hameed Gul former head of Pakistan's ISI.
http://www.robert-fisk.com/hamid_gul_interview_sept26_2001.htm

Michael Meacher recent UK cabinet minister.
http://web.archive.org/web/20040223202712/www.globalfreepress.com/article.pl?sid=03/09/19/1527251

Morgan Reynolds, Ph.D., is professor emeritus at Texas A&M University and former director of the Criminal Justice Center at the National Center for Policy Analysis headquartered in Dallas, TX. He served as chief economist for the US Department of Labor during 2001–2, George W. Bush's first term.

http://www.libertyforum.org/showflat.php?
Cat=&Board=consp_911&Number=293745886#Post293745886

Treasury Secretary Paul O'Neill (not on 9-11 but shows that the Iraq war was in fact planned long in advance, long before 9-11.)
http://www.wsws.org/articles/2004/jan2004/bush-j13.shtml

Stanley Hilton was a senior adviser to Sen Bob Dole (R) and has personally known Rumsfeld and Wolfowitz for decades.
http://www.rense.com/general57/aale.htm

Col. Donn de Grand- Pre of the US army.
http://www.prisonplanet.com/022904degrandpre.html

Lt. Col. Steve Butler of the US airforce.
http://www.rense.com/general40/ecor.htm

David Shayler ex-MI5.
http://www.prisonplanet.com/articles/june2005/270605insidejob.htm

Dr Paul Roberts Assistant Secretary US Treasury under Reagan.
http://www.prisonplanet.com/articles/june2005/240605doubtsstory.htm

Lt. Col. Robert Bowman (Ret.) formerly head of advanced space programs for the Department of Defense.
http://www.rmbowman.com/ssn/Secrecy.htm

Ray McGovern 27 year veteran of the CIA. (not directly mentioning 9-11 but with some interesting comments on that general topic.)
http://www.prisonplanet.com/articles/october2005/191005McGovern.htm

Steven Earl Jones Professor of Physics at Brigham Young University, Utah.
http://www.arcticbeacon.com/articles/article/1518131/37124.htm

Uzbekistan

Craig Murray, the former UK ambassador to Uzbekistan, writing in The Guardian 19 Oct 2005:

"Ms Blears was trotting out the Uzbek government version of events in March 2004. But this string of alleged suicide bombings does not appear to have been anything of the kind. As Britain's ambassador, I visited the site of each of the bombings within a few hours – or, in one case, minutes – of the alleged explosion.

The physical evidence on the ground did not coincide with the official explanation. For example, each suicide bomber was alleged to be using explosives equivalent to 2kg of TNT. But nowhere, not even at the site of an alleged car bomb, was there a crater, or even a crack in a paving stone. In one small triangular courtyard area a bomb had allegedly killed six policemen. But windows on all sides, at between 10 and 30 metres from the alleged blast, were not damaged; nor was a tree in the middle of the yard. The body of one of the alleged suicide bombers was unmarked, save for a small burn about the size of a walnut on her stomach.

A full account of my investigations of these bombings is to appear in my forthcoming book: one reason, perhaps, why the Foreign Office will seek to block its publication. There is no more reason to believe this version of events in March 2004 than to believe the Uzbek government's version of the Andijan massacre in May this year. What is more, as ambassador I sent back the details of my investigation to London, and the Joint Terrorism Assessment Centre (Jtac) agreed with my view that there were serious flaws in the Uzbek government account – agreeing with my view that the US was wrong to accept it. I concluded then, and still believe now, that these events were a series of extrajudicial killings covered by a highly controlled and limited agent-provocateur operation."

Venezuela

http://web.archive.org/web/20031008092512/http://www.reuters.com/ne
wsArticle.jhtml?type=worldNews&storyID=3502728

'"Over there, in U.S. territory, people are conspiring against Venezuela, terrorists are being trained," Chavez said.
...
"If they (the U.S. authorities) are really fighting terrorism as they say, they should act against these terrorists who are threatening Venezuela," Chavez said.'

Yemen

http://www.halifaxherald.com/stories/2002/09/21/f118.raw.html

'Yemeni officials retaliate by arguing that the West, and Britain in particular, is not doing much to neutralize the fund raisers, whom they describe as the lifeblood of groups such the Islamic Army of Aden.
Yemeni officials sent Tony Blair a bulging dossier on what they allege
British Muslims (including the notorious cleric Abu Hamza) have been
up to inside their borders. In Sanaa, government officials are astounded
that Britain has not acted on their information.
As one senior figure in Sanaa says, "The really bad men, like bin
Laden, don't fire the guns, they pay others to do it for them." '

Yugoslavia

http://www.emperors-clothes.com/docs/train.htm

Also covers Macedonia.
"The following are some articles dealing with Anglo-U.S. covert and not so covert sponsorship of 'Greater Albanian' terror in the Balkans."

http://balkanpeace.org/hed/archive/july01/hed3807.shtml

Sunday Times July 29 2001: "UN sources believe the suspect [for the Nis bus bombing], Florim Ejupi, who was wearing a bright orange prison uniform when he vanished and was said to have cut his way through four sets of barbed wire fences with a simple tool, had been working for the Central Intelligence Agency (CIA). His trial would have been a serious embarrassment, they claim."

http://www.iacenter.org/kla.htm

Some interesting points on the rise of the KLA.
"The April 18 London Sunday Telegraph reported that SAS, a unit of the British special forces, is running two KLA training camps near Tirana, the Albanian capital. According to the Telegraph, the KLA units trained by SAS are infiltrating Kosovo, using satellite and cellular telephones to help guide NATO bombing missions."

379

This is a fuller account of the leak in Germany of CIA planning as regards Kosovo and Yugoslavia, that was mentioned in the above article, which was passed on to this website by Jurgen Reents, Press-spokesman of PDS at the German parliament:

"This text I am giving to a Catholic priest, who is a member of the Order for Peace [Ordensleute fur den Frieden] here in Germany. I am doing so while maintaining confessional confidentiality, and divulging no information as to my identity. He will transmit this text on my behalf to those who need to know the truth. I hold a high-security post in the government apparatus in Bonn, and for reasons of conscience can no longer remain silent. The facts that I am about to divulge are, for the better informed, examinable and verifiable. Both the entire NATO propaganda staff as well as the Infernal Trio, Schroeder, Scharping and Fischer, here in Germany are unabashedly lying to the public with nearly every "fact" they present about the Balkans War, while a willing media pack is keenly spreading these lies, unverified, as gospel truth. About the current situation: The Federal Government knows the true reasons why the people are fleeing and is cynically playing with the calculated misery of the refugees in the border regions of Kosovo, in order to maintain an image comparable to WW II deportations and "ethnic cleansing". Neither the military intelligence arm of the Bundeswehr nor that of the NATO have at their disposal photographic evidence, intelligence knowledge, indications and proof leading to the conclusion that there is systematic expulsion or deportation of refugees by the Yugoslav special forces, army or police.

...

Furthermore, NATO officers are functioning as liaison commandos for the KLA. The contacts that were necessary for this mission were established by US and German officers, in violation of their mission as OSCE observers, preceding NATO-attacks. Here the German parliament is being as much taken for a fool as the general public.

...

The Chancellor and Foreign Minister knew from the outset that no Yugoslav government could ever sign the occupation statute, as it appeared in articles 6,8 and 10 of Annex B of the Rambouillet Treaty. Both understood clearly that this would mean the end of Yugoslavia as a sovereign state. War was therefore inevitable. Experts of the Justice Ministry poked fun at these passages, these clauses NATO would give NATO the rights of a medieval robber-knight throughout the whole of Yugoslavia.

...

Code named "Roots" – a covert action under which the CIA prepared the war – the objective is the destruction of Yugoslavia through loss of Kosovo, Montenegro and Vojvodina. Under the "Roots" operations, the

USA has since the beginning of the first term of Clinton's Administration been working – in close collaboration with Germany -on this covert action of the CIA and

the DIA, and supported by the German secret service. The objective of "Roots" is the military and ethnic destabilization of Yugoslavia, the last bastion of resistance in the Balkans. The objective of "Roots'" is the dissociation of Kosovo as the principal source of raw materials for Yugoslavia though a comprehensive autonomy, by Albanian annexation or total independence; the secession of Montenegro, its the only remaining access to the Adriatic, and the dislocation of Vojvodina the "bread basket," and another source of raw materials for Yugoslavia leading to the total collapse of Yugoslavia as a viable, industrial state. Behind this action is Germany's and the USA's fear that Yugoslavia will ally itself with Russia and other

former Soviet states once Yeltsin is replaced by communist and nationalist forces in the near future."

[From an automated translation from the german of the original webpage at:

http://web.archive.org/web/19990508061236/http://www2.pds-online.de/bt/themen/99041303.htm

we get this interesting continuation of the above text, the translation is obviously not perfect but the relevant points are I think clear:]

"After old-Roman custom of the "Divide et impera" the operators of roots set on direct promotion of the large Albanian nationalism in the Kosovo, in addition, on the indirect financing of royalistischen Tscherniks and Serbian Ultranationalisten in the Kosovo by rich right exile-Serbian circles in North America and Europe, in order to provoke an ethnical conflict. Disappointing it ran for the "Roots" planners that 1997 appeared again a peaceful solution, when the moderate speaker of the Kosovo Albanians agreed contractually with the systematically daemonisierten Milosevic contractually to re-establish in the public education the autonomy. Now the CIA establishment UCK [KLA], based on the basis of forces of the Albanian Mafia, which, still like their Sicilian counterpart the mountain villages in the border area between Kosovo, controls Macedonia, Montenegro and Albania, in the drug trade, smuggling, in extortion etc. actively is and a Kodex with blood revenge and the law of the silence operated, also in the Albanian civil war captured weapons on the plan called. Activities of peaceful reconciliation between Albanians and Serbs became by notices of the UCK from the ambush against Yugoslav police units prevented. Weapons had been captured sufficient in the Albanian civil war. The civilian population served as sign.

These actions were strengthened after the renewed meeting between Rugova and Milosevic 1998 and led as expected to over reactions of the police and military units in the Kosovo, which could be sold then in the west on the part of the NATO states and the UCK as first signs of ethnical cleanings. Of by the UCK was in this connection the speech, also not of it, murdered like the civilian population was never abused and only quite not from the Serbian-nationalistic chain dogs financed from the west, which were financed by the same circles right exile inheriting as in Bosnia Arkans Tigermilizen and Tschetniks. (similarly one financed from the west of Usta with the fights for the separation Croatia.)

In the same period the basis Montenegro became more American by promotion of NATO-friendly politicians and immense investments and European Union companies into the routistic infrastructure, as well as by structure of so-called "more pro-Western" private stations undertaken and the today's condition reaches that approx. half of the voters supported the present NATO-friendly government.

On the Vojvodina one took Hungary influence over the NATO candidate. Anti-Serbian rushing transmitters in the border area of Hungary to the province with a population of mixing from Serbs, Hungary and small German (more banal), Romanian and Croatian minorities should schueren resentment opposite close Belgrade. The bombs on the Danube bridges separate now purposefully the province from the remainder of Yugoslavia and promote on the one hand inevitably closer relations with the NATO member Hungary, on the other hand one the bombardment shows concentrated on the cities of the Vojvodina with by the majority Serbian population such as Novi Sad and the exception of the cities with by the majority Hungarian population, who now gentleman is in the country. If this preparation of a war of aggression with knowledge and approval of the Kohl government belongs and now with Schroeder, Scharping and Fischer accomplished, not before the international war crimes tribunal, then I know not, what is to be otherwise negotiated there. Conclusion with that NATO and CIA war against sovereigns Yugoslavia. The "Humanisten" is exposed. Bonn, 7 April 1999 sgd. Insider."

http://www.wsws.org/articles/2000/mar2000/koso-m16.shtml

"On Sunday, March 12, Britain's BBC2 television channel ran a documentary by Alan Little entitled "Moral Combat: NATO At War". The program contained damning evidence of how the Clinton administration set out to create a pretext for declaring war against the Milosevic regime in Serbia by sponsoring the separatist Kosovo Liberation Army (KLA), then pressed this decision on its European allies. The revelations in the documentary were reinforced by an accompanying article in the Sunday Times."

The head of Russia's Defense Ministry's Central International Military Cooperation Directorate at the time of the Kosovo war, General "Ivashov testified that the US/NATO plan relied heavily on psychological operations. He said that these "PsyOps" included disrupting the peace negotiations, discrediting the Yugoslav and Serbian leadership, and encouraging terrorism in order to promote Kosovo's secession from Yugoslavia."

Zaire

http://groups.google.ie/group/soc.culture.greek/browse_thread/thread/b
351786606fa063b/d04ae837d16300d4

It seems that the US was meeting some rebel groups in eastern Zaire prior to the large conflict irrupting there. This is testimony given before a committee of the US House of Representatives by ex NSA official Wayne:

"Madsen said the US military worked with Rwanda and the Congolese rebels to overthrow Mobutu. He said they again supported the rebellion against Laurent Kabila because "by 1998, the Kabila regime had become an irritant to the United States, North American mining interests, and Kabila's Ugandan and Rwandan patrons."

...

"The United States has a long history of supporting all sides in the DRC's civil wars in order to gain access to the country's natural resources."

(For more background on US involvement in the Congo see
http://www.foreignpolicy-infocus.org/briefs/vol2/v2n37cz_body.html.
This site confirms that Mobutu was a CIA asset from before he rose to power:
http://web.archive.org/web/20030802233131/http://www.us.net/cip/intelli g.htm. That site also documents the great size and power of the US intelligence agencies.)

William Blum, *Killing Hope* (London, 2003), p.159.

"In an even more marked policy division, US Air Force C-130s were flying Congolese troops and supplies against the Katangese rebels, while at the same time the CIA and its covert colleagues in the Pentagon were putting together an air armada of heavy transport aircraft, along with mercenary units, to aid the very same rebels." (Source cited as: Col. L. Fletcher Prouty, US Air Force Ret., *The Secret Team, the CIA and its Allies in Control of the World*." (Ballantine Books, New York, 1974), pp.26,129-30,438.)"

Index

388

393

394

If you liked this book you might like to read some of the author's other works, including:

In Defence of Conspiracy Theories: with examples from Irish and International History and Politics

This book is an attempt to address the widespread criticism of 'conspiracy theories', raising issues like: the control and negligence of the main organs of the media and police which make it difficult for true information to reach the public (and hence the public remain in ignorance of – and dismiss as a 'conspiracy theory' – the true facts); and the public's habit of underestimating the complexity of modern day politics.

A number of complex political plots and allegations are described in detail including: the 1641 Rebellion, British Intelligence manipulation of the 1919-21 Irish leaders, Secret Societies and the role of Occult organisations in Ireland and around the world, the allegations that Martin McGuinness is a British agent, and the motivation behind large scale immigration into Ireland. The author also addresses the question of value systems in modern Western societies and asks are even these being manipulated in order to assist the process of political control.

9780955681226

An Cṗeroeaṁ

This book seeks to illustrate the type of literature that shaped and influenced the Irish people's faith over the centuries. It is intended as a cornucopia of Catholic writing, a skirl around the kind of books and journals that graced Irish priest's libraries over the years. Outlined in chronological order it gives the full text of the Confession of St. Patrick, the Life of St. Columbanus, an ancient Irish tract on the mass; extracts from the Confessions of St. Augustine, the Irish Annals, and the fiction of Canon Sheehan; some theology from St. Thomas Aquinas, from 'A Handbook of Moral Theology', and the doctrine of Purgatory from an old Maynooth theologian; historical or contemporary accounts from all centuries, all the way from Tertullian, through Lough Derg in the 15th century, the Cromwellian Wars of the 17th century, to the social and economic teachings of the Church in the 19th and early 20th centuries.

978-0-9556812-3-3

Shakespeare was Irish!

As more and more scholars come to realise that the accepted story of William Shakespeare is untenable, this book tries to unmask the covert Irish influence on his work and the remarkable career of William Nugent, the only Irish candidate ever put forward for Shakespeare. It includes the full text of many original documents on Irish history, from the Reformation to the 1641 Rebellion.

978-0-9556812-1-9

www.ingramcontent.com/pod-product-compliance
Lightning Source LLC
Chambersburg PA
CBHW020653270326
41928CB00005B/103